# Scholastic Success With
# GRADE 4
## WORKBOOK

Scholastic Canada Ltd.

Maps workbook copyright © 2002 by Linda Ward Beech
Charts, Tables & Graphs workbook copyright © 2002 by Michael Priestley

Cover art by Jon Buller
Cover design by Anna Christian
Interior illustrations by Elizabeth Adams, Jon Buller, Reggie Holladay,
Anne Kennedy, Kathy Marlin, Bob Masheris, and Sherry Neidigh
Interior design by Quack & Company

ISBN 978-0-545-99026-4
ISBN-10 0-545-99026-2

6  5  4  3  2  1     Printed in Singapore     08  09  10  11  12  13

# Table of Contents

## CHARTS, TABLES & GRAPHS

## ADDITION, SUBTRACTION, MULTIPLICATION & DIVISION

## MATH

## MAPS

## "*Nothing succeeds like success.*"

Alexandre Dumas the Elder, 1854

Dear Parent,

Congratulations on choosing this excellent educational resource for your child. Scholastic has long been a leader in educational publishing—creating quality educational materials for use in school and at home for nearly a century.

As a partner in your child's academic success, you'll want to get the most out of the learning experience offered in this book. To help your child learn at home, try following these helpful hints:

- ✛ Provide a comfortable place to work.

- ✛ Have frequent work sessions, but keep them short.

- ✛ Praise your child's successes and encourage his or her efforts. Offer positive help when a child makes a mistake.

- ✛ Display your child's work and share his or her progress with family and friends.

In this workbook you'll find hundreds of practise pages that keep kids challenged and excited as they strengthen their skills across the classroom curriculum.

The workbook is divided into eight sections: Reading Comprehension; Reading Tests; Grammar; Writing; Charts, Tables & Graphs; Addition, Subtraction, Multiplication & Division; Math; and Maps. You and your child should feel free to move through the pages in any way you wish.

The table of contents lists the activities and the skills practised. And a complete answer key in the back will help you gauge your child's progress.

Take the lead and help your child succeed with the *Scholastic Success With: Grade 4 Workbook!*

The activities in this workbook reinforce age-appropriate skills and will help your child meet the following standards established as goals by leading educators.

## Mathematics

- ★ Uses a variety of strategies when problem-solving
- ★ Understands and applies number concepts
- ★ Uses basic and advanced procedures while performing computation
- ★ Understands and applies concepts of measurement
- ★ Understands and applies concepts of geometry
- ★ Understands and applies properties of functions and algebra

## Writing

- ★ Understands and uses the writing process
- ★ Uses grammatical and mechanical conventions in written compositions

## Reading

- ★ Understands and uses the general skills and strategies of the reading process
- ★ Can read and understand a variety of literary texts
- ★ Can understand and interpret a variety of informational texts

## Geograpy

- ★ Understands the characteristics and uses of maps and globes
- ★ Knows the location of places, geographic features, and patterns of the environment

# Scholastic Success With

# READING COMPREHENSION

# Mail Call

 *The **main idea** tells what a story or paragraph is mostly about.*

**Read the letters Tyler wrote from camp and those he received. Write the main idea for each letter.**

Dear Mom and Dad,                                    Saturday, June 7

Camp is great! I have met a lot of new friends. Jimmy is from California, Eric is from Iowa, and Tony is from Missouri. We have a great time together, swimming, canoeing, hiking, and playing tricks on other campers! Every night, we sneak over to another cabin. We then try to scare the other campers either by making scary noises or by throwing things at their cabin. It's so funny to see them run out screaming! Now don't worry, Mom. I'm not going to get caught like I did last year.

One thing that is different from last year is how many bugs there are! I know that scientists discover 7 to 10 thousand new kinds of insects each year, and I think they could discover even more here! I have at least 100 itchy mosquito bites and about 20 fire ant bites. Every time I go outside, horseflies chase me, too! Other than all these buggy bugs, I'm having the best time!

Love,
Tyler

Main idea _____

Dear Tyler,                                          Tuesday, June 10

Are you sure you are okay? All of those bugs sound awful! Have you used all of the "Itch-Be-Gone" cream I got you? You know how your feet swell if you don't use the cream! How about the "Ants 'R Awful" lotion for the ant bites? You and your Aunt Ethel have always seemed to attract those nasty fire ants.

Now Tyler, I am very happy that you have met some new friends and that you are having fun together. However, you MUST stop trying to scare other campers. Remember, honey, some campers may frighten easily. I want you to apologize for any anxiety you may have caused them and start being the nice, polite boy that I know you are. Do you hear me, Tyler? Please be careful. I want you home safely.

Love,
Mom

Main idea _____

Dear Steven,                                             Saturday, June 7

Camp is amazing this year! Our guides help us do the coolest stuff. Like yesterday, we hiked for six miles until we found this awesome spring. Then we used a rope hanging on a tree to jump in the water. I went so high that I made a huge splash! Thursday, our guides took us rowing. We rowed to this little island where we made a bonfire. We roasted the fish we had caught. My fish was the biggest, of course!

Last night, we collected a big bunch of frogs in a bag. Then we put the bag under a bed in another cabin while they were all at the campfire. When they got back, the frogs were all over their cabin. We laughed so hard! I know they're going get us back. I've seen them planning. I can't wait to see what they try. Hey! How's the leg? Sure wish you were here!

Your friend,

Tyler

Main idea _____

Dear Tyler,                                             Tuesday, June 10

That's great you're having so much fun! I wish I were there. All I do is sit around bumming out, thinking about all the fun you are having. I can't believe I broke my leg two days before camp started. My mom keeps renting me movies and video games, but I think I've seen everything and played everything. I just know I won't be happy again until this cast is off.

Your new friends sound great! Sure wish I was there helping you guys play tricks on the other campers. Remember last year when we smeared honey all over another cabin and all those bees came? That was so funny—except the part where we had to scrub all the cabins clean wearing hot, protective gear. I'm still surprised they let you come back this summer!

Hey! What's up with all the bugs? Your mom called my mom all worried about a bunch of bugs or something. Have fun and write soon!

Your friend,

Steven

Main idea _____

**Read a newspaper article about a foreign place. On another piece of paper, write the main idea for each paragraph.**

# Super Duper Lance

 *The **main idea** tells what a story or paragraph is mostly about.* **Details** *in a story provide the reader with information about the main idea and help the reader better understand the story.*

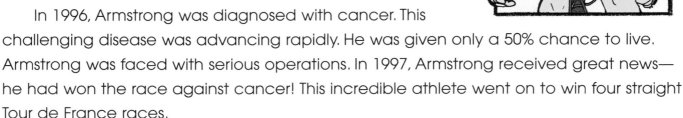

Lance Armstrong is an awesome athlete! This American bicyclist won the Tour de France bicycle race in the summer of 1999. He went on to win it again in 2000, 2001, and 2002. What makes Armstrong's accomplishment even more amazing is that he was battling cancer before competing in the 1999 Tour de France race.

In 1996, Armstrong was diagnosed with cancer. This challenging disease was advancing rapidly. He was given only a 50% chance to live. Armstrong was faced with serious operations. In 1997, Armstrong received great news— he had won the race against cancer! This incredible athlete went on to win four straight Tour de France races.

The Tour de France is the world's premier cycling event. It takes its competitors all over France, even through the Alps and the Pyrenees Mountains. The course changes each year but is always about 3,000 kilometres long and ends in Paris.

**Circle the main idea for each paragraph.**

1. **Paragraph 1:**

   **a. Armstrong was the first American bicyclist to win the Tour de France.**

   **b. Armstrong is an accomplished bicyclist.**

   **c. Armstrong rides all over France in the summer.**

2. **Paragraph 2:**

   **a. Armstrong was the first American bicyclist to win the Tour de France.**

   **b. Armstrong had cancer in 1996.**

   **c. Armstrong won an important "health" race.**

3. **Paragraph 3:**

   **a. Riders in the Tour de France get to see all of France.**

   **b. Tour de France competitors must be very strong to ride through two mountainous regions.**

   **c. The impressive Tour de France runs all over France and ends in Paris.**

Name _____

4. Use details from the story to write why you think Armstrong is an accomplished athlete. _____

_____

_____

_____

_____

_____

_____

5. Write a detail about the Tour de France bicycle race on each tire.

6. What are some of the challenges Armstrong has faced? Which one do you think was the most difficult? _____

_____

_____

_____

 **Read a magazine article about another sports figure. On another piece of paper, write the main idea of the article.**

# A Very Colourful House

 **Context clues** *are words or sentences that can help determine the meaning of a new word.*

Jackson was excited! He and his family were on their way to the White House. Jackson could not wait to see the U.S. President's official **residence**. He had been reading all about it so that he might recognize some things he saw. After standing in a long line, Jackson, his sister, and their parents were allowed to enter the 132-room, six-floor **mansion**. They entered through the East **Wing**. Jackson knew that he and his family were only four of the 6,000 people who would visit this **incredible** house that day.

The first room they were shown by the **guide** was the State Dining Room. Jackson learned that 140 dinner guests could eat there at one time. "What a great place for a huge birthday party!" Jackson thought.

The Red Room was shown next. Red satin **adorned** its walls. The third room the **visitors** entered was the Blue Room. This room serves as the main **reception** room for the President's guests. Jackson wondered when the President would be out to greet him. After all, he was a guest, too.

The Green Room was the fourth room on the **tour**. Jackson and his family were not surprised to find green silk covering the walls in this room.

The last room was the biggest room in the White House. It is called the East Room. Here, guests are **entertained** after **formal** dinners. Jackson wondered if they could **vary** the entertainment by rolling in **huge** movie screens so they could all watch the latest movies. He wondered if kids were invited sometimes; maybe they had huge, bouncy boxes you could jump in. Perhaps they even set up huge ramps so all the kids could practice skateboarding and roller blading. How fun!

Jackson loved his tour of the White House. He was just sorry that he did not get to see the living quarters of the President's family. He wondered if the President had to make *his* bed every day!

Write one of the bolded words from the story to match each definition below. Use context clues to help. Then write each numbered letter in the matching blank below to answer the question and learn an interesting fact.

1. following the usual rules or customs in an exact way  __ __ __ __ __ __
   <br>    1

2. home  __ __ __ __ __ __ __ __
   <br>    12          10

3. a gathering at which guests are received  __ __ __ __ __ __ __ __
   <br>    9              17

4. kept interested with something enjoyable  __ __ __ __ __ __ __ __ __ __ __
   <br>    15                    16      8

5. decorated  __ __ __ __ __
   <br>    13

6. a leader of a tour  __ __ __ __ __
   <br>    4

7. a part that sticks out from a main part  __ __ __ __
   <br>    2

8. a very large, stately house  __ __ __ __ __ __
   <br>    7

9. a trip to inspect something  __ __ __ __
   <br>    6

10. amazing  __ __ __ __ __ __ __ __
    <br>    11

11. very large  __ __ __ __
    <br>    5

12. guests  __ __ __ __ __ __ __
    <br>    3

13. to change  __ __ __ __ __
    <br>    14      18

**How many gallons of paint does it take to paint the outside of the White House?**

__ __ __ __    __ __ __ __ __ __ __    __ __ __ __ __ __ __
1  2  3  4    5  6  7  8  9  10  11    12  13  14  15  16  17  18

# Rattle! Rattle!

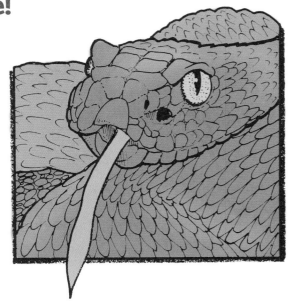

Many kids think Cassidy is crazy! That is okay with her. Cassidy loves rattlesnakes, and that is that. She has every book there is about these fascinating creatures. She loves seeing these animals in the zoo.

Rattlesnakes are extremely poisonous. They often use the rattle in their tails to give a warning sound before they strike. They are classed as pit vipers.

Cassidy has decided her favourite kind of rattlesnake is a diamondback rattlesnake. These snakes can grow to be over two and one-quarter metres long! These large rattlesnakes are the most dangerous of all snakes, and they do not always rattle before striking. Like most rattlesnakes, diamondbacks like to eat birds and small mammals.

Part of the fun of being enamoured with rattlesnakes is learning all kinds of interesting information about them. For example, Cassidy had always heard that you can tell the age of a rattler by the number of rattles in its tail. This, she learned, is not true. Two to four segments are added to the tail each year, one every time the rattler sheds its skin.

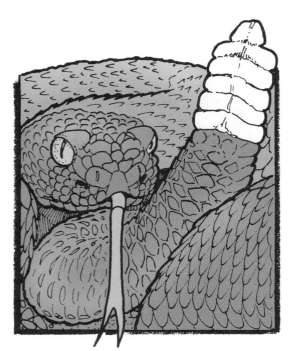

However, once ten have accumulated, they begin to fall off! So you can never be quite sure just how old a rattlesnake is!

Sometimes Cassidy's mom wishes her daughter could love kittens or puppies or ponies instead of poisonous snakes. But actually, Cassidy's love for snakes is definitely what makes her unique.

Find a word in the snake to match each definition.

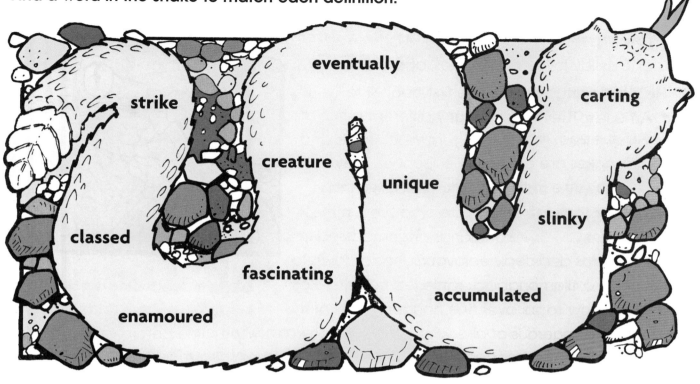

eventually

strike

carting

creature

unique

classed

slinky

fascinating

accumulated

enamoured

1. classified _____
3. interesting _____
5. in love _____
7. collected _____
9. sleek _____

2. one of a kind _____
4. to attack _____
6. sometime _____
8. transporting _____
10. any person or animal _____

11. Check the main idea of the story.
   ☐ Cassidy wants a long snake.
   ☐ Cassidy loves large, dangerous rattlesnakes.
   ☐ Rattlesnakes do not always rattle before striking.

12. What kind of snake does Cassidy like best?

_____

 **Read an article about an animal that fascinates you. Choose five words from the article and write the definition of each on another piece of paper.**

# North America's First Peoples

 *To **compare** and **contrast** ideas in a passage, determine how the ideas are alike and how they are different.*

Native Americans were the first people to live in North America. They lived in many different areas of the continent including the Eastern Woodlands and the Southwest.

The Eastern Woodlands Native peoples had a much different lifestyle than those who lived in the Southwest. The Eastern Woodlands encompassed all of the area from what is now eastern Canada down to the Gulf Coast. The area also extended from the East Coast to the Mississippi River. The northern parts of this area had cold winters, and the whole region had warm summers.

The Southwest Native peoples lived in a large, warm, dry area. Today, Arizona, New Mexico, southern Colorado, and northern Mexico make up this area. In the northern part of this region, wind and water created steep-walled canyons, sandy areas, mesas, buttes, and other interesting landforms. In the southern part, the desert land was flat and dry.

The Iroquois, Ojibwa, and Mi'kmaq are just a few of the major tribes that made their home in the Eastern Woodlands. The Southwest was home to tribes such as the Apache, Navajo, and Pueblo.

Housing was very different for the Native peoples who lived in these two different regions. The Eastern Woodlands natives built a variety of homes, depending on their location. Northern dwellers lived in dome-shaped wigwams covered with sheets of bark or in longhouses. A longhouse was a large, rectangular shelter that was home to a number of related families, each living in its own section. Those in the southeastern area often built villages around a central public square where community events took place.

Many of the Native peoples of the Southwest lived in cliff houses or large, many-storeyed homes built from rock and a mud-like substance called adobe. These adobe dwellings could house many families.

All of the Native peoples living in both regions ate a lot of corn, beans, and squash. Hunting was important in both regions, but fishing was more significant in the Eastern Woodlands.

The tribes living in both regions were excellent craftspeople. Those in the Eastern Woodlands made pottery, wicker baskets, and deerskin clothing. Many tribes in the Southwest also made pottery and were very skilled at spinning cotton and weaving it into cloth. This cloth was made into breechcloths and cotton kilts for the men and a kind of dress for the women.

Learning about the fascinating history of these peoples is important. They have played, and continue to play, a valuable role in the history of North America.

1. **Fill in the Venn diagram using the descriptions below.**

| | |
|---|---|
| wigwams and longhouses | excellent craftspeople |
| made pottery | cold winters, warm summers |
| hunting | buttes |
| many-storeyed homes | Arizona, New Mexico, and southern Colorado |
| steep-walled canyons | corn, beans, and squash |
| fishing | Iroquois and Ojibwa |
| Apache and Navajo | included what is now Canada |

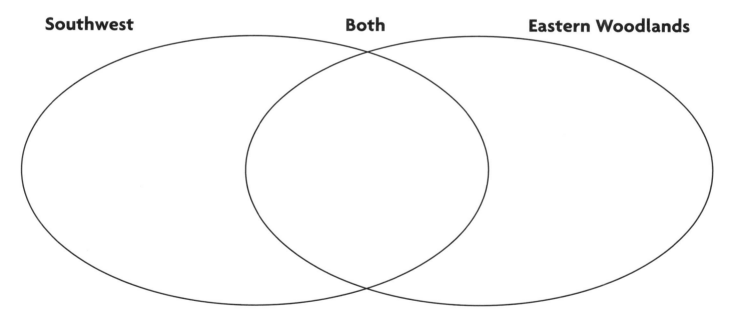

**Southwest**        **Both**        **Eastern Woodlands**

2. **Circle the ways longhouses and adobe houses were alike.**

   large        one-family dwellings        fairly small        multiple-family dwellings

3. **How was the climate in certain parts of the Eastern Woodlands different from other parts in the same region?** _____

_____

# A Difficult Choice

Emily and Zach are confused! Their parents told them they could choose between Massachusetts and Arizona for their vacation this summer, and they think both U.S. states seem pretty awesome. Emily has always wanted to visit Boston, the capital of Massachusetts. Zach and she both agree that strolling along the Freedom Trail would be pretty neat. Walking the trail would enable them to see Boston's most famous historic landmarks, like the site of the school Ben Franklin attended and the Old State House. It was built in 1713 and served as the seat of the colonial government.

Emily and Zach both love the beach. If they went to Massachusetts, they could spend a few days at the beaches on Cape Cod. Emily loves boogie boarding, and Zach is great at body surfing. They both enjoy building sandcastles with their mom and dad.

Zach finds learning about Native peoples fascinating and has always wanted to travel along the Apache Trail in Arizona. This mountain highway passes Native ruins in Tonto National Forest. Emily is not as interested in travelling along this trail as Zach, but they both would like to visit Phoenix, the capital, and then travel to Grand Canyon National Park and Meteor Crater. Zach learned in science class that Meteor Crater is a hole over 1200 metres wide and 156 metres deep that was created when a huge object from space fell to Earth. The object went so deep that it has never been found. Zach would really like to try to locate it. Emily thinks he is crazy! If experienced scientists and researchers cannot find it, Zach might as well not even bother to try.

If Arizona is the chosen state, Emily and Zach would also like to stop at a few other places. Arizona is home to fifteen national monuments. That is more than any other U.S. state.

The only drawback for Zach if they choose Arizona would be the heat. It is very hot and dry in this southwestern state. Arizona has a lot of what Massachusetts does not—desert land. Once in July in Arizona, it got up to 53°C !

Massachusetts, on the other hand, is located in the northeastern United States. Here, Zach and Emily and their parents could enjoy mild temperatures of about 24° C. Their parents love hot weather, but Zach and Emily do not really like to sweat. Therefore, both know that they would prefer the climate of Massachusetts.

How will they ever decide to which state they should travel? If only they could take two trips!

1. "Pack" each suitcase to describe the two regions.

   Tonto National Forest

   Old State House

   Freedom Trail

   mild climate

   Phoenix

   Boston

   very hot

   Cape Cod

   Apache Trail

   Grand Canyon

2. Circle things both Emily and Zach like or would like to see.

   building sandcastles    Apache Trail    hot weather    beach

   Meteor Crater    surfboarding    Freedom Trail    sweating

3. Write one way Zach and Emily are different from their parents. _____

   _____

4. Write one way the Freedom Trail and the Apache Trail are different. _____

   _____

   _____

5. How do Zach and Emily spend their time differently at the beach? _____

   _____

6. How are Zach and Emily's feelings different when it comes to finding the missing

   object at Meteor Crater? _____

   _____

 Read about a province or territory you would like to visit. On another piece of paper, write five differences between the place you chose and the place in which you live.

# A Real Cool Cowboy

 *The events in a story take place in a certain order. This is the **sequence** of events.*

Pecos Bill is a well-known character in American folklore. His legend developed from a magazine article written by Edward O'Reilly in 1923. This cowboy hero is often credited for being the creator of branding, roping, and other cowboy activities. It is also said that Pecos Bill taught broncos how to buck and cowboys how to ride.

Legend has it that Pecos Bill was born in the 1830s in Texas. He teethed on a bowie knife and had bears and other wild animals as friends. On a family trip to the West, little Bill fell out of the wagon near the Pecos River. He was found by coyotes that raised him.

Two famous natural landmarks are also amusingly traced back to Pecos Bill—the Grand Canyon and Death Valley. Supposedly, Pecos Bill once made a bet that he could ride an Oklahoma cyclone without a saddle. The cyclone was not able to throw him off, and it finally "rained out" under him in Arizona. This rain was so heavy that it created the Grand Canyon. When he reached California, Pecos Bill crashed. It was the force of his fall that is said to have created Death Valley. In actuality, some rocks in the deepest part of the Grand Canyon date back about two billion years. The Colorado River began forming the Grand Canyon about six million years ago. Over centuries, the water eroded the

layers of rock, and the walls of the canyon were created. More erosion occurred later as a result of wind, rain, and melting snow. Death Valley is a desert in California and Nevada. It contains the lowest point in the Western Hemisphere at 84.5 metres below sea level.

No one is quite sure how Pecos Bill died. One version says he laughed himself to death after listening to silly questions a man from Boston asked him about the West.

1. Look at each picture. Number the events in the order in which they happened in the story. Write a sentence for each.

_____

_____

_____

_____

_____

_____

_____

_____

_____

_____

_____

_____

2. Four words from the story are hidden in the puzzle. The definition of each word is given below. Shade in the letters for each word, reading left to right and top to bottom. The remaining letters will spell the name of a real cool cowboy two times.

   a piece of writing

   laughingly

   attributed with

   a particular form of something

| a | p | r | t | e | i | c |
|---|---|---|---|---|---|---|
| c | o | l | e | s | a | b |
| m | u | s | i | i | n | l |
| g | l | y | l | c | p | r |
| e | d | e | i | t | c | e |
| o | d | v | s | e | b | r |
| i | s | l | l | i | o | n |

**Read a story about an imaginary character. On another piece of paper, write five events from the character's life in the order in which they happened.**

# Fooled You!

Maria decided to have a Prank Party for her friends on April Fool's Day. She invited five of her best friends to come over for the afternoon. Maria and her mom made some delicious "pranks" for her party. They made treats that looked like one food but tasted like another. For example, Maria and her mom made fried-egg sundaes. These sweet treats looked like a fried egg in a bowl, but they were really made of vanilla ice cream topped with marshmallow fluff and a round blob of yellow pudding.

Another treat looked like a thin-crust pizza with vegetables. However, it was really a tortilla with strawberry and apricot jam, a black licorice stick, a green fruit roll, white chocolate chips, and cashew halves. It was so easy to make that Maria's little brother, Juan, even helped.

To make a "pizza," Juan and Maria first stirred the two jams together. Then Maria spread the jam on a tortilla, being careful not to go all the way to the edge. Maria's mom sliced the licorice stick to resemble black olives and the fruit roll to look like green pepper strips. The cashew halves looked like mushrooms.

Next, Maria melted the white chocolate chips at half power in the microwave for one-minute intervals. Juan stirred the chips after each minute to see if they were completely melted. (Maria's mom made sure he had a dry spoon when he stirred because she said that water makes the chocolate lose its creaminess.) Once it was melted, Maria quickly spread the melted chocolate on the pizza. Then she and Juan topped the "pizza" with the "olives," "peppers," and "mushrooms."

Maria's friends loved the delicious pranks she had made. No one dared to play an April Fool's trick on Maria since her pranks were so tasty and fun!

1. **Number the steps in the order Maria and Juan made a Prank Pizza.**

   ___ **Juan and Maria topped the pizza.**

   ___ **Maria's mom created "olives" and "green peppers."**

   ___ **Maria melted the white chocolate chips.**

   ___ **Maria spread the jam on the tortillas.**

   ___ **Juan and Maria stirred the two jams together.**

   ___ **Juan stirred the chips with a dry spoon.**

   ___ **Maria spread the melted chocolate on the pizza.**

2. On the pizzas below, write one way a real pizza is similar to Maria's Prank Pizza and one way it is different from it.

**Similar**    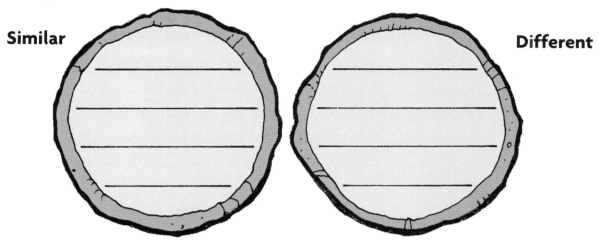    **Different**

3. Write a synonym from the story for each word below.
   trick _____
   celebration _____
   scrumptious _____

4. Why did Maria's mom make sure Juan used a dry spoon to stir the chocolate?

_____

5. Check the ingredients used in making the Prank Pizza.
   ___ crust                  ___ strawberries            ___ tortilla
   ___ apricot jam            ___ red licorice            ___ green fruit
   roll          ___ walnuts  ___ cashews                 ___ chocolate
   chips

6. Circle the main idea of paragraph one.
   Maria is a big prankster.
   Maria "sweetly" tricked her friends on April Fool's Day.
   Maria's mom had great prank ideas for April Fool's Day.

7. What ingredients were in the fried-egg sundaes?

_____

8. If the vegetables on Maria's pizza were real, what would they have been?

 Read the recipe of one of your favourite foods. Write each step on a strip of paper. Mix up the strips and then see if you can put them in the correct sequence.

# A Happy Hero

 *To better understand a character, a reader needs to carefully study, or* **analyze***, a character's traits, personality, motivations, relationships, and strengths and weaknesses.*

One day, Lindsay and Erica were sitting at Lindsay's house working very diligently. Fourth grade was tough, and they were working on a science project about weather. Lindsay was a hard worker like Erica, so the two girls were happy to have each other as partners. They were currently writing about rain and were amazed to learn that Hawaii is the world's wettest place. Lindsay found that Mount Waialeale, on the island of Kauai, gets over 11.5 metres of rain a year! In 1982, Mount Waialeale set an all-time world record when it received almost 17 metres of rain. The girls knew that their classmates would find all these facts interesting.

The girls were enjoying the fun facts they were finding when all of a sudden, Lindsay saw Erica choking. Erica had been chewing on a pen cap and had accidentally swallowed it! Erica started pointing to her neck. Lindsay asked her if she was choking. When Erica nodded to say yes, Lindsay quickly stood up and did the Heimlich maneuvre to try to help Erica stop choking. (The Heimlich maneuvre is a way to save someone from choking. This method is named after the doctor who invented it, Henry Heimlich.)

Lindsay was afraid of hurting her friend, so the first time she tried the Heimlich maneuvre, she did not do it very hard. She tried a second time, and nothing happened. After trying it a third time, the pen cap flew out of Erica's mouth!

Erica was very grateful to Lindsay. She had been terrified when she realized she had swallowed the pen cap and could not breathe. Lindsay was very brave to try to save her friend. This was one science project that both girls would never forget!

1. Circle each word that describes Lindsay.

   hard worker          boring          brave          fast-thinking

   quick-acting          selfish          timid          lazy

2. Circle each word that tells how Erica might have been feeling when she realized she was choking.

   scared          thankful          enthusiastic          helpless

   courageous          sick          alarmed          friendly

3. What do you think Lindsay might be when she grows up? _____

   _____

4. Write *L* for Lindsay, *E* for Erica, or *B* for both.

   ____ good students          ____ frightened          ____ persistent

   ____ courageous          ____ grateful          ____ appreciative

5. What is the name of the doctor who invented the lifesaving maneuvre?

   _____

6. What is the name of the wettest place in the world? _____

7. Circle the average amount of rain Mount Waialeale received each month in 1982.

   just under 2 metres          almost 1 metre          just over 3 metres          about 1/2 metre

8. Why do you think this project will be one neither girl will ever forget? _____

   _____

   _____

   _____

 Choose a character from a book. On another piece of paper, make a list of ten words that describe this character.

# A New Team for Juan

Juan was angry! His mom had signed him up late for baseball, and now he was not on his old team. He would not get to play with Tyler, Joe, and Brad. They had played together for four years! And they all loved Coach Dave—he was one of the best coaches in the league. Juan was not even sure if he wanted to play at all. He just knew it would not be any fun.

At the first practice, Juan walked slowly to the field. He saw one guy pitching and one hitting. The guy hitting struck out. "Great!" thought Juan. "I will be on a team with no hitters!" Juan continued on to the field. He saw some guys playing catch. One guy missed an easy ball. "Perfect!" thought Juan. "I will also have to teach them how to catch!"

Juan thought about calling it quits when he suddenly realized that Eric, a friend from school, was on the team. Eric was a great pitcher! "Well, maybe I will stay for a bit," Juan said to himself.

Juan started looking around some more. He recognized two other kids he had watched when he had been on the other team. One was a fast runner, and one never missed a pop fly. "Hey! This team might be okay after all!" thought Juan.

Eric was excited to see Juan. "Hey, Juan! I'm glad you are on our team. We are going to have a great team. Do you know who our coach is?"

Juan was sure the coach would not be as good as Coach Dave, but Eric was excited. "So, who is the coach, Eric?" Juan asked, somewhat indifferently.

"It's Home Run Harvey!" Eric replied excitedly.

"Home Run Harvey!" exclaimed Juan. "The one and only Home Run Harvey from the university team?"

"That is right," said Eric. "His little brother is on our team, and he wants to coach." Juan could not believe how lucky he was to get on Home Run Harvey's team!

"So who is his brother?" Juan asked.

"Tim is over there," said Eric, pointing to the guy who had not caught what Juan had called an "easy ball."

Juan felt badly for thinking negatively about Tim's missed catch. Everyone misses a ball now and then. Juan could not wait to tell his friends about his new team and coach!

Name _____

1. Check how Juan felt in each situation.

   He could not play baseball with his friends.

   He sees a player on his new team strike out.

   He sees his friend, Eric.

   He learns Home Run Harvey is the coach.

| positive | negative |
|----------|----------|
|          |          |
|          |          |
|          |          |
|          |          |

2. Why was Juan angry that he could not play on his old team? _____

   _____

3. Underline when Juan first started feeling more positive about the new team.

   when he saw a player who was a fast runner

   when he saw a player who never missed a pop fly

   when he saw Eric

4. Why do you think Juan felt badly about what he thought when he saw Tim miss

   a catch? _____

5. Circle the words that describe Juan at the end of the story.

   angry        scared        excited        pessimistic        remorseful        timid

6. Circle the main idea of the story.

   Juan's mom made a terrible mistake, and now Juan had to suffer.

   What Juan thought was going to be a negative experience soon looked
   like it could be a positive one.

   Juan is going to get awesome coaching from a very talented ball player.

7. What kind of season do you think Juan's team will have?_____

   _____

   _____

Choose three characters from a book. On another piece of paper, write two different
words to describe each character.

# Such Choices

 **Making predictions** *is using information from a story to determine what will happen next.*

Hurray! Spring break is here! Tommy's mom and dad are also on vacation from work all week. They want to plan all kinds of fun things to do, like biking, hiking, fishing, swimming, and tennis. They are hoping for some warm, enjoyable weather. However, they just cannot decide which day to do each activity. So, they decided to check the weather forecast in the newspaper before making some final plans.

## THE FIVE-DAY FORECAST

| Monday | Tuesday | Wednesday | Thursday | Friday |
|---|---|---|---|---|
| a beauty with no clouds; high of 28 | partly cloudy with a 40% chance of afternoon thunderstorms; high of 27 | lingering showers until noon; then clearing and cooler with a high of 21 | partly sunny with a high of 15 | partly cloudy with a high of 18 |

1. **Tommy and his dad want to spend one whole day fishing. On which day(s) might they not want to go fishing?** _____

2. **What day would be the best day for swimming?** _____

3. What other activities could Tommy and his family do on Tuesday and Wednesday?

_____

_____

4. On what days do you think the family might wear jeans and jackets?  _____

_____

5. Do you think Tommy and his family are pleased with the forecast? Why or why not?

_____

_____

6. To do the kinds of activities Tommy and his family want to do, which forecast do you think they would like to see every day of spring break? Why?

_____

_____

7. Write the word from the forecast that means "staying." _____

8. Circle the words that describe Tommy's family.

   incompetent          athletic          energetic          listless

9. Circle the things Tommy and his family might want to take with them if they go swimming on Monday.

   jacket                          goggles                          sunglasses

   cooler with drinks              rain umbrella                    sunscreen

10. Write a paragraph about what Tuesday might be like for Tommy.

_____

_____

_____

_____

**Read the weather forecast in the newspaper. Choose four different cities in Canada. On another piece of paper, make a list of the activities you could do in each city, based on the forecast. What other information did you use to make your list?**

# A New Start

*Every story has certain **story elements**. These elements include the characters, the setting, the problem, and the solution.*

In the late 1500s, brave men and women and their children sailed from Europe across the Atlantic Ocean to North America, looking for a better way of life. These people wanted better jobs than they had in their homelands, and many wanted the freedom to choose their own religion. Still others wanted the opportunity to be able to buy land.

This period of time in North America is known as the colonial period. During this time, many colonists worked very hard. The first permanent colony in Canada was founded in 1608 at Quebec. The first colony in the U.S., Jamestown, was established in 1607. Between 1607 and 1733, 13 permanent colonies were established on the east coast of America. These colonies started to grow and prosper as more and more people from other countries began to immigrate. As the population of the colonies grew, trade and manufacturing developed quickly, especially in towns that had good harbours.

Despite the growth and the many successes of the colonies, the colonists also faced their fair share of problems. One very big problem was the friction between the American colonies and Britain. The colonists wanted very much to control themselves and have more say in making decisions that affected them. However, the British Parliament would not allow it. This angered the colonists, so they often ignored British laws.

As Britain imposed more and more taxes on the colonists, the colonists grew angrier and angrier. Acts passed by Parliament, such as the Sugar Act and the Stamp Act, forced the colonists to take action against Britain.

In 1774, delegates from all the American colonies except Georgia met to decide how to gain some independence from Britain. Their attempts failed. They met again in 1775. The delegates helped organize an army and a navy to fight the British soldiers. The colonists wanted freedom from Britain. They outlined this freedom on July 4, 1776, in the Declaration of Independence.

Name _____

List each story element.

main characters: _____

setting: _____

problem: _____

solution: _____

Use words from the story to complete the puzzle.

**Across**

1. Britain _____ many taxes on the colonists, which greatly angered them.

7. People from other countries, looking for better jobs or religious freedom, would _____ to North America.

8. The American colonies decided they wanted to gain _____ from Britain.

**Down**

2. Thirteen _____ colonies were established in America between 1607 and 1733.

3. _____ from almost all of the colonies met to discuss how to gain independence from Britain.

4. The colonists tried to organize an army and a navy to fight the British _____ .

5. The men, women, and children who left their countries to come to North America were very _____ .

6. There was _____ between the American colonies and Britain.

9. As people from other countries moved to North America, the colonies started to grow and _____ .

On another piece of paper, list the story elements from your favourite movie.

# A "Peachy" Beach Day

 *The **cause** is what makes something happen.*
*The **effect** is what happens as a result of the cause.*

The day was beautiful! Janie and Jake's mom decided to take them to the beach. She even told them that since they had finished their chores without complaining, they could each bring a friend. Janie and Jake were excited! They loved the beach.

Janie decided to ask Hayley to go since Hayley had just had her over to play last week. Jake asked his friend Charlie— they went everywhere together. Once both friends had arrived, it was time to load up the van. The kids packed some beach toys they might want—shovels, buckets, beach balls, and flippers. Mom packed a cooler with sandwiches and drinks, towels, sunscreen, and a chair for herself.

On the way to the beach, Jake and Charlie groaned. They had forgotten their boogie boards. Oh well! At least they had buckets and shovels they could use to build a huge sandcastle. Jake and Charlie loved to see how big they could make a sandcastle. They even liked to add roads and moats and lots of other details.

Once they reached the beach, everyone helped unload and set up. Then Mom put sunscreen on everyone. It was going to be a hot one—33° with no clouds! Everyone even put on hats.

Right away, the kids started playing. Jake and Charlie started working on their sandcastle, and Janie and Hayley went looking for shells. What a great day!

1. **By each cause, write the letter of the effect.**

   **Cause:**

   _____ **It was a beautiful, hot day.**

   _____ **They forgot their boogie boards.**

   _____ **Jake and Charlie go everywhere together.**

   **Effect:**

   A. **Jake asked Charlie to go to the beach.**

   B. **Mom put sunscreen on all the kids.**

   C. **Jake and Charlie were disappointed.**

2. Write *C* for cause or *E* for effect for each pair of sentences.

    a. ____ Mom decided to take the kids to the beach.

        ____ The day was beautiful.

    b. ____ They forgot their boogie boards.

        ____ Jake and Charlie would be building sandcastles instead of
            boogie boarding.

    c. ____ Janie and Jake each got to take a friend to the beach.

        ____ The children finished their chores without complaining.

    d. ____ Janie asked Hayley to go with her to the beach.

        ____ Hayley had just had Janie over to play.

3. Circle the main idea of the first paragraph.

    Janie and Jake loved to go to the beach.

    Janie and Jake finished their chores without complaining.

    Since it was a beautiful day, Janie and Jake's mom was taking them to
    the beach.

4. Janie and Jake each asked a friend to go to the beach for a different reason. Write
    each child's reason on the correct sandcastle.

    Janie                                        Jake

5. What might Hayley or Charlie have thought on the way home from the beach?

    _____

    _____

 Simon had to miss baseball practice last night. On another piece of paper, write three
possible causes for this effect.

# Planet Particulars

 *To make an **inference** is to figure out what is happening in a story from clues the author provides.*

There are nine planets that travel around the sun. They are much smaller than the sun and stars which are shining balls of hot gases. The sun and stars produce their own heat and light. The planets do not produce heat or light. They get almost all of their heat and light from the sun. Each planet has features which make it unique.

1. It takes _____ about 248 years to orbit the sun. It is the smallest, a "dwarf planet" and not a real planet. It is located next to Neptune.

2. The largest planet, _____, is the fifth planet from the sun. It is about 1,000 times bigger than Earth. Saturn is next to this planet.

3. _____ rotates while lying on its side. It takes about 84 years to orbit the sun. It is the seventh planet from the sun.

4. _____ 's surface temperature is about 223° C below zero! Brrrrr! It is the eighth planet from the sun. It is located between Pluto and Uranus.

5. We live on _____, the third planet from the sun. It takes this planet 365 days to orbit the sun. It is often called the "living planet."

6. Many rings surround _____. It takes 10,759 days to orbit the sun. It is located between Uranus and Jupiter.

7. _____ is the closest planet to the sun. It is next to Venus, the second planet from the sun. This planet only takes 88 days to orbit the sun.

8. _____ is often called the "red planet." It lies between Earth and Jupiter, the largest planet. This planet has the largest volcano in the solar system— much higher than Mount Everest!

9. _____ was called the "mystery planet" for a long time because it is covered by thick clouds. It is the second planet from the sun.

# Guess the Province

Spencer, Jack, Grant, and Kara are new in Mrs. Steen's Grade 4 class. Each of these students came from one of the following provinces: Ontario, New Brunswick, Quebec, and Prince Edward Island. They are taking turns giving the class clues about the province from which they moved. The other children are trying to guess the province from the clues.

Use the following clues to help you determine which province was the home of each new student. Write each new student's name under the correct province outline below. Label the province in which all the students now live.

1. Spencer is not from the largest province.

2. Grant is not from the north or the east.

3. Kara is not from the north or the west.

4. Jack is not from the north or the west.

5. Grant and Spencer are both from provinces that border another country.

6. Jack and Kara lived the closest to each other before they moved.

7. Grant used to be able to visit Niagara Falls.

8. Many of Spencer's old friends speak French very well.

9. Kara used to live in "the birthplace of Canada."

10. Jack used to vacation at Murray Beach. He also loved fishing on the Miramichi.

11. All four children love their new province. It is located on the western edge of Canada. It is the third largest province. Two adjectives are used to describe it: Super. Natural. The United States lies beyond its southern boundary.

Prince Edward Island

Ontario

Quebec

New Brunswick

# Off to the City

Maura and her grandmother are going into the city today to run some errands and do some shopping. Maura loves spending time with her grandmother. The two of them always have so much to talk about. Maura loves to hear about all the funny things her grandmother did when she was Maura's age. They did some really interesting things way back then when there were no TVs. For example, Maura's grandmother used to play jacks. She and her best friend, Sue, were the best jacks players in their school.

At 10:00 A.M. sharp, Grandma pulled in the driveway to pick up Maura. She honked the horn as she always did on their big shopping days. This was the signal that they had a busy day ahead and could not waste any time.

Maura ran out to the car, dressed in the new jeans and top Grandma bought her on their last trip. Maura knew that Grandma loved to see Maura wearing the clothes she had bought her.

As expected, Grandma told Maura some more funny things she did when she was Maura's age. Today, she told Maura how she and Sue were so hungry for candy one day in July that they decided to put on a performance and charge admission. The two girls dressed up like clowns. Grandma said people laughed so hard that the two girls were able to buy all kinds of fun treats that day. Maura made a note to herself to definitely try that some day.

Before they knew it, Maura and Grandma were in the city. Grandma found a parking spot, and away they went to begin their big day!

1. **Why are Maura and Grandma going to the city?** _____

_____

2. **List something Grandma did for fun when she was a girl. Compare it with something Maura might spend her time doing for fun.**

_____

_____

Name _____

Help Maura and Grandma find their way around the city. Follow the directions to complete the map.

1. Maura wants to go to the mall first. It is just south of the hospital. Cherry Street runs along the western side of the mall. Label the mall.

2. On the southern side of Pine Street and the western side of Oak Street is Grandma's eye doctor. Draw a pair of eyeglasses here.

3. There are five houses on Elm Street east of the hospital. Elm Street is south of the hospital. Label Elm Street and draw five houses across from the library.

4. The supermarket is located on the corner of Holly Street and Evergreen Street. Grandma needs some groceries. Label Evergreen Street.

5. There is a great park where Maura wants to play that is located between Maple and Pear streets. Oak Street runs north/south along the western side of the park. Label Pear Street, and draw three trees in the park.

6. The fire station is located on the western side of Cherry Street, north of Holly Street. Draw and label it.

7. The police station is located to the south of the fire department. Draw and label it.

Draw a map that shows how to get from your house to your favourite fast-food restaurant.

# Food for Fitness

 **Classifying** *means putting things into categories with other similar things.*

Katie knows that it is very important to eat right and to exercise in order to stay healthy. That is why she gets up every morning and has **oatmeal**, a **banana**, and a glass of **milk** for breakfast. Then Katie goes to play kickball.

Katie, Jimmy, Toni, and Anna always organize a two-on-two game of kickball. After playing all morning, the foursome usually sits down for lunch. Katie knows Toni's lunch by heart— **chicken nuggets**, **carrots** and dip, an **apple**, and two **chocolate chip cookies**. Jimmy's lunch varies a little. Some days it is **ham** on **wheat bread**, **grapes**, **yogurt**, and a **candy bar**. Other days his mom will make him come home to eat

a good, hot meal of **peas** and **corn**, **rice**, a **hamburger**, **strawberries**, and homemade **ice cream**. Usually on those days, Jimmy has eaten **doughnuts** for breakfast.

The only meat Anna eats is fish, so she often has **fish sticks**, crunchy **broccoli**, a **pear**,

**cheese** and **crackers** and occasionally a piece of her mom's delicious **chocolate cake**. Katie always wants a bite of the cake. Sometimes Anna shares, and sometimes she does not.

To finish off her day of trying to eat healthy, Katie usually goes home to one of her dad's magnificent meals. Tonight they are having **pork chops**, **pasta**, **cauliflower** with cheese sauce, and her choice of turtle **cheesecake** or a **vanilla milk shake**. Although Katie and her friends eat some sweets, they try not to eat a lot of them, and they exercise each day.

Write each bolded word from the story in the chart under the correct category.

| Dairy | Vegetables | Grains | Fruits | Meat & Fish | Fats/Sweets |
|-------|-----------|--------|--------|-------------|-------------|
|       |           |        |        |             |             |
|       |           |        |        |             |             |
|       |           |        |        |             |             |
|       |           |        |        |             |             |
|       |           |        |        |             |             |

1. What does Katie do to stay healthy? _____

2. Circle the foods Anna would NOT eat.

   hamburger     broccoli     apple     chicken     cheese     ribs     salmon

3. List four foods Katie might have had for a healthy lunch. _____

   _____

4. Write *C* for Cause and *E* for Effect

   ___ Jimmy goes home to eat a good, hot meal.

   ___ Jimmy has probably eaten doughnuts for breakfast.

5. Write *K* for Katie, *J* for Jimmy, *T* for Toni, or *A* for Anna.

   ____ chocolate chip cookies          ____ fish sticks

   ____ candy bar                       ____ chicken nuggets

   ____ banana                          ____ ham

   ____ pear                            ____ corn

   ____ carrots                         ____ oatmeal

On another piece of paper, list all the foods you eat in one day. Classify the foods.

# Flower Fun

 *To **draw conclusions** is to use the information in a story to make a logical assumption.*

Aaaaaahhhhh! It was that time of year again—time to plant flowers. Christina and her dad were trying to decide what kind of flowers to plant this year. Her dad showed her an ad in the morning paper. He wanted Christina to check it out so she could help him determine what they should buy. The two always like to surprise Christina's mom with beautiful flowers before her "big day" in May. Christina was surprised to see Flower Power was having a sale. She knew they had better hurry to the store.

> FLOWER POWER SALE
> Beautiful flowers of all kinds
> — annuals and perennials—
> are all on sale — 25% OFF!
> All pots and hanging baskets
> are on sale, too
> Buy one, get one FREE!
> Reg. $3.99 to $49.99
> Hurry! Sale ends Tuesday!
> Flower Power
> 2418 Harbour Ave.

1. What time of year is it? _____

2. Circle the day in May on which Christina and her dad want her mother to enjoy beautiful flowers.

   Father's Day          Earth Day          Mother's Day          Easter

3. Circle why Christina and her dad will probably go to Flower Power today.

   because they are having a sale

   because they want to plant today

   because the two always plant flowers together

4. Why was Christina surprised that Flower Power was having a sale? _____

   _____

5. Why might Christina and her dad want to buy new pots or hanging baskets? _____

   _____

6. Why does the ad say to hurry? _____

   _____

# On the Move

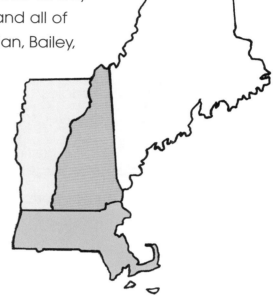

Sam and Danny cannot believe that they have to move away from Florida. Florida is so awesome! They can play outside all day long—every day. It is almost always warm and sunny, and all of their friends live there. What will they do without Brendan, Bailey, John, Alexis, and Brian? They will never have such great friends again. Never!

However, Sam and Danny are very excited for their dad. He has a great new job. The only problem is that the job is in New Hampshire. Danny was not even sure where this state was located. After learning that it is way up north near Canada, both boys did get a little excited about playing in the snow. Danny has always wanted to learn to ski, and Sam thinks playing ice hockey sounds like fun.

Sam and Danny also like the location of New Hampshire. It is between Maine and Vermont and not far from Boston, Massachusetts. Quebec, Canada, borders this state on the north. Neither of the boys has ever visited this part of the country, so they are now looking forward to exploring a new area. If only their friends could come with them! Their parents have promised that they can visit their old friends over spring break and even go to Disney World. The boys think that moving to New Hampshire will not be so bad after all.

1. **How do Sam and Danny feel about Florida?** _____

   _____

2. **Circle how Sam and Danny feel about leaving their friends.**

   **They are sad.**

   **They do not know what they will do without their good friends.**

   **They know they will make a lot of new friends.**

3. **Circle how the boys feel about moving to New Hampshire.**

   **They think it sounds like a fun, interesting part of the country.**

   **They are excited about visiting their old friends on spring break.**

   **They are disappointed that it is next to Vermont.**

4. **On the map above, label New Hampshire and the country and states that border it.**

# The Wonderful Whale

 *A **summary** tells the most important parts of a story.*

**For each paragraph, circle the sentence that tells the most important part.**

**1.** The largest animal that has ever lived is the blue whale. It can grow up to 90 metres long and weigh more than 100 tonnes. Whales, for the most part, are enormous creatures. However, some kinds only grow to be 3 to 4.5 metres long.

**The blue whale is the largest animal.**

**Most whales are enormous creatures.**

**Some whales are only 3 to 4.5 metres long.**

**2.** Whales look a lot like fish. However, whales differ from fish in many ways. For example, the tail fin of a fish is up and down; the tail fin of a whale is sideways. Fish breathe through gills. Whales have lungs and must come to the surface from time to time to breathe. Whales can hold their breath for a very long time. The sperm whale can hold its breath for about an hour.

**Whales and fish do not share similar breathing patterns.**

**Whales can hold their breath for about an hour.**

**Whales might look a lot like fish, but the two are very different.**

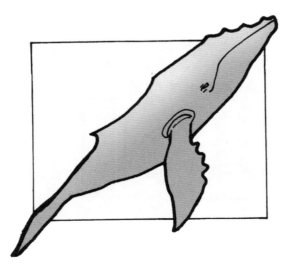

**3.** Baleen whales have no teeth. Toothed whales have teeth. Baleen whales have hundreds of thin plates in their mouth. They use these plates to strain out food from the water. Their diet consists of tiny plants and animals. Toothed whales eat such foods as other fish, cuttlefish, and squid.

**Whales can be divided into two groups— baleen and toothed.**

**Baleen whales have plates in their mouths; toothed whales do not.**

**Toothed whales use their teeth to chew their food.**

4.     Whales have a layer of fat called blubber. Blubber keeps them warm. Whales can live off their blubber for a long time if food is scarce. Blubber also helps whales float, as it is lighter than water.

**Layers of fat are called blubber.**

**Blubber is very important to whales and has many purposes.**

**Blubber is what makes whales float.**

5.  Write the main idea of each paragraph to complete a summary about whales.

_____

_____

_____

_____

_____

6.  Fill in the whale and the fish with the following descriptions. Write what the two have in common in the shared space. Write the descriptions that are specific to each on the spaces that don't overlap.

can hold breath for long time         people love to watch

gills                             tail fin sideways

live in ponds               tail fin up and down

live in oceans              lungs

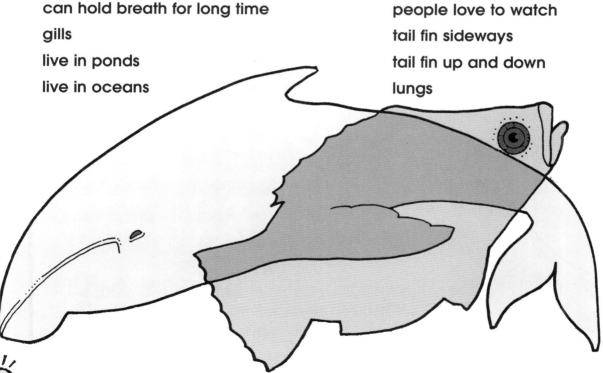

**Read information about another animal. On another piece of paper, write a summary of the information.**

# Climbing Blindly

 A **fact** is information that can be proven.
(Example: Asia is a continent.)

An **opinion** is information that tells what someone thinks.
(Example: Asia is the most interesting continent in the world.)

Mount Everest is the highest mountain in the world. This mountain is located in Asia. Asia is home to all five of the world's highest mountains. Mount Everest's peak is more than 8.8 kilometres above sea level. That is very high!

Many climbers have tried to climb to the top of Mount Everest's approximately 8850-metre peak. The first people to reach the peak were Sir Edmund Hillary and Tenzing Norgay. Since then, about 900 people have survived the climb to Mount Everest's top.

One of the successful climbers is Erik Weihenmayer. Like all who try to climb this huge mountain, Erik faced strong winds, snow, and avalanches. However, what really made Erik's climb unbelievable is the fact that he is blind. After losing his vision at age 13, Erik began climbing at age 16. He has climbed the tallest mountains on five continents. Erik became the first blind person to reach the peak of Mount Everest.

At the age of 32, Erik began his climb as part of a 19-member team. His team wore bells that he could follow during his climb, and fellow climbers were quick to warn him of such things as a big drop on the right or a boulder to the left. Erik also used long climbing poles and an ice axe to feel his way across the ice, rock, and snow on the mountain.

During his climb, Erik encountered many dangers. He struggled through 160 k.p.h. winds and sliding masses of snow, ice, and rock. Because the air became thinner the higher Erik climbed, he wore an oxygen mask, as do many who climb high mountains. This helped him breathe as he climbed higher and higher. It took Erik about two-and-a half months to reach the top of this incredible mountain.

1. Write *F* for fact or *O* for opinion.

___ Erik is very courageous.

___ The bells made Erik's climb a lot easier.

___ Erik is blind.

___ All climbers should use climbing poles and ice axes.

___ Mount Everest is the world's tallest mountain.

___ Erik's oxygen mask helped him breathe.

___ Erik used tools to help him climb.

___ Erik is proud of his achievement.

2. List three interesting facts from the story. _____

_____

_____

3. Write your opinion of Erik's accomplishment. _____

_____

_____

4. Circle words that describe Erik.

brave        foolish        cautious        strong        daring        athletic

5. What are some climbing tools many climbers use? _____

_____

6. Do you think bells are a good idea for all teams of climbers to use? Why or

why not? _____

_____

_____

7. Why do you think Erik attempted this dangerous climb? _____

_____

_____

**Read about another adventurous person. On another piece of paper, write three facts and three opinions about this person.**

# Don't Worry, Be Happy

*Understanding an author's purpose when writing will make appreciating literature easier for the reader. Authors have a purpose when writing such as to **inform** (give readers facts), to **persuade** (convince readers to do or believe something), or to **entertain** (tell an interesting story).*

If I were a bird, I'd fly up high,
Above the clouds, up in the sky.
I'd float and sing and soar and play,
Without any worries to ruin my day.

If I were a dolphin, I'd splash in the sea,
And dive and flip—what fun for me!
I'd play with friends under the sea so blue.
There'd be no chores or homework to do.

If I were a bear, I'd sleep all day,
And then wake up at night to play.
I'd fish and run and jump and climb,
With no one around to ruin my good time.

If I were a dog, during the day I'd rest,
So when my master came home, I'd be at my best—
Ready to run or play ball or catch,
Ready to jump, roll over, or fetch.

But I'm not a dog or a bird or a bear.
I'm not a dolphin who can swim everywhere.
I'm just a kid who wants to have fun,
But I know I can't till my work's all done!

1. Circle why you think the author wrote this poem.

    to persuade            to inform            to entertain

2. Circle what you think the author is trying to tell you.

    The author wants to fly or swim or play all day.

    Working is not what the author would choose to do.

    The author wants to be an animal.

3. Circle why you think the author thinks about being something else.

    The author wants to escape from worries and work and be free like animals.

    The author wants a pet.

    The author would love to be an animal.

4. List three things the author wants to leave behind. _____

    _____

5. Write the following words on the matching animal. Some words will be used more than once.

    | fly | play ball | splash | jump | climb | float | sing |
    | sleep | run | play | flip | roll over | dive | fetch |
    | soar | rest | fish | catch | | | |

6. Write *F* for Fact or *O* for Opinion.

    ___ The author would like to escape worries and work like a bird or a dolphin.

    ___ The author is unhappy as a human and wants to be an animal.

    ___ The author knows work needs to be finished before playing.

    ___ The author just wants to have fun.

    ___ The author feels sorry for all kids who have to do work.

 Find three articles in a newspaper or magazine that are written for different purposes. Share the articles with a friend.

# Improve Learning by Skating

I believe that all students should be able to rollerblade during school. Rollerblading would allow students to get around the school more quickly. This would leave more class time, and thus, students would learn more. It would also get the students outside quicker, so they could enjoy a longer recess. Because everyone would be moving quickly in the hallways, there would be no time for talking or messing around. The teachers would really like that!

Rollerblading is a very good form of exercise. Just think of how physically fit every student would be! Being physically fit often leads to better health. Consequently, students would be absent less and would be learning more.

Finally, rollerblading is fun. More learning, better physical fitness, and fun, I believe, are the keys to a successful school.

1. **Circle the author's purpose for writing this passage.**

   to persuade                to inform                to entertain

2. **Why do you think the author wrote this article?**_____

   _____

3. **List three reasons students should be allowed to rollerblade during school.**

   _____

   _____

   _____

4. **List three reasons students should not be allowed to rollerblade during school.**

   _____

   _____

   _____

 **On another piece of paper, write an article about a change you would like to see take place. Read the article to a friend.**

# Scholastic Success With

# TESTS: READING

# Reading Comprehension

**Read each story. Then fill in the circle that best completes each sentence or answers each question.**

---

**SAMPLE**

Many people like to glide along the sidewalk on roller skates. They owe a vote of thanks to Joseph Merlin of Belgium. He invented a kind of roller skate back in 1760. His skates **provided** a pretty bumpy ride, however.

**1.** What is the best title for this story?
- ○ **A.** "Inventors"
- ○ **B.** "Famous Inventions"
- ○ **C.** "Belgium"
- ○ **D.** "Early Roller Skates"

**2.** In this story, the word **provided** means
- ○ **A.** scraped.
- ○ **B.** invented.
- ○ **C.** gave
- ○ **D.** took

---

**A.** Boston Post Road is the oldest road in the United States. It is more than 300 years old! Colonists made the road in the 1670s, more than 100 years before American Revolution. They needed a way to carry mail and messages between two growing cities—Boston and New York. The road followed trails established over centuries by the Native peoples.

**1.** What is the best title for this story?
- ○ **A.** "Building Roads"
- ○ **B.** "U.S. Mail"
- ○ **C.** "Two Colonial Cities"
- ○ **D.** "America's First Road"

**2.** You can guess that
- ○ **A.** Boston Post Road is still around.
- ○ **B.** Boston is a small city.
- ○ **C.** Boston Post Road is short.
- ○ **D.** New York is older than Boston.

**3.** You would probably find this story in a book about
- ○ **A.** fairy tales.
- ○ **B.** current events.
- ○ **C.** how to build roads.
- ○ **D.** American history.

**B.** In 1271, Marco Polo left Italy and set out for China. He was just 17 years old! Polo's trip took three and a half years. In China, he discovered a black stone that burned and gave heat. It was coal. Polo also learned about paper-making and the compass. When he got home, he wrote a book about his **journey**.

**I.** Marco Polo traveled to
○ **A.** Greece.
○ **B.** Canada.
○ **C.** China.
○ **D.** Africa.

**2.** In this story, the word **journey** means
○ **A.** trip.
○ **B.** findings.
○ **C.** sailboat.
○ **D.** country.

**3.** Which of these is an *opinion* about Marco Polo?
○ **A.** He lived in the 1200s.
○ **B.** He travelled to China
○ **C.** He was the greatest explorer of all time.
○ **D.** He wrote a book.

**C.** When you're hungry, or even just thinking about food, you often hear your stomach growl. Sometimes, your stomach also growls when you're nervous or excited. What you are actually hearing is your stomach muscles pushing air around inside your stomach.

Your stomach also makes noises right after you eat. That's because your stomach muscles move around to mix the food you've eaten with special juices. When they do this, they also move around the air that you swallowed with your food. This causes your stomach to growl, though not as loudly as when your stomach is empty.

**I.** This story is mainly about
○ **A.** how you digest food.
○ **B.** muscles of the human body.
○ **C.** why your stomach growls.
○ **D.** why people get hungry.

**2.** You can guess that your stomach growls the loudest when you
○ **A.** are eating.
○ **B.** are at school.
○ **C.** yell loudly.
○ **D.** need food.

**3.** Which of the following statements is an *opinion*?
○ **A.** Stomach noises are gross.
○ **B.** Your stomach growls when its muscles push air around in your stomach.
○ **C.** Your stomach can growl when it's full.
○ **D.** Sometimes your stomach growls when you're nervous.

**4.** Your stomach growls because
○ **A.** you have eaten too much.
○ **B.** there is air in your stomach.
○ **C.** you feel sick to your stomach.
○ **D.** you are tired.

**D.** More than 40 fish produce electricity. The most dangerous is the electric eel, a long slimy fish that lives in South America. This snakelike fish gives off electric signals to "see" in the dark water where it lives. These signals bounce off underwater objects and help the eel find fish and frogs to eat.

Once the electric eel **locates** its prey, it fills the water with an electric shock. The organs that produce electricity are in the eel's tail. The shock stuns or kills any small animals in the area around the eel. The electric charge is so strong it could also stun a person or knock over a full-grown horse!

**1.** The electric eel looks like a
   ○ **A.** snake.
   ○ **B.** fish.
   ○ **C.** turtle.
   ○ **D.** bird.

**2.** The author wrote this story to
   ○ **A.** tell about different kinds of eels.
   ○ **B.** tell about electric eels.
   ○ **C.** ask people to protect fish.
   ○ **D.** explain electricity.

**3.** In this story, the word **locates** means
   ○ **A.** swims.
   ○ **B.** eats.
   ○ **C.** slides.
   ○ **D.** finds.

**E.** Popcorn is one of the oldest snack foods in the Americas. When European explorers arrived in the 1400s, Native peoples were growing about 700 types of corn. Popcorn probably originated in South America. It came to be used for both food and decoration. Some tribes used it in their headdresses and necklaces.

These early popcorn lovers couldn't plug in the electric popper or zap the popcorn in the microwave. Instead, they popped the kernels in clay pots over an open fire. Some kinds of popcorn were even popped right on the cob.

Ears of popcorn discovered in a cave in New Mexico were found to be 5600 years old!

**1.** What is the best title for this story?
   ○ **A.** "The History of Popcorn"
   ○ **B.** "Native Peoples"
   ○ **C.** "The First Thanksgiving"
   ○ **D.** "Snack Foods"

**2.** Which happened first?
   ○ **A.** European explorers arrived.
   ○ **B.** Electric poppers were invented.
   ○ **C.** Movie theatres served popcorn.
   ○ **D.** Native peoples of the Americas grew corn.

**3.** Popcorn has been used for
   ○ **A.** sewing.
   ○ **B.** making paint.
   ○ **C.** heating homes.
   ○ **D.** making jewelry.

**4.** This story would probably go on to talk about
   ○ **A.** how microwaves work.
   ○ **B.** the popularity of popcorn today.
   ○ **C.** Native customs.
   ○ **D.** snacks of the world.

# Vocabulary

## Synonyms

Read the underlined word in each phrase. Mark the word below it that has the same (or close to the same) meaning.

**Sample:**

damage the building
- ○ **A.** hurt
- ○ **B.** deck
- ○ **C.** anger
- ○ **D.** command

**1.** argue about it
- ○ **A.** laugh
- ○ **B.** pickle
- ○ **C.** fight
- ○ **D.** whisper

**2.** gradually cook
- ○ **A.** boil
- ○ **B.** slowly
- ○ **C.** hot
- ○ **D.** quickly

**3.** a rose's scent
- ○ **A.** red
- ○ **B.** smell
- ○ **C.** stem
- ○ **D.** colour

**4.** annoy her
- ○ **A.** help
- ○ **B.** necklace
- ○ **C.** bother
- ○ **D.** talk

**5.** wicked character
- ○ **A.** sweet
- ○ **B.** boy
- ○ **C.** helpful
- ○ **D.** mean

**6.** unkind words
- ○ **A.** friendly
- ○ **B.** mean
- ○ **C.** happy
- ○ **D.** shy

**7.** wee child
- ○ **A.** small
- ○ **B.** large
- ○ **C.** happy
- ○ **D.** shy

## Antonyms

Read the underlined word in each phrase. Mark the word below it that means the opposite or nearly the opposite.

**Sample:**

silent evening
- ○ **A.** quiet
- ○ **B.** patient
- ○ **C.** noisy
- ○ **B.** perfect

**1.** worthless watch
- ○ **A.** leather
- ○ **B.** ticking
- ○ **C.** valuable
- ○ **D.** cart

**2.** afternoon stroll
- ○ **A.** walk
- ○ **B.** sun
- ○ **C.** pond
- ○ **D.** run

**3.** antique chest
- ○ **A.** brown
- ○ **B.** old
- ○ **C.** case
- ○ **D.** new

**4.** cheap shoes
- ○ **A.** blue
- ○ **B.** strings
- ○ **C.** expensive
- ○ **D.** free

**5.** exit the building
- ○ **A.** enter
- ○ **B.** door
- ○ **C.** roof
- ○ **D.** leave

**6.** vast ocean
- ○ **A.** large
- ○ **B.** tiny
- ○ **C.** deep
- ○ **D.** shallow

**7.** valuable earrings
- ○ **A.** worthless
- ○ **B.** expensive
- ○ **C.** diamond
- ○ **D.** pendant

# Reading Comprehension

**Read each story. Then fill in the circle that best completes each sentence or answers each question.**

**SAMPLE**

Many people get nosebleeds. That's because the lining inside the nose is very **sensitive**. Dry air or sneezing can irritate it. If one of the small blood vessels in the lining should break, the blood starts to flow!

**1.** What is the best title for this story?
○ **A.** "Eyes, Ears, Nose, and Throat"
○ **B.** "How the Nose Works"
○ **C.** "The Sense of Smell"
○ **D.** "Why You Get Bloody Noses"

**2.** In this story, the word **sensitive** means
○ **A.** pinkish-red.
○ **B.** often bloody.
○ **C.** easily hurt.
○ **D.** very tough.

**A.** Labour Day is a special day for many Canadians and Americans. They get to take the day off! The holiday honours everyone who works—even kids!

The first "workingman's demonstration" took place in Toronto, Canada, in 1872. The parade and speeches were attended by a crowd of 10 000. The U.S.'s first Labour Day was celebrated in 1882. Having been invited to Canada's event earlier that year, a carpenter named Peter McGuire planned a parade for all of the workers in his hometown of New York City. Ten thousand people marched proudly through the streets. That day, they enjoyed music, picnics, and fireworks.

In 1894, Labour Day was made a national holiday in both Canada and the U.S. It is always the first Monday in September.

**1.** What is the best title for this story?
○ **A.** "My Favourite Labour Day"
○ **B.** "Hooray for Parades!"
○ **C.** "The History of Labour Day"
○ **D.** "Holidays Around the World"

**2.** Labour Day became a national holiday
○ **A.** in 1882.
○ **B.** in 1994.
○ **C.** last September.
○ **D.** in 1894.

**3.** Which is an *opinion* about Labour Day?
○ **A.** It always takes place on a Monday.
○ **B.** It is a great holiday.
○ **C.** It was started in Canada.
○ **D.** Its purpose is to honour workers.

**B.**    If one of your classmates made fun of you in the schoolyard, or cheated at a game you were playing together, what would you do? Many people would get angry. Some might even start yelling, pushing, or punching.

At 75th Street School in Los Angeles, California, kids in every grade learn how to solve problems without fighting. The school has a team of students called conflict managers who are specially trained.

How do students become conflict managers? First, they must be in Grade 4 or 5. Then, teachers and other students must choose them. In the playground, these conflict managers keep an eye out for arguments. They help solve problems when students disagree.

**1.**  This article is mainly about
○ **A.** why kids argue.
○ **B.** schools in California.
○ **C.** one solution to playground fighting.
○ **D.** violence in the community.

**2.**  The conflict managers are
○ **A.** college students.
○ **B.** teachers at 75th Street School.
○ **C.** in Grade 1 or 2.
○ **D.** in Grade 4 or 5.

**3.**  The story would probably go on to talk about
○ **A.** popular playground games.
○ **B.** how conflict managers handle arguments.
○ **C.** how to do first aid outdoors.
○ **D.** downtown Los Angeles.

**C.**    In honour of Fire Safety Week, here are some fire-safety tips for you to follow:
• Never play with matches or lighters.
• Ask your parents to make sure your home has smoke detectors and a fire extinguisher.
• Make a plan for escaping from your home in case of fire. Learn two ways out of every room. Pick a spot outside where your family will meet.  Practise!
• If there is a fire in your home, get out and stay out! Use a neighbour's phone to call for help.
• Find a **route** out of the building that is free from smoke and flames. If you have to go through a smoky area to escape, crawl on your hands and knees. The air near the floor will be cooler and less smoky.
• If your clothes catch fire, do not run. Drop to the ground, and roll back and forth to put out the flames.

**1.**  The purpose of this article is to
○ **A.** explain why fires start.
○ **B.** teach fire safety.
○ **C.** describe what a fire is like.
○ **D.** show how fire can be used safely.

**2.**  In this story, the word **route** means
○ **A.** path.
○ **B.** place.
○ **C.** door.
○ **D.** air.

**3.**  To escape a smoky area, you should
○ **A.** run.
○ **B.** scream.
○ **C.** crawl.
○ **D.** roll back and forth on the ground.

**4.**  Which is a *fact* about fire safety?
○ **A.** You should have fire drills often.
○ **B.** In case of fire, save your toys first.
○ **C.** In a fire, the air is cooler near the floor.
○ **D.** Children should never use matches.

**D.** Once upon a time, a man lived in a gloomy basement, where he worked all day long. Even so, he was happy because he sang as he worked.

Above the poor man lived a rich man, who worried all day long about his money. This made him miserable. Being in a bad mood, he really hated to hear the poor man singing.

He wanted the poor man to feel bad, like he did. He thought if the poor man felt bad, he might stop singing. He thought if the poor man had money, he too might worry. So the rich man gave the poor man a big sack of money.

The poor man was happier than ever—until he realized that someone might steal the money from him. So he decided to hide it. But no place seemed safe enough. There was nothing he could do—except worry.

The poor man worried until he grew thin and pale. He no longer felt like singing.

One day, he gave the money back to the rich man. "I can live without this money," he said. "But I cannot live without my song."

**1.** This story tells why
○ **A.** a poor man had no money.
○ **B.** money made a poor man unhappy.
○ **C.** a rich man loved his money.
○ **D.** money made a poor man sing.

**2.** The rich man gave the poor man money
○ **A.** to make him happy.
○ **B.** to make him sing more.
○ **C.** to make him worry.
○ **D.** to make him move away.

**3.** Which happened last?
○ **A.** The rich man worried all day long.
○ **B.** The poor man gave back the money.
○ **C.** The poor man stopped singing.
○ **D.** The rich man gave the poor man a big sack of money.

**E.** Once the howl of the wolf was heard all over the United States' wilderness. But by 1900, only a few thousand wolves roamed free in the U.S. In 1973, the government put wolves on the endangered-species list.

Today, animal activists are working to bring back the wolf. As an experiment, 31 wild wolves from Canada were released in Yellowstone National Park. Nine wolf pups were born there. Now, animal activists want to repeat this success story in New York, Maine, New Mexico, and Arizona.

But, some farmers and ranchers worry that this meat eater will hunt their **livestock**. In New York, dairy farmers worry that wolves will attack their dairy cows. In New Mexico, ranchers worry about wolf attacks on their cattle and sheep.

**1.** What is the main idea of this story?
○ **A.** The wolf program in Yellowstone was a big success.
○ **B.** Although wolves are endangered, not everyone wants to help them.
○ **C.** Wolves are meat eaters.
○ **D.** Ranchers and farmer dislike wolves.

**2.** In this story, the word **livestock** means
○ **A.** farmers.   ○ **B.** barns.
○ **C.** farm animals.   ○ **D.** grass.

**3.** From this article, you could guess that wolves
○ **A.** are dangerous to people.
○ **B.** like sheep better than cows.
○ **C.** are happier in Canada.
○ **D.** might roam into ranches or farms.

# Vocabulary

## Synonyms

Read the underlined word in each phrase.
Mark the word below it that has the
same (or close to the same) meaning.

**Sample:**

<u>mend</u> the fence
- ○ **A.** break
- ○ **C.** fix
- ○ **B.** banana
- ○ **D.** climb

**I.** <u>rapidly</u> stir
- ○ **A.** shake
- ○ **C.** mix
- ○ **B.** quickly
- ○ **D.** slowly

**2.** the student's <u>task</u>
- ○ **A.** smart
- ○ **C.** school
- ○ **B.** job
- ○ **D.** book

**3.** <u>tore</u> paper
- ○ **A.** glued
- ○ **C.** ripped
- ○ **B.** sheet
- ○ **D.** wrote

**4.** an <u>imaginary</u> friend
- ○ **A.** best
- ○ **C.** real
- ○ **B.** kind
- ○ **D.** make-believe

**5.** a log <u>cabin</u>
- ○ **A.** wood
- ○ **C.** brown
- ○ **B.** house
- ○ **D.** room

**6.** loud <u>wail</u>
- ○ **A.** song
- ○ **C.** bang
- ○ **B.** siren
- ○ **D.** cry

**7.** <u>tilt</u> sideways
- ○ **A.** hoe
- ○ **C.** straighten
- ○ **B.** lean
- ○ **D.** tile

## Antonyms

Read the underlined word in each phrase.
Mark the word below it that means the
opposite or nearly the opposite.

**Sample:**

<u>useless</u> tool
- ○ **A.** metal
- ○ **C.** helpful
- ○ **B.** sharp
- ○ **B.** hammer

**I.** loud <u>chuckle</u>
- ○ **A.** laugh
- ○ **C.** radio
- ○ **B.** car
- ○ **D.** sob

**2.** feel <u>ashamed</u>
- ○ **A.** embarrassed
- ○ **C.** sick
- ○ **B.** happy
- ○ **D.** proud

**3.** <u>silent</u> classroom
- ○ **A.** noisy
- ○ **C.** warm
- ○ **B.** teacher
- ○ **D.** quiet

**4.** <u>beneath</u> the roof
- ○ **A.** under
- ○ **C.** above
- ○ **B.** raise
- ○ **D.** below

**5.** a sudden <u>shriek</u>
- ○ **A.** scream
- ○ **C.** whisper
- ○ **B.** reply
- ○ **D.** noise

**6.** a great <u>triumph</u>
- ○ **A.** success
- ○ **C.** failure
- ○ **B.** trial
- ○ **D.** finish

**7.** <u>widen</u> the road
- ○ **A.** narrow
- ○ **C.** curve
- ○ **B.** pave
- ○ **D.** straighten

# Reading Comprehension

**Read each story. Then fill in the circle that best completes each sentence or answers each question.**

**SAMPLE**

Being bitten by a bedbug stinks in more ways than one. It hurts and the bug gives off a bad odour. These critters, each about the size of a grain of rice, **nourish** themselves on human blood. Their odour prevents other bugs from feasting on bedbugs!

**1.** What is the best title for this story?
  ○ **A.** "Why Bedbugs Live in Beds"
  ○ **B.** "How Bedbugs Live"
  ○ **C.** "Bugs that Eat Rice"
  ○ **D.** "Bedbugs Stink"

**2.** In this story, the word **nourish** means
  ○ **A.** feed.
  ○ **B.** clean.
  ○ **C.** hungry.
  ○ **D.** stink.

**A.** A club called the Graffiti Grapplers won't stand for a mess—especially not in their hometown of San Antonio, Texas, in the U.S. The group of teachers and kids paint over graffiti and sweep up litter in their community.

Since the club was founded in 1993, the Grapplers have won many awards. One year, they won $32,500! The club members use the money they receive for projects such as planting trees and flowers around San Antonio.

"These kids have good hearts," Grappler and teacher Linda Pruski said. "They are seeing the positive effect they can have on the community."

**1.** What is the best title for this story?
  ○ **A.** "The History of San Antonio"
  ○ **B.** "A Club for Kids Who Care"
  ○ **C.** "The Growing Problem of Graffiti"
  ○ **D.** "How to Win Big Money"

**2.** The Graffiti Grapplers club was founded
  ○ **A.** in 1990.
  ○ **B.** by teachers and business people.
  ○ **C.** by graffiti artists.
  ○ **D.** in Texas.

**3.** Which of the following is an *opinion* about the Graffiti Grapplers?
  ○ **A.** Its members are teachers and kids.
  ○ **B.** It is based in San Antonio, Texas.
  ○ **C.** It is one of the best clubs in San Antonio.
  ○ **D.** Its members clean up litter and graffiti.

**B.** Once upon a time, most people thought the world was flat. Eventually, new discoveries proved them wrong. Scientists have always thought that all planets moved in nearly circular orbits. Now, they believe that idea may be wrong, too.

Why? Just a few years ago, astronomers discovered a planet outside of our solar system that moves around its sun in a very flattened, egg-shaped or oblong path.

The newly discovered planet is 17 times larger than Earth. It was spotted in a constellation called Cygnus, located 600 trillion miles, or about 70 light-years, from Earth. Now scientists are researching to find out what makes this planet move in such a wacky way.

**1.** The purpose of this article is to
○ **A.** explain why Earth may be flat after all.
○ **B.** show that new discoveries can lead to new ideas.
○ **C.** show that scientists are always right.
○ **D.** discuss how humans could visit Cygnus.

**2.** In this story, the word oblong means
○ **A.** orbit      ○ **C.** shaped like a circle
○ **B.** egg-shaped ○ **D.** discovery

**3.** The newly discovered planet was spotted
○ **A.** in our solar system.
○ **B.** herbivores are small animals.
○ **C.** moving around Earth.
○ **D.** in the constellation Cygnus.

**C.** Animals can't speak in words, but they have many other ways to "talk" to each other. Here's a look at how several different creatures communicate in the wild.
- Giant otters speak in a unique language of whistles, whines, squeals, and snorts. Each sound means a different thing. For instance, one type of snort warns other otters of danger, such as a nearby human hunter.
- Red howler monkeys communicate by howling. Their howls can be heard up to three miles away. In fact, these monkeys are the world's noisiest land animals.
- Wolves curl their lips above their teeth and snarl at other wolves to show who's in charge, and to warn other wolves to back off. Wolves will also howl to signal danger.
- The elephant seal uses its amazing inflatable nose and its nostrils as a giant microphone.

**1.** This article is mainly about
○ **A.** why red howler monkeys are so loud.
○ **B.** animals that use their noses to communicate.
○ **C.** ways different animals communicate.
○ **D.** how giant otters stay safe from hunters.

**2.** According to the article, elephant seals communicate by
○ **A.** inflating their noses.
○ **B.** whistling.
○ **C.** snarling.
○ **D.** wagging their tails.

**3.** The story would probably go on to talk about
○ **A.** what red howler monkeys eat.
○ **B.** how other animals communicate.
○ **C.** where giant otters live.
○ **D.** how wolves talk to giant otters.

**4.** Which is a *fact* about animal communication?
○ **A.** The elephant seal's inflatable nose is really strange.
○ **B.** Listening to red howler monkeys all day would really get on your nerves.
○ **C.** Wolves look scary when they snarl.
○ **D.** Whistles and snorts are part of the giant otter's language.

**D.** What's wet and covers three fourths of the Earth's surface? It's the water that makes up the Earth's five oceans. These oceans are the Pacific, the Atlantic, the Indian, the Southern, and the Arctic. The Pacific Ocean is the largest and deepest. The Arctic Ocean is the smallest and shallowest.

Oceans are the **source** of many different things people need. Ocean water contains salt, a basic cooking need. Some ocean plants, like seaweed, are used for medicine and food. Ocean fishing provides many people with work and food.

Oceans can also be fun places to visit. People who visit the ocean might swim in the waves, hunt for shells, and play in the sand.

On a map, the Earth's four oceans may look just like giant pools of water. But they are so much more than that.

**I.** Which ocean is the deepest?
- ○ **A.** the Pacific
- ○ **B.** the Atlantic
- ○ **C.** the Indian
- ○ **D.** the Arctic

**2.** What is one thing people need that they can get from the ocean?
- ○ **A.** ice
- ○ **B.** salt
- ○ **C.** sand
- ○ **D.** waves

**3.** How much of the Earth's surface do oceans cover?
- ○ **A.** one third
- ○ **B.** one half
- ○ **C.** two thirds
- ○ **D.** three fourths

**4.** In this story, the word **source** means
- ○ **A.** store.
- ○ **B.** salty.
- ○ **C.** place to get.
- ○ **D.** place to put.

---

**E.** Ghosts and ghouls have raised more than $100 million to help poor children around the world. How? By trick-or-treating!

They were trick-or-treating for UNICEF. UNICEF is the United Nation's Children's Fund.

Founded in 1946, UNICEF has helped children in more than 150 poor or war-torn countries get food, shelter, and medicine. Every year it adopts a new slogan, such as "Increase the Peace!"

A group of kids from Philadelphia in the U. S. founded the trick-or-treat for UNICEF program in 1950. They raised $17. Ever since, kids dressed in their Halloween best have followed suit—and, as the program has grown, the amount of money kids raise has grown far beyond $17 annually. In fact, in a recent year, kids around the world helped raise $2.7 million. This year, they could raise even more!

**I.** What is the main idea of this story?
- ○ **A.** Halloween is one of kids' favourite holidays.
- ○ **B.** Trick-or-treat for UNICEF is a successful program to raise money for poor children.
- ○ **C.** Trick-or-treat for UNICEF was founded in 1950.
- ○ **D.** Trick-or-treat for UNICEF is no longer a popular program.

**2.** Which happened last?
- ○ **A.** UNICEF was founded.
- ○ **B.** Kids began trick-or-treating for UNICEF.
- ○ **C.** Kids helped raise $2.7 million for UNICEF.
- ○ **D.** A group of kids from Philadelphia raised $17.

**3.** From this article, you could guess that
- ○ **A.** large numbers of children participate in trick-or-treat for UNICEF.
- ○ **B.** kids from Philadelphia are nicer than most other kids.
- ○ **C.** the trick-or-treat for UNICEF program made more money in the 1950s than it does now.
- ○ **D.** kids get more candy when they trick-or-treat for UNICEF.

# Vocabulary

## Synonyms

Read the underlined word in each phrase. Mark the word below it that has the same (or close to the same) meaning.

**Sample:**

argue loudly
- ○ **A.** agree
- ○ **B.** fight
- ○ **C.** toaster
- ○ **D.** shout

**1.** current event
- ○ **A.** funny
- ○ **B.** article
- ○ **C.** recent
- ○ **D.** old

**2.** sharp fang
- ○ **A.** tooth
- ○ **B.** knife
- ○ **C.** mouth
- ○ **D.** eat

**3.** solid foundation
- ○ **A.** rock
- ○ **B.** base
- ○ **C.** breeze
- ○ **D.** ice

**4.** eerie sound
- ○ **A.** loud
- ○ **B.** spooky
- ○ **C.** monster
- ○ **D.** whisper

**5.** stroll downtown
- ○ **A.** appear
- ○ **B.** drive
- ○ **C.** store
- ○ **D.** walk

**6.** false statement
- ○ **A.** loud
- ○ **B.** whispered
- ○ **C.** sworn
- ○ **D.** untrue

**7.** blend in
- ○ **A.** fill
- ○ **B.** mix
- ○ **C.** throw
- ○ **D.** push

## Antonyms

Read the underlined word in each phrase. Mark the word below it that means the opposite or nearly the opposite.

**Sample:**

latch the door
- ○ **A.** unlock
- ○ **B.** slam
- ○ **C.** lock
- ○ **D.** knob

**1.** sturdy table
- ○ **A.** strong
- ○ **B.** dining
- ○ **C.** fragile
- ○ **D.** chair

**2.** descend the staircase
- ○ **A.** go down
- ○ **B.** sweep
- ○ **C.** hide
- ○ **D.** climb up

**3.** nasty person
- ○ **A.** pleasant
- ○ **B.** mean
- ○ **C.** wise
- ○ **D.** human

**4.** widen the path
- ○ **A.** enlarge
- ○ **B.** trail
- ○ **C.** hike
- ○ **D.** narrow

**5.** hero's bravery
- ○ **A.** courage
- ○ **B.** cowardice
- ○ **C.** wealth
- ○ **D.** win

**6.** assist others
- ○ **A.** help
- ○ **B.** talk to
- ○ **C.** ignore
- ○ **D.** follow

**7.** brief recess
- ○ **A.** fun
- ○ **B.** boring
- ○ **C.** short
- ○ **D.** long

# Reading Comprehension

**Read each story. Then fill in the circle that best completes each sentence or answers each question.**

**SAMPLE**

In 1998, Tom Whittaker made history. He became the first disabled person to climb Mount Everest. Ten years earlier, Tom had been in a car accident. He was badly **injured**. He lost both his right foot and his kneecap. Still, Tom wasn't going to let anything keep him from his goal. He was going to climb the world's tallest mountain.

**1.** In this passage, the word **injured** means
○ **A.** ignored.
○ **B.** annoyed.
○ **C.** shaken.
○ **D.** hurt.

**2.** This story is mainly about
○ **A.** how people avoid knee injuries.
○ **B.** why Mount Everest is too dangerous to climb.
○ **C.** a disabled person who climbed Mount Everest.
○ **D.** some very serious car accidents.

**A.** For most of us, headaches aren't a big deal. We get them now and then. They cause a little pain, then they go away. For about one in 10 people, however, headaches are more serious. They get extremely strong headaches called migraines.

Migraine headaches are more than just annoying. They can last for several hours, or even several days. Sometimes, people with migraines have so much pain that they have to stay in bed. They may not be able to do everyday activities. Often, they miss school or work. The problem is larger than you might think. Migraine headaches result in more than one million lost school days every year.

No one knows exactly what causes migraines. In different people, different things can set one off. With some people, eating certain foods can **trigger** a migraine. With others, it may be loud noises or blinking lights.

**1.** Compared to ordinary headaches, migraines are much
○ **A.** less serious.
○ **B.** less painful.
○ **C.** more painful.
○ **D.** more common.

**2.** In this story, the word **trigger** means
○ **A.** stop.
○ **B.** cause.
○ **C.** help.
○ **D.** slow down.

**B.** Wilt Chamberlain was once basketball's greatest superstar. He played in the 1960s and 1970s. The big seven-foot centre was a dazzling scorer. During his career, he had many excellent games. One game, however, stands out above the rest. That was the night he scored 100 points.

Why was the 100-point game so amazing? On most nights, it's not easy for a team to score that many points, let alone a player. Yet on March 2, 1962, Wilt did it all by himself. Wilt's team was the Philadelphia 76ers. The 76ers were playing against the New York Knicks. From the very beginning of the game, the 76ers gave the ball to Wilt. Almost every time they did so, Wilt managed to score. By halftime, Wilt had 41 points. After three quarters, he had 79 points. The fans went crazy as the game came to an end. Wilt had scored a record 100 points. This was the first time that it happened. It's never happened again.

**1.** What is the best title for this story?
- ○ **A.** "Wilt's 100-Point Game"
- ○ **B.** "The Philadelphia 76ers"
- ○ **C.** "How to Play Basketball"
- ○ **D.** "Isn't This Amazing?"

**2.** Which of these is an *opinion*?
- ○ **A.** Wilt played in the 1960s and 1970s.
- ○ **B.** Wilt was playing for the 76ers.
- ○ **C.** The 76ers were playing against New York.
- ○ **D.** Wilt was basketball's greatest superstar.

**3.** How many points did Wilt have at halftime?
- ○ **A.** 41
- ○ **B.** 79
- ○ **C.** 100
- ○ **D.** 141

**C.** In the summer of 1997, a disaster struck Indonesia. The disaster was a series of fires that sent huge clouds of smoke rising into the air. The fires spread across a huge area. Thousands of acres were destroyed by flame. But it wasn't the flames that caused the most serious problems. It was the smoke. The smoke was so thick that it made people sick, even people hundreds of miles away.

The smoke swept over Indonesia. Then it spread to other countries. In Singapore and Malaysia, cities were choked by a thick layer of hazy smog. Millions of people suffered from the air pollution.

The thick smoke also caused accidents. Drivers could barely see the roads through their windshields. One airplane crashed in the haze. Two ships ran into each other in the sea. In November, rains came and put out the raging fires. By that time, tremendous damage had been done.

**1.** Where did the fires begin?
- ○ **A.** Malaysia.
- ○ **B.** Singapore.
- ○ **C.** Indonesia.
- ○ **D.** Indonesia and Singapore.

**2.** The two ships ran into each other because of
- ○ **A.** heavy rain.
- ○ **B.** thick smoke.
- ○ **C.** high waves.
- ○ **D.** hot flames.

**3.** The article's main purpose is to
- ○ **A.** explain how to put out forest fires.
- ○ **B.** tell you about a disaster in Indonesia.
- ○ **C.** persuade you not to start fires.
- ○ **D.** amuse you with a story about accidents.

**D.** All week long, I looked forward to finishing my book. The book was called *The Secret of the Hidden Cave*. It was a mystery, my favourite kind. Because I was busy with homework, I knew I wouldn't get the opportunity to finish it until Friday. Anyway, thinking about the story gave me something to look forward to. It was the most exciting book I had ever **encountered**.

When Friday came, I sat down on the couch and began to read. Each new page was better than the one before. What would the explorers find at the bottom of the cave? This question was driving me crazy! Finally, I got to the next-to-last page. I was about to learn the secret! When I turned the page, I was shocked. The last page was missing!

"It's not fair," I yelled. Then I heard a giggle. Looking into the next room, I saw my little sister. She was running away with something in her hand.

**I.** What is the best title for this story?
- ○ **A.** "The Mystery of the Missing Page"
- ○ **B.** "Why I Read Books"
- ○ **C.** "Too Much Homework"
- ○ **D.** "The Story of Famous Explorers"

**2.** In this story, the word **encountered** means
- ○ **A.** borrowed.   ○ **C.** finished.
- ○ **B.** returned.   ○ **D.** came across.

**3.** What can you guess from this story?
- ○ **A.** Mystery books are always missing a page.
- ○ **B.** The explorers found a skeleton in the cave.
- ○ **C.** The explorers didn't find anything in the cave.
- ○ **D.** The reader's sister tore out the last page.

**E.** August, 1999, was a sad month for the Russian space program. After 13½ years, it finally abandoned the space station *Mir*. The *Mir* had been in space since 1986. For years, it was the pride of the Russian program. Lately, however, the space station had been the scene of many accidents. Three occurred within a single year. First, a fire broke out on board. The crew of the *Mir* almost had to leave the space station. Then, a cargo ship crashed into the side of the space station. The crash caused major damage to the *Mir*'s solar panels. Finally, a computer breakdown nearly caused disaster.

In the end, none of these accidents caused the shutdown. The *Mir* was left behind because it was simply too old. The equipment was getting creaky. If astronauts stayed there, they would probably be risking their lives. The *Mir* had lasted far longer than expected. When it was built, the space station was supposed to last only five years.

**I.** Which of these is an *opinion*?
- ○ **A.** A cargo ship crashed into the space station.
- ○ **B.** The *Mir* had been in space since 1986.
- ○ **C.** August, 1999, was a sad month for the Russian space program.
- ○ **D.** A fire broke out on board.

**2.** What is the best title for this story?
- ○ **A.** "Lost in Space"
- ○ **B.** "A Safe Journey"
- ○ **C.** "The End of the *Mir*"
- ○ **D.** "All About Russia's Space Program"

**3.** The *Mir* closed down because
- ○ **A.** It was more than five years old.
- ○ **B.** The equipment was too old to be safe.
- ○ **C.** A computer broke down.
- ○ **D.** The astronauts had been in space since 1986.

# Vocabulary

## Synonyms

Read the underlined word in each phrase. Mark the word below it that has the same (or close to the same) meaning.

**Sample:**

take a stroll
- ○ **A.** look
- ○ **B.** number
- ○ **C.** board
- ○ **D.** walk

**1.** squirming around
- ○ **A.** standing
- ○ **B.** running
- ○ **C.** laughing
- ○ **D.** wriggling

**2.** nonstop wailing
- ○ **A.** crying
- ○ **B.** speaking
- ○ **C.** talking
- ○ **D.** joking

**3.** a surprising triumph
- ○ **A.** solution
- ○ **B.** victory
- ○ **C.** friend
- ○ **D.** day

**4.** tattered clothing
- ○ **A.** colourful
- ○ **B.** new
- ○ **C.** worn-out
- ○ **D.** clean

**5.** waterfront location
- ○ **A.** central
- ○ **B.** mountainous
- ○ **C.** island
- ○ **D.** shore

**6.** sole survivor
- ○ **A.** first
- ○ **B.** only
- ○ **C.** last
- ○ **D.** oldest

**7.** tilt your head
- ○ **A.** lean
- ○ **B.** nod
- ○ **C.** shake
- ○ **D.** lay

## Antonyms

Read the underlined word in each phrase. Mark the word below it that means the opposite or nearly the opposite.

**Sample:**

nervous feeling
- ○ **A.** calm
- ○ **B.** frightened
- ○ **C.** angry
- ○ **D.** funny

**1.** tighten the hold
- ○ **A.** return
- ○ **B.** remove
- ○ **C.** slow down
- ○ **D.** loosen

**2.** valuable idea
- ○ **A.** useful
- ○ **B.** super
- ○ **C.** worthless
- ○ **D.** certain

**3.** possible solution
- ○ **A.** problem
- ○ **B.** surprise
- ○ **C.** activity
- ○ **D.** idea

**4.** unfamiliar faces
- ○ **A.** pleasant
- ○ **B.** known
- ○ **C.** beautiful
- ○ **D.** strange

**5.** unfortunate event
- ○ **A.** important
- ○ **B.** early
- ○ **C.** late
- ○ **D.** lucky

**6.** tighten your grip
- ○ **A.** brighten
- ○ **B.** loosen
- ○ **C.** increase
- ○ **D.** maintain

**7.** spare part
- ○ **A.** needed
- ○ **B.** extra
- ○ **C.** loose
- ○ **D.** costly

# Reading Comprehension

**Read each story. Then fill in the circle that best completes each sentence or answers each question.**

**SAMPLE**

Some kids in Japan may not have to feed the fish in their aquariums anymore. That's because they may choose to buy robotic fish instead. Robotic fish are little fish robots powered by light. The light causes the fish to move around inside the aquarium. A special design keeps the fish from bumping into the aquarium's walls.

**I.** A good title for this story would be
○ **A.** "New Aquariums."
○ **B.** "Robotic Fish."
○ **C.** "Pets in Japan."
○ **D.** "The Power of Light."

**2.** What causes the robotic fish to move?
○ **A.** light
○ **B.** fish food
○ **C.** robots
○ **D.** water

**A.** Squeezed into a ship called the *Amistad*, the 53 slaves aboard could barely breathe. Each day, the crew gave them sips of water and scraps of food. The slaves were beaten and chained.

They had been kidnapped from Africa. On July 4, 1839, they broke free. They killed the captain and took control of *Amistad* off Cuba's coast, making the ship a famous symbol of freedom.

The *Amistad* story is famous for the rebellion and for what followed. After breaking free, the slaves tried to sail the ship back to their native Sierra Leone, in West Africa. The U.S. Navy captured the ship off the coast of Long Island and charged the slaves with murder.

In 1841, the U.S. Supreme Court ruled that the Africans had been illegally kidnapped. The Court allowed them to return to Africa.

**I.** What did the *Amistad* become a symbol of?
○ **A.** slavery
○ **B.** Africa
○ **C.** the Supreme Court
○ **D.** freedom

**2.** What happened after the U.S. Navy captured the ship?
○ **A.** The slaves were charged with murder.
○ **B.** The slaves were chained and beaten.
○ **C.** The slaves killed the ship's captain.
○ **D.** The slaves tried to sail to Sierra Leone.

**3.** The best title for this story is
○ **A.** "A History of Slavery."
○ **B.** "The Supreme Court."
○ **C.** "The Story of the *Amistad*."
○ **D.** "U.S. Navy Rescues."

**B.** Test your Australia awareness! Known as the "Land Down Under," Australia may be the world's most beautiful country. It's certainly the only country in the world that's both an island and a continent.

Want more Australia facts? It's about four fifths the size of Canada. Nineteen million people live there. Some of these people are Aborigines. Aborigines were Australia's first settlers, like Native peoples in Canada.

Australia is also home to some **unique** and interesting animals. Koala bears are one example. These picky eaters will only eat leaves from eucalyptus trees. They never drink water. Another famous Australian animal is the kangaroo. There are more kangaroos than people in Australia. A newborn kangaroo lives in its mother's pouch for as long as six months.

**I.** Which of these is an *opinion*?
○ **A.** Australia may be the world's most beautiful country.
○ **B.** Australia is about four fifths the size of Canada.
○ **C.** Some Australians are Aborigines.
○ **D.** There are more kangaroos than people in Australia.

**2.** Koala bears are picky eaters because
○ **A.** they never drink water.
○ **B.** they live in Australia.
○ **C.** they only eat kangaroos.
○ **D.** they only eat eucalyptus leaves.

**3.** In this story, the word **unique** means
○ **A.** large.
○ **B.** small.
○ **C.** one-of-a-kind.
○ **D.** popular.

**C.** Have you heard the buzz about bees? It's possible that the common honeybee can help scientists **detect** deadly land mines, or underground bombs.

Land mines kill more than 20,000 people each year. Soldiers bury the mines during wars, but the mines stay even after the wars have ended. People can't tell where land mines are until they explode.

Scientists are hoping that honeybees can help to find buried land mines and save people's lives.

How will it work? Honeybees' fuzzy bodies collect particles from the air, including particles from land mines. Scientists will use special sensors to check the bees for land mine particles. If they find some, the scientists can track the bees back to the mines and destroy them.

**I.** In this story, the word **detect** means
○ **A.** kill.
○ **B.** find.
○ **C.** collect.
○ **D.** bury.

**2.** According to the story, honeybees will
○ **A.** lead scientists to special sensors.
○ **B.** help lead scientists to land mines.
○ **C.** explode land mines.
○ **D.** sting the soldiers who bury land mines.

**3.** Which is the best summary of this article?
○ **A.** Land mines are dangerous weapons that kill people.
○ **B.** No one can find land mines after soldiers bury them.
○ **C.** Honeybees have fuzzy bodies that collect particles from the air.
○ **D.** Honeybees may be able to help scientists detect land mines.

**D.** When Buddy Koerner eats an orange or a banana at school, he doesn't throw the peels into the trash. Buddy and his class have found a better use for fruit peels, limp lettuce, and soggy bread crusts. With the help of a few hundred worms, the class turns food scraps into a nourishing snack for planet Earth.

Each week, Buddy's class dumps food scraps into a special bin in their classroom. Red worms live inside the bin. They eat the scraps and make castings, or worm poop. The castings form compost, which looks like dark soil. Compost is rich in nutrients to help plants and lawns grow better.

Farmers have been making compost for at least 2,000 years. Today, more and more people are learning to compost in homes and schools. This kind of recycling can really help the planet.

**I.** Castings are
○ **A.** food scraps.
○ **B.** worms.
○ **C.** worm poop.
○ **D.** soil.

**2.** Buddy and his classmates make compost from
○ **A.** worms.
○ **B.** food scraps.
○ **C.** soil.
○ **D.** plants.

**3.** This story probably goes on to talk about
○ **A.** other kinds of worms.
○ **B.** other kinds of recycling.
○ **C.** what Buddy has for lunch every day.
○ **D.** the life cycle of worms.

**E.** Exercise helps to keep people healthy. But not everyone wants to play basketball or run marathons. Fortunately, there are plenty of other ways to get exercise. One good way is hiking.

What is hiking? Hiking really just means taking a long walk. Often, hiking involves going up or down a hill. Most people do it in the countryside, but you can also do it in town. And hiking doesn't really require any special equipment. All you need is a comfortable pair of shoes, a nutritious snack, and some water.

The shoes are very important. Uncomfortable hiking shoes can make walking painful. They can cause blisters or worse. It shouldn't hurt to hike, so wear sturdy, comfortable shoes.

The snack and water are also important. Hiking uses up the body's energy and fluids. A snack and some water can replace what you've lost. That means you'll be able to go up that one last hill.

**I.** If you hike in uncomfortable shoes you could
○ **A.** run out of energy.
○ **B.** get blisters.
○ **C.** fall down.
○ **D.** need more water.

**2.** What is the best title for this story?
○ **A.** "All Kinds of Exercise"
○ **B.** "A Guide to Hiking"
○ **C.** "The Importance of Shoes"
○ **D.** "Nutritious Snacks"

**3.** Which of these is not true about hiking?
○ **A.** It's like walking.
○ **B.** You can do it in the country.
○ **C.** You use a lot of special equipment.
○ **D.** It's important to take water on a hike.

# Vocabulary

## Synonyms

Read the underlined word in each phrase. Mark the word below it that has the same (or close to the same) meaning.

**Sample:**

weary legs
- A. tired
- B. long
- C. active
- D. jumpy

1. unexpected defeat
   - A. game
   - B. number
   - C. loss
   - D. win

2. soaring through the air
   - A. falling
   - B. flying
   - C. walking
   - D. blowing

3. family tradition
   - A. party
   - B. gathering
   - C. friend
   - D. custom

4. fierce animal
   - A. huge
   - B. mean
   - C. tiny
   - D. hungry

5. weekly chore
   - A. meal
   - B. meeting
   - C. party
   - D. job

6. feeling uneasy
   - A. unfit
   - B. difficult
   - C. disappointed
   - D. uncomfortable

7. wring the wet clothes
   - A. hang
   - B. wash
   - C. squeeze
   - D. dry

## Antonyms

Read the underlined word in each phrase. Mark the word below it that means the opposite or nearly the opposite.

**Sample:**

talk rapidly
- A. quickly
- B. slowly
- C. funnily
- D. normally

1. sure thing
   - A. tiring
   - B. uncertain
   - C. new
   - D. old

2. airplane takeoff
   - A. wheel
   - B. landing
   - C. ticket
   - D. flight

3. sloppy work
   - A. neat
   - B. good
   - C. hard
   - D. easy

4. back to reality
   - A. life
   - B. fantasy
   - C. school
   - D. work

5. thorough search
   - A. incomplete
   - B. neat
   - C. incorrect
   - D. successful

6. unseen problems
   - A. unknown
   - B. hard
   - C. serious
   - D. visible

7. valuable gift
   - A. expensive
   - B. birthday
   - C. useless
   - D. good

# Reading Comprehension

**Read each story. Then fill in the circle that best completes each sentence or answers each question.**

**SAMPLE**

Do you think you own the world's tiniest dog? *The Guinness Book of World Records* is the place to check! For 40 years, the *Guinness Book* has been **resolving** arguments about the biggest, the smallest, the fastest, and the strangest things in the world. Want to find out who blew the biggest bubble-gum bubble? Now you know where to look.

**I.** In this passage, the word **resolving** means
○ **A.** starting.
○ **B.** settling.
○ **C.** causing.
○ **D.** recording.

**2.** What is the best title for this passage?
○ **A.** "The World's Smallest Dog"
○ **B.** "Arguing for 40 Years"
○ **C.** "How to Blow a Giant Bubble"
○ **D.** "The Book With All the Records"

**A.** One winter day, a young girl named Jenny was walking her dog named Hero. Jenny took Hero's tennis ball and threw it. "Rats!" she thought as the ball rolled onto the frozen pond. Hero ran out after it in a flash. "Hero!" Jenny screamed, running after her dog.

After about three large steps, the ice cracked under Jenny's feet and she fell into the pond. Hero ran to Jenny, but he fell in the water too. Jenny kept slipping as she tried to climb out. So Hero raised his body and slammed it down on the ice like a hammer, again and again, to break the ice and make a path to the shore. That day Hero was a real hero.

**I.** What is the best title for this story?
○ **A.** "Hero Saves the Day "
○ **B.** "Recognizing Thin Ice"
○ **C.** "Favourite Pets"
○ **D.** "They Used to Play Fetch"

**2.** What can you guess from this story?
○ **A.** Hero hates the water.
○ **B.** Jenny can't swim.
○ **C.** Hero is a smart dog.
○ **D.** Jenny plays Little League baseball.

**3.** Why did Jenny go out on the ice?
○ **A.** to save Hero
○ **B.** to slide around on it
○ **C.** to see how strong it was
○ **D.** to play with Hero

**B.** It happened in 1947. For the first time, an African-American was stepping onto the field to play in a major-league baseball game. Jackie Robinson was playing for the Brooklyn Dodgers, the only team with enough courage to let this great athlete play. That day, baseball's colour barrier was broken forever.

Despite the racism he met both on and off the field, Jackie was named Rookie of the Year and led the league in stolen bases. Two years later, he won the National League's Most Valuable Player (MVP) award. Robinson made it to the Baseball Hall of Fame in 1962.

Jackie changed baseball, but he also changed the way people thought. Civil rights leader Martin Luther King Jr. said, "Without Jackie Robinson, I could never have done what I did."

**I.** In 1947, Jackie Robinson
  ○ **A.** made the Baseball Hall of Fame.
  ○ **B.** was honoured by Martin Luther King.
  ○ **C.** became the first African-American to play in the major leagues.
  ○ **D.** won the MVP award.

**2.** You can guess from this story that Robinson is most famous for
  ○ **A.** breaking baseball's colour barrier.
  ○ **B.** leading the league in stolen bases.
  ○ **C.** playing for the Brooklyn Dodgers.
  ○ **D.** being named Rookie of the Year.

**3.** When did Robinson win the MVP award?
  ○ **A.** the year he joined the Dodgers
  ○ **B.** the year after he joined the Dodgers
  ○ **C.** two years after he joined the Dodgers
  ○ **D.** the year he made it to the Baseball

---

**C.** Almost everyone likes bread. But not everyone knows how easy it is to make it. All you need are yeast, flour, and water.

First, mix a package of yeast with two cups of warm water. Let the mixture stand until bubbles form. Then start adding four cups of flour, a half a cup at a time. When the dough gets too thick to stir, scrape it onto a floured board and knead it. To knead, turn the dough in a circle and fold and punch it. Knead it for ten minutes as you add one more cup of flour. The dough is ready when it feels soft and smooth, not sticky.

After kneading, put the dough in a buttered bowl and cover it with a dish towel. Leave it there for an hour or more to rise. It should double in size. Then, knead it for another minute or so, and shape it into a loaf. Let it rise again for 45 minutes. Pop it in the oven to bake for 45 minutes in a 375-degree (190°C) oven. When it's done, let it cool for ten minutes before slicing.

**I.** After the dough has doubled in size, you
  ○ **A.** knead it for ten minutes.
  ○ **B.** mix the yeast with two cups of water.
  ○ **C.** add flour a half a cup at a time.
  ○ **D.** knead it and shape it into a loaf.

**2.** The purpose of this article is to
  ○ **A.** teach you how to make bread.
  ○ **B.** tell you a funny cooking story.
  ○ **C.** persuade you to cook more.
  ○ **D.** make you like bread.

**3.** From this article, you can conclude that
  ○ **A.** bread requires many ingredients.
  ○ **B.** the author doesn't like bread.
  ○ **C.** making bread takes several hours.
  ○ **D.** dough is difficult to knead.

**D.** Put away those surfboards! Even the best surfer wouldn't want to ride a tsunami. The name tsunami comes from the Japanese language. It's the scientific term for a seismic sea wave, a giant wave caused by an undersea earthquake.

Scientists believe tsunamis occur when an earthquake lifts or tilts the ocean floor. The quake creates very long waves that speed across the sea. Tsunamis travel at up to 800 kilometres an hour. The waves grow in height as they reach the shore. Some monster-sized tsunamis can tower 18 metres or more above the ocean's surface.

Tsunamis are sometimes called tidal waves, but that name is misleading. High and low tides never cause tsunamis, only earthquakes or volcanic eruptions do. But by any name, tsunamis can be very dangerous. Hawaii has been hit by over 40 tsunamis!

**1.** What can cause a tsunami?
○ **A.** high and low tides
○ **B.** seismic sea waves
○ **C.** undersea earthquakes
○ **D.** scientific experiments

**2.** Which of these is an *opinion*?
○ **A.** Hawaii has been hit by over 40 tsunamis.
○ **B.** The best surfer wouldn't want to ride a tsunami.
○ **C.** Tsunamis grow in height as they reach the shore.
○ **D.** Tsunamis travel at up to 800 kilometres per hour.

**3.** This article would probably go on to talk about
○ **A.** destruction caused by tsunamis.
○ **B.** destruction caused by earthquakes.
○ **C.** surfers who like to ride tsunamis.
○ **D.** what causes high and low tides.

**E.** At 7:52 a.m. on May 20, 1927, Charles Lindbergh sat in the cockpit of his plane, the *Spirit of St. Louis*. The 25-year-old American was trying to fly nonstop across the Atlantic Ocean, from New York to Paris. The distance was 5760 kilometres. No one had ever done this. If he made it, air travel would never be the same.

After taking off, Lindbergh had to find his way to Paris without the radar, radios, and computer equipment planes use today. Instead, he had a compass, maps, and the stars to help him find his way. Getting lost would be dangerous. He could easily run out of fuel before reaching land.

Finally, over 33 hours after he began his trip, Lindbergh landed in Paris. As he did, 25 000 people cheered. Lindbergh became an instant hero with a new nickname: the Lone Eagle.

**1.** How was Lindbergh's plane different from planes today?
○ **A.** It didn't have a name.
○ **B.** It had to take off and land on water.
○ **C.** It didn't have computer equipment.
○ **D.** It needed two people to fly it.

**2.** What is the best title for this story?
○ **A.** "The Next Plane to Paris"
○ **B.** "Pilots and Their Planes"
○ **C.** "A Trip Across the Atlantic"
○ **D.** "Lindbergh's Famous Flight"

**3.** Which of these is an *opinion*?
○ **A.** Lindbergh's plane was named the *Spirit of St. Louis*.
○ **B.** Lindbergh was the greatest pilot ever.
○ **C.** Lindbergh's trip took over 33 hours.
○ **D.** When he landed in Paris, 25 000 people cheered.

# Vocabulary

## Synonyms

Read the underlined word in each phrase. Mark the word below it that has the same (or close to the same) meaning.

**Sample:**

abandon the ship
- ○ **A.** leave
- ○ **B.** sail
- ○ **C.** board
- ○ **D.** hide

**I.** narrow corridor
- ○ **A.** road
- ○ **B.** minded
- ○ **C.** door
- ○ **D.** hallway

**2.** riding solo
- ○ **A.** quickly
- ○ **B.** alone
- ○ **C.** carefully
- ○ **D.** fast

**3.** unique flavor
- ○ **A.** sweet
- ○ **B.** first-rate
- ○ **C.** one-of-a-kind
- ○ **D.** ordinary

**4.** soothe the pain
- ○ **A.** ignore
- ○ **B.** relieve
- ○ **C.** feel
- ○ **D.** worsen

**5.** unravel the mystery
- ○ **A.** solve
- ○ **B.** enjoy
- ○ **C.** forget
- ○ **D.** notice

**6.** possess a book
- ○ **A.** own
- ○ **B.** lend
- ○ **C.** carry
- ○ **D.** read

**7.** stale ideas
- ○ **A.** fresh
- ○ **B.** original
- ○ **C.** bad
- ○ **D.** old

## Antonyms

Read the underlined word in each phrase. Mark the word below it that means the opposite or nearly the opposite.

**Sample:**

gush out of the tap
- ○ **A.** spill
- ○ **B.** trickle
- ○ **C.** topple
- ○ **D.** flow

**I.** confident character
- ○ **A.** funny
- ○ **B.** unsure
- ○ **C.** smug
- ○ **D.** pesky

**2.** gritty texture
- ○ **A.** smooth
- ○ **B.** stubby
- ○ **C.** tasty
- ○ **D.** bumpy

**3.** expand your horizons
- ○ **A.** visit
- ○ **B.** shrink
- ○ **C.** colour
- ○ **D.** widen

**4.** an agreement between friends
- ○ **A.** apology
- ○ **B.** formula
- ○ **C.** contract
- ○ **D.** dispute

**5.** coastal highway
- ○ **A.** interstate
- ○ **B.** inland
- ○ **C.** frontier
- ○ **D.** circular

**6.** solemn occasion
- ○ **A.** frequent
- ○ **B.** rare
- ○ **C.** sorry
- ○ **D.** cheerful

**7.** elated look
- ○ **A.** happy
- ○ **B.** unsure
- ○ **C.** sad
- ○ **D.** pleased

# Reading Comprehension

**Read each story. Then fill in the circle that best completes each sentence or answers each question.**

Since 1886, the Statue of Liberty has stood on Liberty Island in New York Bay. The beautiful statue was given to the United States by the people of France. With its torch raised high, the statue has welcomed immigrants from all over the world. It has become a **symbol** of American freedom.

**1.** What is the best title for this story?
○ **A.** "Immigrant Land"
○ **B.** "An American Symbol"
○ **C.** "Liberty Island"
○ **D.** "How a Statue Is Made"

**2.** In this story, the word **symbol** means
○ **A.** sculpture.
○ **B.** celebration.
○ **C.** sign.
○ **D.** warning.

**A.** Adobe is a Spanish word meaning "sun-dried brick." Adobe bricks are made by mixing sand, water, and small amounts of straw or grass. The mixture is then shaped into bricks, dried, and baked in the sun for about two weeks. Since sand is widely available in many deserts, desert dwellers have used adobe to make their homes for thousands of years.

**1.** The main idea of this story is that
○ **A.** adobe bricks are difficult to make.
○ **B.** deserts are hot.
○ **C.** people in deserts often build with adobe.
○ **D.** adobe is a Spanish word.

**2.** You would probably find this story in a book about
○ **A.** weather.
○ **B.** the sun.
○ **C.** building materials.
○ **D.** cactuses.

**3.** Which of these is an *opinion*?
○ **A.** Adobe is made from sand.
○ **B.** Adobe homes are beautiful.
○ **C.** Adobe is a Spanish word.
○ **D.** Adobe is used in building.

**B.** Today, when you send a letter to a friend, it can get there in seconds—by electronic mail. However, centuries ago, sending a letter took much longer. About 2,400 years ago, a Persian king named Cyrus the Great **introduced** the first postal system. Messengers on horseback raced from station to station delivering letters. It took weeks or even months to receive a message from far away!

**1.** In this story, the word **introduced** means
○ **A.** met.
○ **B.** mailed.
○ **C.** used.
○ **D.** started.

**2.** The story would probably go on to talk about
○ **A.** other famous kings.
○ **B.** horses throughout history.
○ **C.** advances in sending mail.
○ **D.** the cost of stamps.

**C.** Scientists have been studying volcanoes for many years. They want to find ways to predict when volcanoes will erupt. Such knowledge could help protect people from a volcano's sudden burst of hot lava and ash. Although scientists can't say exactly when a volcano will erupt, they know that a slight change in the shape of the earth is one warning sign. Another is that some volcanoes emit a gas called sulphur dioxide before they erupt.

**1.** This story is mainly about
○ **A.** becoming a scientist.
○ **B.** natural disasters.
○ **C.** the dangers of volcanoes.
○ **D.** predicting volcanic eruptions.

**2.** You can guess that
○ **A.** scientists can predict all volcanic eruptions.
○ **B.** studying volcanoes is important.
○ **C.** volcanoes usually erupt in summer.
○ **D.** all volcanoes are tall.

**D.** As American pioneers headed west in the late 1700s and early 1800s, they used Conestoga wagons. These wagons were named for the valley in Pennsylvania where they were first built. Teams of four to six horses were used to **draw** the wagons. When it was hot or stormy, pioneers put canvas roofs on their wagons. When the pioneers came to rivers, they removed the vehicles' wide wheels, turning the wagons into boats!

**1.** Conestoga wagons were first made
○ **A.** in the West.
○ **B.** on the prairies.
○ **C.** in Pennsylvania.
○ **D.** in the 1800s.

**2.** In this story, the word **draw** means
○ **A.** run.
○ **B.** float.
○ **C.** paint.
○ **D.** pull.

**3.** Pioneers removed wagon wheels because
○ **A.** they had to cross rivers.
○ **B.** the wheels were broken.
○ **C.** the weather was stormy.
○ **D.** they wanted to sell them.

**E.** Have you ever used an encyclopedia? These reference books contain articles about many subjects. The articles are arranged in alphabetical order. To research a subject, follow these steps:

1. Find the encyclopedia index. It is usually in a separate volume. Use the index to find key words related to the subject you are researching.
2. Record from the index the names of articles related to your subject. Jot down the volume and page numbers so you can find the articles.
3. Using your list of articles, find the correct encyclopedia volumes. Then turn to the page on which each article begins.
4. Read each article. Write down the important information you want to remember.
5. Look at the end of the article for cross references. These references will send you to other articles related to your subject.

**1.** What is the best title for this story?
○ **A.** "Using an Encyclopedia"
○ **B.** "Taking Notes"
○ **C.** "Finding Cross References"
○ **D.** "Locating Subjects"

**2.** You can find cross references
○ **A.** in the front of each volume.
○ **B.** at the end of an article.
○ **C.** in your notes.
○ **D.** at the start of an article.

**3.** You can guess that encyclopedias
○ **A.** are useful research tools.
○ **B.** are just like dictionaries.
○ **C.** are difficult to use.
○ **D.** have very short articles.

**4.** What should you do right after you find the correct volume?
○ **A.** Find the index.
○ **B.** Take notes.
○ **C.** Look for cross references.
○ **D.** Find the article.

**F.**  Dear Editor,
    I am a Grade 4 student here in West Elmville. I am writing to respond to last week's article about school lunches. In the article, school officials said they planned to add more vegetables to the school lunch menu. That's a great idea. However, I would like to make a **recommendation**. Instead of adding more mushy canned veggies, our school cafeterias should have salad bars. A fresh salad is tasty and full of vitamins. And with a salad bar, kids can choose the veggies they like best.
                    Sincerely,
                    A Salad Fan

**1.** In this letter, the word **recommendation** means
○ **A.** meal.
○ **B.** suggestion.
○ **C.** vote.
○ **D.** addition.

**2.** You would probably see this letter
○ **A.** in a local newspaper.
○ **B.** on a school principal's desk.
○ **C.** in your mailbox.
○ **D.** in a book about nutrition.

**3.** The author wrote this letter to
○ **A.** get a job in a cafeteria.
○ **B.** share his or her opinion.
○ **C.** entertain readers.
○ **D.** tell how to grow fresh vegetables.

# Vocabulary

## Synonyms

Read the underlined word in each phrase. Mark the word below it that has the same (or close to the same) meaning.

**Sample:**

massive creature
- ○ **A.** huge
- ○ **B.** quiet
- ○ **C.** hungry
- ○ **D.** ugly

**I.** link together
- ○ **A.** key
- ○ **B.** connect
- ○ **C.** blast
- ○ **D.** walk

**2.** important mission
- ○ **A.** secret
- ○ **B.** day
- ○ **C.** task
- ○ **D.** title

**3.** humorous story
- ○ **A.** long
- ○ **B.** funny
- ○ **C.** short
- ○ **D.** sad

**4.** purchase goods
- ○ **A.** clean
- ○ **B.** paint
- ○ **C.** sell
- ○ **D.** buy

**5.** heavy parcel
- ○ **A.** weight
- ○ **B.** rain
- ○ **C.** light
- ○ **D.** package

**6.** cautious driver
- ○ **A.** fast
- ○ **B.** careful
- ○ **C.** unsafe
- ○ **D.** taxi

**7.** conceal a smile
- ○ **A.** hide
- ○ **B.** draw
- ○ **C.** reveal
- ○ **D.** force

## Multiple Meanings

Read each set of sentences. Mark the word that makes sense in both sentences.

**Sample:**

The doctor said her _____ had a stomach flu.
Be _____ while others at the table finish eating.
- ○ **A.** son
- ○ **B.** staff
- ○ **C.** patient
- ○ **D.** kind

**I.** Wheat and corn are both examples of _____.
I found a few _____ of sand in my shoe.
- ○ **A.** plants
- ○ **B.** grains
- ○ **C.** foods
- ○ **D.** pieces

**2.** He works the early _____ at the library.
Mary had to _____ her chair to get a better view.
- ○ **A.** job
- ○ **B.** turn
- ○ **C.** move
- ○ **D.** shift

**3.** The family bought a _____ of farmland.
Did you enjoy that book's exciting _____?
- ○ **A.** piece
- ○ **B.** plot
- ○ **C.** mile
- ○ **D.** hero

**4.** The baby can't walk, but she _____ along the floor.
The scary movie gave me the _____.
- ○ **A.** creeps
- ○ **B.** moves
- ○ **C.** slithers
- ○ **D.** crawls

# Reading Comprehension

**Read each story. Then fill in the circle that best completes each sentence or answers each question.**

**SAMPLE**

Girls are shooting pucks and scoring goals all over Canada. They are skating their way into a sport once thought to be just for boys. The number of Canadian girls playing in organized ice-hockey leagues **increased** from less than 6000 in the mid-1980s to more than 43,000 in 2000.

**I.** What is the main idea of this story?
○ **A.** Ice hockey is a dangerous sport.
○ **B.** Many girls play ice hockey now.
○ **C.** Only boys should play hockey.
○ **D.** Only girls should play hockey.

**2.** In this story, the word **increased** means
○ **A.** gone up.
○ **B.** skated.
○ **C.** fallen.
○ **D.** gone down.

**A.** The next time you pick up a bag of potato chips, read the label. You might notice a new ingredient—Olestra. Olestra was invented as a **substitute** for ingredients that are high in fat, such as butter or oil. But unlike butter and oil, Olestra doesn't add fat or calories to foods. That's because Olestra is not a food. It just passes through the body, without being digested.

Some people say that snacks containing Olestra taste as delicious as the real things. But Olestra can cause stomach cramps and other side effects. "I would rather see kids eat healthy snacks rather than potato chips," says diet expert Jodie Shield. "That's a better goal than choosing Olestra chips over regular high-fat chips."

**I.** What is the best title for this story?
○ **A.** "Everyone Loves Potato Chips"
○ **B.** "Olestra Tastes Great"
○ **C.** "Olestra May Not Be the Answer"
○ **D.** "How to Improve Your Diet"

**2.** In this story, the word **substitute** means
○ **A.** greasy.          ○ **C.** addition.
○ **B.** replacement.    ○ **D.** subtraction.

**3.** Which is an *opinion* about Olestra?
○ **A.** It tastes delicious.
○ **B.** It isn't digested by the body.
○ **C.** It can be used in snack foods.
○ **D.** It may cause stomach cramps.

**4.** Olestra can be used to make foods
○ **A.** taste better.
○ **B.** saltier.
○ **C.** lower in fat.
○ **D.** lower in cost.

**B.** The state of Connecticut in the U.S. used to have one official hero—a man named Nathan Hale. But in 1993, a Grade 4 class from New Canaan Country School decided that their state should have a female hero too. So the students began researching important women in Connecticut's history. They chose Prudence Crandall, a teacher who had let black students attend her school—even though it was against the law—back in 1832. Eventually, Crandall went to jail for her efforts. After the students chose Crandall, they asked lawmakers to introduce a bill recognizing her as a hero. That bill was made a law in 1995.

**1.** Prudence Crandall was a teacher in
○ **A.** 1993.     ○ **C.** 1832.
○ **B.** 1995.     ○ **D.** 1997.

**2.** Which happened last?
○ **A.** Crandall became a state hero.
○ **B.** Crandall went to jail.
○ **C.** The students chose Crandall.
○ **D.** Crandall let black students go to her school.

**3.** From this story, you can guess that
○ **A.** the fourth-graders went to jail.
○ **B.** Nathan Hale is no longer a hero.
○ **C.** only men can be heroes.
○ **D.** women probably aren't recognized as heroes as often as they could be.

---

**C.**               November 20, 1997
Dear Principal,
    I think the students at our school should wear uniforms. Many schools already have them. Uniforms will help our families save money, since we would have to **purchase** only one or two uniforms for the whole year. Uniforms could also give us more pride in our school. And best of all, if we all wore uniforms, kids wouldn't tease each other about their clothes.
    I know some students think uniforms are ugly and uncomfortable. But maybe we can pick a uniform that everyone likes. I think this is a terrific idea for our school.

        Sincerely,
        Justin Jones

**1.** This letter was written by
○ **A.** a father.
○ **B.** a mother.
○ **C.** a teacher.
○ **D.** a student.

**2.** In this letter, the word **purchase** means
○ **A.** wear.     ○ **C.** buy.
○ **B.** see.       ○ **D.** sell.

**3.** Which of these is a *fact* about uniforms?
○ **A.** They are uncomfortable.
○ **B.** Some schools already have them.
○ **C.** They are ugly.
○ **D.** They aren't too expensive.

**4.** Justin wrote this letter to
○ **A.** ask for new clothes.
○ **B.** apologize to the principal.
○ **C.** suggest that students wear uniforms.
○ **D.** thank the principal.

**5.** Some students don't want to wear uniforms because they think
○ **A.** uniforms are expensive.
○ **B.** school pride is silly.
○ **C.** the principal is mean.
○ **D.** uniforms can be ugly and uncomfortable.

**D.**  Zoom! Each spring, dozens of cars race from New York City to Washington, D.C.—without using a single drop of gas! These cars run on electricity.

Most cars run on gasoline. When cars burn this fuel, they pollute the air with smelly exhaust. Electric cars run on batteries. Since they don't burn fuel, they produce much less pollution.

Events, like this 496-kilometre race, give electric carmakers a chance to show off their **vehicles**. They hope to convince people that electric cars are the wave of the future. But so far, electric cars can travel only about 64 kilometres on one charge of electricity. A gasoline-powered car could probably go about 320 kilometres on one tank of gas. That means electric cars require five times as many pit stops—and that may be the reason that these cars haven't caught on yet.

**I.**  What is the main idea of this article?
○ **A.** Gasoline is an expensive fuel.
○ **B.** Electric-car races are exciting.
○ **C.** Everyone wants an electric car.
○ **D.** The electric car is a clean, if slow, way to travel.

**2.**  In this article, the word **vehicles** means
○ **A.** cars.   ○ **C.** speed.
○ **B.** gasoline.   ○ **D.** tires.

**3.**  Cars produce smelly exhaust when they
○ **A.** recharge.   ○ **C.** burn gasoline.
○ **B.** speed.   ○ **D.** use batteries.

**4.**  The next paragraph might talk about
○ **A.** monster trucks.
○ **B.** other ways to cut down on car pollution.
○ **C.** other uses of electricity.
○ **D.** famous race-car drivers.

---

**E.**  Many years ago in Greece, there lived a king named Midas. He wished for the power to turn things to gold simply by touching them. Since Midas was a good king, a god named Dionysus granted his wish. Shouting with joy, Midas ran through his palace, touching everything. And everything he owned became gold. He was rich beyond his wildest dreams.

At dinner time, King Midas reached for some bread, and the bread turned to gold. He reached for some water, and his lips turned the water to gold. King Midas realized he would soon die of hunger or thirst. Weeping gold tears, he went to the god Dionysus and begged the god to remove the golden touch.

"You have been greedy and foolish," scolded Dionysus. But he took pity on Midas, and sent the king to a special river to wash his hands. Midas did so, and the golden touch was washed away.

**I.**  This story is mainly about
○ **A.** how Midas got to be very rich.
○ **B.** how Midas learned a lesson about being greedy.
○ **C.** how Dionysus played a mean trick.
○ **D.** how to cook gold food.

**2.**  Midas got rid of the golden touch by
○ **A.** eating bread and water.
○ **B.** washing his hands in a fountain.
○ **C.** sleeping in a special bed.
○ **D.** washing his hands in a special river.

**3.**  This story teaches that
○ **A.** all wishes are foolish.
○ **B.** some things are more important than gold.
○ **C.** some rivers are cleaner than others.
○ **D.** Greek gods should feel sorry for kings who love gold.

# Vocabulary

## Synonyms

Read the underlined word in each phrase. Mark the word below it that has the same (or close to the same) meaning.

**Sample:**
injure your foot
- ○ **A.** hurt
- ○ **B.** kill
- ○ **C.** toe
- ○ **D.** tickle

1. holler loudly
   - ○ **A.** noisy
   - ○ **B.** whisper
   - ○ **C.** shout
   - ○ **D.** laugh

2. take a ferry
   - ○ **A.** car
   - ○ **B.** boat
   - ○ **C.** grab
   - ○ **D.** taxi

3. faithful dog
   - ○ **A.** brown
   - ○ **B.** furry
   - ○ **C.** collar
   - ○ **D.** loyal

4. bewildered student
   - ○ **A.** smart
   - ○ **B.** book
   - ○ **C.** confused
   - ○ **D.** teacher

5. solid foundation
   - ○ **A.** base
   - ○ **B.** rock
   - ○ **C.** roof
   - ○ **D.** hard

6. essential equipment
   - ○ **A.** necessary
   - ○ **B.** expensive
   - ○ **C.** cheap
   - ○ **D.** sturdy

7. rigid material
   - ○ **A.** stiff
   - ○ **B.** red
   - ○ **C.** natural
   - ○ **D.** soft

## Antonyms

Read the underlined word in each phrase. Mark the word below it that means the opposite or nearly the opposite.

**Sample:**
felt sorrow
- ○ **A.** silly
- ○ **B.** joy
- ○ **C.** saw
- ○ **D.** sadness

1. brief message
   - ○ **A.** short
   - ○ **B.** long
   - ○ **C.** note
   - ○ **D.** funny

2. the nearest exit
   - ○ **A.** entrance
   - ○ **B.** slow
   - ○ **C.** door
   - ○ **D.** leave

3. a harmless spider
   - ○ **A.** safe
   - ○ **B.** ugly
   - ○ **C.** hairy
   - ○ **D.** poisonous

4. a harsh sound
   - ○ **A.** gentle
   - ○ **B.** scream
   - ○ **C.** noise
   - ○ **D.** alarm

5. visit frequently
   - ○ **A.** often
   - ○ **B.** travel
   - ○ **C.** rarely
   - ○ **D.** gladly

6. efficient worker
   - ○ **A.** busy
   - ○ **B.** hard
   - ○ **C.** wasteful
   - ○ **D.** careful

7. defiant attitude
   - ○ **A.** unhappy
   - ○ **B.** respectful
   - ○ **C.** confused
   - ○ **D.** poor

# Reading Comprehension

Read each story. Then fill in the circle that best completes
each sentence or answers each question.

**SAMPLE**

More hurricanes happen in September than in any other month. Why? In the late summer and early fall, ocean water is warm after a summer in the sun. The warm, **moist** air rises off the surface of the ocean and forms thunderstorms. The thunderstorms can spin into powerful hurricanes.

**I.** What is the best title for this story?
○ **A.** "Why Hurricanes Are So Powerful"
○ **B.** "Why Hurricanes Often Happen in September"
○ **C.** "Why the Ocean Is Warm in September"
○ **D.** "Why Late Summer and Early Fall Are Great Seasons"

**2.** In this story, the word **moist** means
○ **A.** makes.
○ **B.** wet.
○ **C.** stops.
○ **D.** hides.

**A.** Kids at Dupuy Elementary school in Birmingham, Alabama, study more than reading, writing, and math. They also take classes in manners! They practise when to say "please" and "thank you" and learn the polite way to pass food at the lunch table.

They also learn to eat with a fork, not fingers; to say "hello" and not "yo" when they answer the phone; to shake hands when meeting someone—especially a grown-up; not to interrupt when others are speaking; and to say "excuse me" instead of pushing.

**I.** This story is mostly about
○ **A.** how to pass food at the lunch table.
○ **B.** a school's classes in manners.
○ **C.** why Alabama students are so polite.
○ **D.** how one school teaches reading, writing, and math.

**2.** At Dupuy Elementary school, kids learn the polite way to
○ **A.** study math.
○ **B.** interrupt when others are speaking.
○ **C.** pass food at the lunch table.
○ **D.** pass food on the school bus.

**3.** Which of the following statements is an *opinion*?
○ **A.** More schools should teach classes in manners.
○ **B.** Dupuy Elementary school teaches classes in manners.
○ **C.** Many schools don't teach classes in manners.
○ **D.** Dupuy's classes teach kids to shake hands when meeting someone.

**B.**   When people think about wildlife, they often think about fields and forests. But many wild animals live in cities. One creature often found in city skies is the peregrine falcon.

In the wilderness, peregrine falcons make their homes on steep, rocky cliffs. In cities, these birds nest on skyscrapers. Peregrine falcons like to be high in the sky so they can spot their favourite food—pigeons. Then the falcons swoop down and snatch their **prey** right out of the sky!

So if you live in a city and you see something whiz by faster than 320 kilometres per hour, it may not be a jet plane. It may be a peregrine falcon—the fastest flying animal alive!

**I.**   In this story, the word **prey** means an animal that
  ○ **A.** can fly.        ○ **B.** is hunted.
  ○ **C.** has wings.      ○ **D.** lives in cities.

**2.**   A peregrine falcon can fly faster than
  ○ **A.** 3200 kilometres per hour.
  ○ **B.** a jet plane.
  ○ **C.** a few other flying animals.
  ○ **D.** 320 kilometres per hour.

**3.**   From this story, you can guess that
  ○ **A.** peregrine falcons eat nothing but pigeons.
  ○ **B.** peregrine falcons build huge nests.
  ○ **C.** peregrine falcons live both in cities and in the wilderness.
  ○ **D.** peregrine falcons live only in cities.

**C.**   If you're a kid under 18, and you live in New Orleans, Louisiana, U.S., you can't be out on the street on a school night after 8 p.m. If you are under 16 and you want to visit the U.S.'s largest mall—the Mall of America in Bloomington, Minnesota—on a Friday or Saturday night, you have to be with your mom or dad, or another grown-up.

Rules like these are called curfews. They prevent people from travelling freely, usually after dark. In many places, curfews are a cause of debate. Many people think curfews are a good way to **reduce** crimes committed by young people. They say curfews make communities safer. But other people say curfews are unfair because they punish all kids for the behaviour of a few troublemakers.

**I.**   In this story, the word **reduce** means
  ○ **A.** make more.
  ○ **B.** stop totally.
  ○ **C.** make fewer.
  ○ **D.** spread.

**2.**   In New Orleans, kids under 18 can't be out on the streets after 8 p.m.
  ○ **A.** on any night.
  ○ **B.** on school nights.
  ○ **C.** on Fridays and Saturdays.
  ○ **D.** near the mall.

**3.**   The story tells
  ○ **A.** why the Mall of America is a safe place to visit.
  ○ **B.** why most people want curfews in their communities.
  ○ **C.** why most people think curfews are unfair.
  ○ **D.** why people disagree about curfews.

**4.**   Which of these is a *fact* about curfews?
  ○ **A.** They are unfair to kids.
  ○ **B.** They prevent people from travelling freely.
  ○ **C.** They always make communities safer.
  ○ **D.** The city of New Orleans is lucky to have one.

**D.** If you saw Stan Herd at work, you'd probably think that he looked like an ordinary farmer. And most of the **materials** he works with—like seeds, soil, and a tractor—are just ordinary farm items. But in one very big way, Stan has little in common with other farmers. Stan Herd doesn't just plant crops, he's a crop artist! Stan plants and shapes crops into pictures so huge you need to view them from an airplane.

Many of Stan's pictures are modelled after famous works of art. For example, he once planted 20 acres of crops in the shape of Vincent van Gogh's painting "Sunflowers." Naturally, Stan used real sunflowers.

Stan does most of his work on his farm in Kansas. But recently, he travelled to New York City to plant a landscape along the East River. No need for an airplane in the city—you can see Stan's work from nearby skyscrapers!

**I.** What is the main idea of this story?
 ○ **A.** Stan Herd is a better artist than Vincent van Gogh.
 ○ **B.** Stan Herd uses some very strange materials on his farm.
 ○ **C.** Stan Herd's art is so big, you must view it from an airplane.
 ○ **D.** Stan Herd is not just a farmer, he's a crop artist.

**2.** In this story, the word **materials** means
 ○ **A.** tools.    ○ **C.** fabrics.
 ○ **B.** crops.   ○ **D.** tractor.

**3.** In this story, where did Stan Herd plant a landscape?
 ○ **A.** along the East River in Kansas.
 ○ **B.** on top of a skyscraper in New York City
 ○ **C.** along the East River in New York City
 ○ **D.** near the Kansas River

**E.** One day the sun and the wind had an argument. The wind claimed that he was stronger than the sun. "Wrong," replied the sun. "I am stronger than you."

As they were disputing, a woman came down the road, wearing a heavy woollen coat.

"Here's how we can decide who is stronger," shouted the wind. "See that woman. Let's see which of us can remove her coat."

"Good idea," the sun replied. "You go first." So the wind started to blow. He blew and blew, as hard as he could. Trees swayed almost to the ground, but the woman only wrapped her coat more tightly around her.

Now the sun began to shine. She shone down on the woman, until the woman grew warm and unbuttoned her coat. The sun kept on shining. Soon, the woman removed her coat and laid it over her arm.

"Alas, you win," said the wind to the sun. "Your gentleness has succeeded where my rudeness failed."

**I.** This story is mainly about
 ○ **A.** solar power.
 ○ **B.** how the wind beat the sun in a contest.
 ○ **C.** how the wind learned a lesson from the sun.
 ○ **D.** why we don't wear coats when it's warm out.

**2.** The woman removed her coat because
 ○ **A.** the wind was blowing it off.
 ○ **B.** she became too warm in the sun.
 ○ **C.** she wanted the wind to lose the contest.
 ○ **D.** she didn't like the coat.

**3.** This story teaches that
 ○ **A.** you shouldn't wear a coat in warm weather.
 ○ **B.** the wind shouldn't blow so hard.
 ○ **C.** bullies often get their way.
 ○ **D.** kindness may get you further than rudeness.

# Vocabulary

## Synonyms

Read the underlined word in each phrase. Mark the word below it that has the same (or close to the same) meaning.

**Sample:**
annoy your brother
- ○ **A.** help
- ○ **B.** bother
- ○ **C.** sister
- ○ **D.** please

**I.** summer drought
- ○ **A.** dry spell
- ○ **B.** rainy season
- ○ **C.** winter
- ○ **D.** sunshine

**2.** brief lesson
- ○ **A.** long
- ○ **B.** tennis
- ○ **C.** teacher
- ○ **D.** short

**3.** strong ability
- ○ **A.** smell
- ○ **B.** muscle
- ○ **C.** skill
- ○ **D.** weakness

**4.** hastily finished
- ○ **A.** quickly
- ○ **B.** completed
- ○ **C.** purple
- ○ **D.** slowly

**5.** soar through the sky
- ○ **A.** run
- ○ **B.** fly
- ○ **C.** float
- ○ **D.** cloud

**6.** became hysterical
- ○ **A.** emotional
- ○ **B.** calm
- ○ **C.** tired
- ○ **D.** energetic

**7.** elevate the temperature
- ○ **A.** read
- ○ **B.** criticize
- ○ **C.** describe
- ○ **D.** raise

## Antonyms

Read the underlined word in each phrase. Mark the word below it that means the opposite or nearly the opposite.

**Sample:**
grandmother's kindness
- ○ **A.** age
- ○ **B.** grandchild
- ○ **C.** meanness
- ○ **D.** happiness

**I.** fortunate event
- ○ **A.** unlucky
- ○ **B.** lucky
- ○ **C.** happening
- ○ **D.** exciting

**2.** student's failure
- ○ **A.** books
- ○ **B.** teacher
- ○ **C.** problem
- ○ **D.** success

**3.** friendly youngster
- ○ **A.** adult
- ○ **B.** puppy
- ○ **C.** child
- ○ **D.** rude

**4.** amuse the child
- ○ **A.** bore
- ○ **B.** scare
- ○ **C.** watch
- ○ **D.** entertain

**5.** fled the disaster
- ○ **A.** ran to
- ○ **B.** caused
- ○ **C.** ran from
- ○ **D.** tragedy

**6.** an earned privilege
- ○ **A.** punishment
- ○ **B.** paycheck
- ○ **C.** treat
- ○ **D.** position

**7.** the courage to persist
- ○ **A.** speak
- ○ **B.** act
- ○ **C.** continue
- ○ **D.** quit

# Reading Comprehension

Read each story. Then fill in the circle that best completes each sentence or answers each question.

**SAMPLE**

For centuries, humans have lived in cities. People came to cities to trade goods, to find jobs, and to be near other people. Today, however, experts are asking if cities are still **necessary**. E-mail and the Internet have changed the way people live. They can work from their homes, even if their homes are far from any town. They can shop over the Internet. They can even use the Internet to talk with friends.

**1.** In this passage, the word **necessary** means
  ○ **A.** growing.
  ○ **B.** fun.
  ○ **C.** needed.
  ○ **D.** uncertain.

**2.** This story is mainly about
  ○ **A.** how to work in a city.
  ○ **B.** how people talk with friends.
  ○ **C.** whether or not people still need cities.
  ○ **D.** what is was like to live in old cities.

**A.**     Are you tired of plain old apples and oranges? Add some spice to your diet by trying tropical fruit! If you look around the supermarket, you'll find flavourful items to give your lunch a whole new twist. Here are some possibilities:

Try a mango. You may already be familiar with mango-flavored food, like candy or ice cream. There's nothing quite like a real mango, however. A fresh ripe mango has sweet orange meat. It's the perfect snack in summer.

There's also the star fruit. Shaped like its name, the star fruit is a special crunchy treat.

The pomelo is another idea. Pomelos are like large grapefruits, but sweeter and drier. Since they don't have too much juice, they're a great fruit to eat when you don't want to get your hands sticky.

If none of these interest you, here are some more **suggestions**: papayas, kumquats, cherimoyas, lychees, or mangosteens.

**1.** Compared to pomelos, grapefruits are
  ○ **A.** crunchier.
  ○ **B.** less sweet.
  ○ **C.** less juicy.
  ○ **D.** larger.

**2.** In this story, the word **suggestions** means
  ○ **A.** answers.
  ○ **B.** flavours.
  ○ **C.** ideas.
  ○ **D.** vegetables.

**B.** Many zoos in the U.S. have opened new attractions.

The San Diego Zoo is famous. Now there's a new reason to visit. It's called Ituri Forest. The forest is modelled after an African river basin. Visitors can watch swimming hippos, otters, and buffalo.

In Philadelphia, the zookeepers built a new home for the gorillas. The gorillas have to share their house. Eleven kinds of animals live there.

The Dallas Zoo was very busy. For starters, they opened the Endangered Tiger area. Tigers roam through an actual rain forest. It's the best place to see big cats. They also have a new hospital. It's 20 times bigger than the old one. It has lots of space to help sick animals.

**1.** What is the best title for this story?
  ○ **A.** "Zoos Get Better"
  ○ **B.** "See the Swimming Hippos"
  ○ **C.** "Tigers in the Zoo"
  ○ **D.** "The Dallas Zoo Hospital"

**2.** Which of these is an *opinion*?
  ○ **A.** Visitors can watch swimming hippos.
  ○ **B.** It's 20 times bigger than the old one.
  ○ **C.** It's the best place to see big cats.
  ○ **D.** The Dallas Zoo opened an Endangered Tiger area.

**3.** Where can a visitor see tigers roam?
  ○ **A.** The Philadelphia Zoo
  ○ **B.** The Dallas Zoo
  ○ **C.** The San Diego Zoo
  ○ **D.** Ituri Forest

**C.** Is there life on other planets? Some scientists think so. They don't expect to find human-like creatures or little green men. If life exists, it's probably tiny bacteria. Discoveries here on Earth have shaped this thinking.

For a long time, scientists thought other planets were too cold for life. Now they've changed their minds. It's because of studies done near the South Pole, one of the coldest places on Earth. They've found bacteria that live in the ice. The bacteria survive in tiny pockets of water.

If there's life near the South Pole, there may be life on cold planets. Mars is one possibility. Europa, a moon of Jupiter, is another. Europa is covered with ice. Beneath the ice, there may be an ocean. Scientists say that this water may support life.

**1.** Which is the best summary of this article?
  ○ **A.** Scientists have been studying the South Pole.
  ○ **B.** Life is found on Mars and Europa.
  ○ **C.** Scientists think there may be life on other planets.
  ○ **D.** Europa, an icy moon, may be covered in water.

**2.** Scientists used to believe that
  ○ **A.** cold planets could not support life.
  ○ **B.** little green men lived on other planets.
  ○ **C.** life could be found on Europa.
  ○ **D.** life could be found on Mars.

**3.** Scientists changed their mind about life on other planets because
  ○ **A.** Mars and Europa are not very cold.
  ○ **B.** of voyages to other planets.
  ○ **C.** of studies done here on Earth.
  ○ **D.** Jupiter's moon is covered in ice.

**D.** "Take your rain gear," Sarah's mom said as Sarah ran out the door to catch her ride. "Don't need it," Sarah yelled back. "It's a beautiful day."

In fact, it was a little bit cloudy, but the sun was out. The nature walk was only supposed to take two hours. Sarah was sure that the weather wouldn't change that quickly. As Sarah and her troop walked through the woods, the sky **became** dark and grey. As they marched up the hill toward Skinner's Lake, the wind howled. "I'm glad I brought my poncho," said Shawn. "You never know around here; the weather can change in a second."

Sarah glared at him. "What do you know? It's a beautiful day, Shawn."

"I agree," he replied. "A beautiful day for a thunderstorm."

**1.** How does Sarah seem to feel toward Shawn?
○ **A.** friendly      ○ **C.** worried about
○ **B.** annoyed      ○ **D.** sorry for

**2.** In this story, the word **became** means
○ **A.** grew.      ○ **C.** sounded.
○ **B.** felt.      ○ **D.** was no longer.

**3.** This story probably goes on to talk about
○ **A.** what Sarah and Shawn ate for lunch.
○ **B.** other nature hikes the troop had taken.
○ **C.** different kinds of insects found in the forest.
○ **D.** whether or not it rained.

---

**E.** People in the United States love their ice cream. The average American eats about 47 pints each year. That's almost two hundred scoops of the frozen stuff! There's no doubt about it. They're the biggest ice cream eaters in the world! Who's next? Believe it or not, New Zealand. New Zealanders **consume** about 40 pints a year. Australians are in third place at 32 pints each.

You might think that Canadians would be big ice cream eaters. After all, Canada is right next to the United States. The average Canadian, however, only eats 27 pints. Maybe it's just too cold in Canada to eat that much ice cream.

The top-selling flavour is vanilla. Some call it boring, but people seem to eat it up. Believe it or not, chocolate is only the fifth favorite flavor. It trails fruit flavors, nut flavors, and candy-mix flavors in popularity.

**1.** Which of these is an *opinion*?
○ **A.** New Zealanders eat 40 pints a year.
○ **B.** Canadians eat 27 pints a year.
○ **C.** It's too cold to eat ice cream in Canada.
○ **D.** The top-selling flavor is vanilla.

**2.** What is the best title for this story?
○ **A.** "Ice Cream Facts and Figures"
○ **B.** "Chocolate Ice Cream"
○ **C.** "New Zealand Takes Second Place in Ice Cream Race"
○ **D.** "How Much Is a Pint?"

**3.** After the United States and New Zealand, which country eats the most ice cream?
○ **A.** Canada
○ **B.** Australia
○ **C.** France
○ **D.** Sweden

**4.** In this story, the word **consume** means
○ **A.** melt.      ○ **C.** make.
○ **B.** eat.      ○ **D.** borrow.

# Vocabulary

## Synonyms

Read the underlined word in each phrase. Mark the word below it that has the same (or close to the same) meaning.

**Sample:**
weary legs
- ○ **A.** tired
- ○ **B.** long
- ○ **C.** active
- ○ **D.** jumpy

**1.** unexpected victory
- ○ **A.** game
- ○ **B.** number
- ○ **C.** loss
- ○ **D.** win

**2.** soaring through the air
- ○ **A.** falling
- ○ **B.** flying
- ○ **C.** walking
- ○ **D.** blowing

**3.** family tradition
- ○ **A.** party
- ○ **B.** gathering
- ○ **C.** friend
- ○ **D.** custom

**4.** giant animal
- ○ **A.** fierce
- ○ **B.** huge
- ○ **C.** tiny
- ○ **D.** hungry

**5.** early sunset
- ○ **A.** meltdown
- ○ **B.** suntan
- ○ **C.** sunrise
- ○ **D.** sundown

**6.** a vague idea
- ○ **A.** bad
- ○ **B.** unclear
- ○ **C.** near
- ○ **D.** great

**7.** an outlandish outfit
- ○ **A.** outgrown
- ○ **B.** handsome
- ○ **C.** silly
- ○ **D.** common

## Antonyms

Read the underlined word in each phrase. Mark the word below it that means the opposite or nearly the opposite.

**Sample:**
walking steadily
- ○ **A.** unevenly
- ○ **B.** quickly
- ○ **C.** slowly
- ○ **D.** normally

**1.** sure thing
- ○ **A.** tiring
- ○ **B.** uncertain
- ○ **C.** new
- ○ **D.** old

**2.** airplane takeoff
- ○ **A.** wheel
- ○ **B.** landing
- ○ **C.** ticket
- ○ **D.** flight

**3.** pleased to meet you
- ○ **A.** lucky
- ○ **B.** surprised
- ○ **C.** happy
- ○ **D.** unhappy

**4.** wicked ways
- ○ **A.** good
- ○ **B.** smart
- ○ **C.** stout
- ○ **D.** awful

**5.** thorough search
- ○ **A.** incomplete
- ○ **B.** neat
- ○ **C.** incorrect
- ○ **D.** successful

**6.** renew the friendship
- ○ **A.** end
- ○ **B.** begin
- ○ **C.** enjoy
- ○ **D.** abuse

**7.** decline the offer
- ○ **A.** ignore
- ○ **B.** accept
- ○ **C.** debate
- ○ **D.** consider

# Reading Comprehension

**Read each story. Then fill in the circle that best completes each sentence or answers each question.**

**SAMPLE**

Are you letting too much water go down the drain in your house? We all know that it's important not to waste water. But most of us use a lot more water than we think. Try these two simple ways to cut your water **consumption.** First, try taking a shower instead of a bath. Showers use a lot less water. You should also turn off the tap while you brush your teeth. Turn it on again to rinse.

**1.** A good title for this story would be
○ **A.** "How to Brush Your Teeth."
○ **B.** "Saving Water."
○ **C.** "Shower Power."
○ **D.** "The World of Water."

**2.** In this story the word **consumption** means
○ **A.** running.  ○ **B.** bill.
○ **C.** action.  ○ **D.** use.

**A.**　Something is happening to kids in Canada today. They are getting more and more out of shape. Why? Today's kids exercise less.

　　Many of them don't spend enough time playing sports and games outside. Instead, they sit inside watching TV or using the computer. This can be bad for their health. It's important to exercise. Exercise helps keep your body running smoothly.

　　Besides, exercise is fun. Playing a sport with other people is much more exciting than watching a TV show alone. So get off that couch and go outside. Join a soccer game or play hide-and-seek. Your body will thank you!

**1.** According to the story, why are today's kids out of shape?
○ **A.** They don't exercise enough.
○ **B.** They don't watch enough TV.
○ **C.** They play too many sports.
○ **D.** They don't eat well.

**2.** The purpose of this story is to
○ **A.** inform you that computers are bad.
○ **B.** entertain you with fun and games.
○ **C.** inform you that kids today are in good shape.
○ **D.** persuade you that it's important to exercise.

**3.** Which of these is an *opinion*?
○ **A.** Many kids today are out of shape.
○ **B.** Not exercising can be bad for your health.
○ **C.** Exercise is fun.
○ **D.** Exercise is good for you.

**B.** STELLA: I wish I knew what to do for that art project about my neighbourhood.

TYRONE: I'm making a collage. I'm going to put in pictures of my neighbours and their homes.

STELLA: That's a great idea. But I don't have any neighbours. In fact, I don't really have a neighbourhood. That's why I'm having trouble.

TYRONE: How can you not have neighbours or a neighbourhood?

STELLA: I live out in the country.

TYRONE: Do you have wild animals where you live?

STELLA: Some. We have raccoons and deer.

TYRONE: Well then, those are your neighbours.

**I.** Why doesn't Stella think she has neighbours?
- ○ **A.** She lives alone.
- ○ **B.** She lives in the country.
- ○ **C.** She lives with too many animals.
- ○ **D.** She doesn't live near Tyrone.

**2.** According to the play, which of the following is probably true?
- ○ **A.** Tyrone lives in the city.
- ○ **B.** Tyrone lives in the country.
- ○ **C.** Stella and Tyrone are neighbours.
- ○ **D.** Stella and Tyrone go to different schools.

**3.** What How are Stella and Tyrone different?
- ○ **A.** One lives in the country and the other doesn't.
- ○ **B.** One has an art project and the other doesn't.
- ○ **C.** One is a raccoon and the other is a deer.
- ○ **D.** One hates animals and the other one loves them.

**4.** What is Tyrone making?
- ○ **A.** a painting
- ○ **B.** a photograph
- ○ **C.** a painting
- ○ **D.** a collage

**C.** Do you think a supermarket is only for shopping? Well, think again. In fact, it's a good place to practise your reading skills. Try reading food labels. They're full of information. A label can tell you a lot about what you're eating.

For instance, a label will tell you the ingredients, or what's in the food. The ingredients are listed from greatest to least amounts. Is sugar first or second on the ingredient list? That means the food has a lot of it.

Labels can also tell you how many calories a serving of food has. But be sure to also look at the serving size. A serving of your favourite cookies may have 100 calories. But the serving size may only be one cookie. If you eat four, you're eating 400 calories!

**I.** If a food has a lot of sugar, where will it be listed on the ingredient list?
- ○ **A.** at the beginning
- ○ **B.** at the end
- ○ **C.** in the middle
- ○ **D.** nowhere

**2.** Why is it important to know a food's serving size?
- ○ **A.** to know how much it costs
- ○ **B.** to know how much to serve others
- ○ **C.** to know how many calories are in what you eat.
- ○ **D.** to know what the food's main ingredients are.

**3.** This story will probably go on to talk about
- ○ **A.** more foods that are 100 calories a serving.
- ○ **B.** popular food ingredients.
- ○ **C.** people's favourite cookies.
- ○ **D.** other information available on food labels.

**4.** What can labels tell you about a food?
- ○ **A.** the size of a serving
- ○ **B.** the number of calories in a serving
- ○ **C.** the ingredients in a food
- ○ **D.** all of the above

**D.**    You're eating pizza at the mall. A friend starts to choke. She is coughing and gasping for air. She can't speak. Would you know what to do?

Carlos Barbosa Jr. did. He performed a lifesaving action called the Heimlich maneuvre when he was only 7 years old. He did it after his dad began to choke on some baby carrots.

"I got behind my father and gave his stomach two squeezes," Carlos said. "The carrot popped out of his mouth and flew across the room."

Dr. Henry Heimlich, an Ohio surgeon, developed the Heimlich maneuvre 25 years ago. It **dislodges** food that gets stuck in the throat and blocks breathing and speaking. Pressing the stomach forces air out of the lungs. This creates an artificial cough. The rush of air from the cough pushes out the food.

**1.** What is the Heimlich maneuvre?
  ○ **A.** a lifesaving action
  ○ **B.** a way of eating
  ○ **C.** a deadly action
  ○ **D.** a way of choking

**2.** What happened after Carlos squeezed his dad's stomach?
  ○ **A.** His dad began to choke.
  ○ **B.** His dad began to laugh.
  ○ **C.** Pizza popped out of his dad's mouth.
  ○ **D.** A carrot popped out of his dad's mouth.

**3.** In this story the word **dislodges** means
  ○ **A.** removes.          ○ **C.** squeezes
  ○ **B.** chokes.           ○ **D.** clogs.

**4.** From this story you can conclude that
  ○ **A.** people choke all the time.
  ○ **B.** Carlos's dad shouldn't eat carrots.
  ○ **C.** the Heimlich maneuvre saves lives.
  ○ **D.** it's dangerous to eat pizza.

**E.**    The movie audience holds its breath. A kid is splashing around in the warm ocean. Suddenly, a shark's fin breaks the surface. It's heading for the unsuspecting swimmer. The background music rises. And then? The kid escapes. And the audience leaves the movie the same way it came in, believing that sharks are evil, people-eating creatures.

The truth is that sharks are neither our enemies nor our friends. Sharks live in every part of the world's oceans, from warm, shallow waters to the darkest depths.  They are not evil. But they are fierce **predators.**

In fact, one of the most amazing sights in nature is to watch a shark hunt its prey. First, the shark cruises slowly. When it has its target in sight, it explodes into action. It charges and attacks. Yikes! No wonder sharks have the reputation they do.

But whatever people think of sharks, they must learn to live with these marine creatures.

**1.** What happens first when a shark hunts?
  ○ **A.** It cruises slowly.
  ○ **B.** It explodes into action.
  ○ **C.** It charges.
  ○ **D.** It attacks.

**2.** What is the best title for this story?
  ○ **A.** "Scary, Scary Sharks"
  ○ **B.** "The Truth About Sharks"
  ○ **C.** "Where Sharks Live"
  ○ **D.** "Good Shark Movies"

**3.** Which of these is <u>not</u> true about sharks?
  ○ **A.** They live in every part of the ocean.
  ○ **B.** They are good hunters.
  ○ **C.** They are evil.
  ○ **D.** They have fins.

**4.** In this story, the word **predators** means
  ○ **A.** hunters.          ○ **C.** swimmers.
  ○ **B.** monsters.         ○ **D.** divers.

# Vocabulary

## Synonyms

Read the underlined word in each phrase.
Mark the word below it that has the same
(or close to the same) meaning.

**Sample:**

adore her
- ○ **A.** help
- ○ **B.** harm
- ○ **C.** love
- ○ **D.** hate

1. herd of cattle
   - ○ **A.** sheep
   - ○ **B.** goats
   - ○ **C.** horses
   - ○ **D.** cows

2. gang of people
   - ○ **A.** group
   - ○ **B.** party
   - ○ **C.** crowd
   - ○ **D.** lack

3. with all his might
   - ○ **A.** will
   - ○ **B.** money
   - ○ **C.** strength
   - ○ **D.** desire

4. squeal with joy
   - ○ **A.** cry
   - ○ **B.** squeak
   - ○ **C.** fill
   - ○ **D.** dance

5. boundless energy
   - ○ **A.** unlimited
   - ○ **B.** violent
   - ○ **C.** bright
   - ○ **D.** silly

6. wool and cotton blend
   - ○ **A.** fabric
   - ○ **B.** material
   - ○ **C.** mix
   - ○ **D.** layer

7. resemble him
   - ○ **A.** look like
   - ○ **B.** resent
   - ○ **C.** hate
   - ○ **D.** watch

## Antonyms

Read the underlined word in each phrase.
Mark the word below it that means the
opposite or nearly the opposite.

**Sample:**

swift runner
- ○ **A.** slow
- ○ **B.** fast
- ○ **C.** front
- ○ **D.** small

1. weak arms
   - ○ **A.** thin
   - ○ **B.** fat
   - ○ **C.** strong
   - ○ **D.** soft

2. busy highway
   - ○ **A.** active
   - ○ **B.** quiet
   - ○ **C.** large
   - ○ **D.** major

3. lean and hungry
   - ○ **A.** good
   - ○ **B.** thin
   - ○ **C.** bad
   - ○ **D.** fat

4. flunk the test
   - ○ **A.** fail
   - ○ **B.** take
   - ○ **C.** miss
   - ○ **D.** pass

5. very ordinary
   - ○ **A.** different
   - ○ **B.** nice
   - ○ **C.** orderly
   - ○ **D.** famous

6. adore her
   - ○ **A.** love
   - ○ **B.** hate
   - ○ **C.** like
   - ○ **D.** dislike

7. wintry day
   - ○ **A.** cold
   - ○ **B.** warm
   - ○ **C.** long
   - ○ **D.** tiring

# Reading Comprehension

Read each story. Then fill in the circle that best completes each sentence or answers each question.

**SAMPLE**

Do you know how to stay safe? The No. 1 safety tip is: Never talk to stangers. When you go out, stick to the safest routes. It's also a good idea to tell a parent or another trusted adult where you'll be. If you're home alone, keep all the doors and windows locked.

**I.** The No. 1 safety tip is
○ **A.** keep doors and windows locked.
○ **B.** stick to the safest routes.
○ **C.** tell you parents where you'll be.
○ **D.** never talk to strangers.

**2.** From this story, you can conclude that talking to strangers is
○ **A.** dangerous.
○ **B.** interesting.
○ **C.** fun.
○ **D.** safe.

**A.** The marine toad looks—and acts—like a creature right out of a horror movie. This fat amphibian from South America weighs 1.4 kilograms and makes a sound like a chugging tractor. When threatened, it oozes poison.

Now, marine toads are terrorizing Florida. They've moved out of the wilds and into the suburbs, where they eat almost anything—small birds, garbage, garden vegetables. They've even developed a taste for pet food!

So how did this monster from South America get to the Sunshine State? In the 1930s, insects were eating the local sugar cane crop. Marine toads were brought to Florida to gobble up the pests. Now the toads have become pests themselves.

**I.** Why were marine toads brought to Florida?
○ **A.** to be pets
○ **B.** to eat garbage
○ **C.** to be food for pets
○ **D.** to eat insects

**2.** What is the best title for this story?
○ **A.** "Insects Damage Crops"
○ **B.** "Horror Movies Are a Scream!"
○ **C.** "How to Grow Sugar Cane"
○ **D.** "Toad Solution Becomes a Problem"

**3.** The next paragraph might talk about
○ **A.** other types of toads.
○ **B.** pets in other countries.
○ **C.** how to solve the marine toad problem.
○ **D.** other crops grown in Florida.

**B.** Who's the biggest athlete in the world? If you're talking size, there's no contest. It's Hawaiian-born sumo wrestler Saleva'a Atisano'e, known in Japan as Konishiki. He tips the scales at 263 kilograms.

Sumo wrestling is the national sport of Japan. Thousands of fans attend sumo matches each week. And wrestlers such as Konishiki are treated like movie stars.

What happens at a sumo match? Two sumo wrestlers face each other. There is a lot of pushing and shoving. One wrestler wins when he forces his opponent out of the 4.5-metre ring, or knocks him to the ground. Each match lasts 20 seconds.

**I.** What happens first during a sumo match?
○ **A.** They push and shove each other.
○ **B.** They face each other.
○ **C.** One forces the other out of the ring.
○ **D.** One knocks the other to the ground.

**2.** Which is a *fact*?
○ **A.** Konishiki is the best sumo wrestler.
○ **B.** Sumo wrestling is a fun sport.
○ **C.** Sumo wrestlers should be treated better than movie stars.
○ **D.** Sumo matches last 20 seconds.

**3.** Saleva'a Atisano'e is also known as
○ **A.** Hawaii.
○ **B.** Konishiki.
○ **C.** Japan.
○ **D.** Sumo.

**C.** Yellowstone National Park contains some of the most beautiful land in the United States. It has more than 800 000 hectares of glorious geysers, deep canyons, and vast forests. No wonder it's a top vacation spot.

But many conservationists fear that Yellowstone is becoming a victim of its own success. Increasing numbers of visitors are overcrowding campgrounds and straining park resources. Last year, more than 3 million people packed into the park.

Yellowstone Park may have its problems, but it is also full of success stories—especially for endangered animals like the grey wolf. Thanks to scientists who set up a wolf-breeding program in 1995, grey wolves are roaming free in Yellowstone for the first time in more than 50 years. Wildlife protection laws have also allowed grizzly bears and bison to bounce back from low numbers in recent years.

**I.** Which of these is an *opinion* about Yellowstone?
○ **A.** It has geysers, canyons, and forests.
○ **B.** It contains some of the most beautiful land in the United States.
○ **C.** Last year, more than 3 million people packed into the park.
○ **D.** Grey wolves are roaming free there.

**2.** How is Yellowstone different now than it was 10 years ago?
○ **A.** It has fewer visitors and forests.
○ **B.** It's smaller than it was.
○ **C.** It has fewer bison and grizzly bears.
○ **D.** It has more visitors and grey wolves.

**3.** The main idea of this story is that
○ **A.** Yellowstone Park has both problems and successes.
○ **B.** Yellowstone is a top vacation spot.
○ **C.** Yellowstone Park contains more than 800 000 hectares.
○ **D.** Grey wolves are endangered.

**D.** It's important to eat a balanced diet. That means plenty of fresh fruit, vegetables, and grains, but less fat and sugar. A **nutritious** diet helps you feel your best. Then you'll be able to do your best in school and in sports. So say goodbye to fatty cheeseburgers and salty french fries! Say hello to pasta with tomato sauce. What's for dessert? How about some fresh fruit topped with yogurt?

You don't have to change your whole diet overnight. A good way to begin is to try substituting one healthful food for one less healthful food each day. Have your cheeseburger with salad instead of with french fries. The next day, try having oatmeal and fruit for breakfast instead of a sugary cereal. You may be surprised one day to find that you have come to like healthful foods as much as the junk food you like now!

**1.** The main purpose of this story is to
- ○ **A.** scare.
- ○ **B.** persuade.
- ○ **C.** sell food.
- ○ **D.** amuse.

**2.** In this story, the word **nutritious** means
- ○ **A.** high-fat.
- ○ **B.** unhealthful.
- ○ **C.** sugary.
- ○ **D.** healthful.

**3.** A good way to begin changing your diet is
- ○ **A.** to eat only candy bars.
- ○ **B.** to eat only healthful food.
- ○ **C.** to eat one healthful food instead of a less healthful food each day.
- ○ **D.** to eat salad at every meal.

**4.** You can conclude from this story that
- ○ **A.** high-fat foods are less healthful than lower-fat foods.
- ○ **B.** everyone likes bananas.
- ○ **C.** candy bars taste better than apples.
- ○ **D.** you should never eat foods you like.

---

**E.** Jim came over for lunch wearing a blue suit with a short brown tie and a green plaid shirt. I couldn't believe this was going to be my new stepfather. It couldn't be true that my beautiful mother would marry someone who dressed like a clown. I hated him.

Lunch was terrible. Mother kept trying to start a conversation, but neither Jim nor I would say much. Finally, I offered to bring in the dessert just to get away from the clown.

I didn't mean to do it. I guess the plate slipped. But one minute I was handing Jim his blackberry pie, and the next, dark purple berries were oozing all over his shirt and tie.

I was **mortified**. My cheeks turned bright red. Jim looked startled at first, but then he began to laugh. I started laughing too. Maybe this guy was all right, after all. Then I glanced at my mother. She looked happier than I had seen her in a long time.

**1.** In this story the word **mortified** means
- ○ **A.** happy.
- ○ **B.** angry.
- ○ **C.** bored.
- ○ **D.** embarrassed.

**2.** The narrator thinks Jim's clothes look
- ○ **A.** nice.
- ○ **B.** expensive.
- ○ **C.** ridiculous.
- ○ **D.** old and worn.

**3.** From the story, you might guess that
- ○ **A.** Jim didn't seem likeable at first.
- ○ **B.** the narrator liked Jim from the start.
- ○ **C.** Jim had no sense of humour.
- ○ **D.** Jim didn't like blackberry pie.

**4.** What is the best title for this story?
- ○ **A.** "I Love Pie"
- ○ **B.** "My New Stepfather"
- ○ **C.** "The World's Best Lunch"
- ○ **D.** "Mothers Shouldn't Marry"

# Vocabulary

In each of the following paragraphs, a word is missing. First, read the paragraph. Then find the missing word in the list of words beneath the paragraph. Fill in the circle next to the word that is missing.

**Sample:**

Jerome's dad belongs to the neighbourhood safety association. Last night, it was his turn to _____ the block. He walked up and down all night, keeping everyone safe.

○ **A.** sweep     ○ **C.** patrol
○ **B.** leave     ○ **D.** study

**1.** When airplanes were first _____ they were small and relatively slow. However, today's jets can go very fast. Some go faster than the speed of sound!

○ **A.** improved     ○ **C.** searched
○ **B.** repaired     ○ **D.** invented

**2.** One thing that hasn't changed is the seriousness of a pilot's job. A pilot should never be _____. Doing careless or dangerous things risks lives.

○ **A.** reckless     ○ **C.** energetic
○ **B.** accurate     ○ **D.** strict

**3.** Passengers are certainly more comfortable than they used to be. Old jet planes were very noisy. People used to wear earplugs to keep out the _____.

○ **A.** filth     ○ **C.** din
○ **B.** music     ○ **D.** moisture

**4.** Airports have changed too. Passengers used to walk onto the runway when getting on and off the plane. Now, upon _____, the plane parks at a gate that leads right inside the airport.

○ **A.** transportation     ○ **C.** publication
○ **B.** landscape     ○ **D.** arrival

**5.** Many people would say that having chocolate cake for _____ is a great treat. They can't think of a better way to end dinner.

○ **A.** lunch     ○ **C.** dessert
○ **B.** delightful     ○ **D.** menu

**6.** It's rare that these people will leave even a _____ of chocolate cake on their plates. They want to eat every bite.

○ **A.** morsel     ○ **C.** mortal
○ **B.** meager     ○ **D.** variety

**7.** For them, a delicious chocolate cake is absolute _____. Nothing could make it better.

○ **A.** elegant     ○ **C.** keen
○ **B.** perfection     ○ **D.** perilous

**8.** Chocolate is native to the Americas. Its delightfully _____ smell has been making people's mouths water for a long time.

○ **A.** fragile     ○ **C.** plentiful
○ **B.** fragrant     ○ **D.** vivid

**9.** Today, a chocolate _____ can produce many different products. A chocolate factory might make candy bars, cocoa powder, chocolate-chip cookies, and lots of other delicious treats.

○ **A.** gourmet     ○ **C.** manufacturer
○ **B.** compound     ○ **D.** provision

# Reading Comprehension

Read each story. Then fill in the circle that best completes each sentence or answers each question.

**SAMPLE**

Have you ever seen someone on the beach with a sunburn? A sunburn can be quite painful. If the burn is really bad, the skin might blister and peel. Sunburn is caused by the sun's powerful ultraviolet (UV) rays. Wearing sunscreen can **shield** your skin from those damaging rays.

**I.** What is the main idea of this story?
  ○ **A.** Ultraviolet rays cause sunburn.
  ○ **B.** Sunburn can cause fever.
  ○ **C.** Sunscreen makes skin peel.
  ○ **D.** The sun is strong at the beach.

**2.** In this story, the word **shield** means
  ○ **A.** burn.
  ○ **B.** lift.
  ○ **C.** protect.
  ○ **D.** open.

**A.** For thousands of years, the Inuit people have lived in what is now the northern part of Canada. For the last 150 years, the Canadian government has ruled the land. Recently, the government agreed to let the Inuit **govern** part of Canada's Northwest Territories.

Since April 1, 1999, the Canadian map has included the new territory of Nunavut, which means "our land" in Inuktitut, the Inuit language. The Inuit wanted control of this land because it is the land of their ancestors. Here they have set up their own territorial government.

**I.** In this story, the word **govern** means
  ○ **A.** build.
  ○ **B.** rule.
  ○ **C.** map.
  ○ **D.** live.

**2.** The Inuit language is called
  ○ **A.** Canadian.      ○ **C.** Nunavut.
  ○ **B.** Inuktitut.      ○ **D.** Inuit.

**3.** You can guess from the story that
  ○ **A.** Canada's government once took over Inuit land.
  ○ **B.** Canada's government is unfair.
  ○ **C.** the Inuit cannot speak English.
  ○ **D.** many Canadian people will soon be homeless.

**4.** Which would come first on a timeline?
  ○ **A.** The Inuit make a deal with Canada's government.
  ○ **B.** The Canadian government begins ruling the Inuit's land.
  ○ **C.** The Inuit settle in Canada.
  ○ **D.** Nunavut appears on a map.

**B.** Animals depend on plants and other animals for food. The relationship among these animals and plants is called a food chain. The food chain keeps nature in balance. Here's how it works:

**1. Producers:** Plants and other organisms that provide food for animals make up the first link in a food chain.

**2. Herbivores:** These are animals that eat only plants. Called "prey," they are hunted by meat eaters.

**3. Carnivores:** These meat eaters feed on herbivores. They are also called "predators." When they die, their remains fertilize the ground and help plants grow.

**I.** What is the best title for this story?
- ◯ **A.** "Plant-Eating Animals"
- ◯ **B.** "Understanding the Food Chain"
- ◯ **C.** "Predators"
- ◯ **D.** "Plants That Need Animals"

**2.** Animals that eat meat are called
- ◯ **A.** herbivores.
- ◯ **C.** prey.
- ◯ **B.** producers.
- ◯ **D.** carnivores.

**3.** You can guess from this story that
- ◯ **A.** herbivores are hungrier than carnivores.
- ◯ **B.** herbivores are small animals.
- ◯ **C.** carnivores eat lots of vegetables.
- ◯ **D.** each link in the food chain is important.

**C.** In Greek mythology, Zeus and Hera were the leaders of the Greek gods. They were husband and wife, and Hera sometimes became angry with Zeus when he spent too much time away from home.

Sometimes, Zeus went to the mountains to play with the forest creatures who lived there. Hera always chased after him because she thought Zeus was wasting time. But every time, a charming creature named Echo chatted with Hera and distracted her until Zeus had escaped.

When Hera figured out that Echo had been tricking her, she was **furious**. "Your talk has made a fool of me!" she screamed. "From now on you will have nothing to say, except what others say to you first!"

From that day on, poor Echo could only repeat the last words of what others said.

**I.** This story is mostly about
- ◯ **A.** Greek gods.
- ◯ **C.** Greece.
- ◯ **B.** forests.
- ◯ **D.** tricks.

**2.** You can guess from this story that
- ◯ **A.** Zeus was tall and handsome.
- ◯ **B.** Echo had a loud voice.
- ◯ **C.** Hera was very gentle.
- ◯ **D.** Echo lived in the forest.

**3.** In this story, the word **furious** means
- ◯ **A.** angry.
- ◯ **C.** happy.
- ◯ **B.** foolish.
- ◯ **D.** tricky.

**4.** Zeus and Hera were
- ◯ **A.** soldiers.
- ◯ **C.** forest creatures.
- ◯ **B.** married.
- ◯ **D.** human.

**5.** This story is an example of a
- ◯ **A.** myth.
- ◯ **C.** news article.
- ◯ **B.** poem.
- ◯ **D.** fairy tale.

**D.** When you play a sport, do you feel that you must win—or else? The Youth Sports Institute in Michigan surveyed 26,000 boys and girls on this topic, and found that many feel pushed to be the best.

Where does the pressure come from? Some kids put pressure on themselves, but many say that parents and coaches are also to blame. They say these adults care only about the final score—not whether kids tried hard or had a good time.

**I.** What is the main idea of this article?
○ **A.** Fewer kids should play baseball.
○ **B.** Youth sports are always fun.
○ **C.** Many kids feel a lot of pressure to win at sports.
○ **D.** Parents should be banned from going to kids' games.

**2.** Which of these statements is a *fact*?
○ **A.** Sports pressure is the worst part of kids' sports.
○ **B.** The Youth Sports Institute surveyed 26,000 kids.
○ **C.** Winning is important.
○ **D.** Coaches should not be allowed to pressure players.

**3.** The author wrote this article to
○ **A.** tell why baseball is good exercise.
○ **B.** tell kids to quit playing sports.
○ **C.** tell about the history of youth sports.
○ **D.** tell about a problem in youth sports.

**4.** The article probably goes on to talk about
○ **A.** solving the problem of sports pressure.
○ **B.** baseball training camps for kids.
○ **C.** ways for teams to win more games.
○ **D.** youth football programs.

---

**E.** In 1844, young Elizabeth Blackwell dreamed of becoming a doctor. There was just one problem: No medical school in the U.S. would accept a woman as a student. Blackwell convinced several doctors to teach her privately. Then, in 1847, she was accepted by a small college in New York. She graduated at the top of her class.

Blackwell travelled to Paris, France, where she studied at a hospital. Even after losing her sight in one eye, Blackwell did not give up her work as a doctor. In the 1850s, she returned to the U.S. and **established** a hospital for women and children. Today, we remember Elizabeth Blackwell as the trailblazer who opened the field of medicine for women in America.

**I.** In this story, the word **established** means
○ **A.** set up.          ○ **C.** named.
○ **B.** cured.          ○ **D.** lost.

**2.** What is the best title for this story?
○ **A.** "Elizabeth Blackwell: Opening College Doors"
○ **B.** "Elizabeth Blackwell: First Woman Doctor"
○ **C.** "The Autobiography of Elizabeth Blackwell"
○ **D.** "Famous Doctors in History"

**3.** Which of these is an *opinion*?
○ **A.** Blackwell lost sight in one eye.
○ **B.** Blackwell became a doctor.
○ **C.** Blackwell lived in the 1800s.
○ **D.** Blackwell was very brave.

**4.** You can guess from this story that Elizabeth Blackwell
○ **A.** got good grades in college.
○ **B.** had French parents.
○ **C.** eventually became totally blind.
○ **D.** died in 1860.

# Vocabulary

In each of the following paragraphs, a word is missing. First, read the paragraph. Then find the missing word in the list of words beneath the paragraph. Fill in the circle next to the word that is missing.

**Sample:**

The car suddenly stopped in the middle of the road. It had run out of ____. The driver had forgotten to fill up the gas tank.

○ **A.** miles      ○ **C.** water
○ **B.** fuel       ○ **D.** popcorn

The driver was late for his soccer game. That was too bad, because he was the best ____ on his team. His teammates counted on him to stop the other team from scoring.

○ **A.** coach      ○ **C.** gardener
○ **B.** goalie      ○ **D.** catcher

**1.** Some really large animals live on the plains of Africa. You might think the biggest ones would be the mightiest hunters, but that's not the case at all. Some of the world's biggest animals eat nothing but leaves, grasses, and shrubs. Instead of hunting other animals, these huge creatures ____ on plant life to survive.

○ **A.** dwell      ○ **C.** grow
○ **B.** sit        ○ **D.** graze

**2.** The largest plant eater of all is the African elephant. In fact, the African elephant is the largest land ____ in the entire world! An adult elephant can weigh as much as 5440 kilograms. And a baby elephant is not exactly tiny: It can weigh up to 113 kilograms at birth!

○ **A.** shark      ○ **C.** mammal
○ **B.** soil       ○ **D.** farmer

**3.** Another very large African plant eater is the white rhinoceros. It is second in size only to the elephant. The adult white rhino can weigh up to 3600 kilograms, or 3.6 ____.

○ **A.** dollars    ○ **C.** litres
○ **B.** tonnes     ○ **D.** metres

**4.** The black rhino is a ____ of the white rhino. Although the two are kin, the black rhino doesn't get nearly as large. At 1360 kilograms, though, the adult black rhino is still pretty big. Both rhinos are very good at using their horns to break off tree branches for dinner.

○ **A.** relative   ○ **C.** friend
○ **B.** neighbour  ○ **D.** killer

**5.** Another African plant eater is the hippopotamus. At 3600 kilograms, the adult hippo often surpasses a white rhino in weight, so you'd feel pretty ____ standing next to either one! The hippo's teeth are excellent tools for munching coarse plants. Its canine teeth are about 50 centimetres long.

○ **A.** gigantic   ○ **C.** small
○ **B.** cold       ○ **D.** loyal

**6.** The hippo's teeth also come in handy for fighting off crocodiles. That's important, because hippos spend lots of time in rivers, where crocs live. Hippos have sensitive skin that can easily get too dry. They hang out in the river to keep their skin ____.

○ **A.** nasty      ○ **C.** brown
○ **B.** moist      ○ **D.** clean

# Reading Comprehension

**Read each story. Then fill in the circle that best completes each sentence or answers each question.**

**SAMPLE**

During a 1992 storm, a ship lost thousands of plastic turtles, frogs, and ducks in the Pacific Ocean. Since then, the toys have drifted thousands of miles. Some have shown up in the ocean off of Alaska. The toys' trip helps scientists study how wind affects drifting objects.

**I.** A good title for this story would be
○ **A.** "Drifting Toys."
○ **B.** "The Great State of Alaska."
○ **C.** "The Big Storm."
○ **D.** "Turtles in the Sea."

**2.** Scientists study the toys to find out about
○ **A.** how turtles swim.
○ **B.** how wind affects drifting objects.
○ **C.** how far it is from Russia to Alaska.
○ **D.** how ducks find food.

**A.** Ten-year-old Caitlin Gionfriddo makes money in a funny way. She chews Gummi Worms, tastes peanut butter, and chomps on chocolate.

Caitlin has more than a big appetite. The Grade 5 student from Cincinnati, Ohio, helps companies dream up new flavours, names, and colours for their products.

"When kids design things, it's what kids want, not what adults want," says Caitlin.

To understand what kids want, companies need to think like kids. So they hire them. For instance, when Curad was looking for a new kid bandage design, they went straight to the experts. They asked 25 kids what they wanted to put on their cuts and bruises. The kids came up with ideas for fun bandages. Then a cartoonist sketched the ideas. The winner? Tattoo bandages.

**I.** Why did Curad hire 25 kids?
○ **A.** They wanted them to taste Gummi Bears.
○ **B.** They wanted them to taste chocolate.
○ **C.** They wanted them to help design a new bandage.
○ **D.** They wanted them to help design a new toy.

**2.** The main purpose of this story is to
○ **A.** inform you about why companies hire kids.
○ **B.** persuade you to eat more peanut butter.
○ **C.** amuse you with details about Caitlin's life.
○ **D.** explain how bandages are designed.

**3.** You can conclude from this story that
○ **A.** Companies don't care what kids think.
○ **B.** Caitlin really hates what she does.
○ **C.** Companies are out of touch with today's kids.
○ **D.** Products designed for kids are important to companies.

**B.** Tiny ocean **creatures** with horse-shaped heads may seem like characters from a fairy tale. But sea horses are real. And, they're in real danger.

The World Conservation Union, a group that protects nature, has said that sea horses are in danger of becoming extinct. That means that soon there may be no more sea horses left in the world's oceans.

Sea horses are curly-tailed fish. They are usually less than 12 centimetres long. Though small, they're in big demand. Some people collect the odd-looking fish. Others eat them. They're also used in Chinese cures for skin diseases and other illnesses.

Fishermen from Florida to the Philippines support their families by selling sea horses. But overfishing causes the loss of at least 20 million sea horses each year. If something isn't done, the only horses on the planet will be the ones left on dry land.

**I.** What is the best title for this story?
○ **A.** "All Kinds of Horses"
○ **B.** "Disappearing Sea Horses"
○ **C.** "What to Do with Sea Horses"
○ **D.** "Fishing Around the World"

**2.** In this story, the word **creatures** means
○ **A.** animals.
○ **B.** plants.
○ **C.** boats.
○ **D.** waves.

**3.** Why are sea horses disappearing?
○ **A.** They are being eaten by other fish.
○ **B.** They are being overfished.
○ **C.** They are too small to survive in the ocean.
○ **D.** They are suffering from a disease.

**C.** Students in the city of Houston, Texas, are climbing the walls. They're not bored. They're working out!

These days, sports like rock climbing are hot in gym class. Hundreds of physical education programs across the country now offer students all sorts of sports. In-line skating, aerobics, mountain biking, and hiking top the list.

According to the experts, kids ages 4 to 12 should exercise for 60 minutes or more each day. But kids won't exercise if they don't enjoy it. So physical education teachers have found new ways to make exercise fun. For some kids, this means harder and more exciting sports, like rock climbing. For others, it means making activities less competitive. One teacher replaced her school's 1.6-kilometre run with a 12-minute run. That way, everyone finishes at the same time. Even slow runners can enjoy themselves.

**I.** According to the story, how long should kids exercise each day?
○ **A.** 12 minutes
○ **B.** 4 minutes
○ **C.** 60 minutes
○ **D.** 30 minutes

**2.** What is the best title for this story?
○ **A.** "Gym Is Great"
○ **B.** "A New Kind of Gym Class"
○ **C.** "Dodge Ball"
○ **D.** "Rainy Day Activities"

**3.** From this story, you can guess that
○ **A.** it's important to exercise.
○ **B.** it's important to be good at sports.
○ **C.** gym classes are boring.
○ **D.** most schools don't have gym classes.

**D.** Stop. Extreme danger. Access strictly **prohibited**. These warnings greet scientist Tim Dixon as he goes to work each day. Dixon works on El Popocatépetl (Poh-poh-kah-tep-eh-tuhl). El Popo, as it's known, is one of the most dangerous volcanoes in the world.

Dixon is putting special equipment on the Mexican volcano. He hopes the equipment will help scientists predict future eruptions. He has already discovered how surprising El Popo can be. "We were up there when, without warning, there was a large blast," he says. "We felt the shock waves hit us. Then, we saw red-hot pieces of rock falling down." But Dixon was fortunate. The eruption was small. It only lasted a few minutes. He wasn't hurt.

El Popo's last big eruption was 1,200 years ago. It killed many people. Dixon and other scientists want to make sure it doesn't happen again. They hope that before the next big eruption, there will be time to warn people.

**1.** What happened after Dixon felt shock waves on El Popo?
○ **A.** Red-hot pieces of rock fell down.
○ **B.** Many people were killed.
○ **C.** There was a large blast.
○ **D.** Dixon's equipment was ruined.

**2.** In this story, the word **prohibited** means
○ **A.** special
○ **B.** expensive
○ **C.** not watched
○ **D.** not allowed

**3.** Why is Dixon putting special equipment on El Popo?
○ **A.** He wants to keep it from erupting.
○ **B.** He wants to collect some red-hot rocks.
○ **C.** He wants to make it erupt more often.
○ **D.** He wants to predict future eruptions.

**E.** How does getting lowered into the ground by your ankles sound? That's what one worker had to do to reach three ancient mummies in Argentina. It was worth it, though. The mummies were in "near-perfect" condition. Now scientists want to use them to learn about the past.

The mummies are the remains of three kids who died 500 years ago. They were buried under dirt and rock on top of a volcano. There are two girls and a boy. It's hard to tell the exact age of a mummy, but scientists know that the kids were between 8 and 15 years old when they died. No one is certain how they died.

Scientists hope the mummies will help them learn more about the Inca civilization. The Inca were an ancient South American people. They had a huge empire that lasted over 100 years. The mummies may reveal new information about the Inca.

**1.** Which of these is an *opinion*?
○ **A.** There are two girls and a boy.
○ **B.** It was worth it, though.
○ **C.** No one is certain how they died.
○ **D.** The Inca were an ancient South American people.

**2.** Which is the best title for this story?
○ **A.** "The Ancient Inca"
○ **B.** "Three New Mummies"
○ **C.** "How Mummies Are Made"
○ **D.** "Volcanoes in Argentina"

**3.** According to the story, why are the mummies important?
○ **A.** They are in "near-perfect" condition.
○ **B.** They are very young.
○ **C.** Scientists don't know how they died.
○ **D.** Scientists can use them to learn more about the Inca.

# Vocabulary

## Synonyms

Read the underlined word in each phrase. Mark the word below it that has the same (or close to the same) meaning.

**Sample:**

<u>tilt</u> the picture
- ○ **A.** straighten
- ○ **B.** turn
- ○ **C.** hang
- ○ **D.** frame

**I.** building <u>site</u>
- ○ **A.** place
- ○ **B.** time
- ○ **C.** event
- ○ **D.** window

**2.** <u>stout</u> person
- ○ **A.** skinny
- ○ **B.** heavy
- ○ **C.** loud
- ○ **D.** small

**3.** big <u>victory</u>
- ○ **A.** loss
- ○ **B.** win
- ○ **C.** smile
- ○ **D.** frown

**4.** <u>uncover</u> the truth
- ○ **A.** hide
- ○ **B.** find out
- ○ **C.** cover up
- ○ **D.** change

**5.** <u>solemn</u> face
- ○ **A.** smiling
- ○ **B.** happy
- ○ **C.** unhappy
- ○ **D.** serious

**6.** <u>shield</u> your face
- ○ **A.** protect
- ○ **B.** hide
- ○ **C.** wipe
- ○ **D.** hurt

**7.** <u>startled</u> expression
- ○ **A.** puzzled
- ○ **B.** surprised
- ○ **C.** unhappy
- ○ **D.** bothered

## Antonyms

Read the underlined word in each phrase. Mark the word below it that means the opposite or nearly the opposite.

**Sample:**

<u>unkind</u> words
- ○ **A.** mean
- ○ **B.** nice
- ○ **C.** angry
- ○ **D.** funny

**I.** <u>bright</u> room
- ○ **A.** dim
- ○ **B.** loud
- ○ **C.** large
- ○ **D.** airy

**2.** <u>thorough</u> cleaning
- ○ **A.** detailed
- ○ **B.** careful
- ○ **C.** careless
- ○ **D.** yearly

**3.** <u>tremendous</u> force
- ○ **A.** great
- ○ **B.** very little
- ○ **C.** scary
- ○ **D.** unbelievable

**4.** <u>unfriendly</u> people
- ○ **A.** mean
- ○ **B.** kind
- ○ **C.** strange
- ○ **D.** unfamiliar

**5.** <u>terrible</u> time
- ○ **A.** happy
- ○ **B.** great
- ○ **C.** boring
- ○ **D.** surprising

**6.** <u>ancient</u> treasure
- ○ **A.** sunken
- ○ **B.** gold
- ○ **C.** new
- ○ **D.** expensive

**7.** <u>graceful</u> dancer
- ○ **A.** clumsy
- ○ **B.** ballet
- ○ **C.** light
- ○ **D.** young

# Reading Comprehension

Read each story. Then fill in the circle that best completes each sentence or answers each question.

**SAMPLE**

The Canadian province of Manitoba has a rather snaky reputation. That's because thousands and thousands of red-sided garter snakes gather there every winter. Most snakes can't live as far north as Manitoba. The winters are just too cold. But red-sided garter snakes have a way of keeping warm. Every year they slither into an area in central Manitoba. There they pack themselves into underground dens. One den might hold more than 20,000 snakes!

**I.** What is the best title for this story?
- ○ **A.** "All About Manitoba"
- ○ **B.** "All About Snakes"
- ○ **C.** "Winter in the Far North"
- ○ **D.** "Red-Sided Garter Snakes"

**2.** Why can't most snakes live in the far north?
- ○ **A.** The winters are too cold.
- ○ **B.** There aren't enough underground dens.
- ○ **C.** The red-sided garters attack other snakes.
- ○ **D.** They are not allowed into Manitoba.

**A.** On May 13, 1607, colonists from England landed their boats on an island that is now part of Virginia in the United States. They built a settlement there. They called it Fort James—and later Jamestown—in honour of the king of England.

Life in Jamestown was difficult. The settlers suffered from disease and hunger. The winters were very cold. **Disputes** with neighbouring settlements made life in Jamestown dangerous. Many people died. But the survivors did not give up. When their fort burned down, they rebuilt it and made it larger. The colonists stayed in Jamestown for almost 100 years.

**I.** What happened first?
- ○ **A.** The colonists built Fort James.
- ○ **B.** The colonists died from disease and hunger.
- ○ **C.** The colonists rebuilt Fort James after it burned down.
- ○ **D.** The colonists landed on an island.

**2.** In this story, the word **disputes** means
- ○ **A.** ceremonies.
- ○ **C.** illnesses.
- ○ **B.** fights.
- ○ **D.** discussions.

**3.** What is the main idea of this story?
- ○ **A.** Life in Jamestown was difficult.
- ○ **B.** The colonists rebuilt the fort that burned down.
- ○ **C.** Winters in Jamestown were very cold.
- ○ **D.** The settlers died from disease and hunger.

**B.** Everyone knows that salads are delicious and good for you. But making a salad can seem tricky to some people. How do you make a good salad? Just follow these tips:

• Always dry your lettuce or spinach after washing it. Salad dressing won't stick to wet leaves.

• Just lettuce and tomatoes make an okay salad. But why not perk it up with some other vegetables? Try carrots, cucumbers, or mushrooms.

• Try adding a can of beans to your salad. They're tasty, and they make the salad even more nutritious.

• Go easy on the salad dressing. It should complement the taste of the vegetables, not **conceal** it.

**I.** What is one reason it's good to add beans to salad?
○ **A.** Salad dressing sticks to them.
○ **B.** Salad isn't tasty without them.
○ **C.** They make salad more nutritious.
○ **D.** They hide the taste of salad dressing.

**2.** In this story, the word **conceal** means
○ **A.** hide.
○ **B.** reveal.
○ **C.** control.
○ **D.** close.

**3.** What is the best title for this story?
○ **A.** "Salad-Making Tips"
○ **B.** "How to Wash Lettuce"
○ **C.** "How to Make Salad Dressing"
○ **D.** "Why Salad Is Good for You"

**C.** Imagine the most famous person you know of. Sidney Crosby. Miley Cyrus. Prince William. Now think of this: Not one of them is as famous as Helen Keller was in her day.

When she was a baby, Helen Keller became blind and deaf because of an illness. Helen's family didn't think she would ever learn to communicate well. But they didn't count on Helen's teacher, Annie Sullivan. Annie taught Helen to speak and to communicate through sign language. She also taught Helen to read and write Braille, an alphabet system used by blind people. Annie made the world open up for Helen.

Word of Helen's learning spread quickly. She became famous, and people all over the country wanted to meet her. Helen went on to graduate from college, travel the world, and write 13 books. When she died, at the age of 87, she had become one of America's great heroes.

**I.** Why did Helen Keller become so famous?
○ **A.** She was a famous author.
○ **B.** She was Annie Sullivan's student.
○ **C.** She did not let disabilities stop her from achieving her goals.
○ **D.** She met famous people and travelled the world.

**2.** What would Helen's life have been like without Annie Sullivan?
○ **A.** She may not ever have been able to communicate.
○ **B.** She would have been famous anyway.
○ **C.** Her parents would have taught her to read and write.
○ **D.** She would have grown up like any other kid.

**3.** Which of these is the best comparison for how Annie Sullivan changed Helen's life?
○ **A.** a car crashing
○ **B.** a bubble bursting
○ **C.** a rock falling
○ **D.** a flower opening

**D.** Mariel didn't see the new girl coming toward her on the sidewalk until it was too late. She bumped right into the girl, sending books flying everywhere.

"Oh excuse me!" she cried. "I'm so sorry. I didn't see you!"

The new girl smiled. "That's okay. I didn't see you either. I'm Shamala. What's your name?"

"I'm Mariel. Where did your family move here from?"

"We came from Toronto. But before that we lived in Montreal. And before that we lived in Halifax. And I was born in India, so I guess we lived there too, but I was too young to remember."

"Wow, you've lived in a lot of places. I've lived here in the same house all my life. You're really lucky."

Shamala laughed. "That's funny. I was just thinking that you're the lucky one!"

**I.** Why did Mariel bump into Shamala?
- ○ **A.** She didn't like Shamala.
- ○ **B.** Shamala was new.
- ○ **C.** She didn't see Shamala coming.
- ○ **D.** Shamala had lived in a lot of places.

**2.** How are Mariel and Shamala alike?
- ○ **A.** They are both new in the neighbourhood.
- ○ **B.** They have both lived in a lot of places.
- ○ **C.** They are both unfriendly.
- ○ **D.** They both envy the other one's life.

**3.** What is most likely to happen next in this story?
- ○ **A.** Mariel and Shamala never see each other again.
- ○ **B.** Mariel and Shamala become friends.
- ○ **C.** Mariel's family moves.
- ○ **D.** Mariel and Shamala become enemies.

---

**E.** The year is 1912. The day is April 10. The *Titanic* sets sail from England. The enormous ship is three football fields long. Eleven storeys high, it is the largest moving object ever built. The ship has elegant restaurants, a swimming pool, and indoor gardens. Some of the world's richest people stroll through its fine rooms. No one seeing it at this moment would guess that tragedy lies ahead.

It is the ship's first voyage. This floating palace is bound for New York City. The crew intends to set a record getting there. The *Titanic* is the most powerful ship on the sea, brags its builder. There is nothing to fear. Let other ships' crews worry about iceberg warnings. Other ships aren't the *Titanic*. The *Titanic* is **unsinkable**.

Sadly, pride goes before the fall. Around midnight on April 14, 1912, a massive iceberg rips open the mighty ship's steel hull. Tons of water gush in. For the *Titanic*, the end has come.

**I.** In this story the word **unsinkable** means
- ○ **A.** luxurious.     ○ **B.** large.
- ○ **C.** heavy.          ○ **D.** buoyant.

**2.** The *Titanic* was
- ○ **A.** made of stone, just like a palace.
- ○ **B.** filled with luxuries such as swimming pools and gardens.
- ○ **C.** a large restaurant that had been fitted to float.
- ○ **D.** just like every other ship of the time.

**3.** Which adjective best describes the Titanic's builder?
- ○ **A.** excited
- ○ **B.** modest
- ○ **C.** proud
- ○ **D.** deceitful

**4.** What is the purpose of this story?
- ○ **A.** to entertain you with details of the *Titanic* tragedy
- ○ **B.** to scare you into avoiding big ships
- ○ **C.** to help you picture what the *Titanic* was like
- ○ **D.** to persuade you that the *Titanic's* builder was cruel.

# Vocabulary

In each of the following sentences, a word is missing. First, read the sentence. Then find the missing word in the list of words beneath the sentence. Fill in the circle next to the word that is missing.

**Sample:**

It was getting late, so they _____ their pace.
- ○ **A.** ambled
- ○ **C.** quickened
- ○ **B.** measured
- ○ **D.** slowed

**1.** He was _____ around new people and didn't talk much.
- ○ **A.** bold
- ○ **C.** angry
- ○ **B.** timid
- ○ **D.** antsy

**2.** If this _____ weather continues, we will need to turn up the heat.
- ○ **A.** balmy
- ○ **C.** frigid
- ○ **B.** pleasant
- ○ **D.** sweltering

**3.** It is good to be _____ of others, no matter how different they are.
- ○ **A.** tolerant
- ○ **C.** suspicious
- ○ **B.** critical
- ○ **D.** wary

**4.** The mystery of who took his lunch continued to _____ him.
- ○ **A.** surprise
- ○ **C.** baffle
- ○ **B.** delight
- ○ **D.** excite

**5.** Their _____ was about whose turn it was to clean up after dinner.
- ○ **A.** dispute
- ○ **C.** assignment
- ○ **B.** occasion
- ○ **D.** encounter

**6.** "Follow that car!" the woman shouted _____.
- ○ **A.** quietly
- ○ **C.** contentedly
- ○ **B.** frantically
- ○ **D.** blissfully

**7.** She was _____ in her decision and never regretted it.
- ○ **A.** wavering
- ○ **C.** discouraged
- ○ **B.** steadfast
- ○ **D.** disappointed

**8.** The beautiful painting was _____ by a large black mark on it.
- ○ **A.** created
- ○ **C.** helped
- ○ **B.** attacked
- ○ **D.** marred

**9.** He was always _____, shaking hands and thanking everyone.
- ○ **A.** tragic
- ○ **C.** tasteful
- ○ **B.** cordial
- ○ **D.** remote

**10.** Despite being dropped three times, the television made it upstairs _____.
- ○ **A.** shattered
- ○ **C.** roundly
- ○ **B.** happily
- ○ **D.** intact

**11.** My friend's _____ the way I draw realistic-looking animals.
- ○ **A.** admire
- ○ **C.** ignore
- ○ **B.** pity
- ○ **D.** scorn

**12.** She was _____ about moving to a new town where she knew nobody.
- ○ **A.** thrilled
- ○ **C.** anxious
- ○ **B.** jealous
- ○ **D.** mean

**13.** He loves to write so much that we _____ he will be a writer when he grows up.
- ○ **A.** explain
- ○ **C.** regret
- ○ **B.** predict
- ○ **D.** ignore

# GRAMMAR

# Types of Sentences

**A. What kind of sentence is each of the following? Write *declarative, interrogative, exclamatory*, or *imperative* on the line.**

1. Merlin carried the baby to safety. _____

2. Why did traitors poison the town's wells? _____

3. Go back and fetch the missing sword. _____

4. Slip the sword into the groove, and pull it out. _____

5. The king was England's bravest ruler! _____

6. Who will follow Selene? _____

**B. Identify which groups of words are incomplete sentences and which are complete sentences. Write *incomplete* or *complete* on the line.**

1. Sarah at the edge of the square. _____

2. The knights fought so bravely! _____

3. How did Kay treat her dog? _____

4. The sword out of the stone. _____

5. Natalie was trained to be a pilot. _____

**C. Correct the incomplete sentences in part B. Add an action word to each one. Then rewrite the complete sentence on the line.**

1. _____

2. _____

# Types of Sentences

**A.** Add the correct end punctuation mark to each sentence. Then write *declarative, interrogative, exclamatory,* or *imperative* to tell what kind of sentence it is.

> **RETEACHING:** A **declarative sentence** makes a statement. An **interrogative sentence** asks a question. An **exclamatory sentence** shows strong feeling. An **imperative sentence** states a command.

1. How do turtles protect themselves_          _____

2. What heavy, hot suits of steel they wore_          _____

3. Pretend that you are an acrobat or juggler_          _____

4. The students sang songs, told stories, and recited poems_          _____

**B.** Use one of the words below to complete each sentence. Then identify each sentence by writing *declarative, interrogative, exclamatory,* or *imperative.*

>    pass        won        listened        play

1. The audience _____ to the bagpipes.          _____

2. What kind of games did pioneers like to _____?          _____

3. Please _____ me the pepper.          _____

4. I've _____ three chess games in a row!          _____

**C.** Write an example of a declarative, interrogative, exclamatory, and imperative sentence. Be sure to use the correct end punctuation.

1. Declarative: _____

2. Interrogative: _____

3. Exclamatory: _____

4. Imperative: _____

# Types of Sentences

**Decide if there is an error in the underlined part of each sentence. Fill in the bubble next to the correct answer.**

1. <u>you do like</u> to see movies about knights and castles?

    ⓐ You do like

    ⓑ Do you like

    ⓒ correct as is

2. Please hand me that mystery book about <u>the Middle Ages?</u>

    ⓐ the Middle Ages!

    ⓑ the Middle Ages.

    ⓒ correct as is

3. Grandfather described life in the early part <u>of the century.</u>

    ⓐ of the century?

    ⓑ of the century!

    ⓒ correct as is

4. Why don't you write about <u>your life!</u>

    ⓐ your life?

    ⓑ your life.

    ⓒ correct as is

5. <u>Begin by describing</u> your very first memory.

    ⓐ begin by describing

    ⓑ By describing

    ⓒ correct as is

6. I had such fun swimming <u>in the ocean?</u>

    ⓐ in the ocean

    ⓑ in the ocean!

    ⓒ correct as is

7. What do you remember about your first day <u>in school?</u>

    ⓐ in school!

    ⓑ in school.

    ⓒ correct as is

8. <u>another story</u> about our relatives in Italy.

    ⓐ Tell me another story

    ⓑ Another story

    ⓒ correct as is

9. The fish looked so colourful swimming in <u>the Caribbean Sea</u>

    ⓐ the Caribbean Sea!

    ⓑ the Caribbean Sea?

    ⓒ correct as is

10. He told us about <u>his trip?</u>

    ⓐ his trip

    ⓑ his trip.

    ⓒ correct as is

# Simple and Complete Subjects and Predicates

**A. Draw a line between the complete subject and the complete predicate. Underline the complete subject once and the simple subject twice.**

1. A small family lived on a faraway planet.

2. The family's two children played near the space launch.

3. The little girl dreamed about life on Earth.

4. Huge spaceships landed daily on the planet.

5. The spaceship mechanics repaired huge cargo ships.

6. Twinkling stars appeared in the black sky.

**B. Draw a line between the complete subject and the complete predicate. Underline the complete predicate once and the simple predicate twice.**

1. The planet's inhabitants lived in underground homes.

2. A special machine manufactures air inside the family's home.

3. The athletic girl jumped high into the air.

4. Many toys and games cluttered the children's playroom.

5. The children's father described weather on Earth.

**C. Circle the complete subject in each sentence. Underline the complete predicate.**

1. The underground home contained large, comfortable rooms.

2. The playful child rolled his clay into a ball.

# Simple and Complete Subjects and Predicates

**A. Read each sentence. Circle the complete subject. Underline the simple subject.**

> **RETEACHING:** The **simple subject** is the main noun or pronoun that tells whom or what the sentence is about. The **complete subject** is the simple subject and all of the words that go with it. The **simple predicate** is the verb that tells what the subject does or is. The **complete predicate** is the verb and all the words that tell what the subject does or is.

1. My whole family had a picnic on Saturday.

2. The warm, sunny day was perfect for an outing in the park.

3. My cousin Fred brought his guitar and harmonica.

4. Everyone sang favourite folk songs.

5. The people in the park applauded us.

**B. Read each sentence. Circle the complete predicate. Underline the simple predicate.**

1. We watched the space shuttle on TV this morning.

2. The huge spaceship rocketed into space at 6:00 A.M.

3. During the flight, the six astronauts released a satellite into space.

4. The space shuttle *Columbia* circled Earth for three days.

5. The spacecraft landed smoothly on Monday at noon.

**C. Write three sentences. Circle the complete subject and underline the complete predicate in each sentence.**

1. _____

2. _____

3. _____

# Simple and Complete Subjects and Predicates

**What part of each sentence is underlined? Fill in the bubble next to the correct answer.**

1. <u>My cousin</u> lives on a big ranch in Montana.
   - ⓐ simple subject
   - ⓑ complete subject
   - ⓒ simple predicate

2. Her family <u>raises cattle on the ranch.</u>
   - ⓐ complete subject
   - ⓑ simple predicate
   - ⓒ complete predicate

3. Rosa's <u>job</u> is feeding the chickens before school.
   - ⓐ simple subject
   - ⓑ complete subject
   - ⓒ simple predicate

4. Her brother John <u>feeds the horses.</u>
   - ⓐ complete subject
   - ⓑ simple predicate
   - ⓒ complete predicate

5. <u>My cousin Rosa</u> rides her horse across the range.
   - ⓐ simple subject
   - ⓑ complete subject
   - ⓒ complete predicate

6. John <u>spreads</u> fresh hay in the pasture.
   - ⓐ simple subject
   - ⓑ simple predicate
   - ⓒ complete predicate

7. Their nearest <u>neighbours</u> often go into town with them.
   - ⓐ simple subject
   - ⓑ complete subject
   - ⓒ simple predicate

8. The dinner bell <u>rings</u> at 6:30 every evening.
   - ⓐ simple subject
   - ⓑ complete subject
   - ⓒ simple predicate

9. <u>The whole family</u> sits on the porch and reads about space.
   - ⓐ simple subject
   - ⓑ complete subject
   - ⓒ complete predicate

10. Rosa <u>searches the Internet for sites about animals.</u>
    - ⓐ complete subject
    - ⓑ simple predicate
    - ⓒ complete predicate

# Compound Subjects and Predicates

**A. Underline the compound subject in each sentence.**

1. Pig One, Pig Two, and Pig Three wrote Goldilocks a letter.

2. The bears, rabbits, and pigs attended a party.

3. Carrots, beets, and squash grow in the garden.

4. Later this month Teddy and Osito will visit Baby Bear.

5. My brothers and sisters really enjoyed the housewarming.

**B. Circle the compound predicate in each sentence.**

1. Peter's mother cleaned and peeled the crispy carrots.

2. The guests laughed and giggled at June's funny jokes.

3. The sly wolves waited and watched for the passing animals.

4. Goldilocks weeds and waters her garden every day.

5. The author writes and edits her amusing fairy tales.

**C. Write the compound subject or compound predicate that completes each sentence. Then write *CS* for compound subject or *CP* for compound predicate.**

> **authors and illustrators**          **buys and reads**

1. My friend _____ all of that author's books.   _____

2. Many _____ visit our school.                          _____

# Compound Subjects and Predicates

> **RETEACHING:** A **compound subject** is two or more subjects in the same sentence, usually joined by a connecting word such as *and* or *or*. A **compound predicate** is two or more verbs in the same sentence, usually joined by a connecting word such as *and* or *or*.

**A. Underline the simple subject in each sentence. Then rewrite the two sentences as one sentence with a compound subject.**

1. The teacher visited the ocean. Her students visited the ocean.

   _____

2. Seagulls flew overhead. Pelicans flew overhead.

   _____

3. Seashells littered the sand. Seaweed littered the sand.

   _____

4. Carlos ran on the beach. Tanya ran on the beach.

   _____

**B. Circle the simple predicate in each sentence. Then rewrite the two sentences as one sentence with a compound predicate.**

1. The artist paints sea life. The artist draws sea life.

   _____

2. I collect driftwood. I decorate driftwood.

   _____

3. Seals swim near the pier. Seals dive near the pier.

   _____

# Compound Subjects and Predicates

**A.** Fill in the bubble next to the compound subject.

1. The deer and bison grazed in the high mountain meadow.
   - (a) deer and bison
   - (b) grazed in
   - (c) high mountain meadow

2. Last weekend Rosa and Kay camped by the lake.
   - (a) Last weekend
   - (b) Rosa and Kay
   - (c) camped by

3. On Friday Alice and I saw a movie about grey wolves.
   - (a) Alice and I
   - (b) saw a movie
   - (c) about grey wolves

4. Last year students and teachers created a wildlife mural.
   - (a) Last year
   - (b) wildlife mural
   - (c) students and teachers

5. My friends and I were hiking in the White Mountains.
   - (a) were hiking
   - (b) friends and I
   - (c) the White Mountains

**B.** Fill in the bubble next to the compound predicate.

1. All night long the chilly wind moaned and howled.
   - (a) All night long
   - (b) chilly wind
   - (c) moaned and howled

2. Joan picked and peeled the apples in the morning.
   - (a) picked and peeled
   - (b) the apples
   - (c) in the morning

3. Last night Ed and Cody washed and dried the dishes.
   - (a) Last night
   - (b) Ed and Cody
   - (c) washed and dried

4. Many students wrote and revised their book reports.
   - (a) Many students
   - (b) wrote and revised
   - (c) their book reports

5. The famous sculptor cut and polished the cold, grey granite.
   - (a) famous sculptor
   - (b) cut and polished
   - (c) cold, grey granite

# Compound Sentences

**A. Read each sentence. Decide if it is a simple sentence or a compound sentence. Write *simple* or *compound* on the line.**

> **RETEACHING:** A **compound sentence** joins two simple sentences with a comma and a **coordinating conjunction**. *And, but,* and *or* are commonly used coordinating conjunctions.

1. Dad had been horseback riding before. _____

2. Lizzie felt a little nervous on a horse, but he would never admit it. _____

3. He discovered that riding was a lot of fun, and he couldn't wait to tell his friends about it. _____

4. There don't seem to be many bears in the national park this year. _____

5. Suddenly Mom pointed out the car window toward some trees. _____

6. We all looked out the window, but the bears turned out to be people in brown coats. _____

**B. Underline the simple sentences that make up each compound sentence.**

1. Connor had seen many parks in his life, but he never had seen a park like this one.

2. Dad brought a pair of binoculars, and Nate used them to look for animals.

3. He saw his first live bear, and the hair stood up on his arms.

4. It was an exciting moment, but it only lasted a second.

5. The bear was no bear at all, and Felicia was embarrassed.

6. He hadn't seen a bear, but he kept looking.

# Compound Sentences

**A. Read each sentence. Underline the simple sentences that make up the compound sentence. Circle the coordinating conjunction in each sentence.**

> **RETEACHING:** A **compound sentence** joins two simple sentences with a comma and a **coordinating conjunction**. *And, but,* and *or* are commonly used coordinating conjunctions.

1. One day we were in the park, and we saw two ducks swimming by.

2. We watched the ducks for a while, but they disappeared into the tall grass.

3. The ducks might have gone to a nest, or they could have swum to the shore.

4. We walked along the grassy bank, but we could not find them anywhere.

5. We sat down on the dock, and out came the ducks again.

6. One adult duck led six ducklings around the pond, and the other adult followed behind the babies.

**B. Read each compound sentence. Choose the coordinating conjunction that makes sense and write it on the line.**

1. The ducklings are brown, _____ the adult ducks are white. (but, or)

2. The ducklings were playing, _____ they were learning, too. (but, or)

3. The ducklings ate a lot, _____ they grew quickly. (but, and)

4. We brought bread with us, _____ we fed the ducks. (and, but)

5. Maybe they knew us, _____ maybe they just liked the food we fed them. (and, or)

**C. Write a compound sentence. Underline the simple sentences, and circle the coordinating conjunction you used.**

_____

_____

# Compound Sentences

**A. Fill in the bubble that tells whether the sentence is a simple sentence or a compound sentence.**

1. There are nine planets in our solar system, but there is only one sun.
   - ⓐ simple
   - ⓑ compound

2. The sun is a star, and a star is a giant ball of burning gases.
   - ⓐ simple
   - ⓑ compound

3. A moon is a satellite that moves around a planet.
   - ⓐ simple
   - ⓑ compound

4. Earth has only one moon, but the planet Mars has two moons.
   - ⓐ simple
   - ⓑ compound

5. The word *orbit* means "to travel around something."
   - ⓐ simple
   - ⓑ compound

**B. Is the underlined part correct? Fill in the bubble next to the right answer.**

1. The sun is <u>a star, but It is not</u> the biggest star.
   - ⓐ a star, but it is not
   - ⓑ a star but, it is not
   - ⓒ correct as is

2. Some stars are bigger than <u>the sun and, some stars</u> are smaller.
   - ⓐ the sun and some stars
   - ⓑ the sun, and some stars
   - ⓒ correct as is

3. Other stars seem smaller than <u>the sun, they are</u> just farther away.
   - ⓐ the sun, but they are
   - ⓑ the sun, They are
   - ⓒ correct as is

4. Do hot stars give off <u>blue light or do they</u> give off red light?
   - ⓐ blue light or, do they
   - ⓑ blue light, or do they
   - ⓒ correct as is

5. Our sun is not the <u>hottest star, but it</u> is not the coolest star either.
   - ⓐ hottest star but it
   - ⓑ hottest star but, it
   - ⓒ correct as is

# Common and Proper Nouns

**A. Circle the common nouns in each sentence.**

1. The farmer lives in the green house down the road.

2. The farmer grows wheat, soybeans, and corn.

3. The fields are plowed before he plants the crop.

4. Crops are planted in rows so that they can be watered easily.

5. As the plants grow, the farmer removes weeds and looks for bugs.

**B. Underline the proper nouns in each sentence.**

1. John Varley grows soybeans and alfalfa on a 12-hectare farm near Terra, Ontario.

2. The Varley Farm is next to the Rising J Horse Ranch.

3. Mr. Varley and his daughter Sally sell alfalfa to the owner of the ranch.

4. Sometimes Joker, a quarter horse, knocks down the fence to get the alfalfa.

5. Every October people come to the Varley Farm for the annual Harvest Celebration.

**C. Rewrite each sentence. Replace each underlined common noun with a proper noun.**

1. We walked down the street to the park.

_____

2. My aunt lives in the city.

_____

# Common and Proper Nouns

**A. Circle the common nouns in each sentence. Underline the proper nouns.**

1. *Toronto Life* published a story about celebrations.

2. *Three Dogs on a Summer Night* is a movie about poodles.

3. We like to sing "She'll Be Comin' 'Round the Mountain" at the campfire.

4. Last August my friend John went to Germany with his grandparents.

5. My family always goes to the beach for Victoria Day.

**B. Complete the chart below by writing each common and proper noun in the correct column. Then add three common nouns and three proper nouns to the chart.**

| newspaper | The Sun News |
|---|---|
| city | Cobblestone |
| day | book |
| magazine | month |
| Calgary | July |
| park | Tuesday |
| Young Arthur | |
| Yellowstone National Park | |

| Common Nouns | Proper Nouns |
|---|---|
| *newspaper* | *The Sun News* |
| | |
| | |
| | |
| | |
| | |
| | |
| | |
| | |
| | |

# Common and Proper Nouns

**Read each sentence. Are the nouns underlined written correctly?
Fill in the bubble next to the right answer.**

1. I go to <u>terry fox school</u>.
   - ⓐ terry fox School
   - ⓑ Terry Fox School
   - ⓒ correct as is

2. I brought <u>a peanut butter sandwich</u>.
   - ⓐ a Peanut Butter sandwich
   - ⓑ a peanut butter Sandwich
   - ⓒ correct as is

3. I sang <u>row, row, row your boat</u> today.
   - ⓐ Row, Row, Row Your Boat today.
   - ⓑ "Row, Row, Row Your Boat" today.
   - ⓒ correct as is

4. My school is located on the <u>corner of Maple Avenue and Elm Street</u>.
   - ⓐ Corner of Maple Avenue and Elm Street
   - ⓑ corner of Maple avenue and Elm street
   - ⓒ correct as is

5. I wrote a book report on *<u>cherokee summer</u>* for reading class.
   - ⓐ *Cherokee Summer*
   - ⓑ *Cherokee summer*
   - ⓒ correct as is

6. <u>My best friend John</u> sits in the third row.
   - ⓐ My Best Friend John
   - ⓑ My best Friend John
   - ⓒ correct as is

7. My <u>french class begins at noon</u>.
   - ⓐ French class begins at Noon
   - ⓑ French class begins at noon
   - ⓒ correct as is

8. That painting <u>is called "Sunflowers."</u>
   - ⓐ is Called sunflowers.
   - ⓑ is called <u>Sunflowers</u>.
   - ⓒ correct as is

9. I wrote <u>about ottawa, ontario</u>.
   - ⓐ about Ottawa, Ontario.
   - ⓑ about Ottawa, ontario.
   - ⓒ correct as is

10. Later I'll go to <u>austin's better books</u>.
    - ⓐ Austin's Better Books
    - ⓑ austin's Better Books
    - ⓒ correct as is

# Singular and Plural Nouns

**A.  Underline the singular nouns in each sentence.**

1.  I opened the door and found the shoes, cap, and bat I needed for the game.

2.  I headed down to the fields with my bat on my shoulder.

3.  My friends were standing by the fence near the dugout.

4.  We were playing on the same team.

5.  That day I hit two grounders, a foul, and a homer.

**B.  Underline the plural nouns in each sentence.**

1.  My uncles taught me to stand with my feet closer together.

2.  The first time I hit a home run, I danced on each of the bases.

3.  In the third game, all the players hit the ball.

4.  My brothers, sisters, and cousins came to every game.

5.  Four teams were in the playoffs, but our team won the championship.

**C.  Circle the singular nouns in each sentence. Underline the plural nouns.**

1.  The teams and players received awards when the season ended.

2.  In the games to come, I will try to be a better hitter, catcher, and teammate.

3.  My mother and father were the proudest parents at the assembly.

4.  They gave me a new glove for my achievements.

# Singular and Plural Nouns

> **RETEACHING:** A **singular noun** names one person, place, thing, or idea. A **plural noun** names more than one person, place, thing, or idea. Add -s to form the plural of most nouns. Some plural nouns are irregular, and their spellings need to be memorized.

**A.** Circle the singular nouns in each sentence.
Underline the plural nouns in each sentence.

1. My homework last night was to write a story about friends.

2. At home I thought about the people who are my friends.

3. My three dogs, one cat, and four birds are also my pals.

4. I wrote about adventures with my pets and my buddies.

5. My teacher liked my story so much that he read it to his classes.

**B.** Write each noun in the box in the correct column on the chart. Remember that some nouns keep the same form in the singular and plural.

| chair | mice |
|-------|-------|
| mouse | chairs |
| teeth | tooth |
| sheep | men |
| foot | feet |
| man | |

| Singular Nouns | Plural Nouns |
|----------------|--------------|
| 1. _____ | _____ |
| 2. _____ | _____ |
| 3. _____ | _____ |
| 4. _____ | _____ |
| 5. _____ | _____ |
| 6. _____ | _____ |

**C.** Write two sentences. Use one singular noun and one plural noun from the chart in each sentence.

1. _____

2. _____

# Singular and Plural Nouns

**Decide if the underlined part of the sentence has an error.**
**Fill in the bubble next to the correct answer.**

1. I read seven <u>chapter in my book</u> last night.
   - ⓐ chapter in my books
   - ⓑ chapters in my book
   - ⓒ correct as is

2. In chapter one, <u>a father and a son</u> went to the mountains.
   - ⓐ a fathers and a son
   - ⓑ a father and a sons
   - ⓒ correct as is

3. They built their campsite under some <u>trees near a creeks</u>.
   - ⓐ tree near a creeks
   - ⓑ trees near a creek
   - ⓒ correct as is

4. The first night the father saw <u>a bear eating nut</u>.
   - ⓐ a bear eating nuts
   - ⓑ a bears eating nuts
   - ⓒ correct as is

5. Two <u>bear cubs</u> were in the bushes hiding.
   - ⓐ bear cub
   - ⓑ bears cub
   - ⓒ correct as is

6. The <u>bear cubs' mother</u> helped them find berries to eat.
   - ⓐ bear cub's mother
   - ⓑ bear cubs mother
   - ⓒ correct as is

7. In the morning, there were four <u>deers and a sheep</u> nearby.
   - ⓐ deers and a sheeps
   - ⓑ deer and a sheep
   - ⓒ correct as is

8. The <u>son's teeths</u> were red after eating berries.
   - ⓐ son's teeth
   - ⓑ son's tooths
   - ⓒ correct as is

9. A bird flew <u>by Dads head</u> and into the tent.
   - ⓐ by Dad's head
   - ⓑ by Dads' head
   - ⓒ correct as is

10. It took almost an hour to get that <u>bird out of the tent's</u>.
    - ⓐ birds out of the tents
    - ⓑ bird out of the tent
    - ⓒ correct as is

# Subject and Object Pronouns

**A. Read the sentences. Circle the subject pronoun in the second sentence that replaces the underlined word or words.**

> **RETEACHING:** A **subject pronoun** —*I, you, he, she, it, we,* or *they*—can replace the subject of a sentence. An **object pronoun**—*me, you, him, her, it, us,* or *them*—can replace a noun that is the object of an action verb or that follows a preposition.

1. The <u>Grade 4s</u> read a book about the rain forest.

   They read a book about the rain forest.

2. Then <u>Ada</u> wrote a poem about a huge kapok tree.

   Then she wrote a poem about a huge kapok tree.

3. <u>Juan, Jill, and I</u> painted a mural of rain forest mammals.

   We painted a mural of rain forest mammals.

**B. Read the sentences. Draw two lines under the object pronoun in the second sentence that replaces the underlined word or words.**

1. Mr. Patel's class sent a fan letter to <u>the author</u>.

   Mr. Patel's class sent a letter to her.

2. Ms. Torres, a rain forest expert, visited <u>the Grade 4s</u> last week.

   Ms. Torres, a rain forest expert, visited them last week.

3. She said, "You can find <u>information</u> in the library.

   She said, "You can find it in the library."

**C. Circle the subject pronoun and underline the object pronoun in each sentence.**

1. I saw you at the library yesterday.

2. You can call me tonight about our class project.

3. Will he make an informative poster for us?

# Subject and Object Pronouns

> **RETEACHING:** A **subject pronoun** —*I, you, he, she, it, they,* or *we*—can replace the subject of a sentence. An **object pronoun**—*me, you, him, her, it, us,* or *them*—can replace a noun that is the object of an action verb or that follows a preposition.

**A. Choose the pronoun in parentheses ( ) that completes each sentence, and write it on the line. Then identify the kind of pronoun in the sentence by writing *S* for *subject* or *O* for *object*.**

1. _____ took a boat trip through the Everglades. (We, Us) _____

2. The boat's captain gave _____ a special tour. (we, us) _____

3. The captain said, " _____ will love the wildlife here!" (You, Us) _____

4. _____ brought an instant camera in my backpack. (I, Me) _____

5. I used _____ to photograph birds, turtles, and alligators. (he, it) _____

6. My sister Kit carried paper and pencils with _____ . (she, her) _____

7. Kit used _____ to sketch scenes of the Everglades. (they, them) _____

8. _____ is an excellent artist. (She, Her) _____

**B. Rewrite each sentence. Replace the underlined words with the correct subject or object pronoun.**

1. Our grandparents sent a postcard to my sister, my brother, and me.

_____

2. The postcard was addressed to my older brother.

_____

**C. Write two sentences. In the first, use a subject pronoun. In the second, use an object pronoun.**

1. _____

2. _____

# Subject and Object Pronouns

**A.** Fill in the bubble next to the pronoun that can replace the underlined words.

1. <u>Carlos and Sue</u> have a very popular pet-care service.
   - (a) They
   - (b) Them
   - (c) He

2. Many people hire <u>Carlos and Sue</u> to feed their cats.
   - (a) her
   - (b) they
   - (c) them

3. Carlos asked <u>Jenna and me</u> to help out for a day.
   - (a) we
   - (b) us
   - (c) me

4. <u>Jenna and I</u> were delighted to help.
   - (a) We
   - (b) Us
   - (c) They

5. I agreed to meet <u>Sue</u> at the Chans' house this afternoon.
   - (a) she
   - (b) her
   - (c) them

**B.** Fill in the bubble next to the pronoun that correctly completes each sentence.

1. Dot, Ed, and _____ visited the Air and Space Museum recently.
   - (a) I
   - (b) me
   - (c) us

2. Fortunately, _____ knew his way around the huge exhibition hall.
   - (a) her
   - (b) he
   - (c) him

3. _____ really wanted to see the biplanes.
   - (a) She
   - (b) Them
   - (c) Her

4. Then Ed told Dot and _____ about the Wright Brothers' flight.
   - (a) I
   - (b) me
   - (c) she

5. I persuaded Dot and _____ to visit the museum again soon.
   - (a) he
   - (b) him
   - (c) we

# Possessive Pronouns

**A.** **Underline the possessive pronoun in each sentence.**

> RETEACHING: A **possessive pronoun** is a pronoun that shows ownership or belonging.

1. I miss my best friend, Carlos, because he is spending the summer in Toronto, Ontario.

2. He is staying with his favourite cousins, Blanca and Eduardo, during July and August.

3. The cousins have been showing Carlos around their city.

4. When I opened my e-mail this morning, I read about the ferry ride they took to Centre Island.

5. Blanca also showed Carlos her favourite beach for clam digging.

6. Eduardo said, "Carlos, this will be your best vacation ever!"

7. Then Blanca added, "Our next stop will be the Space Needle."

**B.** **Write the possessive pronoun from the box that completes each sentence. Use the underlined word or words to help you.**

| my | her | his | their | our |
|----|-----|-----|-------|-----|

1. _____ grandparents sent me a long letter in French.

2. They said that _____ goal was to help me learn the language.

3. Grandmother included the words to _____ favourite French song.

4. Grandfather wrote a list of _____ special tips for learning a language.

5. During _____ next visit, we will try to speak as much French as possible.

6. I know that _____ speaking ability will improve with this kind of help.

# Possessive Pronouns

**A.** Write the possessive pronoun in parentheses ( )
that correctly completes each sentence.

> **RETEACHING:** A **possessive pronoun** is a pronoun that shows ownership or belonging.

1. The sports magazine and newspaper are _____. (my, mine)

2. Where is _____ atlas of Canada? (your, yours)

3. Which of the mysteries on the shelf is _____? (your, yours)

4. These new dictionaries will soon be _____. (our, ours)

5. Where is _____ copy of *Charlotte's Web*? (her, hers)

**B.** Write the possessive pronoun that completes each sentence.

1. My brother and I really enjoy visiting _____ neighbourhood library.

2. Every year Ms. Lee, the librarian, displays _____ choices for the year's best reading.

3. Then all the library users vote for _____ favourite books, too.

4. For _____ favourite, I chose a photo biography about Wayne Gretzky.

5. Luke said that _____ first choice was Jerry Spinelli's new novel.

6. _____ friends Sue and Ed told me that they voted for the same book.

7. I asked them, "What is _____ reason for choosing this book?"

8. They replied, "It's because _____ taste in books is the best."

**C.** Write three sentences about something you treasure.
Use a possessive pronoun in each sentence.

1. _____

2. _____

3. _____

# Possessive Pronouns

**Look at the underlined words in each sentence. Fill in the bubble next to the possessive pronoun that refers back to the underlined word or words.**

1. <u>I</u> love baseball, and _____ hobby is collecting baseball cards.

   ⓐ his        ⓒ your

   ⓑ our        ⓓ my

2. Many <u>baseball-card collectors</u> buy _____ cards from special dealers.

   ⓐ your       ⓒ their

   ⓑ his        ⓓ her

3. A <u>classmate named Ralph</u> keeps _____ cards in an album.

   ⓐ my         ⓒ our

   ⓑ his        ⓓ your

4. <u>Sue</u> treasures that rare Jackie Robinson card of _____ .

   ⓐ ours       ⓒ hers

   ⓑ mine       ⓓ his

5. On Saturday <u>Mom and I</u> packed _____ lunch and ate it at the ballpark.

   ⓐ his        ⓒ your

   ⓑ their      ⓓ our

6. Once <u>all the players</u> signed _____ names on a baseball for me.

   ⓐ his        ⓒ my

   ⓑ their      ⓓ her

7. "<u>I</u> exclaimed, "This signed baseball is _____ greatest treasure!"

   ⓐ theirs     ⓒ ours

   ⓑ my         ⓓ yours

8. Grandfather asked <u>me</u> whether this new baseball cap was _____ .

   ⓐ her        ⓒ you

   ⓑ your       ⓓ mine

9. When the players scored, <u>people in the audience</u> waved _____ baseball caps.

   ⓐ his        ⓒ their

   ⓑ my         ⓓ her

10. I just read a book about <u>Roberto Clemente</u> and _____ amazing career.

   ⓐ his        ⓒ their

   ⓑ my         ⓓ your

# Action Verbs

**A. Underline the action verb in each sentence, and then write it on the line.**

> **RETEACHING:** An **action verb** is a word that shows action. Some action verbs, such as *jump*, name actions you can see. Others, such as *think*, name actions you can't see.

1. Judy Hindley wrote a book about the history of string. _____

2. An illustrator painted funny pictures about string. _____

3. Long ago people twisted vines into long, strong ropes. _____

4. People still weave long, thin fibres into cloth. _____

5. My sister knits sweaters from thick wool yarn. _____

6. We stretched the rope hammock from tree to tree. _____

7. I always tie a ribbon around a birthday package. _____

8. We learned about different kinds of knots. _____

9. He made a belt from three different colours of string. _____

10. We wished for another book by Judy Hindley. _____

**B. Underline the action verb that is more vivid.**

1. The rabbit quickly (moved, hopped) across the lawn.

2. I (pounded, touched) the nail with my hammer.

3. The thirsty dog (drank, slurped) the water noisily.

4. I (made, sewed) a quilt from scraps of fabric.

**C. Write two sentences about how someone did something. Include a vivid action verb in each sentence.**

1. _____

2. _____

# Action Verbs

**A. Circle the action verb in each sentence.**

1. People use string in many different ways.

2. Fran and I tie the packages with string.

3. We imagine people from earlier times.

4. These people invented rope, string, and cord.

5. The lively, happy tone of this story amazes me.

**B. For each sentence, underline the action verb in parentheses that creates a more vivid picture.**

6. We (sit, lounge) on the big chairs near the pool.

7. The horses (go, gallop) across the field.

8. Minna and Max (gulp, eat) their sandwiches in a hurry.

9. The workers (drag, move) the heavy load across the yard.

10. Rosa and I (put, staple) the parts together.

 **Use each of these action verbs in a sentence: follow, shout, rush, slip, pound. Write your sentences on another sheet of paper.**

# Action Verbs

**A. Fill in the bubble next to the action verb in each sentence.**

1. The space shuttle circled the Earth twenty times.
   - ⓐ space
   - ⓑ circled
   - ⓒ twenty

2. Yesterday morning my class watched the newscast on TV.
   - ⓐ morning
   - ⓑ class
   - ⓒ watched

3. I think about space exploration all the time.
   - ⓐ think
   - ⓑ exploration
   - ⓒ time

4. Before a mission, astronauts train for months.
   - ⓐ mission
   - ⓑ train
   - ⓒ months

5. She read a biography about the first woman in space.
   - ⓐ read
   - ⓑ about
   - ⓒ space

**B. For each sentence, fill in the bubble next to the more vivid action verb.**

1. At the beach, we _____ for pieces of driftwood.
   - ⓐ looked
   - ⓑ hunted

2. We _____ into the foamy waves.
   - ⓐ walked
   - ⓑ plunged

3. Several artists _____ a huge castle out of sand.
   - ⓐ sculpted
   - ⓑ made

4. I _____ my beach towel under a large umbrella.
   - ⓐ put
   - ⓑ spread

5. The wild horses _____ along the sandy seashore.
   - ⓐ galloped
   - ⓑ ran

# Verb Tenses

> **RETEACHING: Present tense verbs** show action that is happening now or on a regular basis. Present tense verbs agree in number with who or what is doing the action. **Past tense verbs** show action that took place in the past. Most past tense verbs end in *-ed*. **Future tense verbs** show action that will happen in the future. The future tense is formed with the verb *will*.

**A.** Write *present* if the underlined word is a present tense verb, *past* if the underlined word is a past tense verb, and *future* if it is future tense.

1. The story of sneakers <u>started</u> with the development of rubber. _____

2. People in Central and South America <u>melted</u> gum from trees. _____

3. On Friday she <u>will celebrate</u> her tenth birthday. _____

4. Rubber <u>protected</u> the wearer's feet. _____

5. Gum <u>acts</u> as an eraser. _____

6. Everyone <u>will carry</u> a small backpack. _____

7. Unfortunately, pure rubber <u>cracks</u> in cold weather. _____

8. Charles Goodyear <u>believed</u> in a solution. _____

9. We <u>will visit</u> two museums. _____

10. Goodyear <u>licenses</u> the process to shoe companies. _____

11. The shoe companies <u>manufactured</u> shoes with rubber soles. _____

**B.** Look at the sentences with present tense verbs in part A. Then rewrite each one with the past tense form of the verb.

1. _____

2. _____

3. _____

# Verb Tenses

> **RETEACHING:** **Present tense verbs** show action that is happening now or on a regular basis. Present tense verbs agree in number with who or what is doing the action. **Past tense verbs** show action that took place in the past. Most past tense verbs end in *-ed*. **Future tense verbs** show action that will happen in the future. The future tense is formed with the verb *will*.

**A.** Underline each subject. Decide whether it is singular or plural. Then circle the present tense verb that correctly completes the sentence, and write it on the line.

1. Anna _____ dark purple sneakers.                  wear      wears

2. The sneakers _____ a squeaky sound on the floor.      make      makes

3. The girl _____ her sister how to tie her sneakers.      teach      teaches

4. Tight sneakers _____ your feet.                  hurt      hurts

5. Loose sneakers _____ blisters.                  cause      causes

6. Joe _____ his new sneakers under his bed.          place      places

7. Rachel _____ new sneakers before the race.          buy      buys

8. The students _____ comfortable sneakers.          want      wants

**B.** Look at the present tense verbs in the box. Decide whether they agree in number with a singular or a plural subject. Then write each word in the correct column on the chart. An example is given.

| lace | laces |
|------|-------|
| design | designs |
| reach | reaches |
| erase | erases |

| Present-Tense Verbs | |
|---|---|
| **With Most Singular Subjects and *he, she, it*** | **With Plural Subjects and *I, we,* and *you*** |
| laces | lace |
| _____ | _____ |
| _____ | _____ |
| _____ | _____ |

# Verb Tenses

**A. Look at the underlined verb or verbs. Fill in the bubble next to the correct tense.**

1. Tomorrow we <u>will march</u> in the Canada Day parade.

   ⓐ past
   ⓑ present
   ⓒ future

2. Last week my sister and I <u>sewed</u> our old-fashioned costumes.

   ⓐ past
   ⓑ present
   ⓒ future

3. Many townspeople <u>will dress</u> as Western pioneers.

   ⓐ past
   ⓑ present
   ⓒ future

4. Everyone <u>participates</u> in the celebration.

   ⓐ past
   ⓑ present
   ⓒ future

5. <u>Will</u> local cowhands <u>ride</u> their horses?

   ⓐ past
   ⓑ present
   ⓒ future

**B. Decide if the underlined verbs are correct. Fill in the bubble next to the right answer.**

1. The parade <u>will began</u> at 10:00 tomorrow morning.

   ⓐ will begin
   ⓑ will begins
   ⓒ correct as is

2. The marching bands <u>will arrive</u> in town this afternoon.

   ⓐ will arrives
   ⓑ will arrived
   ⓒ correct as is

3. One parade float <u>will shows</u> an old-time newspaper office.

   ⓐ will showed
   ⓑ will show
   ⓒ correct as is

4. When <u>will</u> the square dancers <u>performed</u>?

   ⓐ will perform
   ⓑ will performs
   ⓒ correct as is

5. Later we <u>will celebrate</u> with a picnic.

   ⓐ will celebrates
   ⓑ will celebrated
   ⓒ correct as is

# Main and Helping Verbs

**A. Read each sentence. Underline the helping verb once and the main verb twice.**

> **RETEACHING: Main verbs** show the main action in a sentence. **Helping verbs** help the main verb show tense. Helping verbs, such as *am, is, are, was, were, has, have, had,* or *will,* work with main verbs to tell when an action occurs.

1. What will happen to the doughnuts?

2. Uncle Ulysses has equipped the lunchroom with labour-saving devices.

3. Homer was polishing the metal trimmings.

4. Uncle Ulysses had tinkered with the inside workings.

5. The Ladies' Club was gathering.

6. Homer will handle everything.

7. Mr. Gabby was talking to Homer about his job.

8. A chauffeur had helped a woman out of a black car.

9. Now she is wearing an apron.

10. She will need some nutmeg.

**B. In each sentence, circle the main verb and underline the helping verb. Then identify when the action occurs by writing *past, present,* or *future.***

1. The lady had asked for baking powder.  _____

2. The rings of batter will drop into the hot fat.  _____

3. Homer is learning about the doughnut machine.  _____

4. People will enjoy the doughnuts later.  _____

5. Everyone has eaten Homer's doughnuts.  _____

6. We are taking doughnuts for friends.  _____

# Main and Helping Verbs

**A.** Read each incomplete sentence. Underline the main verb. Then circle the helping verb that correctly completes the sentence, and write it on the line.

> **RETEACHING: Main verbs** show the main action in a sentence. **Helping verbs** help the main verb show tense. Helping verbs, such as *am*, *is*, *are*, *was*, *were*, *has*, *have*, *had*, or *will*, work with main verbs to tell when an action occurs.

1. Justin _____ cooking seafood stew. (will, was)

2. He _____ added spices and lemon juice. (had, is)

3. Sally and Mick _____ prepared stew before. (will, have)

4. Justin _____ tasting the broth. (is, had)

5. "I _____ add a little more pepper," Justin says. (will, has)

6. His friends _____ just arrived for dinner. (are, have)

**B.** Underline the main verbs, and write the helping verbs on the lines.

1. On Saturday Betty will bake rye bread.  _____

2. Henry has pickled some fresh cucumbers.  _____

3. Gertrude is picking raspberries and blackberries.  _____

4. Alison had planted an herb garden.  _____

5. Marie and Harry have tossed the salad.  _____

6. They are planning another picnic.  _____

**C.** Write sentences using the main and helping verbs below.

1. will meet _____

2. had arrived _____

3. is listening _____

# Main and Helping Verbs

**Decide if the underlined verbs in each sentence are correct.**
**Then fill in the bubble next to the correct answer.**

1. Today Francesca <u>will travelled</u> to Peru by plane.

   - ⓐ is travelling
   - ⓑ am travelling
   - ⓒ correct as is

2. She <u>is photograph</u> the stone ruins of Machu Picchu next week.

   - ⓐ will photograph
   - ⓑ had photographed
   - ⓒ correct as is

3. An American explorer <u>had discovered</u> the ancient Incan city in 1911.

   - ⓐ has discovered
   - ⓑ is discovering
   - ⓒ correct as is

4. Since then, many people <u>will visited</u> the ruins of the city.

   - ⓐ have visited
   - ⓑ have visiting
   - ⓒ correct as is

5. Yesterday Francesca's brothers <u>had looking</u> at pictures of Machu Picchu.

   - ⓐ have looking
   - ⓑ were looking
   - ⓒ correct as is

6. They <u>were wondering</u> about the Incan civilization.

   - ⓐ had wondering
   - ⓑ has wonder
   - ⓒ correct as is

7. Centuries ago the Inca <u>had creating</u> a great empire.

   - ⓐ have creating
   - ⓑ had created
   - ⓒ correct as is

8. What <u>had happening</u> to them?

   - ⓐ has happening
   - ⓑ had happened
   - ⓒ correct as is

9. The Spanish explorers <u>will conquered</u> the Inca in 1532.

   - ⓐ had conquered
   - ⓑ are conquered
   - ⓒ correct as is

10. Francesca <u>will discover</u> Incan culture in present-day Peru.

   - ⓐ has discovering
   - ⓑ was discover
   - ⓒ correct as is

# Linking Verbs

**A.** **Underline the linking verb in each sentence, and circle the words it links.**

1. I am an enthusiastic reader.

2. My favourite books are nonfiction.

3. This bookstore is the best one in town.

4. The nonfiction books here are always interesting.

5. The store's owner is very knowledgeable.

6. His name is Terry Baldes.

7. Mr. Baldes was once an inventor and a scientist.

8. The bookstore's windows were very attractive last month.

9. Last Saturday's main event was an appearance by my favourite author.

10. My friends are big admirers of Mr. Baldes.

**B.** **Write the linking verb in each sentence on the line.**

1. An important invention is the telephone. _____

2. The telephone's inventor was Alexander Graham Bell. _____

3. At one time, most telephones were black. _____

4. Today cellular phones are very popular. _____

5. Cell phones and beepers were uncommon ten years ago. _____

**C.** **Write two sentences. Include a linking verb in each one.**

1. _____

2. _____

# Linking Verbs

**A. Underline the correct linking verb in ( ). Write *S* if the subject is singular and *P* if it is plural.**

> **RETEACHING:** A **linking verb** links the subject of a sentence to other words in the sentence. A linking verb does not show action. It tells what the subject is, was, or will be.

1. The natural history museum (was, were) very busy last weekend. _____

2. Many visitors (was, were) tourists. _____

3. The new displays of rocks and gems (is, are) very popular. _____

4. One amazing rock (is, are) bright blue. _____

5. My favourite gems (was, were) the purple amethysts. _____

6. The gold nuggets (is, are) bright yellow. _____

7. The museum's first floor (is, are) full of Native peoples' artifacts. _____

8. The carved wooden canoes (is, are) enormous. _____

9. The Tlingit woodcarvers (was, were) true artists. _____

10. This canoe (was, were) hand-painted over a hundred years ago. _____

11. I (am, is) a big supporter of the museum. _____

**B. Complete each sentence. Write *is* or *are* on the line.**

1. The apatasaurus skeleton _____ gigantic.

2. These saber-toothed tigers _____ very impressive.

3. The exhibit cards _____ most informative.

4. The tiny dinosaur _____ really cute.

**C. Write a sentence with a singular subject and a sentence with a plural subject. Include a linking verb in each sentence.**

1. _____

2. _____

# Linking Verbs

**Read each incomplete sentence below. Then fill in the bubble next to the linking verb that correctly completes the sentence.**

1. Denver, Colorado, _____ a large city.

   (a) were

   (b) are

   (c) is

2. This growing metropolis _____ a mile high.

   (a) are

   (b) is

   (c) were

3. Gold prospectors _____ the city's founders in 1858.

   (a) is

   (b) was

   (c) were

4. From 1860 to 1945, Denver _____ a mining and agricultural community.

   (a) were

   (b) was

   (c) will be

5. Today many local residents _____ government workers.

   (a) are

   (b) is

   (c) was

6. Now the automobile _____ the quickest way to travel.

   (a) were

   (b) is

   (c) are

7. In earlier times, horses and buggies _____ popular modes of transportation.

   (a) were

   (b) is

   (c) was

8. I _____ a student in a Denver public school.

   (a) were

   (b) am

   (c) is

9. Last year my school's sports teams _____ very successful.

   (a) was

   (b) were

   (c) is

10. I _____ a spectator at the local games.

   (a) was

   (b) were

   (c) is

# Irregular Verbs

**A. Underline the irregular verb in each sentence.**

> **RETEACHING:** An **irregular verb** does not form the past tense by adding *-ed.*

1. This morning Mom bought a red and a green toothbrush.

2. Pat made a tuna sandwich in the kitchen.

3. Mom quickly came into the dining room.

4. Deever rode her bicycle over to Pat's house.

5. Deever shook her head in great amusement.

6. They heard a great deal of noise in the kitchen.

7. Deever took a close look at the bright red toothbrush.

8. Pat carefully thought about the green and red toothbrushes.

9. Deever broke the silence with a sly laugh.

**B. Circle the irregular past tense verb in parentheses ( ). Then write it on the line to complete the sentence.**

1. We _____ a funny story about two toothbrushes. (hear, heard)

2. Pat _____ his decision after fifteen long minutes. (made, make)

3. Mom finally _____ E.J. an orange toothbrush. (buy, bought)

4. E.J. _____ into a song with a big smile on his face. (broke, break)

5. We all _____ to the nearest supermarket on our bikes. (ride, rode)

6. Deever _____ to the store with us. (came, come)

7. E.J. _____ with laughter at Pat's joke. (shook, shake)

# Irregular Verbs

**A.** **Underline the helping verb and the irregular past participle in each sentence.**

1. We have chosen a fantastic day for our school picnic.

2. Mr. Torres has brought all the food and beverages in his van.

3. We have eaten all of the carrots on the table.

4. Ms Chang has hidden the prizes for the treasure hunt.

5. By noon our teacher had taken over forty photographs.

6. All the Grade 4s have gone on a short walk to the lake.

7. They had heard about the great paddleboats there.

8. Some of my friends have ridden in the boats.

9. The school has bought new sports equipment for our afternoon game.

**B.** **Circle the irregular past participle in parentheses ( ). Then write it on the line to complete the sentence.**

1. By May I had _____ about an amazing automobile. (hear, heard)

2. Test drivers have _____ it on experimental runs. (taken, took)

3. My friend's family has _____ to Utah to see it. (went, gone)

4. My friend has _____ in the automobile, too. (ridden, rode)

5. I have _____ this car as a research topic. (chose, chosen)

6. My mom has _____ photos of the car, too. (bought, buy)

7. I have also _____ home articles and books about the car. (bring, brought)

# Irregular Verbs

**A. Complete each sentence. Fill in the bubble next to the irregular past-tense verb.**

1. Last week, we _____ the news about our baseball team's victory.
   - ⓐ hear
   - ⓑ heard
   - ⓒ hears

2. Yesterday morning, Mom and I _____ the bus downtown.
   - ⓐ rode
   - ⓑ rides
   - ⓒ ride

3. Then we _____ in line for an hour.
   - ⓐ stand
   - ⓑ stands
   - ⓒ stood

4. We finally _____ four tickets to the first game in the playoffs.
   - ⓐ bought
   - ⓑ buys
   - ⓒ buying

5. Then we _____ lunch to celebrate.
   - ⓐ eat
   - ⓑ ate
   - ⓒ eats

**B. Complete each sentence. Fill in the bubble next to the correct helping verb and past participle.**

1. That old adobe house _____ on top of the mesa for a century.
   - ⓐ has stood
   - ⓑ has stand
   - ⓒ has stands

2. We _____ up there many times.
   - ⓐ have rode
   - ⓑ have ride
   - ⓒ have ridden

3. Our great-grandfather _____ pictures of the house long ago.
   - ⓐ had drawn
   - ⓑ had draw
   - ⓒ had drew

4. We _____ the sketches for many years.
   - ⓐ have keep
   - ⓑ have kept
   - ⓒ have keeps

5. Fortunately, my family _____ very good care of the drawings.
   - ⓐ has took
   - ⓑ has take
   - ⓒ has taken

# Adjectives

**A.** In the following sentences, circle the adjectives that tell what kind. Underline the adjectives that tell how many.

> **RETEACHING:** An **adjective** is a word that tells more about a person, place, or thing.

1. We watched many colourful creatures swim through the dark water.

2. A few tilefish were building small burrows.

3. Suddenly one strange and unusual fish swam by us.

4. Eugenie swam over to the mysterious fish.

5. It looked like a jawfish with a big head and four dark patches on its back.

6. Was this rare fish a new species?

7. We put the tiny fish in a large bucket of cold seawater.

8. Eugenie has made several amazing discoveries.

**B.** Complete each sentence with an adjective that tells what kind or how many.

1. The _____ fish was named after David.

2. The fish had a _____ head.

3. The fish lived in a _____ burrow at the bottom of the ocean.

4. The tiny fish turned out to be a _____ species.

5. David took _____ photographs that appeared in magazines.

**C.** Write two sentences. Use adjectives that tell what kind and how many in each sentence.

1. _____

2. _____

# Adjectives

**RETEACHING:** An **adjective** is a word that tells more about a person, place, or thing.

**A. Write an adjective to complete each sentence.**

1. The _____ dog ate most of the cat's food.

2. The _____ cat found a nearly empty bowl.

3. The cat ate what remained of her _____ meal.

4. The cat pushed the _____ dish over to where a _____ girl was sitting.

5. The girl refilled the dish with _____ food.

**B. Read each sentence. Circle the adjective that describes each underlined noun.**

1. The grey <u>cat</u> saw the shaggy <u>dog</u> sitting in the dark <u>corner</u>.

2. The cat saw some <u>cat food</u> on the dog's droopy <u>mouth</u>.

3. The cat slipped out of the little <u>kitchen</u> and went into the quiet <u>backyard</u>.

4. She started digging in the soft <u>dirt</u> under a shady <u>tree</u>.

5. The dog looked out the enormous <u>window</u> and saw the cat with a large <u>bone</u>.

**C. Write two sentences that tell what happened next. Use vivid adjectives in your writing.**

1. _____

_____

2. _____

_____

# Adjectives

**Fill in the bubble next to the word in each sentence that is an adjective.**

1. I had an important decision to make this morning.
   - (a) important
   - (b) decision
   - (c) morning

2. I wanted to buy an appropriate pet for my sister.
   - (a) wanted
   - (b) buy
   - (c) appropriate

3. First, I looked at a striped lizard.
   - (a) First
   - (b) striped
   - (c) lizard

4. Then, I considered getting two hamsters.
   - (a) considered
   - (b) two
   - (c) hamsters

5. The white hamster was named George.
   - (a) white
   - (b) hamster
   - (c) George

6. I admired the noisy parrot.
   - (a) I
   - (b) noisy
   - (c) parrot

7. I watched a gigantic turtle on a rock.
   - (a) gigantic
   - (b) turtle
   - (c) rock

8. Several gerbils ran on a wheel.
   - (a) Several
   - (b) gerbils
   - (c) wheel

9. I finally decided to get a saltwater aquarium.
   - (a) decided
   - (b) saltwater
   - (c) aquarium

10. I'm sure my family will enjoy the colourful fish.
    - (a) sure
    - (b) family
    - (c) colourful

# Adjectives That Compare

**A.** **In each sentence, underline the adjective that compares.**

1. Anna is older than her brother Caleb.

2. That was the loudest thunderstorm of the entire summer.

3. Seal is the biggest cat that I have ever seen.

4. Papa is quieter than Sarah.

5. The roof of the barn is higher than the top of the haystack.

6. The kitten's fur was softer than lamb's wool.

7. Sarah pointed to the brightest star in the sky.

8. What is the saddest moment in the story?

**B.** **Underline the adjective in parentheses ( ) that completes each sentence correctly. On the line write *two* or *more than two* to show how many things are being compared.**

1. On the (hotter, hottest) day in July, we went swimming. _____

2. Today is (warmer, warmest) than last Tuesday. _____

3. Is winter (colder, coldest) on the prairie or by the sea? _____

4. This is the (taller, tallest) tree in the entire state. _____

5. Sarah's hair is (longer, longest) than Maggie's. _____

6. Of the three dogs, Nick was the (friendlier, friendliest). _____

7. Caleb's horse is (younger, youngest) than Anna's pony. _____

8. The new foal is the (livelier, liveliest) animal on the farm. _____

# Adjectives That Compare

**Choose the adjective that completes each
sentence and write it on the line.**

> **RETEACHING: Comparative adjectives** compare
> two things by adding *-er* to the adjective or by
> using the word *more.* **Superlative adjectives**
> compare three or more things by adding *-est* or
> by using the word *most.*

**funnier**          **funniest**

1. The _____ book I've ever read is about a family of mice.

2. The book is much _____ than the movie.

**busier**          **busiest**

3. The book department is _____ than the shoe department.

4. The _____ bookstore in the city is on King Street.

**more exciting**          **most exciting**

5. Hiking in the woods is _____ than watching TV.

6. This is the _____ ride at the amusement park.

**more challenging**          **most challenging**

7. Is a game of checkers _____ than a game of chess?

8. I think that soccer is the _____ of all the field games.

**more tiring**          **most tiring**

9. We found that swimming was _____ than walking.

10. Of all the afternoon's activities, tennis was the _____.

**more delicious**          **most delicious**

11. The strawberries are _____ than the green grapes.

12. This is the _____ apple that I have ever eaten.

# Adjectives That Compare

**Fill in the bubble next to the correct comparative or superlative adjective.**

1. I believe that a dog is much _____ than a cat.

    ⓐ friendlier
    ⓑ friendliest

2. My poodle is the _____ dog of all the dogs in the dog-training class.

    ⓐ more intelligent
    ⓑ most intelligent

3. The gazelle is the _____ animal in the animal park.

    ⓐ more graceful
    ⓑ most graceful

4. The movie about turtles is _____ than the book about frogs.

    ⓐ more fascinating
    ⓑ most fascinating

5. The diamondback rattler is _____ than a bull snake.

    ⓐ more dangerous
    ⓑ most dangerous

6. I think that the jaguar is the _____ of all the big cats.

    ⓐ more beautiful
    ⓑ most beautiful

7. Did you know that a cheetah is _____ than a lion?

    ⓐ swifter
    ⓑ swiftest

8. Your parrot is _____ than my cockatoo.

    ⓐ noisier
    ⓑ noisiest

9. This chimpanzee is _____ than that gorilla.

    ⓐ more playful
    ⓑ most playful

10. That polar bear is the _____ mammal I've ever seen.

    ⓐ larger
    ⓑ largest

# Prepositions

**A. Read each sentence. Underline each group of words that begins with a preposition, and circle the preposition. Some sentences have more than one prepositional phrase.**

> **RETEACHING: Prepositions** show the relationship between a noun or pronoun and another word or group of words in a sentence such as *in, on, of, for,* or *at.* Groups of words introduced by a preposition are called **prepositional phrases.**

1. The boy cut out pictures of mountains, rivers, and lakes.

2. He enjoyed pasting them on the walls of his room.

3. His father responded to the scenes in the pictures.

4. He decided that he would take his son on a camping trip.

5. They carried supplies in a backpack and knapsack.

6. The boy drank a hot drink from his father's mug.

7. That afternoon they hiked in the mountains for hours.

8. They were disappointed when they found many campers at the Lost Lake.

9. The boy and his father continued on their journey.

10. Finally, they stopped at a quiet place for the night.

11. The boy and his father ate and slept in a tent.

12. The tent kept them safe from the wind and rain.

13. Will this trip make the boy feel closer to his father?

14. What else will they see on their camping trip?

**B. Complete each sentence with a prepositional phrase.**

1. Let's go to the store _____

2. I just received a letter _____

3. Eduardo found his missing sneaker _____

4. Tanya always plays soccer _____

# Prepositions

**A. Circle the preposition in each sentence.**

> **RETEACHING: Prepositions** show the relationship between a noun or pronoun and another word or group of words in a sentence such as *in*, *on*, *of*, *for*, or *at*. Groups of words introduced by a preposition are called **prepositional phrases**.

1. Herb often goes hiking in the Rocky Mountains.

2. He always carries a water jug and a compass with him.

3. Today he saw wild columbines growing on the mountainsides.

4. Then he passed a doe and her fawn searching for food.

5. The deer stood very still and stared at him.

6. Then the two creatures disappeared into the woods.

**B. Complete each sentence with a prepositional phrase. You may wish to use some of the prepositions from part A or the prepositions *from, over, under, to,* or *by.***

1. Each summer Suzanne goes camping _____

2. Usually they camp _____

3. They pitch their small, green tent _____

4. Her mother cooks _____

5. Suzanne sometimes hears ravens cawing _____

6. Once she saw a black bear running very quickly _____

**C. Use the prepositions *of, with,* and *at* in three sentences of your own.**

1. _____

2. _____

3. _____

# Prepositions

**Fill in the bubble next to the word from the sentence that is a preposition.**

1. Last summer the Camachos took a trip to three national parks in the U.S.

   (a) to
   (b) trip
   (c) Last

2. The family was from San Antonio, Texas.

   (a) family
   (b) was
   (c) from

3. The family left their home on a Saturday morning.

   (a) family
   (b) on
   (c) left

4. First they headed for Carlsbad Caverns, New Mexico.

   (a) for
   (b) First
   (c) Caverns

5. Rita saw bats fly over her head.

   (a) saw
   (b) bats
   (c) over

6. Next the family visited cliff dwellings left by the Anasazi people.

   (a) Next
   (b) cliff
   (c) by

7. Then they camped at Arches National Park.

   (a) at
   (b) they
   (c) Then

8. Edwin sat under a sandstone formation called Delicate Arch.

   (a) sat
   (b) under
   (c) called

9. Rita and Edwin took photographs of their favourite sites.

   (a) took
   (b) their
   (c) of

10. They talked with their friends the next week.

    (a) talked
    (b) with
    (c) their

# Subject-Verb Agreement

**A. Underline the subject once and the verb twice. Write *present* if the verb is in the present tense and *past* if the verb is in the past tense.**

> **RETEACHING:** **Subjects** and **verbs** in a sentence must agree in number. Add *–s* or *–es* to present tense verbs used with *he, she, it,* or a singular noun. Do not add *–s* or *–es* to present tense verbs used with *I, you, we, they,* or a plural noun.

1. Tucker lives in a drain pipe.                                    _____

2. It opens into a pocket.                                          _____

3. Tucker collected stuffing for the pocket.                       _____

4. The mouse filled the pocket with paper and cloth.              _____

5. Tucker sits at the opening of the drain pipe.                  _____

6. He watches the people in the subway station.                  _____

7. The young boy worked at his father's newsstand.               _____

8. They sell papers there on weekdays.                            _____

**B. Underline the subject once and the verb twice. Then write *singular* if the subject and verb are singular and *plural* if the subject and verb are plural.**

1. The nighttime crowd passes by quickly.                         _____

2. Trains run less often at that time.                            _____

3. Papa waits for business.                                       _____

4. The station feels quiet and lonely.                            _____

5. People rush home at the end of the day.                        _____

6. Mama and Papa make very little money.                          _____

# Subject-Verb Agreement

**A. Underline the subject. Then circle the verb in parentheses ( ) that agrees with the subject.**

> **RETEACHING: Subjects** and **verbs** in a sentence must agree in number. Add *−s* or *−es* to present tense verbs used with *he, she, it,* or a singular noun. Do not add *−s* or *−es* to present tense verbs used with *I, you, we, they,* or a plural noun.

1. Crickets _____ a musical sound. (make, makes)

2. Actually, only the males _____ sounds. (produce, produces)

3. I _____ for the sound of crickets on a summer night. (listen, listens)

4. You _____ them in places outside the city. (hear, hears)

5. Mario _____ a cricket in the subway station. (find, finds)

6. His mother _____ the cricket a "bug." (call, calls)

**B. Underline the subject and verb in each sentence. Then rewrite each sentence in the present tense. Be sure your subjects and verbs agree.**

1. Mario wanted the cricket for a pet.

   _____

2. He wished for a pet of his own.

   _____

3. Crickets seemed like unusual pets to his mother.

   _____

4. Maybe insects scared her!

   _____

# Subject-Verb Agreement

**A. Fill in the bubble next to the verb that agrees with the subject of the sentence.**

1. Chester _____ tall buildings for the first time.
   - ⓐ see
   - ⓑ sees

2. The city _____ him.
   - ⓐ surprise
   - ⓑ surprises

3. The stars _____ Chester's attention.
   - ⓐ catch
   - ⓑ catches

4. Maybe he _____ for his home in Connecticut.
   - ⓐ wish
   - ⓑ wishes

5. One star _____ familiar to Chester.
   - ⓐ is
   - ⓑ are

**B. Is the underlined verb correct? Fill in the bubble next to the right answer.**

1. Now the animals <u>crouch</u> against the cement.
   - ⓐ crouches
   - ⓑ crouched
   - ⓒ correct as is

2. At this moment, their eyes <u>is</u> on the sky.
   - ⓐ are
   - ⓑ were
   - ⓒ correct as is

3. The sky <u>looks</u> so beautiful right now.
   - ⓐ look
   - ⓑ looked
   - ⓒ correct as is

4. Last night the cricket <u>view</u> Times Square for the first time.
   - ⓐ views
   - ⓑ viewed
   - ⓒ correct as is

5. One week ago, Chester <u>experiences</u> a much different world.
   - ⓐ experience
   - ⓑ experienced
   - ⓒ correct as is

# Punctuating Dialogue

**A.** **Underline the exact words of the speaker. Circle the quotation marks.**

> **RETEACHING: Quotation marks** show the beginning and end of a speaker's exact words. When the speaker comes first, place a comma between it and the beginning quotation mark. When a quotation comes first, use a comma, question mark, or exclamation point before the end quotation mark. Use a period at the end of the sentence.

1. Eva exclaimed, "I really like tall tales!"

2. "Davy Crockett is my favourite character," said Juan.

3. I asked, "Who likes Sally Ann Thunder Ann Whirlwind?"

**B.** **Add the missing quotation marks to each sentence.**

1. __I am a big fan of hers,__ replied Shavon.

2. I added, __Sally can even sing a wolf to sleep.__

3. __How did Sally tame King Bear?__ asked our teacher.

4. __Sally really ought to be in the movies,__ said Don.

**C.** **Write the missing punctuation marks in each sentence.**

1. __What kind of person is Sally __ __ asked Davy Crockett__

2. The schoolmarm replied__ __Sally is a special friend__ __

3. __She can laugh the bark off a pine tree__ __ added Lucy__

4. The preacher said__ __She can dance a rock to pieces__ __

5. __I'm very impressed__ __ exclaimed Davy__

**D.** **Write two sentences of dialogue between Davy Crockett and Sally.**

1. _____

2. _____

# Punctuating Dialogue

**A. Add the missing commas to the sentences.**

1. "Well__ we are having a canned-food drive next week."

2. "Oh__ Ed__ can you bring some containers to school?"

3. "Yes__ I have several at home, Jody."

4. "Thank you__ Mr. Poole, for all your suggestions."

**B. Add the missing quotation marks and/or commas to each sentence.**

1. __ Kim, your posters for the talent contest are terrific!__ I exclaimed.

2. She replied, __ Thank you, Doug, for your kind words.__

3. Our teacher asked, __ Meg__ will you play your guitar or sing?__

4. "Oh__ I plan to do both,__ said Meg.

5. __ Will you perform your juggling act this year, Roberto?__ Jay asked.

6. __ No__ I want to do a comedy routine,__ he replied.

**C. Add the missing punctuation to each sentence.**

1. __ Kit__ which act did you like best__ __ asked Mina__

2. He replied__ __ Oh__ I enjoyed the singing pumpkins and the tap dancing elephants__ __

3. __ Well__ I liked the guitar player__ __ said Mina__

**D. Write two more sentences of dialogue about a school talent show.**

1. _____

2. _____

# Punctuating Dialogue

**Decide if there is an error in the underlined part of each sentence.**
**Fill in the bubble next to the correct answer.**

1. "Rosa, tell me one of your <u>favourite jokes</u>" said Ken.

   ⓐ favourite jokes."
   ⓑ favourite jokes,"
   ⓒ correct as is

2. "What do <u>sharks eat?</u> she asked.

   ⓐ sharks eat?"
   ⓑ sharks eat"
   ⓒ correct as is

3. <u>Ken replied "tell</u> me. I don't know.

   ⓐ Ken replied. "Tell
   ⓑ Ken replied, "Tell
   ⓒ correct as is

4. "They eat peanut butter and jellyfish <u>sandwiches," replied</u> Rosa.

   ⓐ sandwiches" replied
   ⓑ sandwiches." replied
   ⓒ correct as is

5. <u>Oh, that</u> was funny!" exclaimed Ken.

   ⓐ "Oh, that
   ⓑ Oh that
   ⓒ correct as is

6. <u>"Rosa? tell</u> me another one," he said.

   ⓐ "Rosa tell
   ⓑ "Rosa, tell
   ⓒ correct as is

7. "What years do frogs <u>like best</u> asked Rosa smugly.

   ⓐ like best?"
   ⓑ like best,"
   ⓒ correct as is

8. "Frogs like Hoppy New <u>Years," laughed</u> Ken.

   ⓐ Years" laughed
   ⓑ Years, laughed
   ⓒ correct as is

9. <u>"No frogs</u> like leap years," insisted Rosa.

   ⓐ "No, frogs
   ⓑ No frogs
   ⓒ correct as is

10. "Ken <u>said. "my</u> joke is funnier."

    ⓐ said "My
    ⓑ said, "My
    ⓒ correct as is

# Adverbs

**A. Underline the verb. Then circle the adverb that tells when.**

> **RETEACHING:** An **adverb** is a word that describes a verb, an adjective, or another adverb. Some adverbs tell when or where something happens.

1. Later, newsboys shouted the weekend forecast.

2. That night, a huge snowstorm hit New York City.

3. It got very cold soon.

4. A train tried to plow through the snow earlier.

5. Then the train went off the track.

**B. Underline the verb. Then circle the adverb that tells where.**

1. Snow fell everywhere.

2. Drifts of snow piled up.

3. People were trapped inside.

4. Some people tunnelled out from their homes.

5. People there travelled by sled.

**C. Underline the adverb in each sentence. Write *when* if the adverb tells when or *where* if it tells where.**

1. People had never seen a storm so bad.          _____

2. Pipes burst underground.                        _____

3. The water inside had frozen.                     _____

4. Soon people started to freeze, too.              _____

# Adverbs

**A. Underline the verb once. Then circle the adverb that describes the verb and tells how.**

> **RETEACHING:** An **adverb** describes a verb, an adjective, or another adverb. Some adverbs tell how. Many adverbs that tell how end in -ly.

1. Grandma talked happily to the frolicking sea lions.

2. The seabirds squawked sharply as they dived.

3. Andy greeted the girl and Grandma warmly.

4. He guided them expertly through the Galápagos Islands.

5. Grandma wrote about the islands regularly in her diary.

6. The girl recorded the trip faithfully in her diary.

7. She responded personally to everything she saw.

8. Andy and the girl looked eagerly at the creatures on the shore.

9. Grandma and the girl jumped quickly off the boat.

10. They snorkelled easily with their breathing tubes and fins.

11. The girl saw sea creatures clearly through her face mask.

12. She gazed intently at the yellow-tailed surgeonfish.

13. Swiftly the sea lions surrounded Grandma and the girl.

14. The sea lion pups chased and nipped one another playfully.

**B. Complete each sentence with an action verb and an adverb that describes it and tells how.**

1. The big male sea lion _____

2. The girl and her grandmother _____

# Adverbs

**A. Fill in the bubble next to the adverb that tells how.**

1. Carolina and Gabriella dove rapidly under a big wave.
   - ⓐ rapidly
   - ⓑ under
   - ⓒ big

2. Then a wave crashed loudly against the shore.
   - ⓐ crashed
   - ⓑ loudly
   - ⓒ against

3. Both Carolina and Gabriella were very strong swimmers.
   - ⓐ Both
   - ⓑ very
   - ⓒ strong

4. At the beach, the tide was somewhat low.
   - ⓐ At
   - ⓑ low
   - ⓒ somewhat

5. Carolina quickly spotted a group of bottlenose dolphins.
   - ⓐ quickly
   - ⓑ spotted
   - ⓒ bottle-nose

**B. Fill in the bubble next to the word that is <u>not</u> an adverb.**

1. Gabriella and Carolina swam very slowly toward the playful mammals.
   - ⓐ very
   - ⓑ slowly
   - ⓒ playful

2. "They are so curious!" Carolina exclaimed excitedly.
   - ⓐ so
   - ⓑ curious
   - ⓒ excitedly

3. One baby dolphin came very close.
   - ⓐ One
   - ⓑ very
   - ⓒ close

4. The mother dolphin nudged Carolina so gently.
   - ⓐ nudged
   - ⓑ so
   - ⓒ gently

5. Then swiftly and mysteriously, the dolphins disappeared.
   - ⓐ swiftly
   - ⓑ disappeared
   - ⓒ mysteriously

# WRITING

# Sassy Sentences

 *A **sentence** is a group of words that expresses a complete thought. When you write a sentence, you put your thoughts into words. If the sentence is complete, the meaning is clear. It contains a subject (the naming part) and a predicate (an action or state of being part).*

*These are sentences.*
**Sally sells seashells at the seashore.**
**Betty Botter bought a bit of better butter.**

*These are not sentences.*
**Peck of pickled peppers.**
**Flying up a flue.**

Make complete sentences by adding words to each group of words. Try to create tongue twisters like the sentences above.

1. _____ flips fine flapjacks.

2. Sixty slippery seals _____.

3. _____ fed Ted _____.

4. Ruby Rugby's baby brother _____.

5. _____ managing an imaginary magazine.

6. Sam's sandwich shop _____.

7. _____ back blue balloons.

8. _____ pink peacock pompously _____.

9. Pete's pop Pete _____.

10. _____ sawed Mr. Saw's _____.

11. A flea and a fly _____.

12. _____ black-backed bumblebee.

 **Create your own tongue twisters to share with friends. Make sure each one expresses a complete thought.**

Name _____

# Link It Together

 A sentence needs two parts, a subject and a predicate, to express a complete thought.
The **subject part** tells whom or what the sentence is about.
The **predicate part** tells what the subject is or does.

| One picture | is worth a thousand words. |
| **subject part** | **predicate part** |

| Birds of a feather | flock together. |
| **subject part** | **predicate part** |

**A.** Read the subject and predicate parts from some other famous sayings. Write *S* next to each subject part. Write *P* next to each predicate part.

_____ half a loaf                   _____ must go on

_____ one good turn                 _____ gathers no moss

_____ spoils the whole barrel       _____ has a silver lining

_____ the show                      _____ makes waste

_____ every cloud                   _____ one rotten apple

_____ deserves another              _____ a rolling stone

_____ catches the worm              _____ is better than none

_____ the early bird                _____ haste

**B.** Now combine the subject and predicate parts to create these famous sayings.

1. _____

2. _____

3. _____

4. _____

5. _____

6. _____

7. _____

8. _____

 **Make up some sayings of your own. Then circle the subject part and underline the predicate part of each sentence.**

Name _____

# That's Groovy!

 *There are four kinds of sentences. Each one does something different.*

A **declarative sentence** *tells something.*
*It is a* **statement** *and ends with a period.*
> **My grandparents grew up during the 1960s.**

An **interrogative sentence** *asks something.*
*It is a* **question** *and ends with a question mark.*
> **Do you know who the hippies were?**

An **imperative sentence** *tells someone to do something.*
*It is a* **command** *and ends with a period.*
> **Check out this photo of my grandmother.**

An **exclamatory sentence** *shows strong feeling.*
*It is an* **exclamation** *and ends with an exclamation mark.*
> **Now that's one strange-looking outfit she has on!**

Read the following sentences. Identify what kind of sentence each one is. Write *S* for statement, *Q* for question, *C* for command, and *E* for exclamation.

_____ 1. Grandma says there was a fashion revolution in the 1960s.

_____ 2. What an amazing time it must have been!

_____ 3. Here's a photo of my grandfather in his teens.

_____ 4. How do you like those sideburns and the long hair?

_____ 5. Take a look at what he's wearing.

_____ 6. I don't believe those bellbottoms and sandals!

_____ 7. Please tell me he's not wearing beads.

_____ 8. I'm glad these fashions are no longer in style!

_____ 9. Have you ever seen anything so funny?

_____ 10. Try not to laugh too hard.

_____ 11. One day our grandchildren may laugh at us.

_____ 12. What's so funny about what we're wearing?

Now, look at other "photos" from the sixties and write a statement (S), a question (Q), a command (C), and an exclamation (E) about each one. Make sure to begin and end your sentences correctly.

S _____

Q _____

C _____

E _____

S _____

Q _____

C _____

E _____

S _____

Q _____

C _____

E _____

 **Invite someone to listen as you expressively read aloud the sentences that you wrote, showing what kind of sentences they are by the way that you read them.**

Name _____

# A Whale of a Fish

*When you write, the words and phrases in your sentences must be in an order that makes sense. Compare the sentences in each pair. Which ones make more sense?*

**An enormous fish what the whale shark is!**
**What an enormous fish the whale shark is!**

**The largest fish in the world the whale shark is.**
**The whale shark is the largest fish in the world.**

Use each group of words to write a sentence that makes sense.

**1.** of 18 metres?    that the whale shark    Did you know    to a length    can grow

_____

**2.** two school buses    end to end!    That's about    parked    as long as

_____

**3.** are not a threat    These huge creatures    like some other sharks are.    to humans

_____

**4.** to look for    float near the surface    plankton and tiny fish.    Whale sharks

_____

**5.** it must be    alongside a whale shark.    Imagine    to swim    how amazing

_____

Now rewrite the following sentences so that the words and phrases are in an order that makes better sense.

**6.** An estimated 20,000 known species of fish there are in the world.

_____

**7.** Of all these species the smallest is the dwarf pygmy goby?

_____

**8.** When it is fully grown is one centimetre long this species of goby!

_____

**9.** In the massive Indian Ocean makes its home this tiny fish.

_____

# Number Sentences

*Words such as* who, what, where, why, when, *and* how, *and helping verbs such as* is, are, was, were, do, did, *and* can *at the beginning of sentences, signal interrogative sentences, or questions.*

> **What** *is an odd number?*
> **Do** *you know what an even number is?*
> **Is** *2 an odd number or an even number?*

Change each statement below into a question. Remember to begin and end each sentence correctly.

**1.** Numbers that cannot be divided evenly by 2 are called odd numbers.

_____

**2.** All even numbers can be divided evenly by 2.

_____

**3.** Zero is considered an even number.

_____

**4.** Numbers that have 0, 2, 4, 6, or 8 in the ones place are even numbers.

_____

**5.** Odd numbers end in 1, 3, 5, 7, or 9.

_____

**6.** The number 317,592 is an even number because it ends in 2.

_____

**7.** The sum is always an even number when you add two even numbers.

_____

**8.** The sum of two odd numbers is also an even number.

_____

**9.** The same rule applies if you subtract an odd number from an odd number.

_____

**10.** You can figure out all the rules for working with odd and even numbers.

_____

# Proofing Pays

 *Capitalization and end punctuation help show where one sentence ends and the next one begins. Whenever you write, proofread to make sure each sentence begins with a capital letter and ends correctly. Here's an example of how to mark the letters that should be capitalized.*

have you ever heard of a Goliath birdeater? it is
the world's largest spider. this giant tarantula can grow
to 28 centimetres in length and weigh about 170 grams. now
that's a big spider! although it is called a birdeater, it usually
eats small reptiles and insects. these spiders are
mostly found in rain forests .

Read the passage below. It is about another amazing animal, but it is not so easy to read because the writer forgot to add end punctuation and to use capital letters at the beginning of sentences. Proofread the passage. Mark the letters that should be capitals with the capital letter symbol. Put the correct punctuation marks at the ends of sentences. Then reread the passage.

think about the fastest car you've ever seen in the Indianapolis 500 race

that's about how fast a peregrine falcon dives it actually reaches speeds up to

280 kilometres an hour how incredibly fast they are peregrine falcons are also

very powerful birds did you know that they can catch and kill their prey in the air

using their sharp claws what's really amazing is that peregrine falcons live in

both the country and in the city keep on the lookout if you're ever in New York

City believe it or not, it is home to a very large population of falcons

 **What do you know about the bee hummingbird, atlas moth, or capybara? Choose one, do some research, and write several sentences about it on a piece of paper. Then proofread your writing. Does every sentence begin and end correctly? Are all the words spelled correctly?**

# Spout Some Specifics

*To be a good writer, it is important to know what you are writing about, to be specific, and to include details. All this helps to create a picture for your readers and will make your writing more interesting and informative. Compare the two phrases below. Which one is more specific, interesting, and informative? Which one creates a more vivid picture?*

*a vehicle*   or   *an old, rusty, dilapidated pick-up truck with flat tires and a shattered windshield*

For each general word or phrase, write a more specific word. Then add details to describe each specific word.

|  | | Specific Word | Details |
|---|---|---|---|
| 1. | a body of water | _____ | _____ |
| 2. | a piece of furniture | _____ | _____ |
| 3. | an article of clothing | _____ | _____ |
| 4. | a child's toy | _____ | _____ |
| 5. | a noise or sound | _____ | _____ |
| 6. | a tool | _____ | _____ |
| 7. | a group of people | _____ | _____ |
| 8. | a reptile | _____ | _____ |
| 9. | garden plants | _____ | _____ |
| 10. | a kind of fruit | _____ | _____ |
| 11. | a kind of vegetable | _____ | _____ |
| 12. | a drink | _____ | _____ |
| 13. | footwear | _____ | _____ |
| 14. | musical instrument | _____ | _____ |
| 15. | a holiday | _____ | _____ |

**Look at yourself in the mirror. Then write on a piece of paper as many words and phrases as you can to describe yourself so that someone who does not know you would get a clear, vivid picture of what you look like.**

# Make It Interesting

*A sentence can be very simple. This sentence tells who did what.*
   **The crew worked.**

*As you write and revise your writing, add details about people, places, or things, or about where, when, and what happens. This will make your writing more interesting. Here's how the sentence above was revised several times. Each sentence gives a little more information.*

**The construction crew worked.**
**The construction crew worked quickly.**
**The construction crew worked quickly to clear the rubble.**
**The construction crew worked quickly to clear the rubble at the building site.**
**The construction crew worked quickly yesterday to clear the rubble at the building site.**

Rewrite each sentence four times. Add new details each time to tell more about whom or what, how, where, and when.

### The children played.

1. _____
   _____

2. _____
   _____

3. _____
   _____

4. _____
   _____

### A package arrived.

1. _____
   _____

2. _____
   _____

3. _____
   _____

4. _____
   _____

**Rewrite the following sentence several times on a piece of paper. Remove a detail each time until you are left with a very simple sentence.**

**The excited team cheered wildly after winning the championship basketball game.**

# Order the Combination

*Have you ever noticed how short sentences can make your writing sound choppy? When two sentences have different subjects and the same predicate, you can use the conjunction* and *to combine them into one sentence with a compound subject.*

**My friends ordered a pepperoni pizza. I ordered a pepperoni pizza.**
**My friends and I ordered a pepperoni pizza.**

*When two sentences have the same subject and different predicates, you can use* and *to combine them into one sentence with a compound predicate.*

**My mom ordered. She had pasta instead.**
**My mom ordered and had pasta instead.**

*When two sentences have the same subject and predicate and different objects, you can combine them into one sentence with a compound object using* and.

**My dad wanted anchovies on his pizza. He also wanted onions.**
**My dad wanted anchovies and onions on his pizza.**

Fill in the missing subject, object, or predicate in each set of shorter sentences. Then combine the sentences by making compound subjects, objects, or predicates using *and*.

1. _____ are sweet and juicy.

_____ are sweet and juicy.

_____

2. I _____ about the history of basketball for homework.

I _____ about the history of basketball for homework.

_____

3. _____ is so much fun!

_____ is also so much fun! (Change *is* to *are*.)

_____

4. I like _____ more than broccoli or cauliflower.

I like _____ more than broccoli or cauliflower.

_____

5. I'd like to have _____ for breakfast.

I'd also like to have _____ for breakfast.

_____

# A New Challenge

*When you write, you may want to show how the ideas in two simple sentences are related. You can combine the two sentences by using a comma and the conjunctions* and, but, *or* or *to show the connection.* And *shows a link between the ideas,* but *shows a contrast, and* or *shows a choice. The new sentence is called a* **compound sentence**.

**My sister wants to join a football team. My parents aren't so happy about it.**
**My sister wants to join a football team,** but **my parents aren't so happy about it.**

**Annie is determined. Her friends think she'd make a great place kicker.**
**Annie is determined,** and **her friends think she'd make a great place kicker.**

**Should Annie play football? Should she try something else?**
**Should Annie play football,** or **should she try something else?**

Combine each pair of sentences. Use *and, but,* or *or* to show the connection between the ideas and make a compound sentence.

**1.** My sister Annie has always participated in sports. Many say she's a natural athlete.

_____

_____

**2.** Soccer, basketball, and softball are fun. She wanted a new challenge.

_____

_____

**3.** My sister talked to my brother and me. We were honest with her.

_____

_____

**4.** I told Annie to go for it. My brother told her to stick with soccer or basketball.

_____

_____

**5.** Will Dad convince her to try skiing? Will he suggest ice skating?

_____

_____

**Continue the story about Annie's choice on another piece of paper. Include some compound sentences to tell what happens. Make sure your sentences begin and end correctly. Remember to check for spelling errors.**

# Hot Subjects

*If two sentences share the same subject, information about the subject can be written as a phrase after the subject in the new sentence. Be sure to use commas to set apart the phrase from the rest of the sentence.*

Sentence 1: **The CN Tower is North America's tallest free-standing structure.**

Sentence 2: **The structure rises 553 metres above the ground.**

Combined: **The CN Tower, North America's tallest free-standing structure, rises 553 metres above the ground.**

Read the sentences. Combine the ideas in each pair into one sentence by including information in a phrase after the subject in the sentence.

1. The Caspian Sea is the world's largest lake.
   The lake covers an area about the same size as Japan.

   _____

2. The Komodo dragon is a member of the monitor family.
   It can grow to a length of 3 metres.

   _____

3. Our closest star is the sun.
   It is estimated to be more than 15 000 000°C.

   _____

4. Ronald W. Reagan was the 40th president of the United States.
   He worked as a Hollywood actor for almost 30 years.

   _____

5. Prince Edward Island is the province that grows the most potatoes.
   It harvests more than a billion kilograms each year.

   _____

6. Hank Aaron is major league baseball's all-time home-run hitter.
   He broke Babe Ruth's record in 1974.

   _____

# Sentence Building

 *When you write about something, try to include interesting details. Sometimes you can take the important details from several related sentences and add them to the main sentence.*

**Kyle and Jim had a great plan.**
**They're my brothers.**
**The plan was for a tree house.**

*Now here's a sentence that combines all the important details.*
**My brothers Kyle and Jim had a great plan for a tree house.**

Read each group of sentences. Take the important details from the two related sentences and add them to the main sentence to make one sentence.

**1.** My brothers built a tree house. They built it in the old oak tree. It's in our backyard.

_____

**2.** Jim made a ladder for the tree house. He made it out of rope. It is sturdy.

_____

**3.** Kyle bought paint. The paint was brown. He bought a gallon.

_____

**4.** Kyle and Jim finished painting. They painted the walls. It took an hour.

_____

**5.** Jim painted a sign. He painted "no trespassing." The sign is on the tree house door.

_____

**6.** A squirrel leaped into their tree house. It leaped from a branch. It was curious.

_____

**7.** The visitor startled my brothers. It was unexpected. My brothers were unsuspecting.

_____

**8.** The squirrel leaped out of the tree house. It was frightened. It was in a big hurry.

_____

 **Write three short sentences on a piece of paper about a funny experience. Then try to combine them into one sentence. Which sounds better, one sentence with lots of details or two or three shorter sentences each with one detail? Why?**

# Applause for the Clause

 *Sometimes you can use words such as* when, because, while, *and* before *to combine two sentences with related ideas into one sentence with a main clause and a dependent clause. A* **clause** *is a group of words with a subject and a predicate. A* **dependent clause** *cannot stand alone. An* **independent clause** *can stand alone.*

> **Lee woke up late today. He realized he hadn't set the alarm last night.**
> **When Lee woke up late today, he realized he hadn't set his alarm last night.**
>      ↑                                                    ↑
> *This is a dependent clause.*        *This is a independent clause.*

*When the dependent clause comes before the main clause as in the above sentence, add a comma after the dependent clause. If the dependent clause follows the main clause, you do not need a comma. Here's an example.*

> **Lee was upset. He was going to be late for school.**
> **Lee was upset** because **he was going to be late for school.**

Use the word inside the parentheses to combine each pair of sentences into one.

1. I waited for my parents to get home. I watched a movie. **(while)**

   _____

2. My brother was in his room. He had homework to do. **(because)**

   _____

3. The movie was over. The power went out. **(before)**

   _____

4. This happens all the time. I wasn't concerned. **(since)**

   _____

5. I didn't mind the dark at first. I heard a scratching sound. **(until)**

   _____

6. I found my flashlight. I started to look around. **(when)**

   _____

7. I was checking the living room. I caught Alex trying to hide. **(when)**

   _____

# Triple the Fun

 *When you write, you may want to list three or more items or ideas in a series in a single sentence. Be sure to use a comma after each item in a series except after the last item.*

**Max dressed quickly, ate breakfast, and raced out the door.**
**Luis, Jamie, Leroy, and Sam met Max at the baseball field.**
**They were hopeful, excited, and nervous about their first game.**

Answer each question below in a complete sentence. Use commas where they are needed. Make sure each sentence begins and ends correctly. Remember to check your spelling.

1. What are the titles of three books you've read recently or would like to read? Remember to underline the title of each book.

   _____

2. What are four of the planets in our solar system closer to the sun than Neptune?

   _____

3. What are three green, leafy vegetables?

   _____

4. What countries would you like to visit? Include at least three in your answer.

   _____

5. What months fall between January and July?

   _____

6. What three things have you done today to help out at home?

   _____

7. What provinces or bodies of water border your province?

   _____

8. What activities do you and your friends enjoy in the summer?

   _____

9. Who are some of the most important people in your life?

   _____

 Make up some questions like the ones above and challenge someone you know to answer them on a piece of paper. Correct the sentences.

# Comma Capers

 *You know that you must use commas in a series of three or more items.*
**Max, Sam, and Alex ordered burgers, fries, and milkshakes for lunch.**

*Here are some additional rules you need to know about commas.*
*Use commas*

— *to set off the name of the person or group you are addressing.*
**Here's your order, boys.**

— *after words like* yes, no, *and* well.
**Well, what do you want to do now?**

— *before a conjunction that joins two sentences.*
**The boys finished lunch, and then they went to a movie.**

Read the sentences below. Decide which ones need commas and which ones do not.
Use this symbol ⋏ to show where commas belong.

1. I'd like a bike a pair of in-line skates and a snowboard for my birthday.

2. Well my friend you can't always have what you want when you want it.

3. No but I can always hope!

4. My friends and I skate all year long and snowboard during the winter.

5. I used to like skateboarding but now I prefer snowboarding and in-line skating.

6. What sports games or hobbies do you enjoy most Jody?

7. I learned to ski last year and now I'm taking ice-skating lessons.

8. Skiing ice skating and skateboarding are all fun things to do.

Review the four rules above for using commas. Then write an original sentence for each
rule. Begin and end each sentence correctly. Remember to check your spelling.

9. _____

10. _____

11. _____

12. _____

 **Writers use commas for other reasons. As you read a newspaper, an article in your favourite magazine, a letter, or a book, look for examples of commas in sentences and jot them down on a piece of paper. Then see if you can figure out the rules.**

# Show Time

*Sometimes a writer can change the order of the words in a sentence to make it more interesting.*

**The telephone rang just as the girls were about to leave.**
**Just as the girls were about to leave, the phone rang.**

**Gina decided to answer it in spite of the time.**
**In spite of the time, Gina decided to answer it.**

*Do not forget to add a comma when you begin a sentence with a clause or a phrase that cannot stand alone as in the second and last sentences.*

Rewrite each sentence by changing the order of the words.

**1.** Marta watched for the bus while Gina answered the phone.

_____

**2.** The caller hung up just as Gina said, "Hello."

_____

**3.** The girls were going to miss the one o'clock show unless they hurried.

_____

**4.** The bus had already come and gone by the time they got to the corner.

_____

**5.** The next bus to town finally showed up after the girls had waited a half hour.

_____

**6.** The girls decided to catch the four o'clock show since they missed the earlier show.

_____

**7.** They wouldn't have to stand in line later since Gina bought the tickets first.

_____

**8.** Gina and Marta were at the theatre by three o'clock even though it was early.

_____

**9.** They bought a tub of popcorn and drinks once they were inside.

_____

# Keeps On Going

 *Writers sometimes make the mistake of running together two or more sentences without telling how the ideas are related. This kind of sentence is called a* **run-on sentence**.

> **Kansas holds the record for having the largest ball of twine in the United States can you believe it weighs over 7700 kilograms in fact, the giant ball is 12 metres in circumference, 3.3 metres tall, and made up of more than 1760 kilometres of twine!**

*To fix a run-on sentence, identify each complete thought or idea and break it into shorter sentences.*

> **Kansas holds the record for having the largest ball of twine in the United States. Can you believe it weighs over 7700 kilograms? In fact, the giant ball is 12 metres in circumference, 3.3 metres tall, and made up of more than 1760 kilometres of twine!**

Rewrite each run-on sentence correctly. Remember to begin and end each sentence correctly.

**1.** Did you know that the United States is the top meat-eating country in the world each person consumes about 118 kilograms of meat each year beef is the most commonly eaten meat.

_____

_____

_____

**2.** Have you ever noticed that Abraham Lincoln faces right on a U.S. penny he is the only president on a U.S. coin who does Sacagawea faces right on the new dollar coin, but she was not a president?

_____

_____

_____

**3.** It would be fantastic to have a robot to do all my chores, help do my homework, and play games I really think the day will come unfortunately, it won't come soon enough for me.

_____

_____

_____

# A Long School Year

 *Have you ever accidentally left out words when you write? Whenever you write, it is always a good idea to proofread for words that may be missing. Here is an example of what to do when you want to add a missing word as you proofread.*

**I got an** ^e-mail^ **from my friend last night.**

**We** ^met^ **last summer when my family was in Japan.**

Read the passage below about school in Japan. Twenty words are missing. Figure out what they are and add them to the sentences. Use the ∧ symbol to show where each missing word belongs. Then write each missing word above the sentence.
Hint: Every sentence has at least one missing word.

**How would like to go to school on Saturdays? If you lived in the of Japan,**

**that's just where you'd be each Saturday morning. I have a who lives in Japan.**

**Yuichi explained that attend classes five and one-half a week. The day is on**

**Saturday. I was also surprised to that the Japanese school is one of the longest**

**in the world – over 240 days. It begins in the of April. While we have over two**

**months off each, students in Japan get their in late July and August. School**

**then again in fall and ends in March. The people of believe that a good is very**

**important. Children are required to attend school from the age of six to the of**

**fifteen. They have elementary and middle just like we do. Then most go on to**

**school for another three years. Yuichi says that students work very because the**

**standards are so high. He and some of his friends even extra classes after**

**school. They all want to get into a good someday.**

 *Write several sentences about something that interests you on a piece of paper. Rewrite the sentences on another piece of paper, this time leaving out a key word in each one. Challenge someone you know to add the missing words. Then compare the two sets of sentences.*

# Parts of a Paragraph

 A **paragraph** is a group of sentences that tells about one main idea. The **topic sentence** tells the main idea and is usually the first sentence. **Supporting sentences** tell more about the main idea. The **closing sentence** of a paragraph often retells the main idea in a different way. Here are the parts for one paragraph.

*Paragraph Title:*                  **Starting Over**

*Topic Sentence:*            **Today started off badly and only got worse.**

*Supporting Sentences:* 
1. **Everyone in my family woke up late this morning.**
2. **I had only 15 minutes to get ready and catch the bus.**
3. **I dressed as fast as I could, grabbed an apple and my backpack, and raced to get to the bus stop on time.**
4. **Fortunately, I just made it.**
5. **Unfortunately, the bus was pulling away when several kids pointed out that I had on two different shoes.**

*Closing Sentence:*         **At that moment, I wanted to start the day over.**

When you write a paragraph, remember these rules:

- **Indent** *the first line to let readers know that you are beginning a paragraph.*
- **Capitalize** *the first word of each sentence.*
- **Punctuate** *each sentence correctly (? ! . ,).*

Use all the information above to write the paragraph. Be sure to follow the rules.

_____
**paragraph title**

_____

_____

_____

_____

_____

_____

_____

# What's the Topic?

 *Every paragraph has a topic sentence that tells the main idea of the paragraph, or what it is about. It usually answers several of these questions:*

**Who?   What?   Where?   When?   Why?   How?**

*Here are some examples.*

**The doe and her fawn faced many dangers in the forest.**
**We were amazed by our guest's rude behaviour.**
**Baking bread from scratch is really not so difficult, or so I thought.**
**Getting up in the morning is the hardest thing to do.**

*Did these topic sentences grab your attention? A good topic sentence should.*

Here are some topics. Write a topic sentence for each one.

**1.** convincing someone to try octopus soup

_____

**2.** an important person in your life

_____

**3.** an embarrassing moment

_____

**4.** the importance of Canada Day

_____

**5.** lunchtime at the school cafeteria

_____

Now list some topics of your own. Then write a topic sentence for each one.

_____
**Topic #1**

_____          _____
**Topic #2**                                    **Topic #3**

_____
**Topic sentence #1**

_____
**Topic sentence #2**

_____
**Topic sentence #3**

# Topic Talk

 *Most paragraphs begin with a topic sentence, but it can appear elsewhere in a paragraph. Sometimes a topic sentence is located at the end of a paragraph or even in the middle.*

**A boiling mass of clouds was almost overhead. A bolt of lightning streaked across the darkened sky. Thunder boomed, and it began to rain and hail. <u>We had to find a safe place quickly!</u> There wasn't a moment to spare because early summer storms sometimes turn into tornadoes.**

*Read the paragraph again. This time try the topic sentence elsewhere in the paragraph.*

Read each paragraph. Notice that each one is missing a topic sentence. Think about the supporting sentences. What main idea do you think they support? Write a topic sentence to tell the main idea of each paragraph. Remember that a topic sentence is not always the first sentence of a paragraph.

**1.** **The days are growing longer. The winter snows are melting as the temperatures rise. Colourful crocuses are popping up here and there. Robins have begun to return north, and creatures are beginning to come out of their winter burrows.**

_____

**2.** _____

**It was fun and easy. Students, parents, and teachers began saving the box tops from all Healthful Foods products. After we collected 100,000 box tops, we mailed them to Healthful Foods headquarters. We earned 10 cents for each box top for a total of $10,000. Our school will use the money to buy computers.**

**3.** **The last weekend in June is quickly approaching. You know what that means.**

_____

**This year the festivities will begin at 10:00 A.M. at Twin Lakes Picnic Grove, pavilion 12. As always, there will be music, dancing, lots of great food, games, and some new surprises! We look forward to seeing you.**

# A Lot of Details

 *When you are ready to write a topic sentence, think about the main topic or idea of the paragraph you will be writing and the details you plan to include. Then jot down several possible sentences and choose the best one. Remember that a topic sentence can answer several questions: Who? What? Where? When? Why? How?*

*Tony Hawk*
- *skateboarder*
- *in his thirties*
- *turned professional at age 14*
- *has won more skateboarding contests than anyone*
- *made history at Summer X Games in 1999—landed a "900"*
*(a complete somersault done 2 ¹/₂ times in midair)*

*Possible topic sentences:*   **There is no other skateboarder like Tony Hawk.**
**Tony Hawk is an extraordinary skateboarder.**
**Tony Hawk is the "old man" of skateboarding.**

Here are some topics with details. Write two topic sentences for each one on the lines below.

| 1. **Pet Rocks** | 2. **Komodo Dragon** | 3. **A Great Dessert** |
|---|---|---|
| — fad in the 1970s<br>— idea came from Gary Dahl, a salesman<br>— sold rocks as pets<br>— came with a manual<br>— manual had tips on how to teach a pet rock tricks | — member of monitor family<br>— grows to 3 metres and weighs 136 kilograms<br>— meat eater<br>— dangerous to humans<br>— largest lizard in the world<br>— long neck and tail, strong legs<br>— found on Komodo Island | — slice a banana<br>— add vanilla ice cream<br>— sprinkle on some walnuts<br>— cover with lots of hot fudge sauce<br>— top with mounds of whipped cream and a cherry |

1. _____

_____

2. _____

_____

3. _____

_____

Remember that the supporting sentences you write support or tell more about the main idea in your topic sentence. Read the paragraph below. Draw one line under the topic sentence. Draw two lines under the supporting sentences. Check (√) the closing sentence.

### Tony Hawk

Tony Hawk is an extraordinary skateboarder. He turned professional when he was only 14 years old. Now in his thirties, Tony has won more skateboarding contests than anyone else has. He even made history in 1999 by landing a trick called the "900" at the Summer X Games. Tony Hawk may just be the greatest skateboarder in the world.

Now, review the topics on page 200. Choose one. Then review the details listed about the topic in the box. Next, use the information to write at least three supporting sentences to support the topic sentence you wrote. Include a closing sentence and a title. Write the paragraph below.

_____

_____

_____

_____

_____

_____

_____

 **Make a list of topics you would like to write about. Choose one. Then list on a piece of paper details you know about the topic. Do some research if necessary. Then write a topic sentence and several supporting sentences.**

# Drizzle With Details

*A good paragraph needs supporting sentences that tell more
about the main idea of the topic sentence. Supporting sentences
are sometimes called detail sentences. Every detail sentence in a
paragraph must relate to the main idea. In the following paragraph,
the one supporting sentence that does not relate to the main idea
has been underlined.*

**My first day of softball practice was a total disaster!
Not only was I ten minutes late, but I also forgot my glove.
Then during batting practice, I missed the ball every time I
took a swing. <u>I definitely have improved on my catching skills.</u>
To make matters even worse, I tripped in the outfield and
twisted my ankle. I was definitely not off to a very good start.**

Read the following paragraph. Underline the topic sentence.
Then cross out any supporting sentences that do not relate to
the main idea.

Yesterday our science class went on a field trip to a pond. Next month we're
going to the ocean. That will be fun. We've been studying the pond as an
ecosystem in class. Our teacher wanted us to observe firsthand all the different
habitats in and around the pond. She had us keep a checklist of the different
kinds of plants and animals in each pond habitat. One of the boys accidentally
fell in. He was really embarrassed. Along the water's edge I saw several kinds of
plants partly underwater, two salamanders, snails, and water bugs. I observed
many different habitats.

Name _____

Read the title and topic sentence for each of the following paragraph plans. Then write four supporting sentences that relate to and support each one.

**1.** **Paragraph Title:**       Uniforms – To Wear or Not to Wear?
   **Topic Sentence:**    Our school should require all students to wear uniforms.

   **Supporting Sentences:**

   1. _____

   2. _____

   3. _____

   4. _____

**2.** **Paragraph Title:**       An Adventure in Dreamland
   **Topic Sentence:**    Last night I had the most incredible dream.

   **Supporting Sentences:**

   1. _____

   2. _____

   3. _____

   4. _____

**3.** **Paragraph Title:**       A Sad Day
   **Topic Sentence:**    I will always remember how sad I was that day.

   **Supporting Sentences:**

   1. _____

   2. _____

   3. _____

   4. _____

 Choose one of the titles and topic sentences above. On a piece of paper, write a paragraph using the supporting sentences you wrote above. Include more supporting sentences that relate to the topic sentence if you want. Then add a closing sentence. Remember to indent, begin and end sentences correctly, punctuate correctly, and check your spelling.

# A Musical Lesson

 *There are many kinds of paragraphs. When you write a **comparison paragraph**, you compare by telling how things are similar and contrast by telling how things are different. You can use a Venn diagram to help organize your ideas. Here is an example.*

| Trumpet | Both | Violin |
|---|---|---|

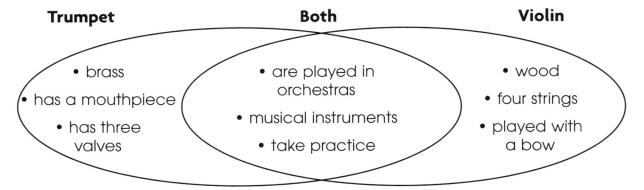

- brass
- has a mouthpiece
- has three valves
- are played in orchestras
- musical instruments
- take practice
- wood
- four strings
- played with a bow

Complete the paragraph using details to compare and contrast the trumpet and violin. Remember to capitalize and punctuate correctly.

## Trumpet Versus Violin

The trumpet and violin are both musical instruments that are_____

_____. However, there are some

important differences. The trumpet_____

_____

_____

On the other hand, the violin_____

_____

_____

_____

Both instruments_____

_____

 **Make a list on a piece of paper of things to compare and contrast such as a house and an apartment building, ice skating and skateboarding, or spinach and broccoli. Choose one pair. Make and complete a Venn diagram like the one above. Then write a paragraph to tell how they are similar and different.**

# Is That a Fact?

*What is the difference between a fact and an opinion? A **fact** can be checked or proven. An opinion is what someone believes or feels about something. An **opinion** cannot be proven.*

Fact → **Cocoa beans are used to make chocolate.**
Opinion → **Chocolate pudding is better than chocolate ice cream**.

Read each sentence. Write *F* next to each fact. Write *O* next to each opinion.

_____ **1. Everyone in the world thinks chocolate makes the best candy.**

_____ **2. In Switzerland, the average person eats about 10 kilograms of chocolate in a year.**

_____ **3. That means the Swiss eat more than 72 million kilograms of chocolate annually.**

_____ **4. I think Americans eat more chocolate than that.**

_____ **5. People also use chocolate to make drinks and to flavour recipes.**

_____ **6. There's nothing better than a chocolate donut with chocolate glaze.**

Look at the pictures. Then write two facts and two opinions about each snack food. Use clue words such as *think, best, believe, like,* and *dislike* to signal an opinion.

**1. Fact:** _____

_____

_____

**Opinion:** _____

_____

_____

**2. Fact:** _____

_____

_____

**Opinion:** _____

_____

_____

**3. Fact:** _____

_____

_____

**Opinion:** _____

_____

_____

As you listen to a conversation among your friends about an issue that is important to them, try to identify the facts and opinions you hear and write them down on a piece of paper. Then ask, "Can this statement be proven?" If the answer is yes, then it is a fact. If not, then it is an opinion. Circle any clue words or phrases that signal opinions.

# I'm Convinced!

*In a **persuasive paragraph**, you give an opinion about something and try to convince readers to think or feel the way you do. A convincing persuasive paragraph includes*

— **a topic sentence that clearly states your opinion.**
— **reasons that support your opinion.**
— **facts to back up your opinion.**
— **a strong closing sentence that summarizes your opinion.**

Pretend you are a world famous chef who prepares dishes that include edible insects—insects that you can eat. You want to persuade people to include insects in their diet. Here is a topic sentence for a persuasive paragraph.

**Everyone should try cooking with insects.**

Here are some reasons and facts.
• Many insects like mealworms, crickets, and weevils are edible.
• People in many cultures around the world eat insects.
• Many insects are low in fat and rich in vitamins.
• Lots of tasty recipes include insects.
• Insects are really quite delicious.

Now put it all together. Write a persuasive paragraph that includes a title and a strong closing sentence. Remember the rules for writing a paragraph.

**Paragraph Title:** _____

**Topic Sentence:** _____

_____

**Reasons/Facts:** _____

_____

_____

_____

_____

_____

_____

**Closing Sentence:** _____

_____

# Step by Step

*When you write an **expository paragraph**, you give facts and information, explain ideas, or give directions. An expository paragraph can also include opinions. Here are some topic ideas for an expository paragraph.*

**Explain how to play the flute.**　　　　**Explain how to bathe a dog.**
**Tell why you do not like brussels sprouts.**　**Tell what skills you need to skateboard.**
**Give facts about yourself.**　　　　　　**Give the facts about your favourite band.**

*Here is an example of an expository paragraph. It explains how to fry an egg.*

**Frying an egg is not all that difficult. After melting a little bit of butter in a frying pan, just crack the eggshell along the rim of the pan and let the egg drop into the pan. Do it gently so the yolk does not break. Let the egg fry over a low heat for about a minute or so. That is all it takes.**

Complete the following topics for expository paragraphs with your own ideas.

**Explain how to**　　　　**Give facts about**　　　　**Tell why**

_____　　　_____　　　_____

_____　　　_____　　　_____

_____　　　_____　　　_____

Use the form below to develop one of your ideas for an expository paragraph.

**Paragraph Title:** _____

**Topic Sentence:** _____

_____

**Details/Facts/Steps:** _____

_____

_____

_____

_____

**Closing Sentence:** _____

_____

Now, use the plan above to write a paragraph on a piece of paper. If you are giving directions for doing or making something, include words such as *first, next, after that,* and *finally* to make the steps clear for your readers.

# A Sentence Relationship

*You can write sentences about cause and effect relationships. A **cause** is the reason something happens. An **effect** is the result of the cause, or what actually happens. Words such as* so, because, *and* since *are used in cause and effect sentences.*

      *effect*                       *cause*
**School was cancelled today** because **the storm dumped two feet of snow**.

      *cause*                            *effect*
**The snow and wind knocked out power lines,** so **many homes were without electricity.**

      *cause*                           *effect*
Since **there was no school today, I went back to bed and slept another hour.**

Add a cause to each of the following sentences about the day that school was cancelled because of snow.

**1.** Many shops, stores, and offices were closed _____

_____

**2.** My friends and I love snow days _____

_____

**3.** It took several minutes to open the back door _____

_____

**4.** Our snow blower would not start _____

_____

Add an effect to each of the following sentences.

**5.** I shovelled snow for two hours, _____

_____

**6.** My sister could not find her boots, _____

_____

**7.** Since our street was finally plowed by noon, _____

_____

**8.** By late afternoon it began snowing again, _____

_____

# What a Mess!

 *You can write a paragraph using a cause and effect relationship. One way to begin is to state a cause. Then you write about the effects that happen as a result of that cause.*

**The piercing sound of the smoke alarm reminded Max that he had forgotten to check the pot of stew heating up on the stove. The stew had boiled over, the bottom of the pot was scorched, and smoke was filling the kitchen. Dinner was obviously ruined, and Max was in big trouble. What a mess!**

Answer each question about the paragraph above.

**1.** **What is the cause?** _____

_____

**2.** **What were the effects? List them.** _____

_____

_____

Read the first sentence of the following paragraph. It states a cause. What might happen as a result? Continue the paragraph. Write what you think the effects will be.

**I walked into my room just as Sebastian, our very inquisitive cat, managed to**

**tip over the goldfish bowl that had been on my desk.** _____

_____

_____

_____

_____

_____

_____

 Brainstorm a list of causes on a piece of paper. Here are some to get you started:
eating too many cookies     staying up too late     not studying for a test
Then list some possible effects. Develop your ideas into a paragraph.

# A Vivid Picture

 A **descriptive paragraph** creates a vivid image or picture for readers. By choosing just the right adjectives, you can reveal how something looks, sounds, smells, tastes, and feels. Compare the sentences from two different paragraphs. Which one creates a more vivid picture?

**The pizza with sausage and onions tasted so good.**

**The smooth, sweet sauce and bubbly mozzarella topped with bite-sized chunks of extra hot sausage and thin slivers of sweet onion on a perfectly baked, thin crust delighted my taste buds.**

Cut out a picture of something interesting and paste it in the box. Then brainstorm a list adjectives and descriptive phrases to tell about it.

_____  _____

_____  _____

_____  _____

_____  _____

_____  _____

Now, write a paragraph about the picture. Begin your paragraph with a topic sentence that will grab readers. Add supporting sentences that include the adjectives and descriptive phrases listed to create a vivid picture.

_____

_____

_____

_____

_____

 **Here is a set of adjectives: bumpy, dusty, narrow, steep, curvy, unpaved, well-worn. Think about what they might describe. Then, on a piece of paper use the words to write a descriptive paragraph that paints a picture.**

# Numerous, Spectacular Words

*When you write, do you sometimes overuse descriptive words like* good, bad, nice, *or* wonderful?
*Overused words can make your writing boring.*

> The weather was **good** for our first camping trip. *(fair)*
> A ranger gave us some really **good** tips about the park. *(useful)*
> Mom thought the campsite near the stream was **good**. *(lovely)*
> My older brother is a **good** fly fisherman. *(skilled)*
> He said his equipment is too **good** for me to use, though! *(valuable)*

*Now reread the sentences. This time use the words in parentheses in place of the word* good.
*You can use a thesaurus to help find words. A thesaurus is a reference book that gives synonyms
and antonyms for words.*

Identify eight frequently overused descriptive words in the passage below and list them
in the answer spaces. Next, use a thesaurus to write three synonyms for each word, or
write three synonyms you know. Then revise the passage. Use editing symbols to cross out
the overused words and add the more effective synonyms to replace them.

> **Our family has a dog named Scooter. He's normally very good until it's time
> to bathe him. That's when our nice, little terrier turns into a big, furry monster.
> Scooter isn't really bad. He's just hard to handle when he doesn't want to do
> something. I think he's afraid of water. You should see how sad he looks once we
> manage to get him into the tub.**

1. _____    _____

2. _____    _____

3. _____    _____

4. _____    _____

5. _____    _____

6. _____    _____

7. _____    _____

8. _____    _____

**Reread a composition you have recently written. Look for overused words and then
use a thesaurus to find other words that you could use instead to make your writing
more interesting.**

# Action Alert

 *When you write, think about the verbs that you choose to express action in your sentences. Are they as exact as they can be? Do they tell your readers exactly what you want to say?*

The child **broke** the plastic toy.
The child **smashed** the plastic toy.
The child **cracked** the plastic toy.

*Each verb creates a different picture of what happened.*

Read each sentence. Underline the verb. Then rewrite each sentence using a more exact verb. You may want to use a thesaurus.

**1.** Three young hikers went up the steep hill.

_____

**2.** A lone runner ran around the track.

_____

**3.** The wind blew through the treetops.

_____

**4.** The janitor cleaned the scuff marks off the floor.

_____

**5.** The audience laughed at the hilarious scene.

_____

**6.** The diners ate the delicious meal.

_____

**7.** The young tourists liked the castle most of all.

_____

**8.** The children slept for about an hour.

_____

**9.** The biologist looked at the unusual specimen.

_____

 Here are some commonly used verbs: make, tell, say, speak, ride. On a piece of paper, list as many exact verbs as you can think of for each one. Use a thesaurus for additional words. Then write several sentences using the exact words on your list.

# Colourful Clues

*You can compare two things that are not alike in order to give your readers a clearer and more colourful picture. When you use* like *or* as *to make a comparison, it is called a* **simile***.*

**Max is as slow as molasses when he doesn't want to do something.**
**My sister leaped over the puddles like a frog to avoid getting her shoes wet.**
**The angry man erupted like a volcano.**

*When you make a comparison without* like *or* as*, it is called a* **metaphor***. You compare things directly, saying the subject is something else.*

**The disturbed anthill was a whirlwind of activity.**
**The oak trees, silent sentries around the cabin, stood guard.**
**Jenny and I were all ears as we listened to the latest gossip.**

Finish the metaphors and similes.

**1.** Crowds of commuters piled into the subway cars like _____

_____

**2.** Chirping crickets on warm summer night are _____

_____

**3.** After rolling in the mud, our dog looked like _____

**4.** Happiness is _____

**5.** Just learning to walk, the toddler was as wobbly as _____

_____

**6.** After scoring the winning point, I felt as _____

_____

**7.** Having a tooth filled is about as much fun as _____

_____

**8.** A summer thunderstorm is _____

_____

**9.** _____ is _____

**10.** _____ is like _____

# Adding Spice

 *Sometimes you can spice up your writing by giving human characteristics and qualities to non-human things such as animals and objects. This is called* **personification**.

**The sagging roof groaned under the weight of all the snow.**
**The falling leaves danced in the wind.**

*You can also use* **hyperbole**, *or deliberate exaggeration, to make a point clearer or to add drama to your writing.*

**The lost hiker is so hungry he could eat a bear.**
**Yesterday was so hot, we could have fried eggs on the sidewalk.**

Personify the animal or object in each sentence by giving it human qualities.

1. The rusted hinges on the old wooden door _____

_____

2. As several birds began feasting on the farmer's corn, the scarecrow _____

_____

3. A gentle summer breeze _____

_____

4. Just as I walked past the statue of Ben Franklin, it _____

_____

Complete each sentence with an example of a hyperbole.

5. The salsa was so spicy hot _____

_____

6. The pumpkin grew so large _____

_____

7. If we placed all the books in the library end to end, they _____

_____

8. My room was so cold last night that by morning _____

_____

 **Listen for examples of hyperbole in the conversations that you hear throughout the day. Jot them down in a notebook. Then make up some of your own.**

# Daily Notes

*When you keep a journal, you can record the facts and details about events that happen in your life and your feelings or opinions about them. Your journal entries can be a valuable resource when you are looking for writing ideas.*

**3/9 We had to take Fuzzer to his new home today. Our new landlord said he could not stay with us at our apartment anymore. I know Fuzzer will be much happier at the farm where he can run and play, but I still felt so sad. I tried not to cry, but I could not help it. Fuzzer has been part of our family for nine years. We grew up together. I will miss him very much!**

**3/15 I had to go to my sister's dance recital at the Palace Theatre last night. She performed in three numbers. At first I didn't want to go because I thought it would be boring, but it wasn't. I actually felt really proud of my sister! She was fantastic. I guess I really should tell her.**

**3/19 Today, the entire Grade 4 class went on a field trip to the capital of the province. It was incredible! We met a member of the Legislative Assembly. She showed us around the Legislative building. We even got to listen to the MLAs discuss a new law. Later, we saw the Speaker's Reception Room. Boy, is this an awesome building!**

Think about the events that have happened in your life over the last several days. Did anything of special importance happen at home, on the way to or from school, or in your community, the country, or the world? Record the facts, details, and your feelings or opinions about two events on the journal page below. Write the date for each entry.

_____ / _____ / _____

_____

_____

_____

_____

_____ / _____ / _____

_____

_____

_____

_____

# Story Time

 A story has **characters**, a **setting** (where and when the story takes place), and a **plot** (the events that happen in a story). The main story character often faces a problem which is introduced at the **beginning** of a story, developed in the **middle**, and solved at the **end**.

Develop your own story about the picture. First, answer the questions.

**1.** **What or who is the story about?** _____

_____

_____

_____

**2.** **Where and when does it take place?** _____

_____

_____

_____

**3.** **How will the story begin?** _____

_____

_____

_____

_____

**4.** **What happens in the middle?** _____

_____

_____

**5.** **How will the story end?** _____

_____

_____

Use your answers to write a story on another sheet of paper. Include a title. Be sure to tell the events in the order they happen. Remember the rules for writing a paragraph.

 **Compile magazine pictures that spark story ideas. From time to time choose one of the pictures and make up an oral story about it. If you have an audiocassette recorder, tape your story and save it. Use it to write a story at another time.**

# What Did You Say?

 *Some stories may include dialogue, or the exact words of story characters. Dialogue lets readers know something about the characters, plot, setting, and problem or conflict in a story. Use quotation marks around a speaker's exact words and commas to set off quotations. Remember to put periods, question marks, exclamation points, and commas inside the quotation marks.*

**"Get away from my bowl!" yelled Little Miss Muffet when she saw the approaching spider.**

**"Please don't get so excited," replied the startled spider. "I just wanted a little taste. I've never tried curds and whey before."**

Use your imagination to complete the dialogue between the fairy tale or nursery rhyme characters. Include quotation marks and commas where they belong and the correct end punctuation.

**1.** When Baby Bear saw the strange girl asleep in his bed, he asked his parents, _____

_____

His mother replied, _____

**2.** Humpty Dumpty was sitting on the wall when he suddenly fell off. On the way down

he shouted, _____

Two of the king's men approached. One whispered nervously to the other, _____

_____

**3.** When Jack realized he was about to fall down the hill with a pail of water, he yelled,

_____

_____cried Jill,

as she went tumbling down the hill after Jack.

**4.** The wolf knocked on the door of the third little pig's house. When there was no

answer, the wolf bellowed, _____

Knowing that he and his brother were safe inside his sturdy brick house, the third

little pig replied, _____

_____

# Let's Get Organized

 *When you write a report or story, it helps to review your notes and organize them into an outline to show the order in which you want to discuss them.*

**Chester Greenwood** → **subject of the report**

I. **Who was Chester Greenwood?** → **main idea becomes topic sentence**
   A. **born in 1858** → **supporting details become supporting sentences**
   B. **grew up in Farmington, Maine, U.S.**
   C. **as a child had ear problems in winter**

II. **His first invention—earmuffs**
   A. **needed a way to protect ears from cold**
   B. **1873 at age 15 began testing his ideas**
   C. **idea for fur-covered earflaps worked**
   D. **people saw and also wanted earflaps**
   E. **grandmother helped produce them**

III. **His later accomplishments**
   A. **founded a telephone company**
   B. **manufactured steam heaters**
   C. **over 100 inventions**

Study the outline above. Then answer the questions.

1. What is the topic of the report? _____

2. How many paragraphs will there be? _____

3. What is main topic of the first paragraph? _____

   _____

4. How many details tell about the second main idea? _____

Use the form on the next page to develop an outline for preparing an interesting and unusual dish that your family enjoys.

**How to Prepare** _____

**I.** **Background about the dish**

    **A.** _____

    **B.** _____

    **C.** _____

    **D.** _____

    **E.** _____

**II.** **Ingredients**

    **A.** _____

    **B.** _____

    **C.** _____

    **D.** _____

    **E.** _____

**III.** **Equipment**

    **A.** _____

    **B.** _____

    **C.** _____

    **D.** _____

    **E.** _____

**IV.** **Steps**

    **A.** _____

    **B.** _____

    **C.** _____

    **D.** _____

    **E.** _____

 Share your outline with someone you know.

# Read All About It

 A **news story** *reports just the facts about an event and answers the questions* who, what, when, where, why, *and* how. *The most important information is included at the beginning of the article in a paragraph called the* **lead**.

**Grass Fires Burn Out of Control**      headline

WHERE did it happen? ⟶ GREENSBURG—Grass fires, fueled by wind gusts up to 50 miles per hour, spread into a — **WHY did it happen?** residential area early Tuesday morning. All residents had to be evacuated. Within min- — **WHEN did it happen?** utes over 25 homes were engulfed by flames and destroyed. According to officials, no — **WHO was affected?** injuries have been reported.

Planes and helicopters battling the blaze had to be grounded because the heat of the flames was so intense.

Write a news story using the information below. Remember to write about the facts and events in the order they occurred. Follow the model lead above.

Who: Roseville Emergency Rescue Team
When: April 10, 2003; 5 A.M.
Where: Slate Run River
What: team and rescue vehicles sent;
    worked for three hours; rescued residents
How: used helicopter and boats
Why: residents along river stranded by flash flood after storm

_____

_____  —  _____

_____

_____

_____

_____

_____

_____

_____

 Use your imagination to write a news story on a piece of paper for one of the following headlines or one of your own.

Mystery of the Missing Dinosaur Solved          Students Protest School Lunch Menu
City High Wins Championship          Second Female Elected Prime Minister

# Scholastic Success With

# CHARTS, TABLES & GRAPHS

# The Winning Team

This table displays the win-loss record for five major-league baseball teams in 2000. Use the table to choose the best answer to each question below.

| BASEBALL STANDINGS: AMERICAN LEAGUE EAST | | | | |
|---|---|---|---|---|
| Team | Wins | Losses | Percent | Games Behind |
| New York Yankees | 87 | 74 | .540 | — |
| Boston Red Sox | 85 | 77 | .525 | $2\frac{1}{2}$ |
| Toronto Blue Jays | 83 | 79 | .512 | $4\frac{1}{2}$ |
| Baltimore Orioles | 74 | 88 | .457 | $13\frac{1}{2}$ |
| Tampa Bay Devil Rays | 69 | 92 | .429 | 18 |

1. Which team had the most wins?
   - (a) Baltimore Orioles
   - (b) Boston Red Sox
   - (c) New York Yankees
   - (d) Toronto Blue Jays

2. How many games did the Boston Red Sox lose?
   - (a) 74
   - (b) 77
   - (c) 79
   - (d) 85

3. Which team had 74 wins and 88 losses?
   - (a) New York Yankees
   - (b) Boston Red Sox
   - (c) Toronto Blue Jays
   - (d) Baltimore Orioles

4. How many games did the Tampa Bay Devil Rays win?
   - (a) 69
   - (b) 74
   - (c) 83
   - (d) 92

5. How many of these teams won more than half of their games?
   - (a) 2
   - (b) 3
   - (c) 4
   - (d) 5

# Measuring Up

Mrs. Umberto made this table to use when she buys clothing for her children. Use the table to answer the questions below.

| MY CHILDREN'S CLOTHING SIZES | | | |
|---|---|---|---|
| **Child** | **Height (centimetres)** | **Weight (kilograms)** | **Size** |
| Emilio | 150 | 46 | 14 |
| Teresita | 135 | 34 | 12 |
| Pablo | 132 | 27 | 8 |
| Juana | 109 | 23 | 5 |

1 How tall is Emilio? _____

2 How much more does Teresita weigh than Juana?

_____

3 Which two children are about the same height?

_____

4 What size clothing does Juana wear?

_____

5 According to this table, how do children's clothing sizes change as children grow taller?

_____

# Tori's Sandwich Study

Tori asked her classmates to name their favourite sandwiches. She made a tally chart showing how many kids chose each kind. Use the chart to choose the best answer to each question below.

| OUR FAVOURITE SANDWICHES | |
| --- | --- |
| KIND OF SANDWICH | NUMBER OF KIDS |
| Ham and cheese | ✓✓✓✓ |
| Tuna fish | ✓✓✓ |
| Peanut butter and jelly | ✓✓✓✓✓ |
| Egg salad | ✓✓ |

**1** How many kids named tuna fish as their favourite kind of sandwich?

ⓐ 2   ⓒ 4
ⓑ 3   ⓓ 5

**2** How many kids named egg salad?

ⓐ 2   ⓒ 4
ⓑ 3   ⓓ 5

**3** Which kind of sandwich was named by the most kids?

ⓐ ham and cheese   ⓒ peanut butter and jelly
ⓑ tuna fish   ⓓ egg salad

**4** If each kid named only one favourite sandwich, how many kids in all answered Tori's question?

ⓐ 4   ⓒ 12
ⓑ 5   ⓓ 14

Name _____

# Pete's Chores

Pete made this tally chart to show how often he did chores around the house. He recorded his chores for one week. Use the chart to choose the best answer to each question below.

| MY WEEKLY RECORD | |
|---|---|
| CHORE | NUMBER OF TIMES |
| Making bed | ✓✓✓✓✓✓ |
| Taking out garbage | ✓ |
| Setting table | ✓✓✓✓✓ |
| Picking up toys | ✓✓✓✓ |
| Feeding cats | ✓✓✓ |
| | |

**1** Which chore did Pete do most often?
   (a) making bed      (c) picking up toys
   (b) setting table     (d) feeding cats

**2** How many times did Pete take out the garbage?
   (a) 5           (c) 3
   (b) 4           (d) 1

**3** How many times did Pete set the table?
   (a) 4           (c) 6
   (b) 5           (d) 7

**4** How many times in all did Pete do chores?
   (a) 13         (c) 17
   (b) 14         (d) 20

# Drew's Newspaper Route

Drew made a pictograph to show how many newspapers he delivers on each street of his newspaper route. Use the graph to choose the best answer to each question below.

| MY DAILY DELIVERIES | |
|---|---|
| Golet | 🗞🗞🗞🗞🗞🗞🗞 |
| Harold Street | 🗞🗞🗞🗞🗞🗞🗞🗞🗞 |
| Lower Road | 🗞🗞🗞 |
| Morris Drive | 🗞🗞🗞🗞🗞🗞 |
| Burnham Street | 🗞🗞🗞🗞🗞🗞🗞🗞 |

Each 🗞 stands for one newspaper.

**1** How many newspapers does Drew deliver on Morris Drive?
    (a) 6           (c) 8
    (b) 7           (d) 9

**2** On which street does Drew deliver the most newspapers?
    (a) Harold Street     (c) Morris Drive
    (b) Gold Street       (d) Lower Road

**3** How many more newspapers does Drew deliver on Burnham Street than on Lower Road?
    (a) 7           (c) 3
    (b) 5           (d) 1

**4** What is the total number of newspapers Drew delivers on his newspaper route?
    (a) 38          (c) 33
    (b) 36          (d) 30

# Cool Inventions

The Grade 4 class in the Town School asked all the students in the school to name the most important invention of the last 200 years. This pictograph shows how many students chose each of the inventions listed. Use the graph to answer the questions below.

### KIDS' CHOICES

| | |
|---|---|
| Automobile | 𝕩 𝕩 𝕩 𝕩 |
| Computer | 𝕩 𝕩 𝕩 𝕩 𝕩 𝕩 𝕩 |
| Electric light | 𝕩 𝕩 𝕩 |
| Telephone | 𝕩 𝕩 𝕩 𝕩 |
| Television | 𝕩 𝕩 𝕩 𝕩 𝕩 𝕩 |

**KEY**

𝕩 = 5 students

**1** Which invention was named by the most students?

_____

**2** How many students named television as the most important invention?

_____

**3** Which two inventions were named by an equal number of students?

_____

**4** How many more students named the computer than the electric light?

_____

# The Class Field Trip

Mrs. Smith's class took a field trip to the park, and a park ranger explained how different trees grow to different heights. This bar graph shows the trees' heights. Use the graph to choose the best answer to each question below.

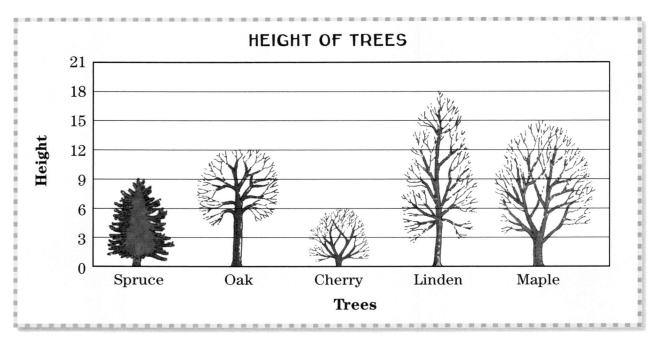

**HEIGHT OF TREES**

**1** Which tree is the shortest?
     (a) cherry            (c) maple
     (b) linden           (d) spruce

**2** How tall is the oak tree?
     (a) 6 metres         (c) 12 metres
     (b) 9 metres         (d) 15 metres

**3** Which tree is twice as tall as the spruce?
     (a) maple            (c) cherry
     (b) linden           (d) oak

**4** How much taller is the maple tree than the cherry tree?
     (a) 12 metres        (c) 6 metres
     (b) 9 metres         (d) 3 metres

# Hannah and Her Cousins

Hannah's cousins live in five different provinces. She made this bar graph to show how many cousins live in each province. Use the graph to answer the questions below.

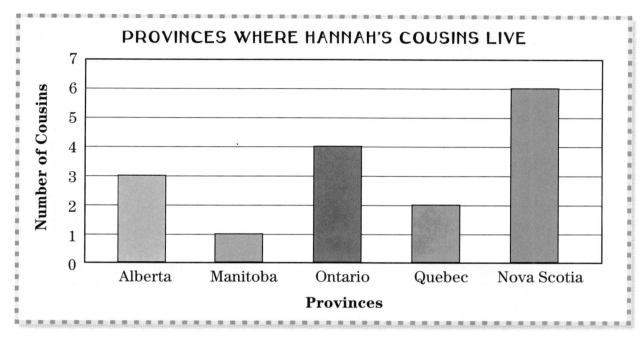

**PROVINCES WHERE HANNAH'S COUSINS LIVE**

1 How many cousins live in Quebec?

_____

2 The greatest number of Hannah's cousins live in which province?

_____

3 How many more cousins live in Ontario than in Alberta?

_____

4 How many cousins does Hannah have altogether?

_____

# Soccer Contest

Five friends held a contest to see how far they could kick a soccer ball. The bar graph below shows the results of their contest. Use the graph to choose the best answer to each question.

THE BEST KICKS

Players

Distance (metres)

**1** Who won the contest?
- (a) Derek
- (b) Elise
- (c) Lori
- (d) Shaka

**2** How far did Jaime kick the ball?
- (a) 8 metres
- (b) 10 metres
- (c) 12 metres
- (d) 14 metres

**3** Who kicked the ball half as far as Shaka?
- (a) Elise
- (b) Lori
- (c) Jaime
- (d) Derek

**4** Compared with Derek, how much farther did Elise kick the ball?
- (a) 12 metres
- (b) 10 metres
- (c) 8 metres
- (d) 6 metres

# Scouts' Honours

The Adventure Scouts earn badges by doing special projects. Their scout leader made this bar graph to show how many scouts have earned each type of badge. Use the graph to answer the questions below.

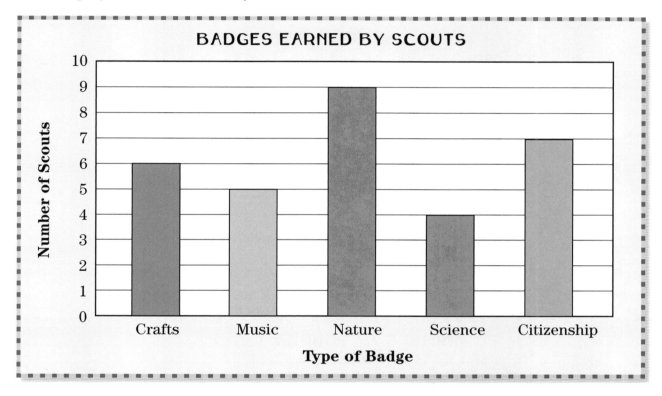

1. How many scouts have earned a music badge? _____

2. How many more scouts have earned citizenship badges than science badges?

_____

3. Which badge has been earned by the most scouts?

_____

4. How many badges have been earned altogether? _____

5. Which type of badge is most difficult to earn? Explain your thinking below.

_____

_____

# Zack's Lazy Afternoon

Zack spent an afternoon at Sunrise Pond. He made this tally chart to show how many animals he saw at the pond.

| KIND OF ANIMAL | NUMBER |
|---|---|
| Turtle | ✓ |
| Duck | ✓✓✓✓✓ |
| Frog | ✓✓✓ |
| Beaver | ✓✓ |
| Fish | ✓✓✓✓✓✓✓ |

Then Zack started making a bar graph of the animals he saw at the pond, but didn't have time to finish it. Use the tally chart to finish Zack's bar graph.

# The Class Takes a Trip

Mrs. Fieldstone's students live in Calgary, Alberta. They took a vote to decide where to go for their class trip in June and made a circle graph to help analyze the results. Use the graph to answer the questions.

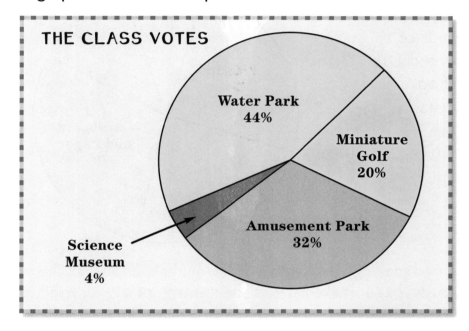

**1** Which choice received the fewest votes?

_____

**2** If there are 25 students in the class, how many voted for miniature golf?

_____

**3** Which two activities together were picked by about $\frac{3}{4}$ of the students?

_____

**4** Which activity was chosen by about $\frac{1}{3}$ of the students?

_____

**5** How do you think the votes would be different if the class trip took place in February instead of June?

_____

_____

# Recycling Efforts

Every week, the town of Galway collects trash for recycling. The circle graph on the right shows what kinds of items are collected. Use the graph to choose the best answer to each question below.

**ITEMS COLLECTED FOR RECYCLING**

Other 10%

Aluminum and Tin 12%

Plastic 25%

Cardboard and Paper 29%

Glass 24%

**1** Cardboard and paper make up what percentage of the recycled items?
  (a) 12%
  (b) 24%
  (c) 25%
  (d) 29%

**2** What fraction shows what part of the recycled items are plastic?
  (a) $\frac{1}{4}$
  (b) $\frac{1}{3}$
  (c) $\frac{1}{2}$
  (d) $\frac{2}{3}$

**3** Of every 100 items recycled, how many are glass?
  (a) 10
  (b) 12
  (c) 15
  (d) 24

**4** What percentage of the recycled items are aluminum and tin?
  (a) 10%
  (b) 12%
  (c) 24%
  (d) 25%

**5** One half of the items in the "Other" category were batteries. If batteries were shown on the graph, what percentage would they represent?
  (a) 50%
  (b) 10%
  (c) 5%
  (d) 3%

# Best-Selling Books

The line graph below shows how many books were sold each day at a school book fair. Use the graph to answer the questions.

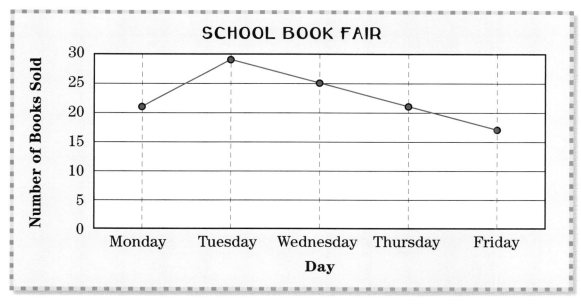

**SCHOOL BOOK FAIR**

1 How many books were sold on Monday? _____

2 On what day were the same number of books sold as on Monday?

_____

3 How many more books were sold on Tuesday than on Thursday?

_____

4 What was the greatest number of books sold in one day?

_____

5 If the sales trend continued to Saturday, how many books would you expect to sell on Saturday?

_____

# Compare the Squares

The line graph below shows the areas of squares of different sizes. Use the graph to answer the questions.

**AREA OF A SQUARE**

1 What is the area of a square with sides that are 4 centimetres long?

_____

2 If the area of a square is 25 square centimetres, how long are its sides?

_____

3 What is the approximate area of a square with 4.5-centimetre sides?

_____

4 About how long are the sides of a square with an area of 12 square centimetres?

_____

5 Write one or two sentences describing the trend shown on this line graph.

_____

_____

# Adorable Animals

Do you know what a baby goat is called? The chart below provides the names for many baby animals. Use the chart to choose the best answer to each question.

| NAMES FOR BABY ANIMALS | | | |
| --- | --- | --- | --- |
| Animal | Name for Baby | Animal | Name for Baby |
| Bear | Cub | Fox | Kit |
| Cow | Calf | Goat | Kid |
| Deer | Fawn | Kangaroo | Joey |
| Dog | Pup | Sheep | Lamb |

1 What is the name for a baby deer?
   (a) cub    (c) fawn
   (b) calf    (d) pup

2 What is a baby fox called?
   (a) kit    (c) cub
   (b) kid    (d) lamb

3 Which kind of animal has cubs?
   (a) goat    (c) kangaroo
   (b) sheep    (d) bear

4 A "joey" is what kind of animal?
   (a) cow    (c) kangaroo
   (b) fox    (d) sheep

5 A baby goat is a —
   (a) kid    (c) pup
   (b) lamb    (d) calf

# Joel's Trip Planner

Joel made a chart for his family to help them plan trips to local parks. Use the chart to answer the questions below.

| THINGS TO DO AT LOCAL PARKS | |
|---|---|
| Blue Summit Park | |
| Lilac Lake Park | |
| Mead Canyon Park | |
| Pinetop Park | |
| Underwood Park | |

**KEY**

Hiking Trails

Picnic Area

Swimming Beach

Campground

1 What can visitors do at Underwood Park?

_____

2 How many parks have a picnic area? _____

3 Which parks have a swimming beach?

_____

4 Which park offers the most activities?

_____

5 In which park can you ONLY camp or hike?

_____

# Ordering Dinner

The Magic Meal Restaurant has a special children's menu. Use the chart to choose the best answer to each question below.

## CHILDREN'S MENU

**Sandwiches**   *Served with potato chips and a pickle*

Egg Salad............................................................$2.50
Ham Salad .........................................................$3.00
Tuna Fish ...........................................................$2.75
Grilled Cheese ...................................................$2.50

**Dinners**   *Served with salad and a dinner roll*

Macaroni and Cheese .......................................$3.75
Spaghetti ............................................................$3.00
Chicken Pot Pie .................................................$4.00
Beef Stew ...........................................................$4.00

**Drinks**

Milk, Chocolate Milk, Lemonade ......................$1.00

**Desserts**

Dish of Ice Cream or Pudding ...........................$1.50

**1** How much does a grilled cheese sandwich cost?
- a $2.50
- b $2.75
- c $3.00
- d $3.50

**2** Which food is served with any dinner on the menu?
- a ice cream
- b potato chips
- c salad
- d pudding

**3** Which drink is listed on the menu?
- a milk shake
- b lemonade
- c orange juice
- d hot chocolate

**4** How much does a spaghetti dinner cost?
- a $4.00
- b $3.75
- c $3.00
- d $2.50

# The Bookworm Club

Use this chart from the Bookworm Club to answer the
questions below.

| OUR BOOKS OF THE MONTH | | |
|---|---|---|
| Item Number | Title | Price |
| 1 | *Amy Grows Up* | $3.25 |
| 2 | *Beginner's Luck* | $2.95 |
| 3 | *Dinosaur Dig* | $4.50 |
| 4 | *Famous Firsts* | $3.95 |
| 5 | *Jump Rope Games* | $4.25 |
| 6 | *Lightning and Thunder* | $2.95 |
| 7 | *Never Say Never* | $3.50 |
| 8 | *Queen Mary of Scotland* | $2.95 |
| 9 | *Science in Your Kitchen* | $3.25 |
| 10 | *Grasslands National Park* | $4.50 |

1 What is the title of item number **1** on the book list?

_____

2 How much does the book *Queen Mary of Scotland* cost?

_____

3 What is the item number of the book *Jump Rope Games*?

_____

4 Look at this part of a book order form. Fill in the missing information.

| Item Number | Title | Price |
|---|---|---|
| 3 | | |

# Niko's Aquarium

Niko wants to set up an aquarium for tropical fish. He is reading a library book about aquariums before he begins this project. Use the table to choose the best answer to each question below.

## TROPICAL FISH AQUARIUMS
### Contents

**1** Niko wonders which fish get along well in an aquarium. Which chapter should he read to find this information?

   (a) chapter 1       (c) chapter 5
   (b) chapter 3       (d) chapter 6

**2** Which of Niko's questions about tropical fish aquariums is probably answered in Chapter 2?

   (a) How much gravel should I put in the bottom of the tank?
   (b) How often should I feed my fish?
   (c) How can I be sure I'm buying healthy fish?
   (d) How much will a five-gallon tank cost?

**3** Where should Niko start reading to find out how to clean the sides of his aquarium?

   (a) page 5       (c) page 21
   (b) page 11       (d) page 29

**4** Which chapter explains how to find information about tropical fish online?

   (a) chapter 2       (c) chapter 5
   (b) chapter 4       (d) chapter 6

# Card Sharks

Do you like to play cards? Use the table to choose the best answer to each question below.

## LET'S PLAY CARDS
### Contents

**1** Which chapter has information about games for two players?
  (a) chapter 1      (c) chapter 3
  (b) chapter 2      (d) chapter 4

**2** Where should you start reading if you need to find out what a "wild card" is?
  (a) page 7      (c) page 21
  (b) page 12      (d) page 24

**3** Which game might be a good one to play with three friends?
  (a) *Beehive*      (c) *Hit or Miss*
  (b) *Jacks*      (d) *Gops*

**4** The directions for playing *Spade Oklahoma* begin on which page?
  (a) page 14      (c) page 17
  (b) page 15      (d) page 19

# School Birthdays

The table below shows how many students in Grades 3 and 4 at the Rand School were born during each month. Use the table to answer the questions.

## BIRTHDAY UPDATE

| Month of Birth | Sep. | Oct. | Nov. | Dec. | Jan. | Feb. | Mar. | Apr. | May | June | July | Aug. |
|---|---|---|---|---|---|---|---|---|---|---|---|---|
| Number of Students | 2 | 1 | 2 | 3 | 2 | 4 | 6 | 9 | 6 | 5 | 4 | 3 |
| Season | Fall | | | Winter | | | Spring | | | Summer | | |

1 How many students were born in November? _____

2 What month had the same number of births as February?

_____

3 How many students were born in the fall?

_____

4 During which season were the most students born?

_____

5 In which month would it be most likely to have two students share the same birthday?

_____

# Beautiful Bridges

The chart below lists six of the longest suspension bridges in the United States. Use the chart to answer the questions.

| SUSPENSION BRIDGES OF THE UNITED STATES | | | |
|---|---|---|---|
| Year Completed | Bridge | Location | Main Span (metres) |
| 1931 | George Washington | New York–New Jersey | 1067 |
| 1937 | Golden Gate | California | 1280 |
| 1950 | Tacoma Narrows | Washington | 853 |
| 1957 | Mackinac Straits | Michigan | 1158 |
| 1964 | Verrazano–Narrows | New York | 1298 |
| 1968 | Delaware Memorial | Delaware | 655 |

**1** Which bridge has the longest main span?

_____

**2** Which bridge was completed in 1957, and where is it located?

_____

**3** Where is the Golden Gate Bridge, and when was it completed?

_____

**4** How long is the main span of the George Washington Bridge?

_____

**5** If the chart listed these bridges from shortest to longest, which two bridges would be listed first?

_____

# Six Super Provinces

The chart below provides information about six provinces in Canada. Use the chart to answer the questions.

| SIX PROVINCES | | | | |
|---|---|---|---|---|
| Province | Capital | Year Joined Canada | Provincial Bird | Provincial Flower |
| New Brunswick | Fredericton | 1867 | black-capped chickadee | purple violet |
| Saskatchewan | Regina | 1905 | sharp-tailed grouse | western red lily |
| British Columbia | Victoria | 1871 | Steller's jay | Pacific dogwood |
| Manitoba | Winnipeg | 1870 | great grey owl | prairie crocus |
| Nova Scotia | Halifax | 1867 | osprey | mayflower |
| Alberta | Edmonton | 1905 | great horned owl | wild rose |

**1** What is the capital of Saskatchewan?_____

**2** In what year did British Columbia become a province? _____

**3** Which two provinces joined Canada first? _____

**4** What is New Brunswick's provincial bird? _____

**5** Halifax is the capital of which province? _____

**6** What is Alberta's provincial flower? _____

**7** Which provinces have an owl as a provincial bird, and what owls are they?

_____

# The Story of Paper

The flow chart below shows how paper is made. Use the chart to answer the questions.

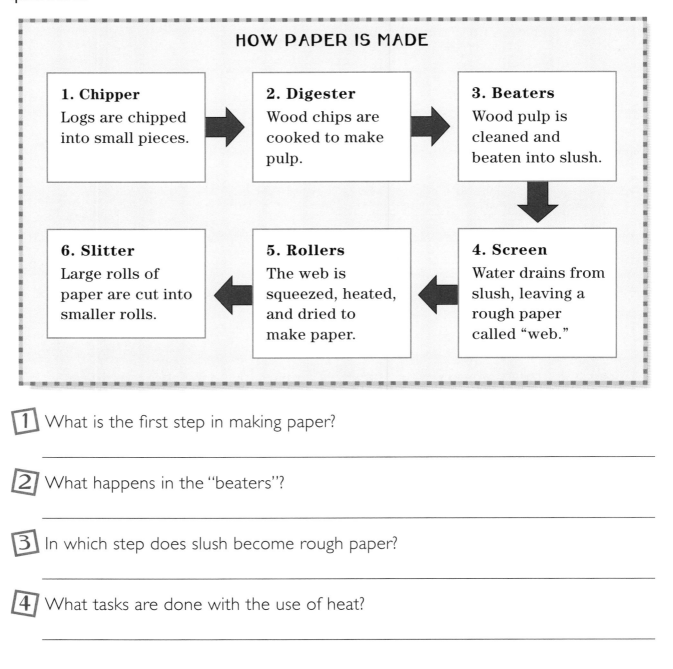

HOW PAPER IS MADE

**1. Chipper**
Logs are chipped into small pieces.

**2. Digester**
Wood chips are cooked to make pulp.

**3. Beaters**
Wood pulp is cleaned and beaten into slush.

**4. Screen**
Water drains from slush, leaving a rough paper called "web."

**5. Rollers**
The web is squeezed, heated, and dried to make paper.

**6. Slitter**
Large rolls of paper are cut into smaller rolls.

**1** What is the first step in making paper?

_____

**2** What happens in the "beaters"?

_____

**3** In which step does slush become rough paper?

_____

**4** What tasks are done with the use of heat?

_____

_____

# Building Houses

The pictograph below shows the number of new houses built in five different counties last year. Use the graph to answer the questions.

## HOUSE CONSTRUCTION

| County | Number of Houses Built |
|--------|------------------------|
| Chilton | 🏠🏠🏠🏠🏠🏠 |
| Essex | 🏠🏠🏠🏠🏠🏠🏠🏠 |
| Franklin | 🏠🏠🏠🏠🏠🏠🏠🏠🏠🏠 |
| Langham | 🏠🏠🏠🏠🏠 |
| Peterson | 🏠🏠🏠🏠🏠🏠🏠🏠 |

**KEY**

🏠 = 10 houses

1. How many houses were built in Chilton County last year?

_____

2. In which county were the most houses built?

_____

3. In which county were the fewest houses built?

_____

4. How many more houses were built in Peterson County than in Langham County?

_____

5. A total of 42 houses were built in Winwood County last year. How would this number be shown on the graph? (Draw a picture on the back of this paper.)

Name _____

# How Does Susan's Garden Grow?

Susan made a bar graph showing the heights of the flowers in her garden. Use the graph to choose the best answers to the questions below.

**1** How tall is the coneflower?
- (a) 90 centimetres
- (b) 120 centimetres
- (c) 150 centimetres
- (d) 180 centimetres

**2** Which plant is tallest?
- (a) lavender
- (b) coneflower
- (c) butterfly bush
- (d) sunflower

**3** Which plant is 120 centimetres tall?
- (a) petunia
- (b) lavender
- (c) coneflower
- (d) butterfly bush

**4** Which plant is three times as tall as the petunia?
- (a) lavender
- (b) coneflower
- (c) butterfly bush
- (d) sunflower

**5** Which plant is closest in height to the lavender?
- (a) petunia
- (b) coneflower
- (c) butterfly bush
- (d) sunflower

# Alex the Sports Reporter

Alex conducted a survey of his classmates about their favourite team and individual sports. He made these charts to show the results of his survey. Use the charts to make your own bar graphs.

| FAVOURITE TEAM SPORTS | |
|---|---|
| Basketball | ЖЖ ЖЖ lll |
| Soccer | ЖЖ ЖЖ ll |
| Hockey | ЖЖ lll |
| Softball | ЖЖ l |

| FAVOURITE INDIVIDUAL SPORTS | |
|---|---|
| Tennis | ЖЖ ЖЖ lll |
| Running | ЖЖ |
| Golf | ЖЖ l |
| Swimming | ЖЖ ЖЖ ЖЖ |

1. On the grid below, make a bar graph to show how many students picked each *team* sport. Be sure to include labels and a title.

2. On the grid below, make a bar graph to show how many students picked each *individual* sport. Be sure to include labels and a title.

# Mindy Minds the Money

Mindy and her Dad made a circle graph to show how the family's money was spent each month. Use the graph to choose the best answer to each question below.

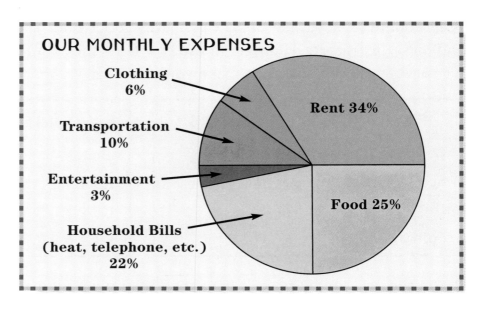

OUR MONTHLY EXPENSES

Clothing 6%
Transportation 10%
Entertainment 3%
Household Bills (heat, telephone, etc.) 22%
Rent 34%
Food 25%

1. Which is the largest cost each month?
   a. food
   b. rent
   c. clothing
   d. transportation

2. How much of the money spent each month goes to food?
   a. More than $\frac{1}{2}$
   b. $\frac{1}{3}$
   c. Less than $\frac{1}{6}$
   d. $\frac{1}{4}$

3. The least amount of money is spent on _____.
   a. household bills
   b. clothing
   c. transportation
   d. entertainment

4. What part of the family's money is spent on clothing each month?
   a. 3%
   b. 6%
   c. 10%
   d. 22%

5. When Dad takes the bus to work each day, that cost is part of what category?
   a. transportation
   b. household bills
   c. clothing
   d. entertainment

6. Which cost is probably higher in winter than in summer?
   a. rent
   b. transportation
   c. household bills
   d. entertainment

# Population Growth

The line graph below shows the number of people living in Newtown between 1900 and 2000. Use the graph to answer the questions.

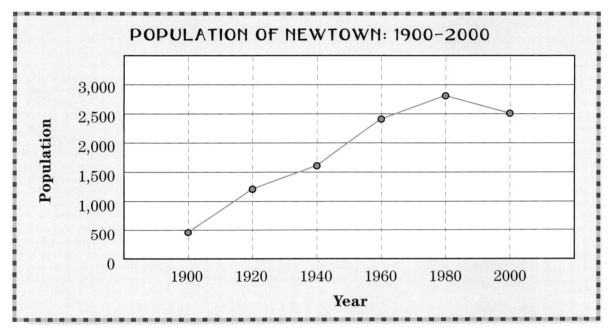

POPULATION OF NEWTOWN: 1900–2000

[1] What was the population of Newtown in 1920? _____

[2] How much did the population increase from 1920 to 1940?

_____

[3] What was the population in 1960? _____

[4] In which 20-year period did the size of the population change the most?

_____

[5] Describe the general changes in Newtown's population from 1900 to 2000.

_____

_____

[6] If this trend continues, what will the population of Newtown be in 2020?

_____

# A Trip Through Time

The timeline below shows when different ways of telling time were invented. Use the timeline to answer the questions.

## TIME MACHINE TIMELINE

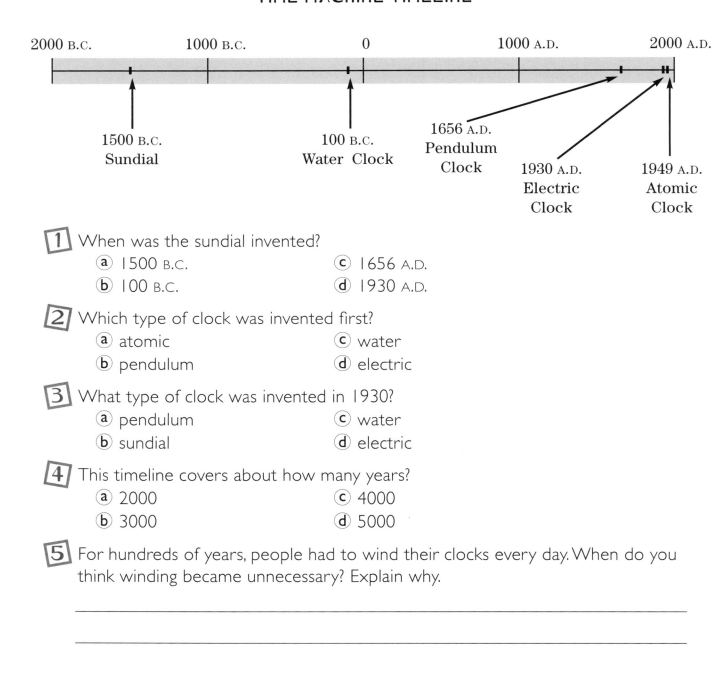

[1] When was the sundial invented?
   ⓐ 1500 B.C.          ⓒ 1656 A.D.
   ⓑ 100 B.C.           ⓓ 1930 A.D.

[2] Which type of clock was invented first?
   ⓐ atomic             ⓒ water
   ⓑ pendulum           ⓓ electric

[3] What type of clock was invented in 1930?
   ⓐ pendulum           ⓒ water
   ⓑ sundial            ⓓ electric

[4] This timeline covers about how many years?
   ⓐ 2000               ⓒ 4000
   ⓑ 3000               ⓓ 5000

[5] For hundreds of years, people had to wind their clocks every day. When do you think winding became unnecessary? Explain why.

_____

_____

# Mimi's Sunny Vacation

Mimi made a table to show when the sun rose and set each Saturday during her summer vacation. Use the table to answer the questions below.

| SUNRISE AND SUNSET ON SUMMER SATURDAYS | | | | | |
|---|---|---|---|---|---|
| Date | Sunrise | Sunset | Date | Sunrise | Sunset |
| June 23 | 5:08 AM | 8:25 PM | July 28 | 5:33 AM | 8:08 PM |
| June 30 | 5:11 AM | 8:25 PM | August 4 | 5:40 AM | 8:00 PM |
| July 7 | 5:14 AM | 8:23 PM | August 11 | 5:47 AM | 7:51 PM |
| July 14 | 5:20 AM | 8:20 PM | August 18 | 5:55 AM | 7:41 PM |
| July 21 | 5:26 AM | 8:15 PM | August 25 | 6:02 AM | 7:30 PM |

1 What time did the sun rise on July 21?

_____

2 On which date did the sun set at exactly 8:00 PM?

_____

3 Which Saturday had the earliest sunrise?

_____

4 How much earlier did the sun set on August 18 than on August 11?

_____

5 Which Saturday had exactly 15 hours between sunrise and sunset?

_____

6 How do the times of sunrise and sunset change from June 23 to the end of August?

_____

# Weather Reporting

Grade 4 students involved in a nation-wide project recorded the weather conditions each day for a week. Use the table to answer the questions below.

| | | | | | |
|---|---|---|---|---|---|
| WEATHER DATA: SEPTEMBER 24–30 | | | | | |
| Day | High Temperature | Low Temperature | Wind Speed (knots) | Precipitation | Conditions |
| Sunday | 19°C | 5°C | 0–5 | 0 | Sunny |
| Monday | 20°C | 7°C | 0–5 | 0 | Sunny |
| Tuesday | 22°C | 6°C | 5–10 | 0 | Cloudy |
| Wednesday | 21°C | 3°C | 10–15 | 0 | Partly Cloudy |
| Thursday | 17°C | 2°C | 25–30 | 3 centimetres | Rainy |
| Friday | 11°C | -1°C | 20–25 | .75 centimetre | Rainy |
| Saturday | 11°C | 0°C | 10–15 | 0 | Partly Cloudy |

1 What were the high and low temperatures on Sunday?

_____

2 Which day was warmest? _____

3 On which days did the temperature go as low as the freezing point of 0°C?

_____

4 What were the weather conditions on Wednesday?

_____

5 In all, how much rain fell during the week? _____

6 Write one or two sentences describing how the weather changed from Sunday to Saturday.

_____

_____

# Dining With Dinosaurs

This "Dino" chart provides specific information about different kinds of dinosaurs. Use the chart to choose the best answer to each question below.

## DINOSAUR FACTS

| Name | What It Means | Size | Weight | Food |
|------|---------------|------|--------|------|
| *Ankylosaurus* | Stiff lizard | 7 metres | 4500 kilograms | plants |
| *Baryonyx* | Heavy claw | 10 metres | 2000 kilograms | fish |
| *Eoraptor* | Dawn thief | 1 metre | 10 kilograms | meat, insects |
| *Maiasaura* | Good mother lizard | 9 metres | 3600 kilograms | plants |
| *Plateosaurus* | Broad lizard | 7 metres | 700 kilograms | plants |
| *Seismosaurus* | Earthquake lizard | 35 metres | 60 000 kilograms | plants |
| *Spinosaurus* | Spined lizard | 18 metres | 8000 kilograms | fish |
| *Velociraptor* | Fast thief | 1.8 metres | 14 kilograms | meat |

1 How much did the dinosaur called *Maiasaura* weigh?

- ⓐ 14 kilograms
- ⓑ 3600 kilograms
- ⓒ 8000 kilograms
- ⓓ 60 000 kilograms

2 Which dinosaur's name means "broad lizard?"

- ⓐ *Ankylosaurus*
- ⓑ *Eoraptor*
- ⓒ *Plateosaurus*
- ⓓ *Spinosaurus*

3 How many metres long was the dinosaur called *Velociraptor?*
- ⓐ 1 metre
- ⓑ 1.8 metres
- ⓒ 7 metres
- ⓓ 9 metres

4 Which of these dinosaurs ate fish?

- ⓐ *Ankylosaurus*
- ⓑ *Maiasaura*
- ⓒ *Velociraptor*
- ⓓ *Spinosaurus*

5 Which is the largest, heaviest dinosaur listed in the chart?

- ⓐ *Seismosaurus*
- ⓒ *Eoraptor*

# How Hurricanes Get Their Names

When hurricanes form each year, the National Hurricane Center in Florida, U.S., gives each one a name. The chart below shows some of the names for hurricanes in the Atlantic Ocean in the years 2002, 2003, and 2004. Use the chart to answer the questions.

| HURRICANE NAMES: ATLANTIC OCEAN | | |
|---|---|---|
| **2002** | **2003** | **2004** |
| Arthur | Ana | Alex |
| Bertha | Bill | Bonnie |
| Cristobal | Claudette | Charley |
| Dolly | Danny | Danielle |
| Edouard | Erika | Earl |
| Fay | Fabian | Frances |
| Gustav | Grace | Gaston |
| Hanna | Henri | Hermine |
| Isidore | Isabel | Ivan |
| Josephine | Juan | Jeanne |
| Kyle | Kate | Karl |

1   What name was given to the first hurricane in 2003?

_____

2   What name was given to the fifth hurricane in 2004?

_____

3   What name came after Gustav in 2002?

_____

4   What name beginning with the letter "D" was used in 2004?

_____

5   From this chart, what can you tell about the "rules" used in naming hurricanes? Explain your idea.

_____

_____

_____

# Speedy Animals

The bar graph below shows how fast some animals can run. Use the graph to answer the questions.

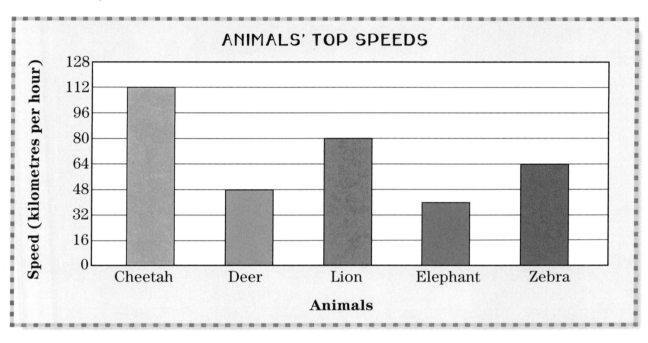

ANIMALS' TOP SPEEDS

Speed (kilometres per hour)

128
112
96
80
64
48
32
16
0

Cheetah    Deer    Lion    Elephant    Zebra

**Animals**

[1] How fast can a lion run? _____

[2] How fast can an elephant run? _____

[3] Which animal runs the fastest? _____

[4] What is a zebra's top speed? _____

[5] List all five animals in order from slowest to fastest.

_____

_____

_____

_____

# All About Energy

The circle graph below shows the sources of energy used in the United States today. Use the circle graph to choose the best answer to each question.

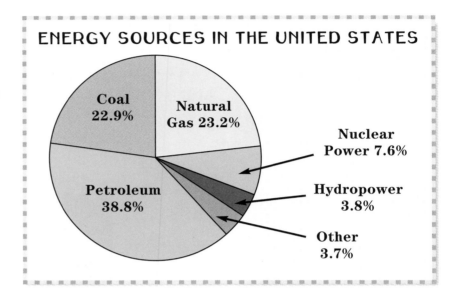

**ENERGY SOURCES IN THE UNITED STATES**

Coal 22.9%

Natural Gas 23.2%

Nuclear Power 7.6%

Hydropower 3.8%

Other 3.7%

Petroleum 38.8%

1 Which energy source provides about 8% of the power in the United States?
- (a) petroleum
- (b) coal
- (c) nuclear power
- (d) hydropower

2 What portion of the energy used in the United States comes from hydropower?
- (a) 38.8%
- (b) 23.2%
- (c) 7.6%
- (d) 3.8%

3 More than one third of the energy used in the United States comes from which source?
- (a) petroleum
- (b) natural gas
- (c) nuclear power
- (d) hydropower

4 About what percentage of energy used in the United States comes from fossil fuels (petroleum, natural gas, and coal)?
- (a) 65%
- (b) 75%
- (c) 85%
- (d) 95%

5 From this graph, you can conclude that the energy in the United States provided by solar power is _____.
- (a) less than 4%
- (b) about 4%
- (c) about 10%
- (d) more than 10%

# Cleveland's Weather Update

The line graph below shows the average temperature each month in Cleveland, Ohio, in the United States. Use the graph to answer the questions.

1 What is the average temperature in Cleveland in March? _____

2 What is the average temperature in Cleveland in September? _____

3 Which is the warmest month? _____

4 Which is the coldest month? _____

5 What is the difference in average temperature
between the warmest month and the coldest? _____

6 Write one or two sentences that describe the changes in temperature during
the year.

_____

_____

_____

# Scholastic Success With

# ADDITION, SUBTRACTION, MULTIPLICATION & DIVISION

Name _____

Name _____

Name _____

# A Sick Riddle

## Riddle: What sickness can't you talk about until it's cured?

Find each sum. Then use the Decoder to solve the riddle by filling in the spaces at the bottom of the page.

**1** $12 + 7$ = _____

**2** $32 + 10$ = _____

**3** $50 + 4$ = _____

**4** $13 + 22$ = _____

**5** $47 + 19$ = _____

**6** $97 + 68$ = _____

**7** $204 + 41$ = _____

**8** $37 + 331$ = _____

**9** $670 + 98$ = _____

**10** $857 + 466$ = _____

### Decoder

| | |
|---|---|
| 66 | I |
| 57 | W |
| 42 | I |
| 216 | M |
| 19 | Y |
| 97 | C |
| 768 | G |
| 35 | S |
| 46 | E |
| 100 | X |
| 245 | R |
| 1,257 | D |
| 54 | A |
| 52 | O |
| 368 | L |
| 82 | P |
| 1,323 | T |
| 155 | Q |
| 165 | N |

___ ___ ___ ___ ___ ___ ___ ___ ___ ___
 8   3   7   1   6   9   5   10  2   4

260   Scholastic Success With Addition, Subtraction, Multiplication & Division • Grade 4

# Blooming Octagon

Solve the problems. ◆ If the answer is between 1 and 300, colour the shape yellow. ◆ If the answer is between 301 and 600, colour the shape blue. ◆ If the answer is between 601 and 1000, colour the shape orange. ◆ Finish by colouring the outer shapes with the colours of your choice.

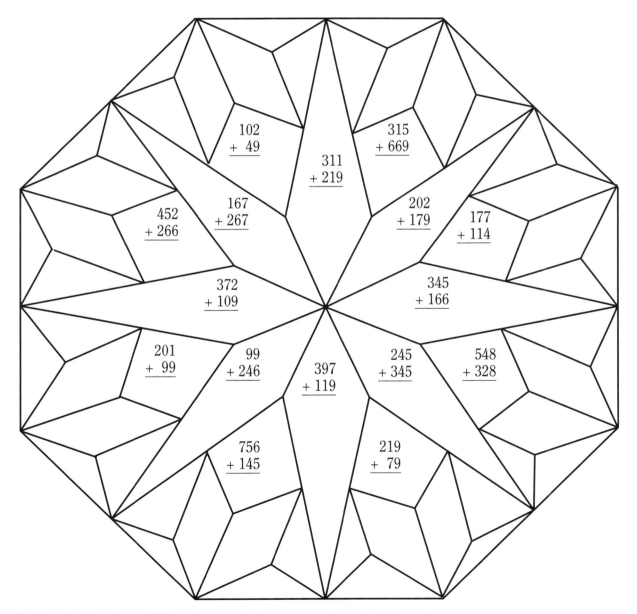

Taking It Further: Fill in the next three numbers in this pattern.

150, 300, 450, 600, _____, _____, _____.

# The Big Cheese

 *Always complete the operation inside the parentheses ( ) first. Then complete the rest of the problem.*

$$7 + (3 + 6) =$$
$$7 + 9 = 16$$

$$(4 + 4) + 8 =$$
$$8 + 8 = 16$$

Add.

**A.** (7 + 2) + 4 = _____          (3 + 4) + 7 = _____

**B.** (5 + 4) + 9 = _____          9 + (2 + 3) = _____

**C.** 8 + (3 + 5) = _____          6 + (2 + 4) = _____

**D.** (2 + 6) + (5 + 2) = _____    (5 + 1) + (4 + 4) = _____

**E.** (3 + 3) + (5 + 4) = _____    (4 + 3) + (6 + 2) = _____

**F.** (6 + 6) + 3 = _____          4 + (5 + 4) = _____

**G.** 5 + (4 + 8) = _____          (3 + 7) + 7 = _____

**H.** (2 + 9) + 8 = _____          5 + (5 + 5) = _____

**I.** (8 + 5) + 4 = _____          (9 + 3) + 2 = _____

**J.** (8 + 2) + (3 + 2) = _____    (5 + 7) + (4 + 4) = _____

**K.** (2 + 5) + (5 + 8) = _____    (6 + 5) + (7 + 4) = _____

 The director ordered a big piece of cheese for each actor in the movie. He ordered 6 pieces from Charlie's Cheese Shop, 3 pieces from Holes and More, and 7 pieces from Mouse Munchers. Write a number sentence using parentheses to solve the problem.

Name _____

# A-Mazing Eighteen

 *The answer to an addition problem is called the* **sum**.

Find the path that leads from the mouse to the cheese by following the sums of eighteen. Add.

| (5 + 4) + (3 + 6) | (7 + 6) + 5 | (5 + 6) + (4 + 2) | (7 + 5) + 7 | 3 + (7 + 5) |
|---|---|---|---|---|
| 4 + (6 + 6) | 3 + (8 + 7) | (5 + 3) + (3 + 4) | (4 + 6) + 5 | (5 + 9) + 3 |
| (9 + 2) + 6 | (5 + 3) + (6 + 4) | 2 + (8 + 8) | 8 + (6+ 2) | (4 + 5) + (2 + 5) |
| 5 + (6 + 6) | (6 + 6) + (4 + 6) | (2 + 3) + (9 + 4) | 3 + (7 + 5) | (6 + 7) + 6 |
| (7 + 8) + 2 | 5 + (4 + 6) | 7 + (4 + 7) | (5 + 6) + (4 + 3) | (8 + 4) + 6 |

 **Write another number sentence with 18 as the sum. Do not use a number sentence from above.**

# Climbing High

 To add multiple-digit numbers without regrouping, follow these steps.
1. Add the ones column.
2. Add the tens column.
3. Add the hundreds column.
4. Continue working through each column in order.

Add.

**A.**
```
   1,136          9,025
+  2,433        +   851
_____        _____
```

**B.**
```
   8,730          2,928          3,650         80,662
+  1,252        + 5,021        + 4,210       + 11,136
_____        _____        _____       _____
```

**C.**
```
  55,100         60,439         81,763         36,034
+ 31,892        + 30,310       +  8,231       + 41,753
_____        _____       _____       _____
```

**D.**
```
 321,957        623,421        264,870        592,604        127,094
+ 260,041       + 151,441      + 303,120      + 102,335      + 832,502
_____       _____      _____      _____      _____
```

 **Mount Everest is the highest mountain in the world. To find the height of Mount Everest in feet, begin climbing in Row D. Write the underlined numbers in order. Continue writing the numbers in Row C, Row B, and Row A. How many feet did you climb?**

# Reaching New Heights

*To add multiple-digit numbers with regrouping, follow these steps.*
1. *Add the ones column.*
2. *If the sum is greater than 9, regroup to the tens column.*
3. *Add the tens column.*
4. *If the sum is greater than 9, regroup to the hundreds column.*
5. *Continue working through each column in order.*

Which of these mountains is the tallest? To find out add. The sum with the greatest number in each row shows the height of the mountain in feet. Circle the height for each mountain.

**Kilimanjaro**

**A.**

|  |  |  |  |
|---|---|---|---|
| 7,542 | 9,831 | 6,905 | 4,671 |
| + 8,439 | + 9,510 | + 3,492 | + 4,319 |

**Mount Cook**

**B.**

|  |  |  |  |
|---|---|---|---|
| 5,725 | 3,642 | 4,863 | 5,677 |
| + 6,624 | + 8,546 | + 7,066 | + 5,307 |

**Mount McKinley**

**C.**

|  |  |  |  |
|---|---|---|---|
| 10,375 | 12,575 | 18,410 | 8,754 |
| + 8,615 | + 4,192 | + 1,910 | + 8,217 |

**Mount Elbrus**

**D.**

|  |  |  |  |
|---|---|---|---|
| 13,825 | 13,257 | 8,251 | 9,060 |
| + 3,934 | + 2,727 | + 6,236 | + 9,450 |

**Find the total height of the two mountains with the greatest heights.**

# Wild Birds

 Some addition problems will require regrouping several times. The steps look like this.

1. Add the ones column. Regroup if needed.
2. Add the tens column. Regroup if needed.
3. Add the hundreds column. Regroup if needed.
4. Continue working through each column in order.

```
     1              11             111            111
 37,462         37,462         37,462         37,462
+  22,798      +  22,798      +  22,798      +  22,798
─────────      ─────────      ─────────      ─────────
      0             60            260         60,260
```

Add. Then use the code to finish the fun fact below.

**bald eagle**

| Z. | 953 | B. | 295 | R. | 418 | Q. | 565 | S. | 862 | X. | 478 |
|---|---|---|---|---|---|---|---|---|---|---|---|
| + | 418 | + | 337 | + | 793 | + | 957 | + | 339 | + | 283 |

**falcon**

| I. | 2,428 | C. | 1,566 | Y. | 3,737 | A. | 9,289 | Y. | 8,754 |
|---|---|---|---|---|---|---|---|---|---|
| + | 6,679 | + | 2,487 | + | 6,418 | + | 4,735 | + | 368 |

**vulture**

| L. | 57,854 | P. | 29,484 | E. | 36,238 | F. | 67,139 |
|---|---|---|---|---|---|---|---|
| + | 45,614 | + | 46,592 | + | 46,135 | + | 25,089 |

**owl**

| D. | 240,669 | O. | 476,381 | R. | 882,948 |
|---|---|---|---|---|---|
| + | 298,727 | + | 175,570 | + | 176,524 |

**What do all of these birds have in common?**

They are ____ ____ ____ ____ ____     ____ ____

632   9,107   1,211   539,396   1,201     651,951   92,228

____ ____ ____ ____ .

76,076   1,059,472   82,373   10,155

# The Majestic Bald Eagle

 *To add numbers that require regrouping in more than one column, follow these steps.*
1. *Add the ones column. Regroup if needed.*
2. *Add the tens column. Regroup if needed.*
4. *Add the hundreds column. Regroup if needed.*
5. *Continue working through each column in order.*

Add. Then use the code to finish the fun fact below.

| | | | | | |
|---|---|---|---|---|---|
| **H.** | 8,754<br>+ 368 | **L.** | 7,789<br>+ 4,759 | **I.** | 8,997<br>+ 9,978 |
| **A.** | 8,599<br>+ 8,932 | **E.** | 5,476<br>+ 4,846 | **O.** | 9,475<br>+ 7,725 |
| **C.** | 8,838<br>+ 9,668 | **T.** | 6,867<br>+ 7,256 | **M.** | 9,891<br>+ 3,699 |

| | | | | | | | |
|---|---|---|---|---|---|---|---|
| **N.** | 92,854<br>+ 37,898 | **U.** | 25,748<br>+ 85,362 | **Y.** | 99,977<br>+ 82,943 | **R.** | 57,544<br>+ 78,587 |

**The bald eagle is found** _____ _____ _____ _____   _____ _____
17,200   130,752   12,548   182,920   17,200   130,752

_____ _____ _____   _____ _____ _____ _____ _____
14,123   9,122   10,322   130,752   17,200   136,131   14,123   9,122

_____ _____ _____ _____ _____ _____ _____ _____
17,531   13,590   10,322   136,131   18,975   18,506   17,531   130,752

_____ _____ _____ _____ _____ _____ _____ _____ _____ .
18,506   17,200   130,752   14,123   18,975   130,752   10,322   130,752   14,123

# Funny Bone

*Use the same steps to add several addends. Some columns will require regrouping, and some will not.*

Add. Then use the code to find the answer to the riddle below.

| W. | T. | P. | N. | O. | E. |
|---|---|---|---|---|---|
| 1,233 | 6,314 | 2,305 | 1,238 | 3,541 | 3,525 |
| 1,442 | 3,380 | 2,404 | 6,281 | 309 | 2,213 |
| + 5,226 | + 2,606 | + 2,439 | + 5,366 | + 7,845 | + 9,281 |

| H. | R. | S. | ! | A. | U. |
|---|---|---|---|---|---|
| 444 | 4,327 | 4,024 | 5,441 | 2,653 | 5,560 |
| 7,283 | 4,331 | 678 | 421 | 3,338 | 4,202 |
| + 8,217 | + 1,746 | + 4,505 | + 3,954 | + 2,924 | + 1,541 |

## What is the difference between a man and a running dog?

11,695   12,885   15,019

7,901   15,019   8,915   10,404   9,207

12,300   10,404   11,695   11,303   9,207   15,019   10,404   9,207 .

12,300   15,944   15,019

11,695   12,300   15,944   15,019   10,404

7,148   8,915   12,885   12,300   9,207   9,816

# Canine Calculations

The numbers being added together are called **addends**.

Use the sum to help you find the missing numbers of each addend.

**A.**

```
    1 1                1 1                                1 1 1
    6, 7 4 □           9, 4 4 3         □, 5 □ 8          □, 2 2 7
 + □, 3 8 2         + 9, □ 1 □       + 5, 3 6 1        + 6, □ 7 3
 ───────────        ───────────      ───────────       ───────────
   10, 1 2 3          19, 2 6 0          9, 9 3 9          9, 2 0 0
```

**B.**

```
      1                    1            1                 1
    3, 8 4 1           7, 0 □ 4        □, □ 1 0          □, 4 2 6
 + □, 0 6 □         + 9, □ 3 8       + 9, 3 8 5        + 7, 9 2 □
 ───────────        ───────────      ───────────       ───────────
    7, 9 0 5          16, 4 6 2         19, 1 9 5         15, 3 4 9
```

**C.**

```
    1 1               1 1              1 1               1       1
    1, 7 □ 3           3, □ 5 4        □, 2 8 4           8, 8 6 □
 +    □ 5 8         + 6, 4 □ 4       + 3, □ 2 1        + □, 3 1 7
 ───────────        ───────────      ───────────       ───────────
    1, 9 3 1          10, 1 2 8          8, 1 0 5         11, 1 8 0
```

**D.**

```
  1 1 1              1     1          1 1 1             1 1 1
  3, □ 4 □          □, 7 □ 9          7, 5 5 □          4, □ 9 5
+ 9, 2 □ 5        + 8, □ 2 □       + □, □ 4 8        + □, 6 □ 8
 ───────────        ───────────      ───────────       ───────────
  13, 2 1 3          18, 4 8 3         17, 5 0 6         11, 2 2 3
```

 Wag'n Tail Kennels bought two enormous bags of dog treats. One bag had 38, □69 dog treats in it. The other bag had 4 □,510 pieces of dog treats. Altogether the bags had 80,879 treats. On another piece of paper, find the number of dog treats in each bag.

# Money Fun

 *Remember to include a decimal point and a dollar sign in the answer when adding money.*

Add. Then use the code to answer the riddle below.

| | | |
|---|---|---|
| **A.** $63.54<br>+ 29.29 | **G.** $65.35<br>+ 27.18 | **U.** $24.12<br>+ 90.48 | **O.** $15.79<br>+ 48.08 |

| | | |
|---|---|---|
| **B.** $27.60<br>+ 44.65 | **N.** $77.88<br>+ 92.90 | **E.** $86.91<br>+ 70.44 | **R.** $39.75<br>+ 29.62 |

| | | |
|---|---|---|
| **M.** $103.90<br>+ 64.82 | **C.** $291.26<br>+ 473.83 | **S.** $485.13<br>+ 494.92 | **T.** $630.57<br>+ 39.52 |

| | | |
|---|---|---|
| **D.** $184.64<br>+ 292.43 | **Y.** $354.60<br>+ 261.74 | **F.** $964.36<br>+ 252.04 | **W.** $904.86<br>+ 95.82 |

## Why are birds poor?

____ ____ ____ ____ ____ ____ ____
$72.25 $157.35 $765.09 $92.83 $114.60 $980.05 $157.35

____ ____ ____ ____ ____
$168.72 $63.87 $170.78 $157.35 $616.34
　　　　　　　　，

____ ____ ____ ____ ____ ____ ____ ____ ____ ____ ____ ____
$477.07 $63.87 $157.35 $980.05 $170.78 $670.09 $92.53 $69.37 $63.87 $1,000.68
　　　　　　　　　　　　　　　　　　　　　　　　　　　　　　！

____ ____ ____ ____ ____ ____ ____
$63.87 $170.78 $670.09 $69.37 $157.35 $157.35 $980.05

## Bathtub Brunch

# Riddle: What's the best thing to eat in a bathtub?

Find each sum. Then use the Decoder to solve the riddle by filling in the spaces at the bottom of the page.

**Decoder**

| | |
|---|---|
| 5,429 | A |
| 10,493 | F |
| 2,133 | S |
| 14,983 | R |
| 10,439 | P |
| 712 | U |
| 3,489 | K |
| 1,840 | M |
| 1,063 | E |
| 4,523 | W |
| 689 | N |
| 2,009 | B |
| 8,292 | O |
| 3,234 | I |
| 7,538 | G |
| 1,804 | C |
| 4,708 | H |
| 6,521 | L |
| 8,234 | E |

❶ $1,004 + 800$ = _____

❷ $512 + 177$ = _____

❸ $364 + 699$ = _____

❹ $1,245 + 888$ = _____

❺ $1,876 + 1,613$ = _____

❻ $2,010 + 6,224$ = _____

❼ $5,470 + 2,068$ = _____

❽ $4,526 + 3,766$ = _____

❾ $1,017 + 4,412$ = _____

❿ $2,588 + 7,851$ = _____

___ ___ ___ ___ ___ ___   ___ ___ ___ ___
 4   10   8   2   7   6    1   9   5   3

# Food to Go

**Figure it out!**

**1.** Woovis the Dog found a $5 bill. Which item can he buy from the menu that will give the least change?

_____

DOGGIE DINER
BREAKFAST SHOP

**MENU**

Kibble . . . . . . . . . . . . . . . $1.79
Mouse Crumbs . . . . . . . . $1.39
Table Scraps . . . . . . . . . $2.49
Crumbs & Cheese . . . . . . $3.19
Deluxe Scraps . . . . . . . . $3.79

**2.** Molly Mouse gets Crumbs & Cheese for breakfast. She pays with the $5 bill. With the leftover money, what can Woovis buy to eat?

_____

**3.** Which item can Woovis buy with the $5 bill that will give the most change?

_____

**4.** Which two items can Woovis buy with the $5 bill so that he gets about $1 back in change?

_____

**5.** Woovis ordered two items from the menu and gave the cashier the $5 bill. But the two items cost more than $6.50. Which two items did Woovis order?

_____

SUPER CHALLENGE: Can Woovis use the $5 bill to buy three different items from the menu? Why or why not?

# A Penny Saved Is a Penny Earned

Write a number sentence for each problem. Solve.

| | |
|---|---|
| **A.** Aimee and her 2 sisters are saving to buy a camera. Aimee has $12.89. Each of her sisters has $28.53. How much money do all the girls have combined? | **B.** Katie has $23.95 in her purse, $17.23 in her bank, and $76.82 in her savings account. What is the total amount of Katie's money? |
| **C.** Jonah worked in the yard for 3 days. The first day he earned $7.96. The second day he earned $2.00 more than the first day. The third day he earned $2.00 less than the first day. How much did Jonah earn altogether? | **D.** Jack has $9.29. He also has 79 dimes and 139 pennies. How much money does he have altogether? |
| **E.** Kelsey has 478 coins in her collection. The silver dollars equal $79.00, and the quarters equal $99.75. How much is Kelsey's collection worth in all? | **F.** Claire bought lemonade for herself and two friends. Each cup costs $1.75. How much did Claire spend in all? |

 **On another piece of paper, write a word problem with a sum equal to $41.68.**

# Reach for the Stars

*Always complete the operation inside the parentheses ( ) first. Then complete the rest of the problem.*

$(18 - 9) - 3 =$ _____
$9 - 3 = 6$

$18 - (9 - 3) =$ _____
$18 - 6 = 12$

Subtract. Then use the code to answer the question below.

**N.** $(16 - 8) - 5 =$ _____          **T.** $(18 - 6) - 2 =$ _____

**B.** $17 - (12 - 4) =$ _____          **L.** $19 - (10 - 6) =$ _____

**U.** $(23 - 4) - 5 =$ _____          **E.** $(13 - 5) - (10 - 9) =$ _____

**D.** $(12 - 3) - (16 - 7) =$ _____          **O.** $(14 - 7) - (12 - 6) =$ _____

**L.** $(17 - 5) - (12 - 8) =$ _____          **I.** $(16 - 8) - (11 - 9) =$ _____

**W.** $13 - (11 - 3) =$ _____          **D.** $17 - (14 - 9) =$ _____

**R.** $(22 - 6) - 5 =$ _____          **N.** $(21 - 2) - (15 - 9) =$ _____

**I.** $(21 - 1) - (16 - 12) =$ _____          **O.** $(10 - 3) - (11 - 6) =$ _____

**H.** $(11 - 3) - 4 =$ _____

**How many stars are in the Milky Way Galaxy?**

___ ___ ___      ___ ___ ___ ___ ___ ___ ___      ___ ___ ___ ___ ___ ___ ___
10  5   1        4  14  13  0  11  7  12       9  16  8  15  6   2   3

# Moon Madness

 *The answer to a subtraction problem is called the **difference**.*

Subtract. Then write the  differences in order to answer the fun fact.

How fast does the moon travel in its orbit?  ____ ____ ____ ____ m.p.h.

A. 11 − (15 − 9) = ____

14 − (18 − 9) = ____

B. (15 − 7) − (11 − 5) = ____

17 − (14 − 6) = ____

C. 16 − (15 − 8) = ____

18 − (16 − 7) = ____

D. 15 − (15 − 8) = ____

(16 − 8) − (10 − 4) = ____

E. (13 − 9) − (11 − 8) = ____

13 − (14 − 7) = ____

F. 12 − (13 − 6) = ____

17 − (12 − 3) = ____

G. (17 − 9) − (13 − 8) = ____

(15 − 6) − (12 − 5) = ____

H. 18 − (13 − 4) = ____

16 − (17 − 9) = ____

I. 14 − (13 − 5) = ____

15 − (16 − 8) = ____

J. 12 − (18 − 9) = ____

(20 − 7) − (6 − 2) = ____

 **On another piece of paper, write subtraction problems with a code to answer this question: What is the diameter of the moon? (2,160 miles) Have a friend solve the problems.**

# Chess, Anyone?

 To subtract multiple-digit numbers without regrouping, follow these steps.

1. Subtract the ones column.

2. Subtract the tens column.

3. Subtract the hundreds column.

4. Subtract the thousands column.

$$6,48\boxed{9}$$
$$-\ 2,16\boxed{5}$$
$$\boxed{4}$$

$$6,4\boxed{8}9$$
$$-\ 2,1\boxed{6}5$$
$$\boxed{2}4$$

$$6,\boxed{4}89$$
$$-\ 2\boxed{1}65$$
$$\boxed{3}24$$

$$\boxed{6},489$$
$$-\ \boxed{2},165$$
$$\boxed{4},324$$

Subtract.

|  |  |  |  |
|---|---|---|---|
| 6,518 − 1,414 | 9,842 − 621 | 7,966 − 3,234 | 6,549 − 21 |
| 4,916 − 4,113 | 8,385 − 7,224 | 3,309 − 203 | 5,977 − 2,863 |
| 9,459 − 300 | 7,749 − 7,637 | 4,969 − 2,863 | 3,496 − 3,260 |
| 6,839 − 5,324 | 1,578 − 1,241 | 8,659 − 46 | 9,481 − 9,240 |

# Checkmate

 To subtract with regrouping, follow these steps.

1. Subtract the ones column. Regroup if needed.

```
      2 11
    4 3 1
  −  2 6 6
  ─────────
          5
```

2. Subtract the tens column. Regroup if needed.

```
       12
    3 2 11
    4 3 1
  −  2 6 6
  ─────────
        6 5
```

3. Subtract the hundreds column. Regroup if needed.

```
       12
    3 2 11
    4 3 1
  −  2 6 6
  ─────────
      1 6 5
```

Subtract. Cross out the chess piece with the matching difference. The last piece standing is the winner of the match.

63

464

```
    956        239        842
  − 492      − 176      − 426
```

179

```
    153        351        983
  −  80      − 172      − 284
```

416

```
    526        643        258
  − 286      − 479      − 139
```

699

73

240

506

119

```
    932        852
  − 426      − 476
```

164

479

⬚ is left standing.

376

# Out of the Park!

To subtract with regrouping, follow these steps.

| 1. | 2. | 3. | 4. |
|---|---|---|---|
| 5 10 | 15 | 13 15 | 13 15 |
| 3,4̸6̸0̸ | 3 ̸5 10 | 2 ̸3 ̸5 10 | 2 ̸3 ̸5 10 |
|  | 3,4̸6̸0̸ | 3̸,4̸6̸0̸ | 3̸,4̸6̸0̸ |
| −    876 | −    876 | −    876 | −    876 |
| 4 | 84 | 584 | 2,584 |

Subtract. Then use the code to solve the riddle below.

**E.**   4,622
−  1,284

**E.**   5,198
−     469

**H.**   3,469
−     890

**T.**   6,077
−  1,258

**A.**   9,617
−     759

**R.**   3,804
−     115

**H.**   8,941
−  1,895

**N.**      952
−       95

**C.**   7,263
−  4,772

**B.**   7,603
−  3,728

**E.**   9,550
−  4,298

**L.**   6,451
−     868

**S.**   2,850
−  1,976

**I.**   2,972
−     984

## In what part of the ballpark do you find the whitest clothes?

____ ____   ____ ____ ____
1,988  857    4,819  2,579  5,252

____ ____ ____ ____ ____ ____ ____ ____ ____!
3,875  5,583  4,729  8,858  2,491  7,046  3,338  3,689  874

**On another piece of paper, write a subtraction problem that requires regrouping two times. Ask someone at home to solve it.**

Name _____

# Touchdown!

Subtract. The final score of the game will be written in the footballs at the bottom of the page.

**Colts**

**Panthers**

| Colts tens | Colts ones | Panthers tens | Panthers ones |
|---|---|---|---|
| 7,694<br>− 1,986 | 8,049<br>− 862 | 9,217<br>− 972 | 5,473<br>− 864 |
| − 874 | − 1,479 | − 1,366 | − 1,953 |
| − 3,782 | − 2,896 | − 3,899 | − 1,838 |
| − 561 | − 1,778 | − 1,597 | − 692 |
| − 488 | − 1,027 | − 1,379 | − 117 |

**tens**        **ones**        **tens**        **ones**

**Who won?** _____

**On another piece of paper, write a series of four subtraction problems that have a final difference equal to your age.**

# A Funny Fixture

 *Continue regrouping into the ten thousands column if necessary.*

Subtract. Then use the code to find the answer to the riddle below.

| E. 63,210 − 11,799 | I. 41,392 − 38,164 | R. 76,146 − 34,982 | E. 12,388 − 9,891 |
|---|---|---|---|
| P. 54,391 − 23,689 | H. 68,612 − 59,446 | T. 97,413 − 89,608 | L. 32,602 − 19,561 |
| A. 18,546 − 11,798 | G. 92,475 − 76,097 | S. 29,816 − 17,909 | ! 78,752 − 69,275 |

## Why did the man climb up the chandelier?

,

____ ____ ____     ____
9,166  51,411  11,907     6,748

____ ____ ____ ____ ____
13,041  3,228  16,378  9,166  7,805

____ ____ ____ ____ ____ ____ ____ ____
11,907  13,041  2,497  51,411  30,702  2,497  41,164  9,477

# Bright Idea!

 *Each part of a subtraction problem has a name:*

$$
\begin{array}{r}
3,486 \leftarrow \textbf{minuend} \\
-\ 2,371 \leftarrow \textbf{subtrahend} \\
\hline
1,115 \leftarrow \textbf{difference}
\end{array}
$$

Find each missing subtrahend by subtracting the difference from the minuend.

|  |  |
|---|---|
| 9,416<br>− ☐<br>812 |  9,416<br>− 812<br>8,604 |
| 32,194<br>− ☐<br>5,778 |  |
| 63,417<br>− ☐<br>21,759 |  |
| 91,753<br>− ☐<br>18,475 |  |
| 8,110<br>− ☐<br>3,794 |  |
| 17,942<br>− ☐<br>8,786 |  |
| 49,234<br>− ☐<br>39,741 |  |
| 23,976<br>− ☐<br>18,687 |  |

 **On another piece of paper, write two subtraction problems with missing subtrahends. Ask a friend to solve the problems.**

# Cross-Number Puzzle

Subtract. Complete the puzzle.

### Across

2.  3,016
    − 1,209

6.  246,342
    − 156,129

8.  64,293
    − 28,318

9.  5,249
    − 3,928

10. 36,425
    − 18,929

11. 5,264
    − 3,192

12. 818,462
    − 131,910

14. 3,642
    − 1,813

15. 7,645
    − 1,328

### Down

1.  6,429
    − 3,298

3.  9,145
    − 2,189

4.  9,142
    − 1,381

5.  58,142
    − 13,098

7.  76,418
    −39,291

10. 31,642
    − 18,945

13. 814,603
    −148,231

# Map It Out

 *Always write a long subtraction problem vertically before solving it. When subtracting decimals, write each place value column so the decimal points are aligned.*

$82.17 - 74.16 =$

$$\begin{array}{r} 82.71 \\ - \quad 74.16 \\ \hline \end{array}$$

Write each subtraction problem vertically. Subtract.

$107.5 - 71.4 =$

**Region A**

$99.85 - 56.37 =$

**Region B**

$78.94 - 59.54 =$

$91.6 - 12.7 =$

**Region C**

**Region D**

$84.57 - 32.98 =$

$548.3 - 282.6 =$

**Region E**

**Region F**

 **Mary travelled to two regions. Their difference is 24.08. What two regions did she visit?**

# Sums & Differences

> ### Point-scoring in the Inter-Galaxy Football League
> Touchdown . . . . . . . . . . . . . . . . . . . . . . . . . . . . . . . . . . . 6 points
> Touchdown with an extra point . . . . . . . . . . . . . . . . 7 points
> Touchdown with a 2-point conversion . . . . . . . . . . 8 points
> Field Goal . . . . . . . . . . . . . . . . . . . . . . . . . . . . . . . . . . . . 3 points

The Asteroids played the Constellations. Each team scored a field goal in the first quarter. In the second quarter, the Asteroids scored a touchdown, but missed the extra point. At the half, the Constellations led by 1 point. In the third quarter, the Asteroids made a touchdown with the extra point. The Constellations matched them, and made a field goal, as well. In the fourth quarter, following a Constellation field goal, the Asteroids scored a touchdown with a 2-point conversion.

Who won? _____

By what score? _____

> Point-scoring in the Inter-Galaxy Basketball League consists of
> 1-point free throws, 2-point goals, 3-point goals, and 4-point goals
> (those made without looking at the basket!).

The Comets, playing the Meteors, led 22–9 at the end of the first quarter. They led by 7 at the half after scoring two 4-point goals, two 3-point goals, four 2-point goals, and three free throws. In the third quarter, the Meteors had six 2-point goals and four free throws. They also had one more 4-point goal, but one less 3-point goal than the Comets. The Comets had five 2-point goals and no free-throws. They scored 20 points in the quarter. In the last quarter, each team scored the same number of 4-point, 3-point, and 2-point goals. The Comets scored 31 points in that quarter, including four free throws. The Meteors made two fewer free throws than the Comets.

Who won? _____

By what score? _____

# Follow the Map

Write a number sentence for each problem. Solve.

**A.** Hannah's family drove 1,246 kilometres in 2 days. They drove 879 kilometres the first day. How far did they drive the second day?

**B.** Joplin is between Wells and Greenville. The distance from Wells to Greenville is 4,128 kilometres. The distance from Wells to Joplin is 1,839 kilometres. How far is it from Joplin to Greenville?

**C.** The Midnight Express travels 6,283 kilometres. When the train reaches Springfield, it has travelled 2,496 kilometres. How much farther will the Midnight Express travel?

**D.** Jacob's scout troop is going camping 947.6 kilometres from home. The bus breaks down after 289.9 kilometres. How far is the bus from the campgrounds?

**E.** Jonesburgh is between Johnsonville and Piper. Johnsonville is 8,612 kilometres from Piper. Piper is 4,985 kilometres from Jonesburgh. How far is it from Jonesburgh to Johnsonville?

**F.** Lola's family drove 2,391 kilometres to go to the beach. They drove home using another route that was 3,290 kilometres. How much longer was the second route?

Name _____

# It's a Circus in Here!

 To multiply is to use repeated addition. Basic multiplication facts
are learned by memorizing.

$3$ groups of $5 = 5 + 5 + 5 = 3 \times 5 = 15$

Multiply.

| $2$ | $3$ | $9$ | $5$ | $6$ |
|---|---|---|---|---|
| $\times\ 2$ | $\times\ 3$ | $\times\ 6$ | $\times\ 4$ | $\times\ 7$ |

| $6$ | $4$ | $5$ | $9$ | $2$ |
|---|---|---|---|---|
| $\times\ 4$ | $\times\ 1$ | $\times\ 8$ | $\times\ 3$ | $\times\ 4$ |

| $8$ | $9$ | $1$ | $3$ | $9$ |
|---|---|---|---|---|
| $\times\ 6$ | $\times\ 5$ | $\times\ 0$ | $\times\ 5$ | $\times\ 7$ |

| $8$ | $4$ | $9$ | $0$ | $3$ |
|---|---|---|---|---|
| $\times\ 8$ | $\times\ 7$ | $\times\ 9$ | $\times\ 8$ | $\times\ 4$ |

| $5$ | $6$ | $7$ | $5$ | $8$ |
|---|---|---|---|---|
| $\times\ 5$ | $\times\ 6$ | $\times\ 7$ | $\times\ 2$ | $\times\ 4$ |

**On another piece of paper, draw a picture to match this problem:
There are 6 clowns. Each clown is holding 7 balloons. Then write the
multiplication fact that tells the total number of balloons.**

Name _____

# Under the Big Top

*The answer to a multiplication problem is called the **product**. The numbers being multiplied are called **factors**.*

Multiply. Then use each product and the code to answer the riddles.

## What happened to the human cannonball at the circus?

____ ____     ____ ____ ____     ____ ____ ____ ____ ____
4 x 6   6 x 3     7 x 7   3 x 4   8 x 8     8 x 3   6 x 8   7 x 9   2 x 9   8 x 7

____ ____ ____     ____ ____ ____ ____ ____     ____ ____
6 x 2   8 x 9   7 x 8     9 x 9   8 x 6   9 x 7   3 x 6   7 x 8     7 x 6   9 x 8

____ ____ ____     ____ ____ ____ ____     ____ ____ ____!
5 x 9   6 x 4   9 x 2     8 x 8   4 x 3   6 x 6   6 x 3     8 x 7   2 x 6   5 x 5

## What happened to the kid who ran away with the circus?

____ ____     ____ ____ ____
3 x 8   2 x 9     4 x 6   3 x 4   8 x 7

____ ____     ____ ____ ____ ____ ____
9 x 5   6 x 7     9 x 3   7 x 9   8 x 6   9 x 8   5 x 8

____ ____     ____ ____ ____ ____!
6 x 8   5 x 9     3 x 9   2 x 6   5 x 3   9 x 6

| | | | |
|---|---|---|---|
| A = 12 | H = 24 | O = 42 | V = 21 |
| B = 27 | I = 48 | P = 16 | W = 49 |
| C = 15 | J = 4 | Q = 28 | X = 1 |
| D = 56 | K = 54 | R = 63 | Y = 25 |
| E = 18 | L = 8 | S = 64 | Z = 2 |
| F = 81 | M = 36 | T = 45 | |
| G = 40 | N = 72 | U = 0 | |

# Come to Costa Rica

 To multiply with a 2-digit factor, follow these steps.

1.  Multiply the ones
    column.

    $\begin{array}{r} 4\,2 \\ x\quad 3 \\ \hline 6 \end{array}$

2.  Multiply the bottom factor in
    the ones column with the top
    factor in the tens column.

    $\begin{array}{r} 4\,2 \\ x\quad 3 \\ \hline 1\,2\,6 \end{array}$

Multiply. Use the code to fill in the blanks below.

| I. | O. | S. | H. | J. |
|---|---|---|---|---|
| 82 | 91 | 21 | 92 | 73 |
| x  4 | x  9 | x  8 | x  3 | x  2 |

| E. | L. | R. | C. | N. |
|---|---|---|---|---|
| 71 | 53 | 90 | 61 | 11 |
| x  7 | x  3 | x  8 | x  6 | x  5 |

| A. | F. | T. | E. | P. |
|---|---|---|---|---|
| 32 | 41 | 70 | 52 | 40 |
| x  4 | x  9 | x  7 | x  4 | x  8 |

<u>490</u>  <u>276</u>  <u>208</u>

<u>366</u>  <u>128</u>  <u>320</u>  <u>328</u>  <u>490</u>  <u>128</u>  <u>159</u>

<u>819</u>  <u>369</u>    <u>366</u>  <u>819</u>  <u>168</u>  <u>490</u>  <u>128</u>

<u>720</u>  <u>328</u>  <u>366</u>  <u>128</u>    <u>328</u>  <u>168</u>

<u>168</u>  <u>128</u>  <u>55</u>    <u>146</u>  <u>819</u>  <u>168</u>  <u>497</u> .

**Costa Rica is in Central America. If a Costa Rican farmer sells 33 kilograms of coffee
every day for 3 days, how much will he sell altogether?**

# The Faraway Country

 To multiply with a 2-digit factor that requires regrouping, follow these steps.

1. Multiply the ones.
   Regroup if needed.
   7 x 3 = 21

2. Multiply the bottom factor in the ones column with
   the top factor in the tens column. Add the extra tens.
   6 x 3 = 18     18 + 2 = 20

Multiply.

**A.**
```
    48          24          73
x    3      x    7      x    4
```

**B.**
```
    57          63          56
x    7      x    9      x    3
```

**C.**
```
    98          64          57          35          23          82
x    2      x    8      x    8      x    9      x    8      x    6
```

**D.**
```
    95          77          83          96          28          96
x    9      x    6      x    9      x    8      x    4      x    5
```

 **Switzerland is famous for the magnificent Swiss Alps. Waterfalls are formed by many of the mountain streams. The highest waterfall is Giessbach Falls. To find out how many metres high this waterfall is, add the products in Row A.**

# A Multiplication Puzzler

Multiply. Circle each product in the puzzle. The products will go across and down.

| | | | | | |
|---|---|---|---|---|---|
| **A.** | 32 <br> x 8 | 56 <br> x 8 | 70 <br> x 5 | 65 <br> x 4 | 68 <br> x 5 |
| **B.** | 81 <br> x 3 | 89 <br> x 6 | 60 <br> x 5 | 69 <br> x 4 | 96 <br> x 2 |
| **C.** | 49 <br> x 6 | 78 <br> x 4 | 72 <br> x 8 | 68 <br> x 9 | 24 <br> x 9 |
| **D.** | 43 <br> x 5 | 97 <br> x 3 | 91 <br> x 2 | 79 <br> x 3 | 49 <br> x 3 |

| 6 | 1 | 2 | 9 | 6 | 8 | 2 | 3 | 7 |
|---|---|---|---|---|---|---|---|---|
| 9 | 3 | 6 | 3 | 1 | 4 | 7 | 2 | 3 |
| 7 | 1 | 2 | 5 | 6 | 0 | 6 | 1 | 5 |
| 2 | 8 | 3 | 0 | 9 | 5 | 4 | 5 | 7 |
| 6 | 2 | 4 | 3 | 2 | 3 | 2 | 1 | 6 |
| 0 | 7 | 4 | 3 | 4 | 0 | 6 | 9 | 3 |
| 1 | 6 | 8 | 1 | 3 | 3 | 1 | 2 | 0 |
| 7 | 5 | 2 | 9 | 1 | 0 | 4 | 3 | 5 |
| 5 | 3 | 4 | 3 | 8 | 0 | 2 | 9 | 4 |

# The Big City

To multiply with a 3-digit factor that requires regrouping, follow these steps.

| 1. Multiply the ones. Regroup if needed. | 2. Multiply the tens in the top factor. Add the extra tens. Regroup if needed. | 3. Multiply the hundreds in the top factor. Add the extra hundreds. |
|---|---|---|
| 1<br>4 7 3<br>x    6<br>——<br>8 | 4 1<br>4 7 3<br>x    6<br>——<br>3 8 | 4 1<br>4 7 3<br>x    6<br>——<br>2,838 |

Multiply.

**A.**

| 463 | 923 | 194 | 630 | 494 | 604 |
|---|---|---|---|---|---|
| x  3 | x  4 | x  8 | x  5 | x  2 | x  4 |

**B.**

| 325 | 817 | 293 | 168 | 208 | 196 |
|---|---|---|---|---|---|
| x  7 | x  6 | x  9 | x  3 | x  8 | x  6 |

**C.**

| 305 | 815 | 980 | 155 | 626 | 126 |
|---|---|---|---|---|---|
| x  2 | x  5 | x  7 | x  9 | x  3 | x  6 |

**A subway train travels 296 kilometres daily. How far does the train travel in a week?**

# A Changing Reef

 To multiply with zeros, follow these steps.

| 9 0 | 9 x 2 = 18 | 9 0 | 9 x 2 = 18 | 9 0 0 | 9 x 2 = 18 |
|---|---|---|---|---|---|
| x   2 | Add a zero in the ones place to make 180. | x  2 0 | Add 2 zeros—one in the ones place and one in the tens place. | x   2 0 | Add 3 zeros—one in the ones place, one in the tens place, and one in the hundreds place. |

Multiply.

**A.**

| 80 | 60 | 900 | 40 | 120 | 200 |
|---|---|---|---|---|---|
| x   7 | x   50 | x   30 | x   11 | x   2 | x   60 |

**B.**

| 70 | 120 | 60 | 700 | 50 | 30 |
|---|---|---|---|---|---|
| x   7 | x   300 | x   90 | x   60 | x   70 | x   12 |

**C.**

| 600 | 40 | 30 | 90 | 200 | 50 |
|---|---|---|---|---|---|
| x   80 | x   12 | x   8 | x   50 | x   120 | x   8 |

**fringing reef**

**barrier reef**

**atoll**

 The formation of a coral reef starts growing around the top of an undersea volcano forming a fringing reef. As the the volcano sinks, it leaves behind a barrier reef. When the volcano sinks below the ocean's surface, an atoll is left. On another piece of paper, write three problems with products to match those on the pictures.

# Ship Shape

What are the cheapest
ships to buy?

## What To Do

To find the answer to the riddle,
solve the multiplication problems.
Then, match each product with a
letter in the Key below. Write the
correct letters on the blanks below.

**1** 100 x 23 = _____

**2** 200 x 17 = _____

**3** 300 x 31 = _____

**4** 400 x 44 = _____

**5** 500 x 19 = _____

**6** 600 x 27 = _____

**7** 700 x 35 = _____

**8** 800 x 18 = _____

**9** 900 x 50 = _____

## Key

| | | | | | |
|---|---|---|---|---|---|
| 3,200 | D | 16,200 | B | 16,700 | H |
| 17,600 | L | 3,600 | K | 24,500 | O |
| 10,500 | I | 3,400 | T | 12,600 | Y |
| 45,000 | A | 9,300 | E | 14,400 | A |
| 15,300 | R | 9,500 | S | 2,300 | S |

Riddle
Answer:
" ___ ___ ___ ___ " ___ ___ ___ ___ ___
**5** **9** **4** **3** **6** **7** **8** **2** **1**

# Caught in the Web

Why did the
spider join the
baseball team?

## What To Do

To find the answer to the riddle,
solve the multiplication problems. Then, match each product
with a letter in the Key below.
Write the correct letters on the
blanks below.

**1**   **1,000 x 11 =** _____

**2**   **2,000 x 12 =** _____

**3**   **3,000 x 10 =** _____

**4**   **4,000 x 14 =** _____

**5**   **5,000 x 20 =** _____

**6**   **6,000 x 24 =** _____

**7**   **7,000 x 30 =** _____

**8**   **8,000 x 32 =** _____

**9**   **9,000 x 40 =** _____

**10**   **7,500 x 50 =** _____

## Key

| | | |
|---|---|---|
| 56,000 . . . . . . . . H | 65,000 . . . . . . . . M | 30,000 . . . . . . . . C |
| 11,000 . . . . . . . . I | 144,000 . . . . . . . . T | 375,000 . . . . . . . . C |
| 265,000 . . . . . . . . B | 25,000 . . . . . . . . N | 10,000 . . . . . . . . Y |
| 360,000 . . . . . . . . F | 256,000 . . . . . . . . L | 100,000 . . . . . . . . A |
| 210,000 . . . . . . . . E | 90,000 . . . . . . . . Q | 24,000 . . . . . . . . S |

Riddle
Answer:   **TO** ___ ___ ___ ___ ___   " ___ ___ ___ ___ ___ "

# Purple Blossoms

Solve the problems. ◆ If the answer is between 1 and 250, colour the shape yellow. ◆ If the answer is between 251 and 4000, colour the shape purple. ◆ If the answer is between 4,001 and 9,000, colour the shape pink. ◆ Finish by colouring the other shapes with colours of your choice.

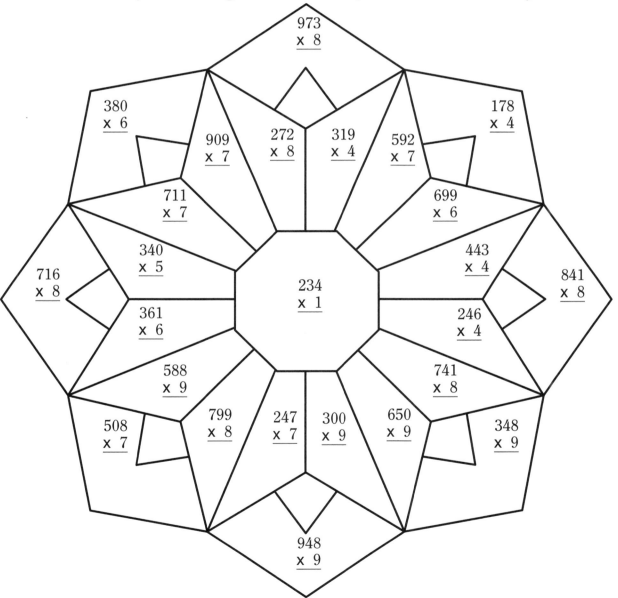

Taking It Further: I am an even number. I have three digits and they are all the same. If you multiply me by 4, all of the digits in the product are 8. What number am I? _____

# Stallions in the Stable

Multiply. Use the products to put each stallion back where he belongs. Write the horse's name on the stall door.

11,284    22,635    7,161    20,130    72,648    7,692

| 3,458<br>x    2 | 4,026<br>x    5 | 2,716<br>x    7 | 1,459<br>x    4 | 5,642<br>x    2 |
|---|---|---|---|---|
| | Lola's Lad | | | Stormy |

| 2,564<br>x    3 | 1,508<br>x    6 | 9,210<br>x    9 | 4,527<br>x    5 | 1,018<br>x    8 |
|---|---|---|---|---|
| Dusty | | | Black Beauty | |

| 1,809<br>x    7 | 2,387<br>x    3 | 9,081<br>x    8 | 7,186<br>x    4 | 7,130<br>x    6 |
|---|---|---|---|---|
| | Midnight | Lightning | | |

# Stop Horsing Around!

To multiply with a 2-digit factor that requires regrouping, follow these steps.

| 1. Multiply by the ones digit. | 2. Place a zero in the ones column.. | 3. Multiply by the tens digit. | 4. Add to find the product. |
|---|---|---|---|

```
    3                3               3              1
                                                   3
   46               46              46             46
 x 26             x 26            x 26           x 26
 ----             ----            ----           ----
  276              276             276            276
                     0           + 920          + 920
                                                -----
                                                1,196
```

Multiply. Then use the code to answer the riddle below.

**G.**  32
      x 48

**T.**  67
      x 14

**S.**  53
      x 27

**I.**  96
      x 52

**A.**  83
      x 33

**D.**  49
      x 72

**M.**  39
      x 28

**E.**  56
      x 15

**N.**  83
      x 24

**R.**  75
      x 46

**K.**  96
      x 51

**H.**  84
      x 62

## What horses like to stay up late?

___ ___ ___ ___ ___ ___ ___ ___ ___ ___!
1,992 4,992 1,536 5,208 938 1,092 2,739 3,450 840 1,431

 **Each of Farmer Gray's 24 horses eat 31 kilograms of hay. How many kilograms of hay do the horses eat altogether?**

# Famous Landmarks

Which of these U.S. landmarks is the tallest? Multiply. Write the ones digit of each product in order to find the height of each landmark in feet. Circle the tallest landmark.

**Gateway Arch**

$$\begin{array}{r} 73 \\ \times\ 42 \\ \hline \end{array} \qquad \begin{array}{r} 49 \\ \times\ 27 \\ \hline \end{array} \qquad \begin{array}{r} 55 \\ \times\ 72 \\ \hline \end{array}$$

= _____ feet tall

**Empire
State
Building**

$$\begin{array}{r} 67 \\ \times\ 42 \\ \hline \end{array} \qquad \begin{array}{r} 25 \\ \times\ 97 \\ \hline \end{array} \qquad \begin{array}{r} 76 \\ \times\ 14 \\ \hline \end{array}$$

= _____ feet tall

$$\begin{array}{r} 83 \\ \times\ 81 \\ \hline \end{array} \qquad \begin{array}{r} 48 \\ \times\ 45 \\ \hline \end{array} \qquad \begin{array}{r} 79 \\ \times\ 65 \\ \hline \end{array}$$

= _____ feet tall

**Statue
of
Liberty**

$$\begin{array}{r} 76 \\ \times\ 86 \\ \hline \end{array} \qquad \begin{array}{r} 65 \\ \times\ 56 \\ \hline \end{array} \qquad \begin{array}{r} 83 \\ \times\ 37 \\ \hline \end{array}$$

= _____ feet tall

**Space
Needle**

 **The Sears Tower in Chicago is 110 storeys tall. If 55 people work on each floor, how many total people work in the building?**

# Soccer Balls

Solve the problems, then choose two colours that you like. ◆ Write the name of one of the colours on each line below. ◆ Colour the design. If the answer is even, colour the shape _____. If the answer is odd, colour the shape _____. ◆ Finish the design by colouring the other shapes with the colours of your choice.

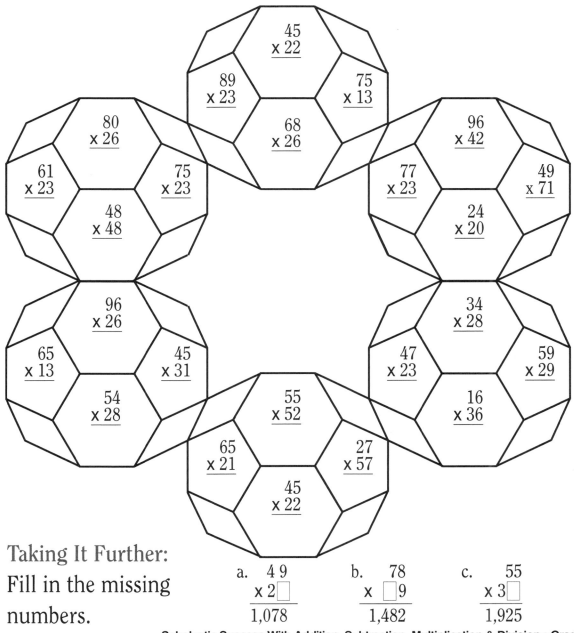

Taking It Further:
Fill in the missing numbers.

a.
```
   4 9
 x 2☐
─────
 1,078
```

b.
```
   7 8
 x ☐9
─────
 1,482
```

c.
```
   5 5
 x 3☐
─────
 1,925
```

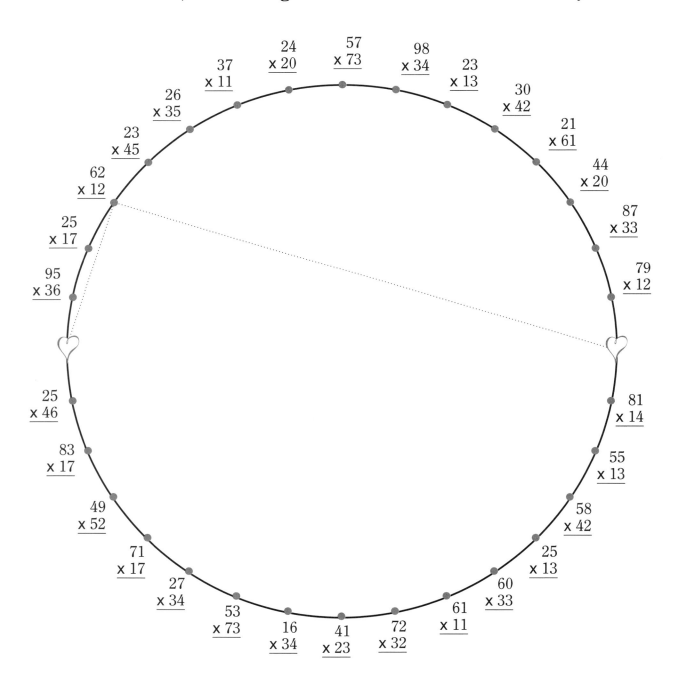
# In the Wink of an Eye

Solve the problems. If the answer is even, connect the dot beside each problem to the heart on the right- and left-hand sides of the circle. If the answer is odd, do nothing. Two lines have been drawn for you.

24
x 20

57
x 73

98
x 34

37
x 11

23
x 13

26
x 35

30
x 42

23
x 45

21
x 61

62
x 12

44
x 20

25
x 17

87
x 33

95
x 36

79
x 12

25
x 46

81
x 14

83
x 17

55
x 13

49
x 52

58
x 42

71
x 17

25
x 13

27
x 34

60
x 33

53
x 73

61
x 11

16
x 34

41
x 23

72
x 32

# Monumental Multiplication

Multiply.

**A.**

| 362 | 602 | 452 | 283 | 918 | 473 |
|---|---|---|---|---|---|
| x   43 | x   18 | x   22 | x   13 | x   27 | x   55 |

**B.**

| 540 | 417 | 308 |
|---|---|---|
| x   38 | x   56 | x   61 |

**C.**

| 692 | 586 | 918 |
|---|---|---|
| x   34 | x   37 | x   86 |

**D.**

| 467 | 598 | 861 |
|---|---|---|
| x   42 | x   29 | x   73 |

 The Washington Monument in the U.S. has 898 steps. If 42 people climb to the top, how many steps have they climbed altogether?

# The Music Store

When a multiplication problem involves money, the product must have a dollar sign and a decimal point. The decimal point is placed between the ones digit and the tenths digit.

```
    6
    2
  $3.71
x     94
  ───────
  14.84
+ 333.90
  ───────
 $348.84
```

Remember to use a dollar sign and a decimal point.

Multiply. Then use the code to answer the riddle below.

| **N.** $1.94 x 23 | **M.** $0.79 x 25 | **I.** $2.06 x 64 | **O.** $0.68 x 45 |
| --- | --- | --- | --- |
| **A.** $3.68 x 32 | **T.** $9.54 x 19 | **F.** $0.88 x 72 | **D.** $0.93 x 94 |
| **E.** $8.15 x 67 | **S.** $7.43 x 92 | **R.** $0.87 x 75 | **H.** $6.92 x 83 |

### Where do musicians buy instruments?

___ ___    ___ ___ ___
$117.76  $181.26    $181.26  $574.36  $546.05

___ ___ ___ ___    ___ ___ ___
$63.36  $131.84  $63.36  $546.05    $117.76  $44.62  $87.42

___ ___ ___ ___    ___ ___ ___ ___ ___!
$87.42  $131.84  $19.75  $546.05    $683.56  $181.26  $30.60  $65.25  $546.05

**Price your favourite CD. Imagine that you buy one for each of your classmates. How much would you spend?**

# The Corner Candy Store

 *Word problems that suggest equal groups often require multiplication.*

Write a number sentence for each problem. Solve.

| | |
|---|---|
| **A.** Sam bought 4 candy bars at $1.23 each. How much did Sam spend altogether? | **B.** Mr. Johnson, the store owner, ordered 48 boxes of jawbreakers. Each box contained 392 pieces of candy. How many jawbreakers did Mr. Johnson order? |
| **C.** Carly's mom sent her to the candy store with 29 party bags. She asked Carly to fill each bag with 45 pieces of candy. How many pieces of candy will Carly buy? | **D.** Thirty-five children visited the candy store after school. Each child spent 57¢. How much money was spent in all? |
| **E.** Mr. Johnson keeps 37 jars behind the candy counter. Each jar contains 286 pieces of candy. How many pieces of candy are behind the counter altogether? | **F.** Nick bought each of his 6 friends a milk shake. Each milk shake cost $2.98. How much did Nick spend in all? |

# What's on the Tube?

*To divide means to make equal groups. Since multiplication also depends on equal groups, you can use the multiplication facts to help you learn the division facts.*

$$\begin{array}{r} 8 \\ \times\ \ 6 \\ \hline 4\ 8 \end{array} \longrightarrow 6\overline{)48}$$

Basic division facts are problems you will learn by memory. Divide.

**A.**  $4\overline{)24}$   $4\overline{)36}$   $7\overline{)56}$   $5\overline{)25}$   $9\overline{)81}$   $8\overline{)24}$

**B.**  $5\overline{)45}$   $8\overline{)72}$   $4\overline{)28}$   $6\overline{)42}$   $6\overline{)36}$   $1\overline{)9}$

**C.**  $3\overline{)12}$   $7\overline{)21}$   $6\overline{)48}$   $3\overline{)24}$   $8\overline{)32}$   $7\overline{)63}$

**D.**  $8\overline{)64}$   $7\overline{)49}$   $5\overline{)30}$   $9\overline{)27}$   $6\overline{)6}$   $3\overline{)15}$

Divide to learn an interesting fact.

### In what year was television invented?

$3\overline{)3}$   $8\overline{)72}$   $7\overline{)14}$   $8\overline{)64}$

 **Research to find the year something else was invented. On another piece of paper, write four division facts with the year hidden in their quotients.**

Name _____

# Television Division

 *Each part of a division problem has a name.*

$$5 \leftarrow \text{quotient}$$
$$\text{divisor} \rightarrow 9\,\overline{)45} \leftarrow \text{dividend}$$

Divide.

**A.**

$6\overline{)24}$  $9\overline{)63}$  $4\overline{)12}$

$9\overline{)45}$  $3\overline{)18}$  $8\overline{)56}$

$8\overline{)64}$  $8\overline{)40}$  $9\overline{)72}$

**B.**

$7\overline{)35}$  $9\overline{)36}$  $7\overline{)21}$

$4\overline{)32}$  $5\overline{)20}$  $6\overline{)36}$

$3\overline{)9}$  $7\overline{)56}$  $9\overline{)81}$

**C.**

$8\overline{)48}$  $5\overline{)25}$  $9\overline{)27}$

$7\overline{)49}$  $9\overline{)54}$  $4\overline{)36}$

$5\overline{)15}$  $7\overline{)63}$  $5\overline{)30}$

**D.**

$6\overline{)54}$  $3\overline{)27}$  $6\overline{)42}$

$3\overline{)21}$  $6\overline{)18}$  $4\overline{)28}$

$7\overline{)28}$  $5\overline{)40}$  $7\overline{)42}$

 **On another piece of paper, write nine division facts with a quotient of 8.**

# Patchwork Diamonds

Solve the problems. ◆ If the answer is between 1 and 6, colour the shape green. ◆ If the answer is between 7 and 12, colour the shape red. ◆ Finish the design by colouring the other shapes with the colours of your choice.

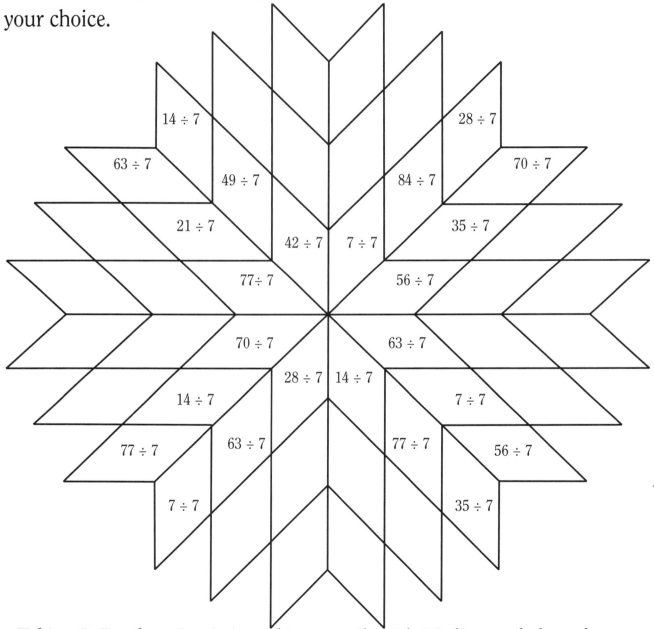

**Taking It Further:** Jamie is making a quilt with 70 diamond-shaped pieces. If 7 pieces make 1 square, how many squares will her quilt have?

# Mirror Image

Solve the problems. Then connect the dot beside each problem to the dot beside its answer.

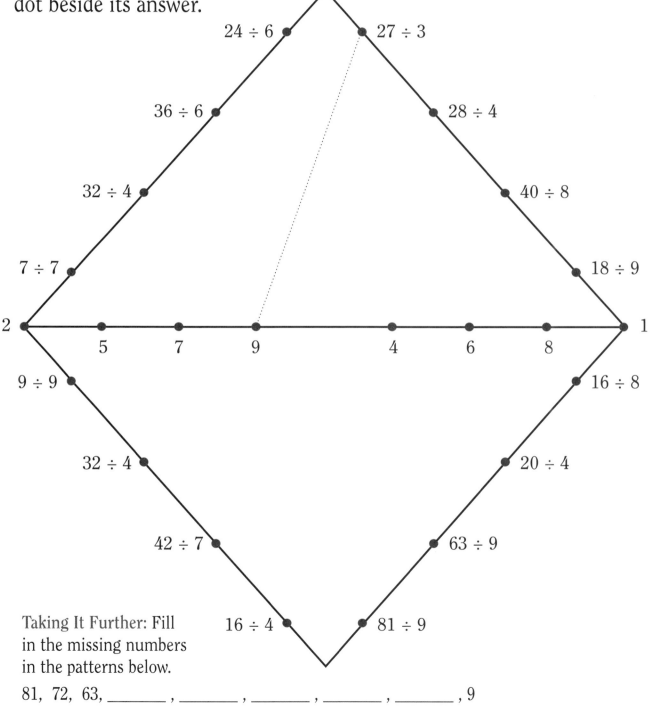

Taking It Further: Fill in the missing numbers in the patterns below.

81, 72, 63, _____ , _____ , _____ , _____ , _____ , 9

63, 56, 49, _____ , _____ , _____ , _____ , _____ , 7

# A Barrel of Monkeys

 To divide with zeros, follow these samples.

$$\begin{array}{r} 80 \\ 8\overline{)640} \end{array}$$
$64 \div 8 = 8$
$0 \div 8 = 0$
Add a zero to make 80.

$$\begin{array}{r} 800 \\ 8\overline{)6400} \end{array}$$
$64 \div 8 = 8$
$0 \div 8 = 0$
$0 \div 8 = 0$
Add 2 zeros to make 800.

Divide.

**A.**    $6\overline{)420}$      $9\overline{)8100}$      $6\overline{)540}$      $5\overline{)4500}$      $3\overline{)2400}$

**B.**    $3\overline{)1800}$      $4\overline{)320}$      $8\overline{)7200}$      $7\overline{)560}$      $5\overline{)400}$

**C.**    $3\overline{)150}$      $4\overline{)360}$      $6\overline{)4800}$      $6\overline{)360}$      $8\overline{)640}$

90      900      9

 **Write three problems with quotients to match those on the barrels.**

# No Way!

*To divide with remainders, follow these steps.*

1. Does 8 x __ = 34? No!

$$8 \overline{)34}$$

2. Use the closest smaller dividend.
8 x 4 = 32

$$\begin{array}{r} 4 \\ 8 \overline{)34} \\ 32 \end{array}$$

3. Subtract to find the remainder.

$$\begin{array}{r} 4 \\ 8 \overline{)34} \\ -32 \\ \hline 2 \end{array}$$

4. The remainder is always less than the divisor.

$$\begin{array}{r} 4\ R2 \\ 8 \overline{)34} \\ -32 \\ \hline 2 \end{array}$$

Divide. Then use the code to complete the riddle below.

| | | | |
|---|---|---|---|
| **E.** $9 \overline{)84}$ | **L.** $3 \overline{)29}$ | **S.** $7 \overline{)67}$ | **O.** $5 \overline{)24}$ |
| **T.** $6 \overline{)23}$ | **N.** $6 \overline{)47}$ | **P.** $6 \overline{)39}$ | **I.** $7 \overline{)52}$ |
| **O.** $4 \overline{)19}$ | **A.** $8 \overline{)70}$ | **T.** $3 \overline{)26}$ | **S.** $9 \overline{)55}$ |
| **H.** $4 \overline{)23}$ | **!** $7 \overline{)45}$ | **R.** $5 \overline{)27}$ | **N.** $8 \overline{)79}$ |

**Emily:** Yesterday I saw a man at the mall with very long arms. Every time he went up the stairs he stepped on them.

**Jack:** Wow! He stepped on his arms?

**Emily:** ____ ____ , ____ ____    ____ ____ ____
        7 R5  4 R4   4 R3  9 R7   8 R2  5 R3  9 R3

____ ____ ____ ____ ____ ____
9 R4  3 R5  8 R6  7 R3  5 R2  6 R1  6 R3

# Honeycomb

Solve the problems. ◆ If the answer has a remainder between 1 and 4, colour the shape black. ◆ If the answer has a remainder between 5 and 8, colour the shape red. ◆ Finish the design by colouring the other shapes with the colours of your choice.

14 ÷ 6

15 ÷ 9

86 ÷ 7

41 ÷ 6

37 ÷ 6

33 ÷ 9

23 ÷ 6

54 ÷ 7

15 ÷ 8

15 ÷ 2

13 ÷ 3

45 ÷ 7

66 ÷ 9

28 ÷ 3

19 ÷ 2

63 ÷ 8

33 ÷ 7

53 ÷ 6

27 ÷ 5   62 ÷ 7      76 ÷ 9   80 ÷ 9      17 ÷ 4   11 ÷ 6

## Division Decoder

# Riddle: What kind of tools do you use for math?

Find each quotient. Then use the Decoder to solve the riddle by filling in the spaces at the bottom of the page.

**Decoder**

| | |
|---|---|
| 8 ..................... | **I** |
| 3 remainder 2 .. | **L** |
| 7 ..................... | **W** |
| 8 remainder 1 .. | **S** |
| 6 ..................... | **U** |
| 9 ..................... | **A** |
| 15 remainder 3 | **B** |
| 4 ..................... | **L** |
| 2 remainder 3 .. | **D** |
| 9 remainder 2.... | **T** |
| 1 ..................... | **F** |
| 7 remainder 6 .. | **N** |
| 6 remainder 6 .... | **I** |
| 2 ..................... | **E** |
| 11 .................... | **O** |
| 15 remainder 2.. | **P** |
| 2 remainder 5 .. | **X** |
| 10 .................... | **C** |
| 5 ..................... | **R** |

❶ 8 ÷ 2 = _____

❷ 10 ÷ 5 = _____

❸ 24 ÷ 4 = _____

❹ 50 ÷ 10 = _____

❺ 72 ÷ 9 = _____

❻ 32 ÷ 10 = _____

❼ 48 ÷ 7 = _____

❽ 29 ÷ 3 = _____

❾ 65 ÷ 8 = _____

❿ 92 ÷ 6 = _____

"M __ __ __ __ " __ __ __ __ __ __
    3  1  8  5    10  6  7  2  4  9

# Mousing Around

 *To divide with a 3-digit dividend, follow these steps.*

1.
$$7\overline{)427}$$ 6 / 42

$7 \times \underline{\quad} = 42$
$7 \times 6 = 42$

2.
$$7\overline{)427}$$ 6
$-42\downarrow$
07

Subtract.

Bring down the ones digit.

3.
$$7\overline{)427}$$ 61
$-42\downarrow$
07
$-\ 7$
0

$7 \times \underline{\quad} = 7$
$7 \times 1 = 7$

Subtract.

Divide. Then use the code to answer the riddle below.

**T.** $4\overline{)208}$      **U.** $6\overline{)306}$      **H.** $9\overline{)819}$      **C.** $3\overline{)246}$      **A.** $4\overline{)368}$

**E.** $8\overline{)648}$      **O.** $7\overline{)497}$      **S.** $4\overline{)248}$      **N.** $2\overline{)168}$      **D.** $4\overline{)288}$

**C.** $4\overline{)328}$      **I.** $3\overline{)159}$      **W.** $5\overline{)305}$      **M.** $9\overline{)279}$      **!** $4\overline{)88}$

## Why did the cat hang out near the computer?

__53__ __52__   __61__ __92__ __84__ __52__ __81__ __72__   __52__ __71__

__82__ __92__ __52__ __82__ __91__   __52__ __91__ __81__

__31__ __71__ __51__ __62__ __81__ __22__

**On another piece of paper, design a mouse pad. Include at least three division problems and their quotients in your design.**

# Surfing the Web

 *When the divisor has a remainder in the middle of a problem, follow these steps.*

1.
$$\begin{array}{r} 10 \\ 8\overline{)816} \\ 80 \end{array}$$
8 x ___ = 81
8 x 10 = 80

2.
$$\begin{array}{r} 10 \\ 8\overline{)816} \\ -\ 80\downarrow \\ \hline 16 \end{array}$$
Subtract.

Bring down
the ones digit.

3.
$$\begin{array}{r} 102 \\ 8\overline{)816} \\ -\ 42\downarrow \\ \hline 07 \\ -\ 7 \\ \hline 0 \end{array}$$
8 x ___ = 16
8 x 2 = 16

Subtract
again.

Divide. Use another piece of paper to work the problems.
Then connect each problem to its answer to learn the definitions of some computer terms.

**A.**  5 )‾375‾   browser

**B.**  6 )‾492‾   byte

**C.**  2 )‾216‾   download

**D.**  3 )‾246‾   gigabyte

**E.**  9 )‾243‾   Internet

**F.**  8 )‾288‾   megabyte

**G.**  4 )‾424‾   network

**H.**  6 )‾564‾   program

**I.**  7 )‾532‾   scanner

**J.**  4 )‾312‾   virus

**K.**  9 )‾486‾   web site

82   an amount of data equal to 8 bits

75   a program to help get around the Internet

54   a place on the Internet's World Wide Web
where text and pictures are stored

106   a group of computers linked together so
they can share information

36   an amount of information equal to
1,048,516 bytes

27   a worldwide system of linked computers

108   to transfer information from a host computer
to a personal computer

82   an amount of information equal to 1,024
megabytes

78   a program that damages other programs
and data; often transmitted through
telephone lines or shared disks

94   instructions for a computer to follow

76   a device that can transfer words and pictures
from a printed page into the computer

# Flying Carpet

Solve the problems. ◆ If the answer is between 100 and 250, colour the shape red. ◆ If the answer is between 251 and 900, colour the shape blue. ◆ Finish the design by colouring the other shapes with the colours of your choice.

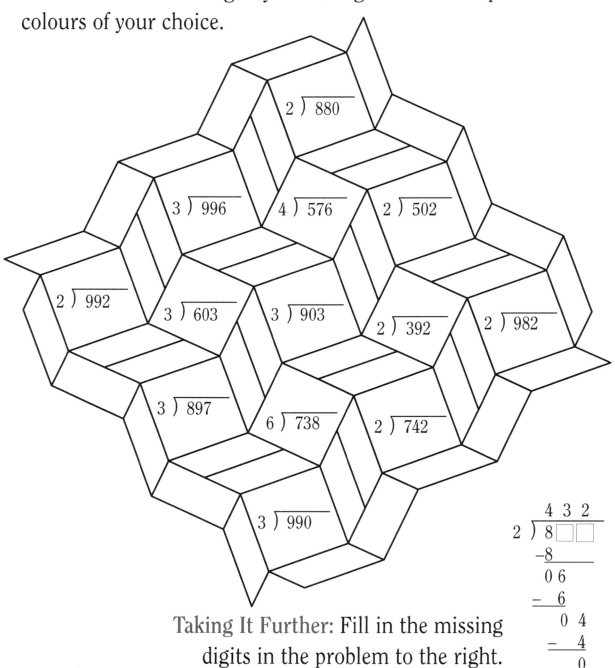

Taking It Further: Fill in the missing digits in the problem to the right.

# Poolside!

➡️ *Remember: The remainder is always less than the divisor.*

Divide. Then use the code to answer the riddle below.

**O.** 4 ) 258

**G.** 7 ) 445

**K.** 6 ) 573

**R.** 9 ) 380

**L.** 8 ) 419

**A.** 9 ) 748

**M.** 5 ) 293

**P.** 8 ) 706

**S.** 3 ) 263

**T.** 6 ) 356

**C.** 7 ) 309

**What kind of pool is not made for swimming?**

___ ___ ___ ___ ___ ___ ___ !
83R1  44R1  83R1  42R2  88R2  64R2  64R2  52R3

# Summer Days

Divide. Then use the code to answer the riddle below.

Z.  3 ) 2226     N.  5 ) 2918     T.  8 ) 2099

S.  4 ) 2992     B.  7 ) 4332     P.  9 ) 3204

D.  6 ) 2364     C.  7 ) 3800     U.  3 ) 2571

O.  9 ) 8289     A.  5 ) 4609     Y.  8 ) 5376

**What is the best day to go to the beach?**

___ ___ ___ ___ ___ ___ !
748   857   583R3   394   921R4   672

 A year has 365 days. Summer is one of the four seasons. On another piece of paper, divide to find the exact number of days that are in each season. Your answer will tell you why our seasons truly change at a specific hour.

Name _____

# Bone Up on Division

 To divide by a 2-digit divisor, follow these steps.

1.
$$15\overline{\smash{)}330}$$ gives 2, with 30 below

15 x ___ = 33
Use the closest smaller dividend.
15 x 2 = 30
Put the 2 above the 3 tens.

2.
$$15\overline{\smash{)}330}$$ with − 30 and 30 below

Subtract.
Bring down the ones digit.

3.
$$15\overline{\smash{)}330}$$ gives 22, with − 30, 30, − 30, 0

15 x ___ = 30
15 x 2 = 30
Subtract again.

Divide. Write the digit in the ones place with the least amount in each row to find out how many bones an adult human body has.

**A.**  $13\overline{\smash{)}559}$  $16\overline{\smash{)}208}$  $39\overline{\smash{)}468}$  $23\overline{\smash{)}874}$

**B.**  $31\overline{\smash{)}682}$  $46\overline{\smash{)}690}$  $26\overline{\smash{)}858}$  $47\overline{\smash{)}940}$

**C.**  $35\overline{\smash{)}630}$  $27\overline{\smash{)}486}$  $28\overline{\smash{)}756}$  $18\overline{\smash{)}828}$

_____ _____ _____ bones

 **How many bones are in a newborn baby's body?**
**Divide to find out: 8,750 ÷ 25 =**

# Let's Go to the Show

 Look at each sample to learn how to finish dividing when there is a zero in the quotient.

Sample 1:

```
      306
8 ) 2448
  − 24↓
     04↓
   −  0↓
      48
    − 48
```

8 x ___ = 4
Since there is no number, record a 0 in the quotient. Subtract and bring down the 8. Continue to divide.

Sample 2:

```
      680
6 ) 4080
  − 36↓
    048↓
   − 48↓
      00
```

Sample 3:

```
       20 R9
44) 889
  − 88↓
     09
   −  0
      9
```

Divide. Then use the code to answer the riddle below.

**S.** 3 ) 1812     **U.** 4 ) 3632     **W.** 18 ) 910     **X.** 25 ) 3250

**G.** 17 ) 356     **B.** 6 ) 1848     **R.** 39 ) 786     **J.** 8 ) 7216

**A.** 7 ) 4207     **E.** 27 ) 562     **Y.** 9 ) 2880     **T.** 9 ) 6345

**What is the name of the movie about frogs in outer space?**

___ ___ ___ ___   ___ ___ ___ ___ ___!
604  705  601  20R6   50R10  601  20R6  705  604

Imagine that you have popped 1,422 pieces of popcorn for you and your 6 friends. How many pieces would each person get?

# MATH

# Comparing & Ordering Numbers

Use the digits in the box to answer each number riddle.
You cannot repeat digits within a number.

**1** I am the number that is 100 greater than 3,362.
*What number am I?* _____

**2** I am the number that is 40 less than the largest number
you can make using five of the digits.
*What number am I?* _____

**3** I am the largest number you can make that is greater than
8,745 but less than 8,750.
*What number am I?* _____

**4** I am the number that is 5,000 greater than the smallest
number you can make using six of the digits.
*What number am I?* _____

**5** I am the smallest number you can make that is greater
than 617,500.
*What number am I?* _____

**6** I am the largest number you can make that is less than
618,400 but greater than 618,300.
*What number am I?* _____

# Sign It!

✏ There are signs with numbers on them almost everywhere you look! They're on street corners and on highways. What if those numbers were written out as words?

Take a look at the street signs below. They all have numbers on them. Each sign has a blank sign next to it. Write the numbers as words on each blank sign. We've done the first one for you.

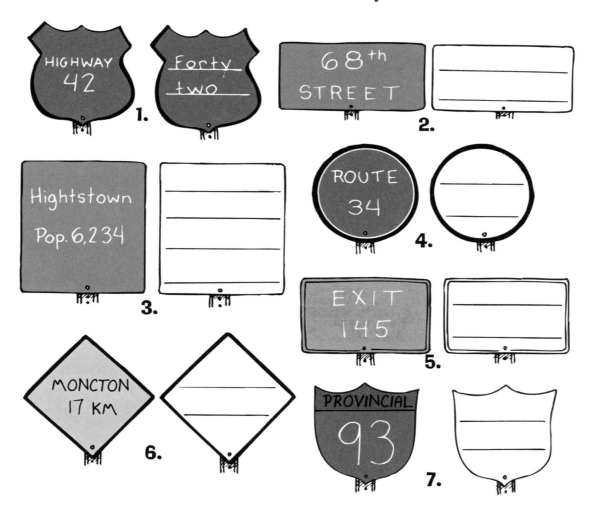

HIGHWAY 42 — Forty two   1.

68th STREET   2.

Hightstown Pop. 6,234   3.

ROUTE 34   4.

EXIT 145   5.

MONCTON 17 KM   6.

PROVINCIAL 93   7.

 **Try writing other numbers as words, such as your address, area code, age, or shoe size.**

# Mystery Number

Use the digits in the box to answer each number riddle. Digits appear only once in an answer. Each answer may not use all digits.

$$2 \quad 4 \quad 9 \quad 6 \quad 7 \quad 3$$

**1** When you subtract a 2-digit number from a 3-digit number, the difference is 473.
*What are the numbers?* _____

**2** The sum of these two numbers is 112.
*What are the numbers?* _____

**3** The sum of these two numbers is 519.
*What are the numbers?* _____

**4** The difference between these two 3-digit numbers is 263.
*What are the numbers?* _____

**5** The sum of these three 2-digit numbers is 184.
*What are the numbers?* _____

**6** The difference between two 3-digit numbers is a palindrome between 200 and 300.
*What are the numbers?* _____

# What Number Am I?

Use the digits in the box to answer each number riddle.
You cannot repeat digits within a number.

1  2  3  4  5  6  7  8  9

**1** I am the largest 4-digit odd number you can make.
*What number am I?* _____

**2** I am the smallest 5-digit even number you can make.
*What number am I?* _____

**3** I am the largest 5-digit even number you can make that has
a 3 in the thousands place.
*What number am I?* _____

**4** I am the smallest 5-digit number you can make that has all
odd digits.
*What number am I?* _____

**5** I am the largest 6-digit number you can make that has a 1
in the thousands place and a 5 in the ten-thousands place.
*What number am I?* _____

**6** I am the smallest 6-digit even number you can make that
has a 6 in the hundreds place.
*What number am I?* _____

# A Place for Every Number

Look at the numbers in 243. Each number in the group has its own "place" and meaning. For instance, the 2 in 243 is in the hundreds place. That stands for 2 hundreds or 200. The 4 is in the tens place, meaning 4 tens or 40. And the 3 is in the ones place, meaning 3 ones or 3.

## DIRECTIONS:

Use a place value chart to put the numbers in this crossnumber puzzle in their places.

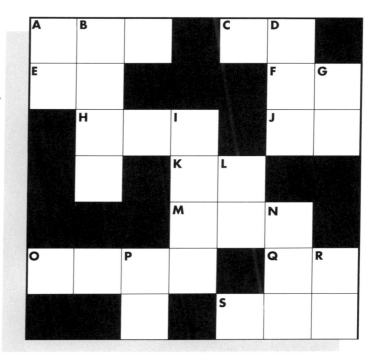

## ACROSS

A. 3 hundreds 2 tens 6 ones
C. 8 tens 1 one
E. 6 tens 4 ones
F. 4 tens 7 ones
H. 5 hundreds 2 tens 6 ones
J. 9 tens 3 ones
K. 8 tens 9 ones
M. 5 hundreds 4 tens 2 ones
O. 2 thousands 8 hundreds 3 tens 1 one
Q. 9 tens 8 ones
S. 6 hundreds 6 tens 4 ones

## DOWN

A. 3 tens 6 ones
B. 2 thousands 4 hundreds 5 tens 7 ones
D. 1 hundred 4 tens 9 ones
G. 7 tens 3 ones
I. 6 thousands 8 hundreds 5 tens 1 one
L. 9 tens 4 ones
N. 2 hundreds 9 tens 6 ones
P. 3 tens 5
R. 8 tens 4 ones

 Make a list of 10 numbers written out in the same way as the clues above. Ask a classmate to write each of those numbers in their own place value box.

# Bee Riddle

## Riddle: What did the farmer get when he tried to reach the beehive?

Round each number. Then use the Decoder to solve the riddle by filling in the spaces at the bottom of the page.

**Decoder**

| | |
|---|---|
| 400 | A |
| 800 | W |
| 30 | O |
| 10 | Y |
| 25 | E |
| 500 | I |
| 210 | J |
| 20 | L |
| 40 | C |
| 700 | U |
| 90 | S |
| 100 | T |
| 600 | G |
| 95 | F |
| 50 | N |
| 550 | V |
| 300 | Z |
| 7 | H |
| 200 | Z |

① Round 7 to the nearest ten _____

② Round 23 to the nearest ten _____

③ Round 46 to the nearest ten _____

④ Round 92 to the nearest ten _____

⑤ Round 203 to the nearest hundred _____

⑥ Round 420 to the nearest hundred _____

⑦ Round 588 to the nearest hundred _____

⑧ Round 312 to the nearest hundred _____

⑨ Round 549 to the nearest hundred _____

⑩ Round 710 to the nearest hundred _____

A "B __ __ __ __ " __ __ __ __ __ __

      10   5   8   1     4   9   7   3   6   2

# When to Estimate

Estimation is a great way to solve many problems.
But some problems need an exact answer. How can you decide?

Read each question below. Think about what kind of answer you need.
Then circle Estimate or Exact Answer.

1. How much sugar do you need to make cookies?    Estimate    Exact Answer

2. How much money could your school play earn?    Estimate    Exact Answer

3. How many plates will you need to serve dinner?    Estimate    Exact Answer

4. How much money will three new tapes cost?    Estimate    Exact Answer

5. How long will it take to get to the airport?    Estimate    Exact Answer

6. How much money is in a bank account?    Estimate    Exact Answer

7. How long would it take you to run a mile?    Estimate    Exact Answer

8. How many kids are in your class?    Estimate    Exact Answer

## How Would You Estimate . . .

On another sheet of paper, write about how you would estimate each of these.

...the height of a tree?

...how long it would take to walk from Miami to Seattle?

...how much water you use in a year?

...the number of gumballs in a gumball machine?

...the number of students in your school?

...how much one million pennies would weigh?

# Super Seven

## How can you make the number seven even?

Find the answer by completing the next step in the pattern. Then use the Decoder to solve the riddle by filling in the blanks at the bottom of the page.

**1** 10, 7, 4, ___

**2** 19, 13, 8, ___

**3** 42, 40, 36, 30, ___

**4** 56, 54, 50, 42, ___

**5** 33, 32, 34, 33, 35, ___

**6** 117, 97, 77, ___

**7** 205, 175, 150, 130, ___

**8** 344, 274, 214, 164, ___

**9** 760, 660, 540, 400, 240, ___

**10** 512, 490, 457, 413, 358, 292, ___

### Decoder

5 ..................... B
1 ..................... A
97 ..................... D
215 ..................... Y
22 ..................... W
124 ..................... H
31 ..................... I
2 ..................... P
115 ..................... A
120 ..................... C
50 ..................... N
4 ..................... E
60 ..................... S
232 ..................... M
26 ..................... T
100 ..................... R
32 ..................... F
57 ..................... E
34 ..................... K

TA __ __  __ __ __ __  __ __ __ " __ ".
   5  2   7  3  1  10   4  8  6    9

# Pansy's Picture Patterns

✏ Pansy Pattern has lots of hobbies. Her favourite hobby, though, is drawing patterns. There's just one problem. Sometimes Pansy forgets to draw the complete pattern. Maybe you can help. Try filling in the missing pieces in the patterns below.

 Draw a picture pattern of your own. Ask a classmate to fill in the missing pictures.

# Root for the Home Team!

## Riddle: What do cheerleaders like to drink?

Use the coordinates to identify points on the graph. Then use the point names to solve the riddle by filling in the blanks at the bottom of the page.

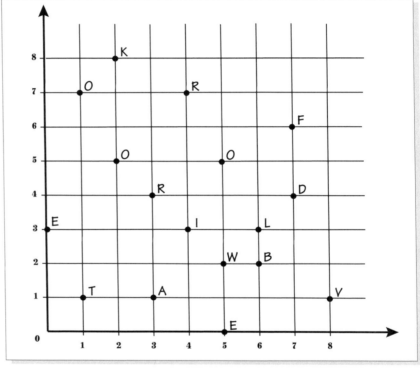

❶ (1,1) _____
❷ (3,4) _____
❸ (4,7) _____
❹ (6,2) _____
❺ (5,5) _____

❻ (2,5) _____
❼ (0,3) _____
❽ (1,7) _____
❾ (7,6) _____
❿ (5,0) _____

**LOTS** __ __ __ __ __ __ __ __ __ __
       5  9  2  6  8  1  4  7  10 3

# Bewitching Math

Solve the problems. Then connect the dot above each problem to the
dot beside its answer. The first line has been drawn for you. Some dots
will not be used.

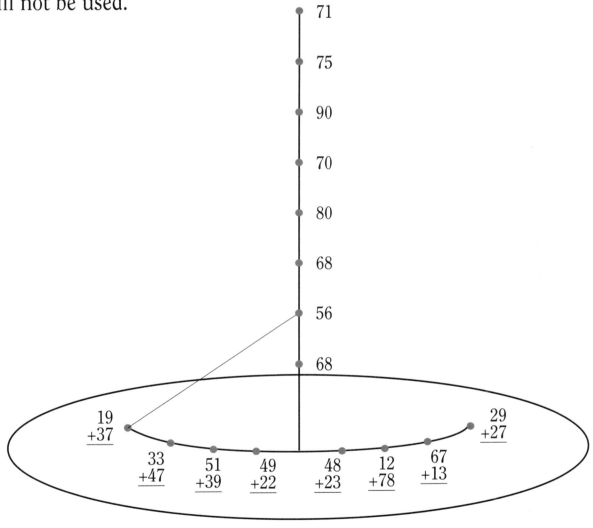

**Taking It Further:** Fill in the missing numbers in the problems below.

a.  $2\square$
   $+27$
   $\overline{50}$

b.  $53$
   $+2\square$
   $\overline{82}$

c.  $56$
   $+1\square$
   $\overline{73}$

d.  $28$
   $+57$
   $\overline{\square\square}$

e.  $43$
   $+\square7$
   $\overline{90}$

f.  $45$
   $+\square\square$
   $\overline{71}$

# Food Fractions

## ACTIVITY GOAL
Identify the fraction represented in each shape to complete a riddle.

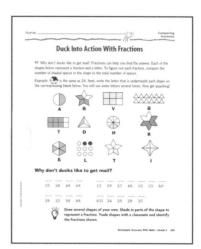

## HELPFUL HINT!
• The **denominator** of each fraction represents the total amount of parts in the shape. The shaded parts represent the **numerator**. A food item can help illustrate this strategy.

## EXAMPLE
There are 8 slices of pie shown here ( /8) the **denominator**. The shaded area represents how many pieces of the pie you can eat (1/ ) the **numerator**. The fraction represented in this picture is 1/8.

## TRY THIS!
Draw a pizza on another piece of paper, then cut out the circle. Cut the pizza into six equal pieces. Using your paper pizza, make the following fractions: 1/2, 2/6, 5/6, 1/3.
Now divide your pizza between you and two imaginary friends. Did you each get the same amount? _____

## MORE SWEET FUN!
Color **1/3** of these **12** pieces of candy. What fraction of the candy is left? _____

Now that you've reviewed fractions, duck into action and name a few fractions to solve the riddle on the following page!

# Duck Into Action With Fractions

✎ Why don't ducks like to get mail? Fractions can help you find the answer. Each of the shapes below represent a fraction and a letter. To figure out each fraction, compare the number of shaded spaces in the shape to the total number of spaces.

Example:  is the same as 2/6. Next, write the letter that is underneath each shape on the corresponding blank below. You will use some letters several times. Now get quacking!

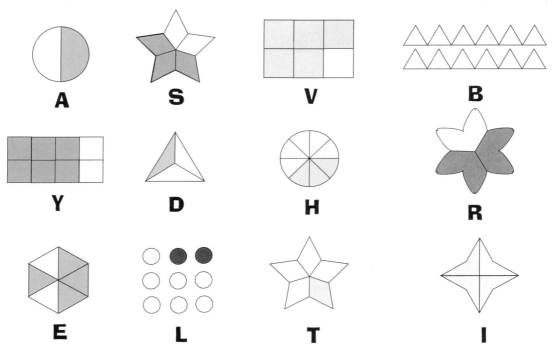

| A | S | V | B |

| Y | D | H | R |

| E | L | T | I |

## Why don't ducks like to get mail?

___ ___ ___ ___    ___ ___ ___ ___ ___ ___ ___
1/5  3/8  4/6  6/8    1/2  2/9  2/3  4/6  1/2  1/3  6/8

___ ___ ___ ___    ___ ___ ___ ___ ___ .
3/8  1/2  5/6  4/6    6/12  3/4  2/9  2/9  3/5

 **Draw several shapes of your own. Shade in parts of the shape to represent a fraction. Trade shapes with a classmate and identify the fractions shown.**

# Into Infinity

Solve the problems. Then rename the answers in lowest terms.

If the answer is $\frac{1}{4}$, $\frac{1}{8}$, or $\frac{1}{16}$, colour the shape purple.

If the answer is $\frac{1}{2}$, $\frac{1}{3}$, or $\frac{1}{7}$, colour the shape blue.

If the answer is $\frac{2}{3}$, $\frac{3}{4}$, or $\frac{7}{8}$, colour the shape green.

If the answer is $\frac{3}{5}$, $\frac{4}{5}$, or $\frac{5}{7}$, colour the shape yellow.

If the answer is $\frac{9}{10}$ or $\frac{11}{12}$, colour the shape red.

Finish the design by colouring the other shapes with colours of your choice.

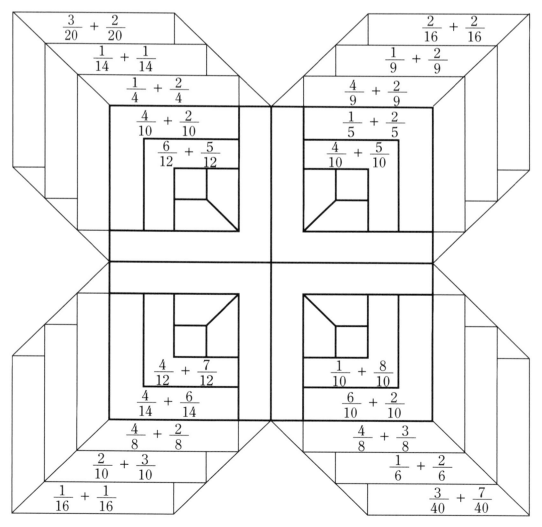

# Trefoil

Solve the problems. ◆ Rename the answers in lowest terms. ◆ If the answer is $\frac{1}{2}$ or greater, colour the shape red. ◆ If the answer is less than $\frac{1}{2}$, colour the shape blue. ◆ Finish the design by colouring the other shapes with the colours of your choice.

# White Socks, Black Socks

**Figure it out!**

**1.** Rowena Pig is wearing 1 white sock and 1 black sock. What fraction of the socks she's wearing is white? What fraction is black?

_____

**2.** Rowena puts 7 socks in the washing machine. Four of them are black and 3 are white. What fraction of the socks is black? What fraction is white?

_____

**3.** Rowena hangs 8 socks out to dry. Two of the socks are black and 6 are white. What fraction is black? Write your answer in simplest form.

_____

**4.** Judy Frog brings 6 socks on a trip. One third of the socks are red. The rest are green. How many socks are red? How many are green?

_____

**5.** Six out of 10 socks are blue. The rest are red. What fraction of the socks is red? Write your answer in simplest form.

_____

SUPER CHALLENGE: Judy has 12 socks. One third of them are white. One fourth of them are red. The rest are yellow. How many socks are yellow? How many socks are white and red?

# Decimals Around the Diamond

Baseball fans always argue who the best player was. Some say it was Ken Griffey, Jr. Others insist it was Cal Ripkin, Jr. Still others claim it was Barry Bonds. Everybody seems to have a favourite!

When it comes to finding the best hitter, though, no one can argue with batting averages. The batting average shows how often a baseball player gets a hit. It is a 3-digit decimal number, and looks like this: .328, .287, .311, .253. The larger the batting average is, the better the hitter is.

Decimals are numbers between 0 and 1. They are written to the right of the ones place. Decimals always have a decimal point to the left of them.

| decimal point | tenths place | hundredths place | thousandths place |

| Rank | Player (Team) | 1995 Batting Average |
|------|---------------|----------------------|
|  | Cal Ripken, Jr. (Baltimore Orioles) | .262 |
|  | Barry Bonds (San Francisco Giants) | .294 |
|  | Mo Vaughn (Boston Red Sox) | .300 |
|  | Barry Larkin (Cincinnati Reds) | .319 |
|  | Kirby Puckett (Minnesota Twins) | .314 |
|  | Tony Gwynn (San Diego Padres) | .368 |
|  | Ken Griffey, Jr. (Seattle Mariners) | .258 |
|  | Mike Piazza (Los Angeles Dodgers) | .346 |
|  | Frank Thomas (Chicago White Sox) | .308 |
|  | David Justice (Atlanta Braves) | .253 |

## What to Do:

Read the chart of baseball players' batting averages from 1995. Rank the batting averages. This means number the batting averages in order from highest to lowest. (See Home Plate for help.) Write the numbers 1 to 10 in the boxes next to the names—1 for the highest average, 10 for the lowest. Ready? Play ball!

### HOME PLATE

To rank decimal numbers:
- Start at the left.
- Compare the digits in the same place.
- Find the first place where the digits are different.
- The number with the smaller digit is the smaller number. Example: Rank .317 and .312

.317
⇕ ⇕ ⇕
.312

So .312 is smaller than .317.

# Across-and-Down Decimals

Complete the crossnumber puzzle as if it were a crossword puzzle. Give each digit and decimal point its own square. Remember to align the decimal points and add any necessary zeros, then proceed as if you were adding whole numbers.

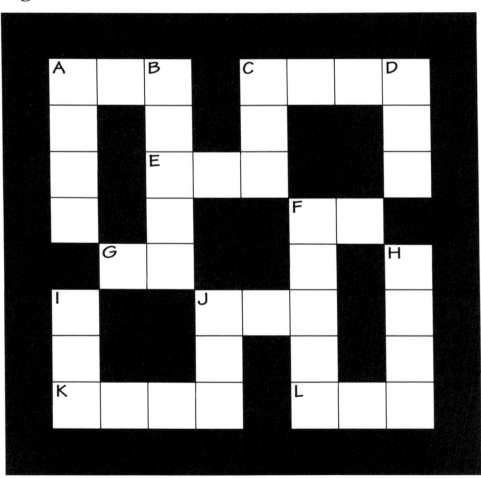

ACROSS

| | |
|---|---|
| A. | 1.3 + 2.4 |
| C. | 2.2 + 2.18 |
| E. | .3 + .25 |
| F. | .3 + .3 |
| G. | .56 + .34 |
| J. | .4 + .17 |
| K. | 6.93 + .23 |
| L. | 1.18 + 3.12 |

DOWN

| | |
|---|---|
| A. | 1.44 + 1.7 |
| B. | 23.11 + 53.18 |
| C. | 2.25 + 2.25 |
| D. | 6.5 + 1.6 |
| F. | .1604 + .11 |
| H. | 20.8 + 3.5 |
| I. | 1.367 + .333 |
| J. | .2 + .16 |

# Change Arranger

When you make change, always start with the price. Count on from the price. Start with the coins that have the least value. Write the change from these purchases.

1. LAWN GAME

AMOUNT GIVEN $5.00
PRICE 3.45

CHANGE $ _____

2. YO-YO

AMOUNT GIVEN $3.00
PRICE 2.77

CHANGE $ _____

3. BIKE HELMET

AMOUNT GIVEN $10.00
PRICE 7.55

CHANGE $ _____

4. SOAP BUBBLES

AMOUNT GIVEN $2.00
PRICE 1.52

CHANGE $ _____

5. VIDEO GAME

AMOUNT GIVEN $20.00
PRICE 7.30

CHANGE $ _____

6. ACTION TOY

AMOUNT GIVEN $10.00
PRICE 6.49

CHANGE $ _____

7. SUNGLASSES

AMOUNT GIVEN $4.00
PRICE 3.68

CHANGE $ _____

8. BACKPACK

AMOUNT GIVEN $20.00
PRICE 9.35

CHANGE $ _____

9. JUMP ROPE

AMOUNT GIVEN $4.00
PRICE 3.17

CHANGE $ _____

10. MARKERS

AMOUNT GIVEN $5.00
PRICE 2.43

CHANGE $ _____

# Money Magic Puzzle

Round your answers to the nearest dollar. Circle the correct amount, then fill in the puzzle.

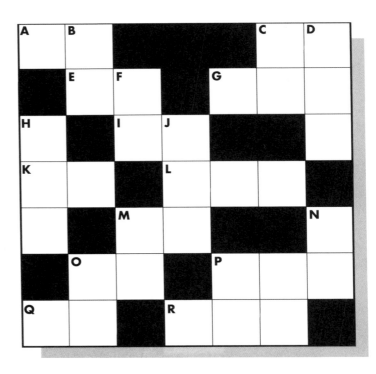

## ACROSS:

| | | | |
|---|---|---|---|
| A. | $16.98 + $18.99 | $36 | $26 |
| C. | $24.85 + $29.99 | $65 | $55 |
| E. | $21.99 + $8.95 | $31 | $41 |
| G. | $218.04 + $67.90 | $286 | $386 |
| I. | $53.75 + $40.98 | $105 | $95 |
| K. | $7.99 + $19.70 | $28 | $22 |
| L. | $99.98 + 99.57 | $300 | $200 |
| M. | $65.75 + $20.90 | $87 | $97 |
| O. | $9.69 + $32.99 | $40 | $43 |
| P. | $588.95 + $14.90 | $704 | $604 |
| Q. | $3.75 + $9.99 | $13 | $14 |
| R. | $428.70 + $50.90 | $480 | $520 |

## DOWN:

| | | | |
|---|---|---|---|
| B. | $28.59 + $33.95 | $69 | $63 |
| C. | $39.25 + $18.70 | $58 | $42 |
| D. | $376.35 + $184.50 | $521 | $561 |
| F. | $7.28 + $11.69 | $19 | $16 |
| H. | $199.80 + $224.99 | $525 | $425 |
| J. | $399.95 + $126.99 | $527 | $566 |
| M. | $5.85 + $76.95 | $83 | $75 |
| N. | $39.80 + $13.99 | $54 | $62 |
| O. | $26.98 + $16.89 | $44 | $49 |
| P. | $48.95 + $18.99 | $68 | $66 |

# Time for Play

✐ The dogs in the neighbourhood play in the park at the same time every day. Today, some are running around trees and others are playing catch with their owners. But most of them are busy doing something else—chasing another dog! What time were they chasing the dog? Equivalent measurements can help you find the answer.

## DIRECTIONS:

- There are two answers next to each question. Circle the letter after the correct answer.
- When you've finished, write each circled letter in the blanks below the riddle. Be sure to write the letters in order.

| | | | | | |
|---|---|---|---|---|---|
| 1. | How many weeks are in a year? | 34 | **L** | 52 | **T** |
| 2. | How many inches are in a foot? | 12 | **W** | 36 | **A** |
| 3. | How many centimetres are in a metre? | 100 | **E** | 1000 | **O** |
| 4. | How many nickels are in a dollar? | 40 | **M** | 20 | **N** |
| 5. | How many days are in a year? | 365 | **T** | 245 | **S** |
| 6. | How many inches are in a yard? | 36 | **Y** | 24 | **B** |
| 7. | How many ounces are in a pound? | 16 | **A** | 12 | **I** |
| 8. | How many hours are in a day? | 48 | **C** | 24 | **F** |
| 9. | How many years are in a decade? | 50 | **H** | 10 | **T** |
| 10. | How many cups are in a pint? | 2 | **E** | 4 | **U** |
| 11. | How many quarts are in a gallon? | 4 | **R** | 8 | **D** |
| 12. | How many feet are in a mile? | 5,280 | **O** | 2,160 | **G** |
| 13. | How many seconds are in a minute? | 30 | **J** | 60 | **N** |
| 14. | How many millimetres are in a metre? | 1,000 | **E** | 1500 | **P** |

## What time is it when twenty dogs run after one dog?

___ ___ ___ ___ ___ ___  ___ ___ ___ ___ ___ ___  ___ ___ ___

**Come up with an equivalent measurement problem of your own.**

# Measure by Measure

✐ Josie is surrounded by all kinds of measuring tools. But she's not sure which tool does what! Sure, she knows that a ruler measures the length of something. But she doesn't realize that all the other tools around her are used for measuring things too. Try giving Josie a hand.

**JOSIE'S TOOL BOX**

Yardstick • Thermometer
Measuring tape • Clock
Measuring cup • Ruler
Scale • Teaspoon

## DIRECTIONS:

Take a look at the list of measuring tools in Josie's Tool Box. Use the list to answer the questions below.

**1.** What tool could Josie use to measure the weight of a pumpkin? _____

**2.** What tool could Josie use to measure the width of her math book?

_____

**3.** Josie plans to watch one of her favourite television shows. What tool could help her measure the length of each commercial that appears during that show?

_____

**4.** Josie has an awful cough. What tool could she use to measure the amount of cough syrup she should take? _____

**5.** If Josie's mom wants to find out Josie's temperature, which tool could she use?

_____

**6.** Say Josie wanted to make a cake. What tool could she use to measure the milk she needs to put in the cake mix? _____

**7.** What tool could Josie use to measure the height of her brother's tree house?

_____

**8.** What tool could Josie give her dad to measure the length of their living room?

_____

 **Choose four of the measuring tools in Josie's Tool Box. Make a list of things you could measure with each of those tools.**

# Picnic Area

## What to Do:

Area measures the number of square units inside a shape. Find the area of each ant family's picnic blanket by counting the number of squares on the blanket. Then answer the following questions.

Remember—area is measured in square units, such as square centimetres. My blanket's area is four square units.

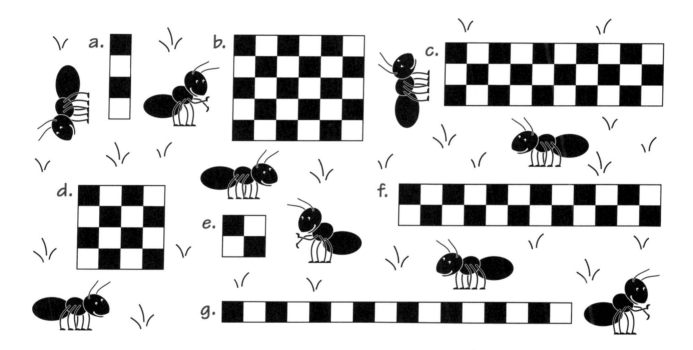

1. Which pairs of blankets have the same area?

   _____ and _____

   _____ and _____

   _____ and _____

2. Which two blankets can you put together to make a rectangle with an area of 20?

   _____

3. Which three blankets can you put together to make a rectangle with an area of 50?

   _____

4. What is the total area of all of the ants' blankets?

   _____

# Perimeter and Area Zoo

A shape doesn't have to be a square or a rectangle to have perimeter and area. The animals in this zoo are different shapes. Can you find each animal's perimeter and area?

**Remember:** To find perimeter, count the sides of the units. To find area, count the number of whole units.

1. Perimeter_____

   Area _____

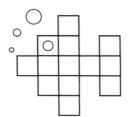

2. Perimeter _____

   Area _____

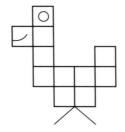

3. Perimeter _____

   Area _____

4. Perimeter _____

   Area _____

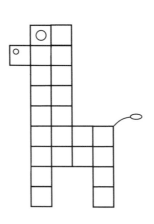

5. Perimeter _____

   Area _____

6. Perimeter_____

   Area _____

# Angles from A to Z

Angles are hiding everywhere—even in the words you're reading now. When two straight lines meet, they make an angle. There are three kinds of angles:

- The corner of a square or rectangle makes a right angle.

- Angles that are smaller than right angles are called acute angles.

- Angles that are larger than right angles are called obtuse angles.

Take a look at the letters below. Circle each angle you see in the letters. Tell whether it is right, acute, or obtuse.

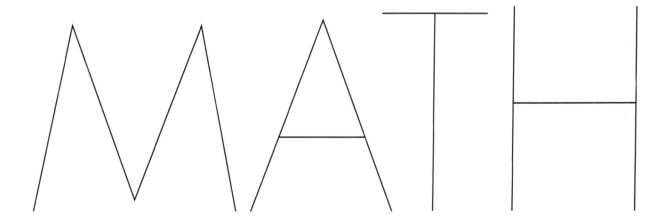

# Flying Through the Air

## What is the last thing that the trapeze flier wants to be?

Find the symmetrical shapes. Then use the Decoder to solve the riddle by filling in the blanks at the bottom of the page.

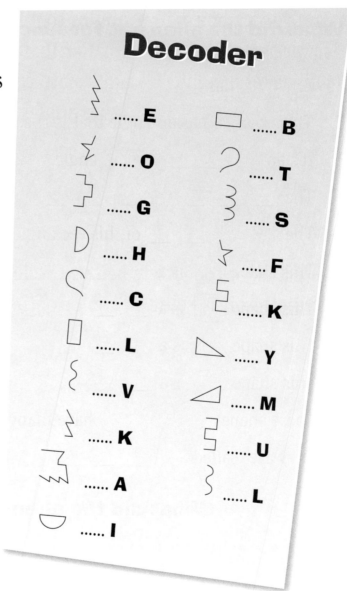

**Decoder**

❶ ▢ _____

❷ ◹ _____

❸ ◖ _____

❹ ☆ _____

❺ ⊏ _____

❻ ⊂ _____

❼ ⌇ _____

❽ ⊐ _____

❾ ⌇ _____

❿ ⌐ _____

____ ____ ____   ____ ____ ____ ____   ____ ____ ____
 6    3    9      4   10   1    7       5    8    2

# Shape Up!

✍ How well do you know geometric shapes? Here's your chance to test yourself. Take a look at the shape in each statement. Fill in the blank spaces with the correct answers. When you're done, write the letters in the shaded squares on the spaces provided to solve the riddle.

## What did the alien eat for lunch?

1. An ⬡ has __ ▨ __ __ ▨ sides.

2. This triangle has an angle that is the opposite of obtuse.

   It's an ▨ __ __ ▨ angle. ◿

3. The __ __ __ ▨ __ __ __ __ __ of this rectangle is fourteen.

4. The ▨ ▨ __ __ of this rectangle is twelve. ³[⎯⁴] ³[⎯⁴]

5. This shape ☐ is a ▨ __ __ __ __ __.

6. This shape ⬓ is a __ __ ▨ __.

7. This shape △ is a __ __ __ ▨ __ __ __ __.

8. This shape ◯ is a __ __ ▨ __ __ __.

9. These shapes ⬡⬠⬡ have many sides.

   They are called __ __ __ __ __ __ __ ▨.

## What did the alien eat for lunch?

__ __ __ __ __ __ __ __ __ __ __ __ __ __ __.

**Draw a geometric shape not included in this activity on a piece of paper. Give it to a friend. See if he or she can name the shape.**

# Terrific Tessellations

## What do math and art have in common? Everything—if you're making tessellations!

A **tessellation** (tess-uh-LAY-shun) is a design made of shapes that fit together like puzzle pieces. People use tessellations to decorate walls and floors, and even works of art.

This sidewalk is formed from rectangles.

Hexagons form this beehive.

Here is a tessellation made from more than one shape.

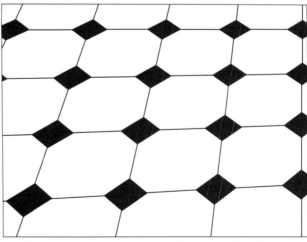

Squares and octagons form a tile floor.

# Terrific Tessellations

## You Need:
heavy paper ◆ scissors
tape ◆ crayons

## What to Do:
Here's how you can make your own tessellation.

1. Start with a simple shape like a square. (Cut your shape from the heavy paper). Cut a piece out of side A . . .

2. . . . and slide it over to side B. Make sure it lines up evenly with the cut out side, or your tessellation won't work. Tape it in place on side B.

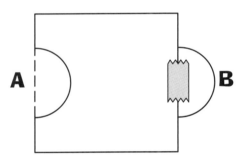

3. If you like, do the same thing with sides C and D. Now you have a new shape.

4. Trace your new shape on paper. Then slide the shape so it fits together with the one you just traced. Trace it again. Keep on sliding and tracing until your page is filled. Decorate your tessellation.

# Kaleidoscope of Flowers

If the number has a 5 in the ones place, colour the shape green.
If the number has a 5 in the tenths place, colour the shape pink.
If the number has a 5 in the hundredths place, colour the shape yellow.
Finish the design by colouring the other shapes with colours of your choice.

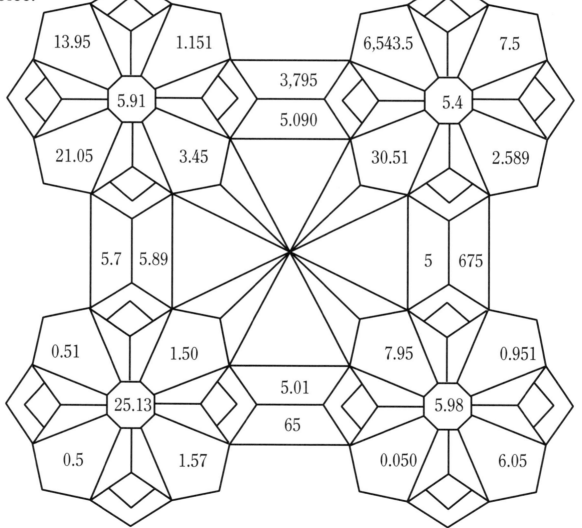

Taking It Further: Place the following decimals in the correct places on the lines below
the dots: 4.9, 1.7, 2.5, and 0.2.

# Scholastic Success With

# MAPS

# What Is a Map?

A map is a flat drawing of a part or all of Earth. A map shows a place from above much as a picture taken high in the sky or from space does. In fact, mapmakers study aerial photographs to help them make more accurate maps.

**S**ince a map shows a large area in a small space, mapmakers use **symbols** to stand for buildings, roads, cities, and other things. A symbol is a drawing or colour that represents something else. You can find out what each symbol means by checking the map key or legend.

map reader's **Tip**

Another word for mapmaker is cartographer. This word comes from the Latin word *carta*, which means "paper" and the Greek word *graphia*, which means "to write."

Study the map key for the map on page 353. Then answer the questions.

**1.** This symbol ------- stands for _____ .

**2.** The capital of Wyoming is _____ .

**3.** Las Vegas is a city in _____ .

**4.** Two states that share a border with Canada are _____ and _____ .

**5.** Boise is the capital of _____ .

**U.S. Mountain States**

**Compass Rose**

**A** map also has a symbol called a **compass rose** that shows directions. The four main directions are north, south, east, and west. These are called the **cardinal directions**. A compass rose might show **intermediate directions** too. They are northeast, southeast, southwest, and northwest. Often, abbreviations are used to show the directions on a compass rose.

Use the compass rose to answer these questions.

**6.** The direction between east and south is _____ .

**7.** The letters NW stand for _____ .

**8.** Colorado is _____ of Idaho.

**9.** Montana is _____ of Wyoming.

**10.** A plane travelling from the capital of Idaho to the capital of Nevada would go in a _____ direction. Draw its route on the map.

# Globes and Hemispheres

As you know, Earth is a large, round planet. To see all of Earth, you would have to orbit it in a spacecraft! An easier way to see Earth is to look at a small model called a globe.

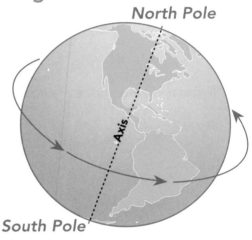

**A** globe shows Earth's four oceans and seven continents. A globe also shows how Earth turns on an imaginary centre line called an **axis**. At the ends of this line are the North and South poles. Pole means "end." These poles help you find directions on Earth. North is toward the North Pole, and south is toward the South Pole.

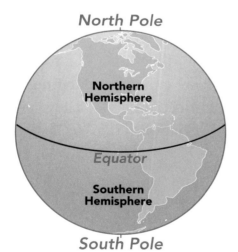

**A**nother imaginary line on a globe is called the **equator**. The equator runs around the centre of Earth and divides it into two halves called **hemispheres**. The northern half is called the Northern Hemisphere, and the southern half is called the Southern Hemisphere.

**S**till another imaginary line divides Earth into the Eastern and Western hemispheres. This line is called the **Prime Meridian**. This line runs from the North Pole to the South Pole.

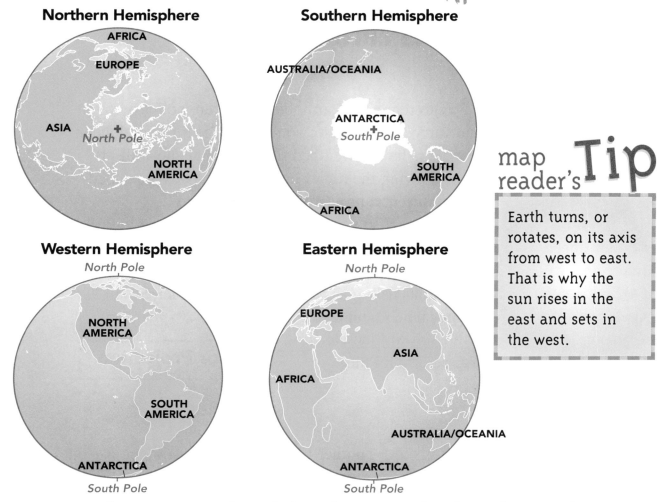

**Northern Hemisphere**

AFRICA
EUROPE
ASIA
North Pole
NORTH AMERICA

**Southern Hemisphere**

AUSTRALIA/OCEANIA
ANTARCTICA
South Pole
SOUTH AMERICA
AFRICA

**Western Hemisphere**

North Pole
NORTH AMERICA
SOUTH AMERICA
ANTARCTICA
South Pole

**Eastern Hemisphere**

North Pole
EUROPE
ASIA
AFRICA
AUSTRALIA/OCEANIA
ANTARCTICA
South Pole

map reader's **Tip**

Earth turns, or rotates, on its axis from west to east. That is why the sun rises in the east and sets in the west.

Here are four views of a globe showing the four hemispheres. Use the pictures on these pages to answer these questions.

1. How many hemispheres does Earth have? _____

2. What is the hemisphere nearest the South Pole? _____

3. What line divides the Eastern and Western hemispheres? _____

4. In which direction is the North Pole from the equator? _____

5. What line divides the Northern and Southern hemispheres? _____

6. What is Earth's axis? _____

7. Name one continent in the Northern Hemisphere. _____

8. Name one continent in the Eastern Hemisphere. _____

# Map Projections

A globe is the best way to represent Earth, but globes are not easy to put in your pocket and carry around. Also, you cannot see all of a globe at one time. So mapmakers have developed flat maps that show all of Earth. The different ways of drawing the round Earth on flat maps are called **projections**. You can see two different projections on these pages.

No flat map can show Earth perfectly. Look at the Mercator projection. It was developed in 1569 by Gerardus Mercator. A Mercator map shows the true shapes of Earth's land, but it distorts sizes, especially near the poles. On a Mercator map, Greenland looks as big as South America. In fact, South America is eight times bigger than Greenland!

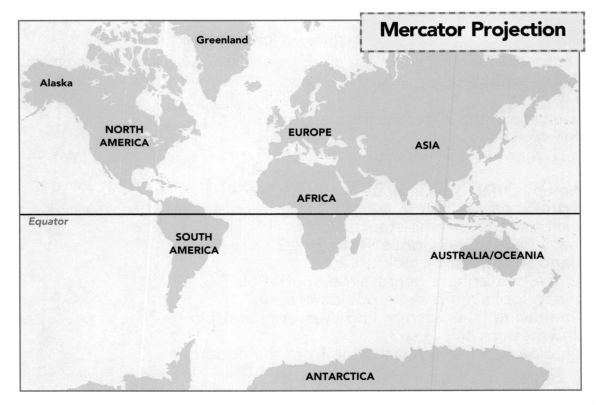

**Mercator Projection**

Greenland

Alaska

NORTH AMERICA

EUROPE

ASIA

AFRICA

Equator

SOUTH AMERICA

AUSTRALIA/OCEANIA

ANTARCTICA

map reader's **Tip**    Other types of projections on world maps include **Mollweide**, **Polar**, and **Interrupted** projections.

The map above shows the Robinson projection. It is used by many geographers today. The land sizes are more accurate on this map, but the shapes get distorted near the outer edges. Compare the shape of Alaska on the two maps. Use the maps to answer the questions.

1. How is a world map different from a globe? _____

2. On which map does Antarctica look bigger? _____

3. Which map is more like a globe? _____

4. On which map does the distance from

   Greenland to Antarctica look greater? _____

5. Which map looks more like a peeled orange? _____

   Why do you think this is so? _____

---

**word scramble** | There are five types of map projections named in this lesson. Can you unscramble them?

**LAROP**      **RATROMEC**      **PETDURNITRE**      **ILEMDEWLO**      **BOSNIRON**

_____      _____      _____      _____      _____

# Using a Map Grid and Index

## Washington, D.C.

sometimes mapmakers place a pattern of lines called a **grid** over a map. The squares formed by the grid are marked with letters and numbers. On this map the letters run across the top; the numbers run down the side. The first square in the top left corner of the map is A1. Can you find it? What is the name of the square immediately to the right of A1?

## Use the map to answer these questions.

1. What landmark is in D3? _____

2. In which grid square is the White House? _____

3. What avenue runs from A1 to C2? _____

4. In which grid squares is Pennsylvania Avenue? _____

5. What body of water do you see in A2? _____

map reader's **Tip**

## Index

| | |
|---|---|
| Arlington Memorial Bridge | A3 |
| The Ellipse | D2 |
| Kennedy Center | A2 |
| Lincoln Memorial | B3 |
| Museum of American History | E2 |
| Reflecting Pool | B3, C3 |
| State Department | B2 |
| Vietnam Veterans Memorial | B2 |
| Washington Monument | D3 |
| White House | D1 |

The D.C. in the city's name stands for District of Columbia. Washington, D.C., is not part of a state, but rather a "federal district." A mayor and city council make laws, but the U.S. Congress has final authority over Washington, D.C.'s government.

Suppose you are visiting the United States and want to see some of the sights in Washington, D.C. A **map index** can help you locate different places. A map index is an alphabetical listing of place names on a map. This index gives the grid square or squares for each place.

## Use the index to answer these questions.

**6.** You are at the Museum of American History.

What is your grid location? _____

**7.** In which square would you look for the State Department? _____

**8.** What place is listed after the Reflecting Pool on the index? _____

**9.** What is the grid location of the Lincoln Memorial? _____

**10.** You are going to a concert at the Kennedy Center.

Where can you find it on the map? _____

# Understanding Latitude

You know that the equator is an imaginary line that runs around the middle of Earth. Mapmakers create other imaginary lines on globes and maps as well. Look at the lines on this globe. These lines run parallel to the equator and are called parallels or lines of **latitude**. You can use lines of latitude to measure places north and south of the equator.

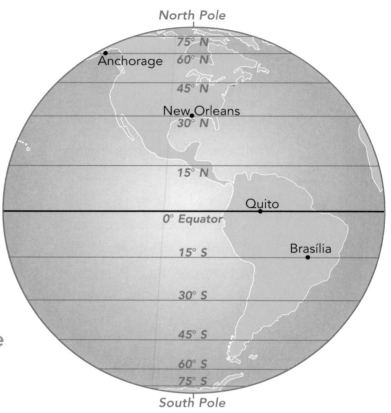

L ines of latitude are measured in degrees, shown by the symbol °. For example, the equator is 0°. Parallels north of the equator are marked in degrees north (N), and parallels south of the equator are marked in degrees south (S). The North Pole is at 90° north and the South Pole is at 90° south. Use the map to answer these questions.

1. Find the 60°N latitude line. What city is located there? _____

2. At what degree of latitude is New Orleans? _____

3. Look at the Southern Hemisphere. What city is at 15°S? _____

4. Quito, a city in Ecuador, is at 0°.
   What is another name for this line of latitude? _____

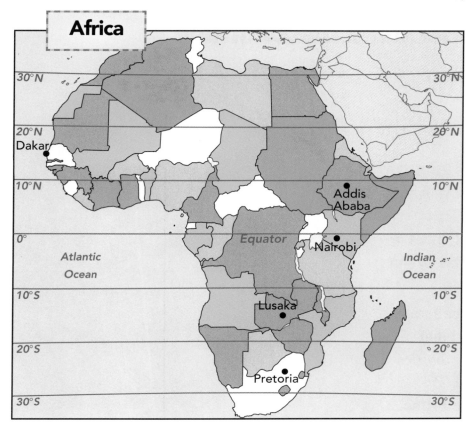

Africa

30°N                     30°N
20°N                     20°N
Dakar
10°N          Addis      10°N
              Ababa
0°      Equator          0°
Atlantic      Nairobi
              Indian
Ocean         Ocean
10°S                     10°S
      Lusaka
20°S                     20°S
      Pretoria
30°S                     30°S

map
reader's **Tip**

The distance
between two
parallels that are
one degree apart is
about III kilometres
or 69 miles. This
distance varies
slightly because
the Earth is not a
perfect sphere.

**M**ost maps do not show every line of latitude. Look at the globe on page 360 again. It shows the lines of latitude for every 15 degrees. How many degrees apart are the lines of latitude on this map of Africa?

5. What city is almost on the equator? _____

6. Find the line of latitude marked 10°N.
   What city is located near this parallel? _____

7. Is Dakar in the northern or southern latitudes? _____

8. Find a city at about 15°S. About how many
   degrees north of Pretoria is it? _____

9. Most of Africa is between _____ and _____ lines of latitude.

10. All in all, Africa covers about _____ degrees of latitude.

# Understanding Longitude

You know that lines of latitude measure the distance north and south on a globe. Lines of **longitude** measure Earth in degrees from east to west.

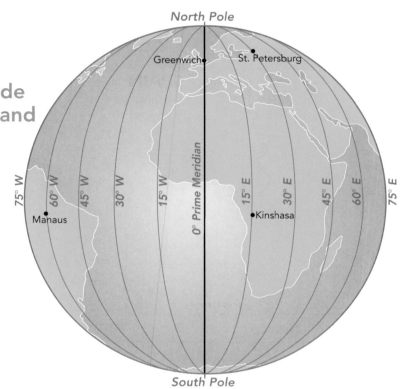

These lines are also called meridians. You read that the Prime Meridian divides Earth into the Eastern and Western hemispheres. The Prime Meridian is 0°. From the Prime Meridian to 180° longitude is exactly halfway around Earth.

1. In which direction do lines of longitude run? _____

2. Find the 15°W longitude line. What does the W stand for? _____

3. Find the 60°W longitude line. What city is located there? _____

4. At what degree of longitude is St. Petersburg? _____

5. Find a city in Africa at 15°E longitude. _____

6. Greenwich, a city in England, is at 0°.

   What is another name for this line of longitude? _____

7. Why can't you see 90° W longitude on this globe? _____

8. Most of Africa is between _____ and _____ lines of longitude.

**map reader's Tip**

Unlike latitude, lines of longitude are not all the same distance apart from each other. They are farthest apart at the equator. At the North and South poles, they all come together.

**M**ost maps do not show every line of longitude. The globe on page 362 shows the lines of longitude for every 15 degrees. How many degrees apart are the lines of longitude on this map of Spain?

**Write True or False before each statement.**

_____ **9.** Spain is entirely in the west longitudes.

_____ **10.** The Prime Meridian runs through Spain.

_____ **11.** Madrid is at about 4°W longitude.

_____ **12.** Spain covers less than 20 degrees of longitude.

**word search**

Find the following words from this lesson: **meridian, longitude, north, south, east, west, earth.**

```
L  H  E  T  M  J  J  O  Z
F  C  S  E  E  A  R  T  H
V  I  O  U  R  T  S  A  E
E  D  U  T  I  G  N  O  L
J  N  T  X  D  B  E  Z  Q
U  E  H  D  I  C  S  A  N
F  K  R  S  A  W  E  S  T
H  T  R  O  N  I  X  P  O
```

# Using a Map Scale

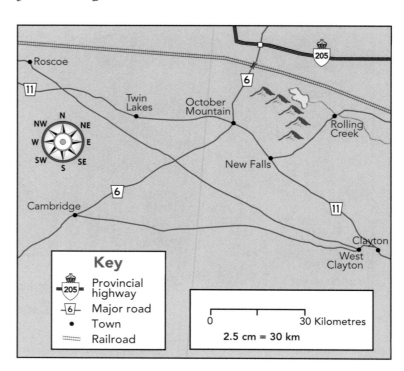

When you are travelling, it is useful to know how far you have to go. To show distances accurately on a map, mapmakers use a **scale**. A map scale helps you measure distance on a map. Look at the scale on this map. It shows that 2.5 centimetres equals thirty kilometres. That means that 2.5 centimetres on the map stands for thirty kilometres on Earth.

Use a ruler to measure distances on the map.
Circle the correct answers.

**1.** From Twin Lakes to October Mountain, it is about _____ .

    a. 30 kilometres      b. 60 kilometres      c. 80 kilometres

**2.** Between Clayton and New Falls there are _____ .

    a. 30 kilometres      b. 50 kilometres      c. 60 kilometres

**3.** The distance from Cambridge to West Clayton is _____ .

    a. 30 kilometres      b. 90 kilometres      c. 120 kilometres

**4.** The distance between Roscoe and West Clayton is less than _____ .

    a. 160 kilometres      b. 30 kilometres      c. 90 kilometres

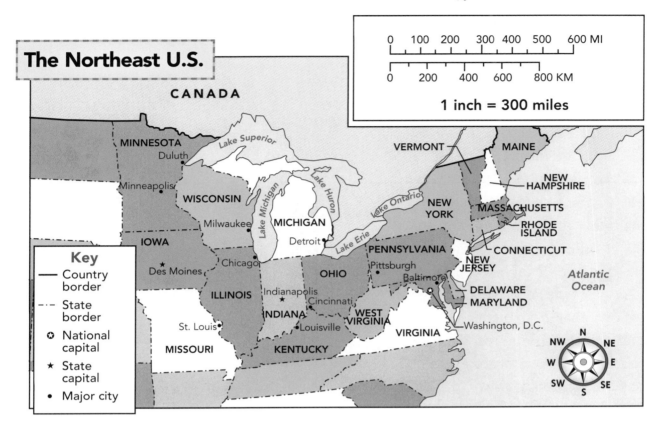

**The Northeast U.S.**

0  100  200  300  400  500  600 MI

0  200  400  600  800 KM

**1 inch = 300 miles**

CANADA

MINNESOTA
Duluth
Minneapolis
WISCONSIN
Milwaukee
IOWA
Des Moines
Chicago
ILLINOIS
Indianapolis
INDIANA
St. Louis
MISSOURI
Louisville
KENTUCKY

Lake Superior
Lake Michigan
Lake Huron
MICHIGAN
Detroit
Lake Erie
OHIO
Cincinnati
WEST VIRGINIA
VIRGINIA

Lake Ontario
VERMONT
NEW YORK
PENNSYLVANIA
Pittsburgh
Baltimore
DELAWARE
MARYLAND
Washington, D.C.

MAINE
NEW HAMPSHIRE
MASSACHUSETTS
RHODE ISLAND
CONNECTICUT
NEW JERSEY

Atlantic Ocean

**Key**
— Country border
-·- State border
✪ National capital
★ State capital
• Major city

N  NE
NW
W   E
SW  SE
S

A map scale usually shows distance in both miles and kilometres. A kilometre is a measurement in the metric system. A mile is a longer distance than a kilometre. On this map scale you can see that 300 miles is a longer distance than 400 kilometres. Notice that the abbreviation for miles is MI and the abbreviation for kilometres is KM. Use the map to answer these questions.

5. How many miles does one inch represent on this map? _____

6. How many miles is it from St. Louis to Cincinnati? _____
   About how many kilometres is this? _____

7. About how many miles is it from Milwaukee to Pittsburgh? _____

8. How many kilometres is it between
   Minneapolis and Des Moines? _____

9. About how many kilometres is it from
   Indianapolis to Washington, D.C.? _____

# Comparing Maps and Scales

Not all maps have the same scale. The maps on this page show the same place, but they have different scales.

Use the map to answer these questions.

1. What does 2.5 centimetres stand for on the Map A scale? _____

2. How many kilometres does 2.5 centimetres stand for on Map B? _____

3. How long is Hall Road on Map A? _____

   How long is it on Map B? _____

4. Which map shows a smaller area? _____

5. Which map shows a larger area? _____

6. Which map would be more useful for getting from the provincial

   highway to Jeb's house? _____

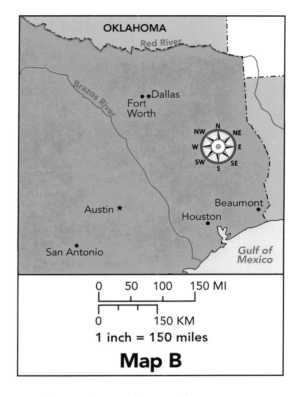

The maps on this page are the same size, but they show areas of different sizes. One map shows the whole state of Texas. The other map shows just the eastern part of the state.

Use the maps to answer the questions.

7. How many miles does one inch stand for on each map? _____

8. Why isn't El Paso on Map B? _____

9. Name two cities on Map B that are not shown on Map A. _____

10. About how many miles is it between El Paso and Lubbock? _____

11. Which map would you use if you were driving all the way across the state of Texas? _____

# A Vegetation Map

The different kinds of trees and plants that grow in an area are called vegetation. This map shows **vegetation** on the continent of Africa.

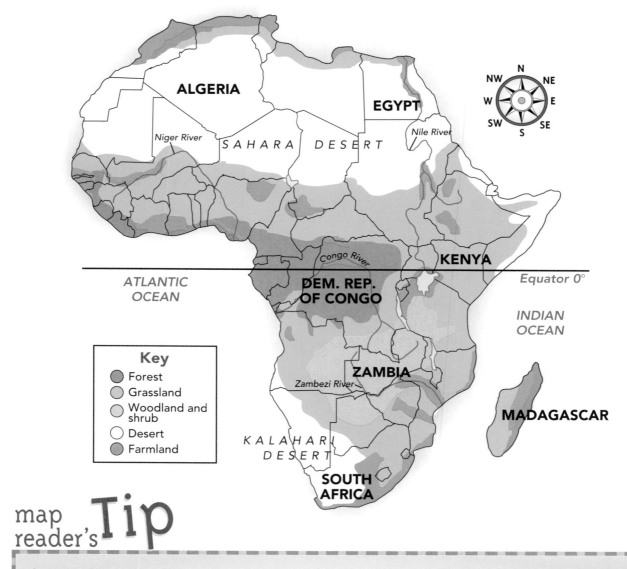

map reader's **Tip**

The cacao tree is one special kind of vegetation that grows in the West African countries of Ghana, Ivory Coast, and Nigeria. The seeds from these trees produce most of the world's chocolate.

**Use the map to answer these questions.**

1. What does this symbol ( ) stand for? _____

2. Deserts cover two-fifths of Africa.

   In what part of Africa do you find the largest desert? _____

3. Would you expect the population in Africa's desert regions to be large

   or small? Why? _____

4. Grasslands also cover much of Africa.

   What is the symbol for this vegetation on the map? _____

5. How would you describe the vegetation in Zambia? _____

6. Name two African nations that are mostly desert. _____

## Crossword Puzzle

Use the map to complete this puzzle.

**Across**

3. desert in southern Africa

4. land where crops are grown

5. a river that runs through large forests

6. a country with farmland and desert

**Down**

1. land that is very dry

2. a river that flows through a desert

3. a country in the east that is almost all grassland

4. land along the Congo River

# Looking at Landforms

As you know, Earth's surface has both land and water. The pictures on this page show some of the landforms found on Earth. Read each of these descriptions. Then write the name of the correct landform on each line under the picture.

**1.** _____

A **canyon** is a deep, narrow valley with high, steep sides.

A **mountain** is high, steep, rugged land that rises sharply from the surrounding area.

A **hill** is an area of raised land that is lower and more rounded than a mountain.

A **plain** is a broad area of open, flat land.

A **plateau** is a large area of high, flat land.

A **valley** is the land that lies between hills or mountains.

A **volcano** is a mountain with a cone shape that is formed by lava that erupts from a crack in the Earth's surface.

**2.** _____

**3.** _____

**4.** _____

**5.** _____

**6.** _____

**7.** _____

**8.** _____

Many landforms are formed where land and water come together. The pictures on this page show some examples. Read the description of each one. Then write the name of each landform under the correct picture.

A **cape** is a small, narrow point of land that sticks out into a body of water.

A **peninsula** is an area of land that is surrounded by water on three sides.

An **isthmus** is a narrow strip of land that connects two large areas of land.

**9.** _____

**10.** _____

Many bodies of water, including oceans, rivers, and lakes, cover Earth. The pictures show still other bodies of water. Read each description and write the name under the correct picture.

A **strait** is a narrow channel that connects two larger bodies of water.

A **gulf** is an arm of an ocean or sea that is partly enclosed by land.

A **bay** is a smaller body of water partly enclosed by land.

**11.** _____

**12.** _____

**13.** _____

# A Profile and Contour Map

You know that mountains are high, but how high are they? The drawing on this page shows the **profile**, or side view, of two mountains.

**Profile Map**

Elevation measured in metres

- 1500 m
- 1200 m
- 900 m
- 600 m
- 300 m
- Sea level

**Cougar Ridge**     **Pine Mountain**

The key tells you the **elevation** of different parts of the mountains. Elevation is the height of any place on land above **sea level**. Sea level is the average height of the ocean's surface. It is zero elevation. Land that rises 150 metres higher than sea level has an elevation of 150 metres.

1. What does the colour yellow stand for on the mountains? _____

2. Which mountain is higher? _____
   What is its elevation? _____

3. What colour represents an elevation of 250 metres? _____

4. Forest rangers are building a hut at the top of Pine Mountain. At what elevation will it be? _____

5. Suppose you are climbing Cougar Ridge and are halfway to the top. What is the elevation? _____

**Cougar Ridge**

**Contour Map**

**Pine Mountain**

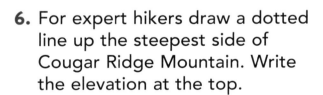

T he map on this page is a **contour map**. It shows the same mountains as the profile on page 372, but it shows the view from above. The lines on the contour map show the elevations of different parts of the mountains. When the lines on a contour map are close together, they show that the land is steep. When the lines are far apart, they show a more gradual slope.

Imagine you are a mountain guide planning treks up these mountains. Draw the following routes on the contour map.

*Elevation measured in metres*

- 1500 m
- 1200 m
- 900 m
- 600 m
- 300 m
- Sea level

**6.** For expert hikers draw a dotted line up the steepest side of Cougar Ridge Mountain. Write the elevation at the top.

**7.** Mark a point halfway up this mountain with an X so the hikers can take a rest.

**8.** For the beginning hikers draw a double line up the least steep side of Pine Mountain. Write the elevation at the top.

**9.** For an all-day hike draw a continuous line from the lowest point on the map to the highest point on the map.

map reader's Tip

Some land on Earth is actually below sea level. For example, Death Valley in California is 86 metres below sea level. It is the lowest land in the Western Hemisphere.

# A Physical Map

A **physical map** shows natural features of a place. These might include lakes, rivers, and the elevation of the land. The physical map on this page shows the main islands of Hawaii.

map reader's **Tip**

The islands of Hawaii were formed by volcanoes. Most of these volcanoes are no longer active, but Mauna Loa and Kilauea on the island of Hawaii still erupt sometimes.

1. What elevation does the colour green stand for?_____

2. Which island has the highest elevation? _____

3. What landforms would you expect to see on the highest island? _____

4. Find Hawaii's capital, Honolulu. What is the elevation of this city?_____

5. Which islands are less than 1500 metres high? _____

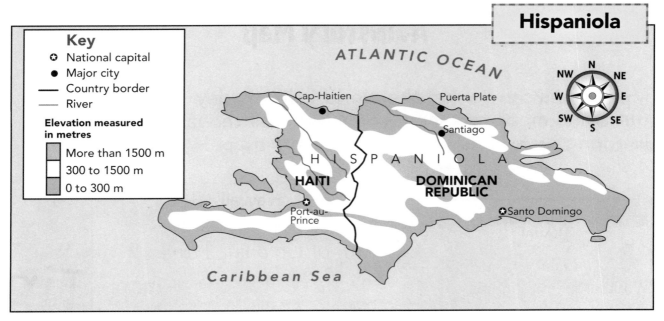

Here is another physical map. It shows the two countries on the island of Hispaniola in the Caribbean Sea.

**1.** What are the two countries shown on this map? _____

**2.** What colour is used to show elevations at sea level on this map? _____

**3.** In which country do you find the highest elevation? What landform would you expect to find there? _____

**4.** Find Santo Domingo, the capital of the Dominican Republic. What is the elevation of this city? _____

**5.** Find the border between the two countries. What is the elevation for most of it? _____

**6.** Rivers flow from high land to lower land. Find the rivers on this map. In which direction are they flowing? _____

map reader's **Tip**    Hispaniola is the second largest island (after Cuba) in the West Indies. The explorer Christopher Columbus landed on Hispaniola in 1492.

# A History Map

A | E

Most maps show what the world is like today. But some maps can show you what a place was like long ago. These are called history maps.

**T**he map on these pages shows Colonial Williamsburg in Virginia in the United States. Some people call this community a "living museum." That's because Colonial Williamsburg was rebuilt to show how people lived in 1775. Looking at this map is like stepping back in time.

### Glossary of Colonial Terms

apothecary . . . . . pharmacy or drugstore

blacksmith . . . . . maker of iron tools, knives, and horsehoes

cooper . . . . . . . . barrelmaker

gaol . . . . . . . . . jail

milliner . . . . . . . hatmaker

rural trades . . . . farm equipment

tavern . . . . . . . . restaurant

wheelwright . . . . wheelmaker

windmill . . . . . . . grinder of grain into flour

SCOTLAND STREET

**1**

PRINCE GEORGE STREET

**2**

College of William and Mary

**3**

BOUNDARY STREET

**4**

Use the glossary and grid to answer the questions. List the name and grid location of each place.

**1.** You drop off your horse's harness for repair. _____

**2.** You pick up some medicines for your mother. _____

**3.** You order a barrel for your father. _____

**4.** You drop off an ad for the newspaper. _____

**Historic Williamsburg**

map reader's **Tip**

Williamsburg was the capital of Virginia from 1699 to 1780. Today, Virginia's capital is Richmond.

**5.** You leave a basket of corn to be ground into corn meal. _____

**6.** You join your father for dinner. _____

**7.** You stop to look at hats in a store window. _____

**8.** You help your father take a horse to get new shoes. _____

**9.** Mmmm. You can't resist those baked apple pies! _____

**10.** You buy a candlestick for your sister's wedding. _____

# A Weather Map

What's the weather like today? One way to find out is to look out the window. Another way to check the weather is to look at a weather map like the one shown here.

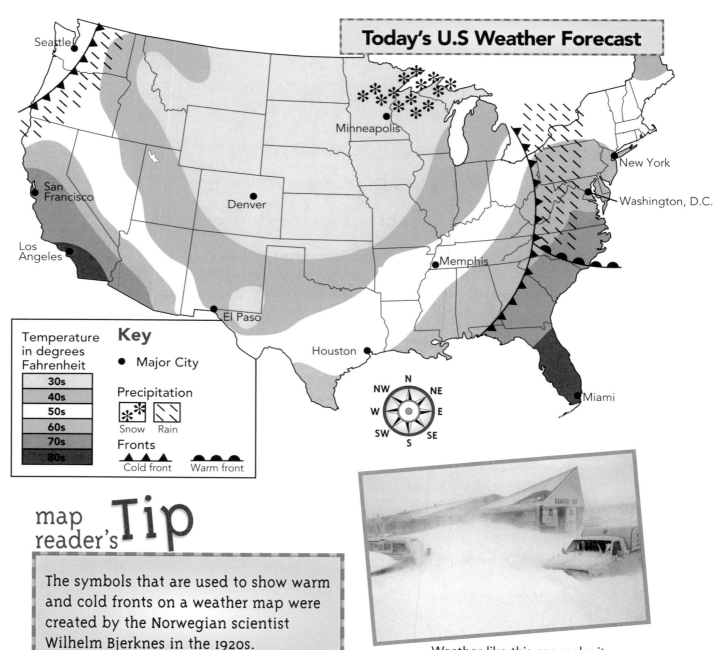

Weather like this can make it dangerous to be outside.

Name _____

**A** cold front is a zone of cold air moving in as warm air retreats. A cold front usually means clouds and showers. A warm front is a zone of warm air advancing as cold air retreats. Clouds and rain often occur just ahead of a warm front. Weather systems usually move from west to east across North America.

**1.** In which part of the U.S. is there a warm front? _____

**2.** What is the temperature in Seattle today? _____

**3.** What city is about to get snow? _____

**4.** Name two cities with temperatures in the 80s. _____

**5.** If you were in Denver today, how would you dress? _____

**6.** What kind of weather is heading toward Washington, D.C.? _____

**7.** Is it cooler in San Francisco or Los Angeles today? _____

**8.** You are visiting Memphis and are planning a hike.

Will you have good weather for this activity? _____

**Weather or Not**

Find the area of your hometown on the weather map. Then fill out the chart below with your prediction for the weather for today and the next two days. Use the symbols provided.

| Today | Tomorrow | Day After Tomorrow |
|-------|----------|--------------------|
|       |          |                    |

# A Climate Map

**Weather changes from day to day, but climate remains more or less the same.**

**C**limate is the pattern of weather that an area has over a period of time. Does an area get a lot of rain during the year? Is it mostly hot or mostly cold? The map shown here is a climate map. It shows the different kinds of climate regions in the United States.

**United States**

map reader's **Tip**

Different factors affect climate. Elevation is one. Another is latitude or how far a place is from the equator. Landforms also affect climate.

1. How would you describe the climate in the northeastern part of the United States?

    _____

    _____

2. Find an area where summers are hot and winters are mild. Where is it? _____

3. How many kinds of climates does Texas (TX) have? _____

4. Describe one climate in Alaska (AK). _____

    _____

    _____

5. What is the climate like along most of the west coast?

    _____

    _____

6. What kind of climate does this color ▦ represent? _____

7. In general, is the western part of the country drier or wetter than the eastern part? _____

## Map Key

- ▢ Cool summers/ cold winters; Very dry
- ▩ Cool summers/ cold winters; Wet
- ▩ Cool summers/ mild winters; Wet
- ▢ Warm or hot summers/ cold winters; Dry
- ▩ Warm or hot summers/ mild winters; Dry or very dry
- ▩ Warm or hot summers/ cold winters; Wet
- ▩ Hot summers/ mild or warm winters; Wet

# A News Map

News maps help readers locate and understand events around the globe. Here is the first paragraph of a news story and a map that goes with it.

**Oldest City in the Americas**
Researchers working at an archaeological site in Peru say that they think it is the oldest city in the Americas. The site, called Caral, dates back to 2600 B.C. Scientists used radiocarbon dating of plant fibres from the site to determine its age. They believe that a civilization existed at Caral for five centuries. Until now, scientists thought that the earliest civilization in Peru was on the coast.

**1.** In which direction is Caral from Lima? _____

**2.** What is the symbol for an archaeological site? _____

**3.** In which valley is Caral? _____

**4.** In which mountain range is the valley located? _____

**5.** Is Caral on the ocean or inland? _____

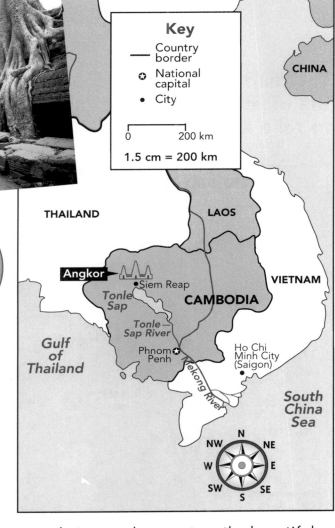

This news story takes place in another part of the world, the country of Cambodia in Southeast Asia.

### Temples and Trees Embrace

Angkor was one of the world's great cities between the ninth and fifteenth centuries. Its huge temples were famous. When the empire at Angkor collapsed, the jungle crept in and the temples lay hidden by trees and undergrowth. Although the temples were rediscovered by explorers many years later, only part of the jungle was cleared away. Today, efforts are being made to restore the beautiful temples. But in many cases the trees have become part of the buildings.

**6.** What countries border Cambodia on the north? _____

What country borders Cambodia on the east? _____

**7.** What city is Angkor near? _____

**8.** In which direction is Angkor from Phnom Penh? _____

**9.** About how far is Angkor from the border of Laos? _____

**10.** What body of water is Angkor near? _____

# Planning With a Map

The map on this page shows Yellowstone National Park, one of the most popular parks in the United States. It's a great place to take a vacation!

1. Yellowstone is located in three different states. What are they? _____

2. How many road entrances are there to the park? _____

3. Old Faithful Geyser is the park's most famous attraction.

   In which direction is the geyser from Yellowstone Lake? _____

map reader's **Tip**

The Continental Divide runs through Yellowstone Park. Rain that falls on the west side of this line flows to the Pacific Ocean. Rain that falls on the east side of this line flows to the Atlantic Ocean.

**Handy Dandy Planning Guide**

Use the guide below to plan a three-day visit to Yellowstone Park.

|  | Day 1 | Day 2 | Day 3 |
|---|---|---|---|
| Sights to See |  |  |  |
| Places to Swim or Fish |  |  |  |
| Mountain to Hike |  |  |  |
| Hotel |  |  |  |

**4.** Which river flows out of the north end of the park? _____

**5.** What is the largest lake in the park? _____

**6.** Look at the scale on this map. About how many kilometres is it from the east side of the park to the west side? _____

# Map Review

**South America: Vegetation**

1. Find the equator. What degree latitude is it? _____

2. Name three countries that the equator runs through.

   _____

   _____

   _____

3. Look at the other lines of latitude. In which hemisphere is most of South America? _____

4. At about what longitude is the westernmost part of Ecuador? _____

5. What does this symbol ⬤ stand for? _____

6. Where are the deserts in South America? _____

7. How would you describe the vegetation in Guyana? _____

8. In which part of Brazil would you expect to find the Amazon Rain Forest? _____

# Thinking About Maps

Use what you have learned about maps
to complete the crossword puzzle.

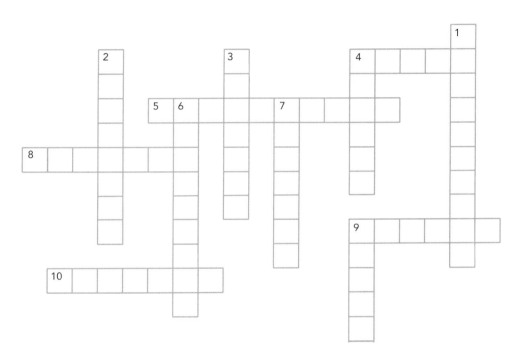

## Across

4. a way to measure
   distance on a map
5. half of Earth
8. a map that is a side view
9. a drawing that stands
   for something on a map
10. 0° latitude

## Down

1. plants that grow in a place
2. A mountain is a kind of
   _____.
3. the pattern of weather
   in a place
4. a narrow channel of water
6. the height of land above
   sea level
7. an area of high, flat land
9. the pole located in
   Antarctica

# Glossary

**axis**
An axis is an imaginary centre line on which Earth turns.

**canyon**
A canyon is a deep, narrow valley with high, steep sides.

**cape**
A cape is a small, narrow point of land that sticks out into a body of water.

**cardinal directions**
Cardinal directions are the four main directions—north, south, east, and west.

**climate**
Climate is the kind of weather that an area has over a period of time.

**compass rose**
A compass rose is a symbol that shows directions.

**contour map**
A contour map has lines that show the elevations of different parts of land.

**elevation**
Elevation is the height of land above sea level.

**equator**
The equator is an imaginary line that runs around the centre of Earth and divides it into the Northern and Southern hemispheres. The equator is 0° latitude.

**grid**
A grid is a pattern of lines that form squares.

**gulf**
A gulf is an arm of an ocean or sea that is partly enclosed by land.

**hemisphere**
A hemisphere is half of Earth. Earth can be divided into Northern and Southern hemispheres or Eastern and Western hemispheres.

**intermediate directions**
Intermediate directions are directions between the four main directions. They are northeast, southeast, southwest, and northwest.

**isthmus**
An isthmus is a narrow strip of land that connects two large areas of land.

**latitude**
Lines of latitude run around Earth parallel to the equator. They are marked in degrees north and south.

**longitude**
Lines of longitude are meridians that measure Earth in degrees from east to west.

**map index**
A map index is an alphabetical listing of place names on a map. A map index gives the grid square for each place.

**peninsula**
A peninsula is an area of land that is surrounded by water on three sides.

**physical map**
A physical map shows natural features of Earth.

**plateau**
A plateau is a large area of high, flat land.

**Prime Meridian**
The Prime Meridian is an imaginary line at 0° longitude. The Prime Meridian divides Earth into Eastern and Western hemispheres.

**profile map**
A profile map shows the side view of a place.

**projections**
Map projections are different ways of showing Earth on a flat surface.

**scale**
A map scale helps you measure distance on a map.

**sea level**
Sea level is the average height of the ocean's surface. It is zero elevation.

**strait**
A strait is a narrow channel that connects two larger bodies of water.

**symbol**
A symbol is a drawing or color that represents something else.

**vegetation**
Vegetation is the different kinds of trees and plants that grow in an area.

**volcano**
A volcano is a mountain with a cone shape that is formed by lava that erupts from a crack in Earth's surface.

# Answer Key

## READING COMPREHENSION

### Pages 12–13

Answers will vary. Sample main ideas: Letter one—Except for the bugs, Tyler and his new friends are having fun at camp.; Letter two—Tyler's mom is worried about his bug bites, and she wants him to start being nice to the other campers.; Letter Three—Tyler is having a great time at camp, has some new friends, and is having fun playing tricks on other campers.; Letter four—Steven is sad he could not go to camp and remembers the fun he had at camp last year.

### Pages 14–15

1. b; 2. c; 3. c; 4. Answers will vary.
5. Answers will vary. Sample answers: The course for the Tour de France changes each year. The course is always about 3000 kilometres long. 6. Armstrong faced the challenges of battling cancer and competing in the Tour de France. Opinions will vary.

### Pages 16–17

1. formal; 2. residence; 3. reception;
4. entertained; 5. adorned; 6. guide; 7. wing;
8. mansion; 9. tour; 10. incredible; 11. huge;
12. visitors; 13. vary; five hundred seventy

### Pages 18–19

1. classed; 2. unique; 3. fascinating; 4. strike;
5. enamored; 6. eventually; 7. accumulated;
8. carting; 9. slinky; 10. creature;
11. Cassidy loves large, dangerous snakes.
12. a diamondback rattlesnake

### Pages 20–21

1. Southwest: many-storeyed homes; steep-walled canyons; buttes; Arizona, New Mexico, and southern Colorado; Apache and Navajo; Both: made pottery; hunting; excellent craftspeople; corn, beans, and squash; Eastern Woodlands: wigwams and longhouses; fishing; cold winters, warm summers; Iroquois and Ojibwa; included what is now Canada; 2. large, multiple-family dwellings; 3. The northern parts had cold winters.

### Pages 22–23

1. Arizona: Tonto National Forest, Phoenix, very hot, Apache Trail, Grand Canyon; Massachusetts: Old State House, Freedom Trail, mild climate, Boston, Cape Cod;
2. building sandcastles, beach, Meteor Crater, Freedom Trail; 3. Their parents love hot weather. Zach and Emily do not. 4. You can walk on the Freedom Trail; you must drive along the Apache Trail. 5. Emily likes to boogie board, and Zach likes to body surf.

6. Zach thinks he might be able to find the missing object. Emily thinks he is crazy to think he might find it.

### Pages 24–25

1. Picture order: 5, 1, 6, 3, 4, 2, Sentences will vary.
2.

| a | p | r | t | e | i | c |
| c | o | l | e | s | a | b |
| m | u | s | i | n | n | l |
| g | l | y | l | c | p | r |
| e | d | e | i | t | c | e |
| o | d | v | s | e | b | r |
| i | s | l | l | i | o | n |

### Pages 26–27

1. 7, 3, 4, 2, 1, 5, 6; 2. Answers will vary. 3. prank, party, delicious; 4. because water makes the chocolate lose its creaminess; 5. tortilla, apricot jam, green fruit roll, cashews, chocolate chips; 6. Maria "sweetly" tricked her friends on April Fool's Day. 7. vanilla ice cream, marshmallow fluff, yellow pudding; 8. black olives, green peppers, mushrooms

### Pages 28–29

1. hard worker, brave, fast-thinking, quick-acting; 2. scared, helpless, sick, alarmed;
3. Answers will vary. 4. Both: good students; Lindsay: persistent, courageous; Erica: frightened, grateful, appreciative; 5. Henry Heimlich; 6. Mount Waialeale; 7. almost 1 m; 8. Answers will vary.

### Pages 30–31

1. positive: He sees his friend, Eric., He learns Home Run Harvey is the coach.; negative: He could not play baseball with his friends., He sees a player on his new team strike out. 2. He would not get to see his friends and have Coach Dave whom he loved. 3. when he saw Eric; 4. Answers will vary. 5. excited, remorseful; 6. What Juan thought was going to be a negative experience soon looked like it could be a positive one. 7. Answers will vary.

### Pages 32–33

1. Tuesday and Wednesday; 2. Monday;
3. Answers will vary. Suggested answers: go to the movies, go to the mall, go bowling, go to a museum, go to the library;
4. Wednesday, Thursday, Friday; 5. Answers will vary. Possible answer: They are probably not pleased. They want to do all kinds of outdoor activities, and it is going to be cold and rainy. 6. no clouds with a high of 28; It is the best forecast for doing outside activities. 7. lingering; 8. athletic, energetic; 9. goggles, sunglasses, cooler with drinks, sunscreen; 10. Paragraphs will vary.

### Pages 34–35

main characters: the colonists; setting: east coast of America; problem: The colonists wanted their independence from Britain. solution: Delegates met to try to help gain independence from Britain. When their efforts did not work, they agreed to go to war.

## Pages 36–37

1. B, C, A; 2. a. E, C; b. C, E; c. E, C; d. E, C;
3. Since it was a beautiful day, Janie and Jake's mom was taking them to the beach.
4. Janie: because Hayley had recently had Janie over to play; Jake: because he and Charlie went everywhere together;
5. Answers will vary.

## Page 38

1. Pluto; 2. Jupiter; 3. Uranus; 4. Neptune;
5. Earth; 6. Saturn; 7. Mercury; 8. Mars;
9. Venus

## Page 39

Grant: Washington; Spencer: Arizona; Kara: Pennsylvania; Jack: Massachusetts; All live in Maine.

## Pages 40–41

1. to run errands and shop;
2. Answers will vary.

## Pages 42–43

Chart: Dairy—milk, yogurt, ice cream, cheese, milkshake; Vegetables—carrots, peas, corn, broccoli, cauliflower; Grains—oatmeal, wheat bread, rice, crackers, pasta; Fruits—banana, apple, grapes, strawberries, pear; Meat & Fish—chicken nuggets, ham, hamburger, fish sticks, pork chops; Fats/Sweets—chocolate chip cookies, candy bar, doughnuts, chocolate cake, cheesecake;
1. She eats right and exercises.
2. hamburger, chicken, ribs;
3. Answers will vary. 4. E, C;
5. Katie: banana, oatmeal; Jimmy: candy bar, ham, corn; Toni: chocolate chip cookies, chicken nuggets, carrots; Anna: fish sticks, pear

## Page 44

1. spring; 2. Mother's Day; 3. because they are having a sale; 4. Answers will vary. Possible answer: It was spring. Many people shop for plants in the spring, so a sale would not be needed. 5. because they are buy one get one free; 6. because the sale ends Tuesday

## Page 45

1. They love it. 2. They are sad., They do not know what they will do without their good friends. 3. They think it sounds like a fun, interesting part of the country.
4.

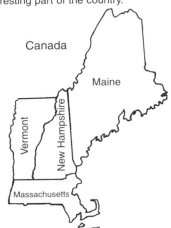

## Pages 46–47

1. Most whales are enormous creatures.
2. Whales might look a lot like fish, but the two are very different. 3. Whales can be divided into two groups—baleen and toothed. 4. Blubber is very important to whales and has many purposes. 5. Most whales are enormous creatures. Whales might look a lot like fish, but the two are very different. Whales can be divided into two groups—baleen and toothed. Blubber is very important to whales and has many purposes. 6. Whale: can hold breath for long time, tail fin sideways, lungs; Fish: gills, live in ponds, tail fin up and down; Both: live in oceans, people love to watch

## Pages 48–49

1. O, O, F, O, F, F, F, O; 2. Answers will vary.
3. Answers will vary. 4. brave, strong, daring, athletic; 5. climbing poles, ice axes, breathing masks; 6. Answers will vary. 7. Answers will vary.

## Pages 50–51

1. to entertain; 2. Working is not what the author would choose to do. 3. The author wants to escape from worries and be free like animals. 4. worries, chores, homework;
5. bird: fly, float, sing, play, soar; dolphin: splash, play, dive, flip; bear: jump, climb, sleep, run, play, fish; dog: play ball, jump, run, roll over, fetch, rest, catch;
6. F, O, F, F, O

## Page 52

1. to persuade; 2. Answers will vary.
3. Answers will vary. Possible reasons: Students would get around more quickly., Students would learn more., It would lead to better health. 4. Answers will vary.

# TESTS: READING

## Test 1: Pages 55–56
*Sample: 1.D  2.C*

**Passage A**
1.D  2.A  3.D

**Passage B**
1.C  2.A  3.C

**Passage C**
1.C  2.D  3.A  4.B

**Passage D**
1.A  2.B  3.D

**Passage E**
1.A  2.D  3.D  4.B

**Vocabulary**
Synonyms
*Sample: A*
1.C  2.B  3.B  4.C
5.D  6.B  7.A
Antonyms
*Sample: C*
1.C  2.D  3.D  4.C
5.A  6.B  7.A

## Test 2: Pages 59–62
*Sample: 1.D  2.C*

**Passage A**
1.C  2.D  3.B

**Passage B**
1.C  2.D  3.B

**Passage C**
1.B  2.A  3.C  4.C

**Passage D**
1.B  2.C  3.B

**Passage E**
1.B  2.C  3.D

**Vocabulary**
Synonyms
*Sample: C*
1.B  2.B  3.C  4.D
5.B  6.D  7.B

Antonyms
*Sample: C*
1.D  2.D  3.A  4.C
5.C  6.C  7.A

## Test 3: Pages 63–66
*Sample: 1.D  2.A*

**Passage A**
1.B  2.D  3.C

**Passage B**
1.B  2.B  3.D

**Passage C**
1.C  2.A  3.B  4.D

**Passage D**
1.A  2.B  3.D  4.C

**Passage E**
1.B  2.C  3.A

**Vocabulary**
Synonyms
*Sample: B*
1.C  2.A  3.B  4.B
5.D  6.D  7.B

Antonyms
*Sample: A*
1.C  2.D  3.A  4.D
5.B  6.C  7.D

## Test 4: Pages 67–70
*Sample: 1.D  2.C*

**Passage A**
1.C  2.B

**Passage B**
1.A  2.D  3.A

**Passage C**
1.C  2.B  3.B

**Passage D**
1.A  2.D  3.D

**Passage E**
1.C  2.C  3.B

**Vocabulary**
Synonyms
*Sample: D*
1.D  2.A  3.B  4.C
5.D  6.B  7.A

Antonyms
*Sample: A*
1.D  2.C  3.A  4.B
5.D  6.B  7.A

## Test 5: Pages 71–74
*Sample: 1.B  2.A*

**Passage A**
1.D  2.A  3.C

**Passage B**
1.A  2.D  3.C

**Passage C**
1.B  2.B  3.D

**Passage D**
1.C  2.B  3.B

**Passage E**
1.B  2.B  3.C

**Vocabulary**
Synonyms
*Sample: A*
1.C  2.B  3.D  4.B
5.D  6.D  7.C

Antonyms
*Sample: B*
1.B  2.B  3.A  4.B
5.A  6.D  7.C

## Test 6: Pages 75–78
*Sample: 1.B  2.D*

**Passage A**
1.A  2.C  3.A

**Passage B**
1.C  2.A  3.C

**Passage C**
1.D  2.A  3.C

**Passage D**
1.C  2.B  3.A

**Passage E**
1.C  2.D  3.B

**Vocabulary**
Synonyms
*Sample: A*
1.D  2.B  3.C  4.B
5.A  6.A  7.D

Antonyms
*Sample: B*
1.B  2.A  3.B  4.D
5.B  6.D  7.C

## Test 7: Pages 79–82
*Sample: 1.B  2.C*

**Passage A**
1.C  2.C  3.B

**Passage B**
1.D  2.C

**Passage C**
1.D  2.B

**Passage D**
1.C  2.D  3.A

**Passage E**
1.A  2.B  3.A  4.D

**Passage F**
1.B  2.A  3.B

**Vocabulary**
Synonyms
*Sample: A*
1.B  2.C  3.B  4.D
5.D  6.B  7.A

Multiple Meanings
*Sample: C*
1.B  2.D  3.B  4.A

## Test 8: Pages 83–86
*Sample: 1.B  2.A*

**Passage A**
1.C  2.B  3.A  4.C

**Passage B**
1.C  2.A  3.D

**Passage C**
1.D  2.C  3.B  4.C  5.D

**Passage D**
1.D  2.A  3.C  4.B

**Passage E**
1.B  2.D  3.B

**Vocabulary**
Synonyms
*Sample: A*
1.C   2.B   3.D   4.C
5.A   6.A   7.A

Antonyms
*Sample: B*
1.B   2.A   3.D   4.A
5.C   6.C   7.B

## Test 9: Pages 87–90
*Sample: 1.B   2.B*

**Passage A**
1.B   2.C   3.A

**Passage B**
1.B   2.D   3.C

**Passage C**
1.C   2.B   3.D   4.B

**Passage D**
1.D   2.A   3.C

**Passage E**
1.C   2.B   3.D

**Vocabulary**
Synonyms
*Sample: B*
1.A   2.D   3.C   4.A
5.B   6.A   7.D

Antonyms
*Sample: C*
1.A   2.D   3.A   4.A
5.A   6.A   7.D

## Test 10: Pages 91–94
*Sample: 1.C   2.C*

**Passage A**
1.B   2.C

**Passage B**
1.A   2.C   3.B

**Passage C**
1.C   2.A   3.C

**Passage D**
1.B   2.A   3.D

**Passage E**
1.C   2.A   3.B   4.B

**Vocabulary**
Synonyms
*Sample: A*
1.D   2.B   3.D   4.B
5.D   6.B   7.C

Antonyms
*Sample: A*
1.B   2.B   3.D   4.A
5.A   6.A   7.B

## Test 11: Pages 95–98
*Sample: 1.B   2.D*

**Passage A**
1.A   2.D   3.C

**Passage B**
1.B   2.A   3.A   4.D

**Passage C**
1.A   2.C   3.D   4.D

**Passage D**
1.A   2.D   3.A   4.C

**Passage E**
1.A   2.B   3.C   4.A

**Vocabulary**
Synonyms
*Sample: C*
1.D   2.A   3.C   4.B
5.A   6.C   7.A

Antonyms
*Sample: A*
1.C   2.B   3.D   4.D
5.A   6.B   7.B

## Test 12: Pages 99–102
*Sample: 1.D   2.A*

**Passage A**
1.D   2.D   3.C

**Passage B**
1.B   2.D   3.B

**Passage C**
1.B   2.D   3.A

**Passage D**
1.B   2.D   3.C   4.A

**Passage E**
1.D   2.C   3.A   4.B

**Vocabulary**
*Sample: C*
1.D   2.A   3.C   4.D   5.C
6.A   7.B   8.B   9.C

## Test 13: Pages 103–106
*Sample: 1.A   2.C*

**Passage A**
1.B   2.B   3.A   4.C

**Passage B**
1.B   2.D   3.D

**Passage C**
1.A   2.D   3.A   4.B   5.A

**Passage D**
1.C   2.B   3.D   4.A

**Passage E**
1.A   2.B   3.D   4.A

**Vocabulary**
*Sample: B; B*
1.D   2.C   3.B
4.A   5.C   6.B

## Test 14: Pages 107–110
*Sample: 1.A   2.B*

**Passage A**
1.C   2.A   3.D

**Passage B**
1.B   2.A   3.B

**Passage C**
1.C   2.B   3.A

**Passage D**
1.A   2.D   3.D

**Passage E**
1.B   2.B   3.D

**Vocabulary**
Synonyms
*Sample: B*
1.A   2.B   3.B   4.B
5.D   6.A   7.B

Antonyms
*Sample: B*
1.A   2.C   3.B   4.B
5.B   6.C   7.A

## Test 15: Pages 111–114
*Sample: 1.D   2.A*

**Passage A**
1.D   2.B   3.A

**Passage B**
1.C   2.A   3.A

**Passage C**
1.C   2.A   3.D

**Passage D**
1.C   2.D   3.B

**Passage E**
1.D   2.B   3.C   4.C

**Vocabulary**
*Sample: C*
1.B   2.C   3.A   4.C   5.A   6.B   7.B   8.D
9.B   10.D   11.A   12.C   13.B

# GRAMMAR

### Page 117
A. 1. declarative
2. interrogative
3. imperative
4. imperative
5. exclamatory
6. interrogative
B. 1. incomplete
2. complete
3. complete
4. incomplete
5. complete
C. 1. Sarah stood at the edge of the square.
2. The sword slid out of the stone.

### Page 118
A. 1. interrogative, ?
2. exclamatory, !
3. imperative, .
4. declarative, .
B. 1. listened, declarative
2. play, interrogative
3. pass, imperative
4. won, exclamatory
C. Answers will vary.

### Page 119
1. b   3. c   5. c   7. c   9. a
2. b   4. a   6. b   8. a   10. b

### Page 120
A. 1. A small family | lived on a faraway planet.
2. The family's two children | played near the space launch.
3. The little girl | dreamed about life on Earth.
4. Huge spaceships | landed daily on the planet.
5. The spaceship mechanics | repaired huge cargo ships.
6. Twinkling stars | appeared in the black sky.
B. 1. The planet's inhabitants | lived in underground homes.
2. A special machine | manufactures air inside the family's home.
3. The athletic girl | jumped high into the air.
4. Many toys and games | cluttered the children's playroom.
5. The children's father | described weather on Earth.
C. 1. The underground home contained large, comfortable rooms.
2. The playful child rolled his clay into a ball.

### Page 121
A. 1. My whole family
2. The warm, sunny day in the park
3. My cousin Fred
4. Everyone
5. The people in

B. 1. watched the space shuttle on TV this morning.
2. rocketed into space at 6:00 a.m.
3. released a satellite into space.
4. circled Earth for three days.
5. landed smoothly on Monday at noon.
C. Answers will vary.

### Page 122
1. b   3. a   5. b   7. a   9. b
2. c   4. c   6. b   8. c   10. c

### Page 123
A. 1. Pig One, Pig Two, and Pig Three
2. bears, rabbits, and pigs
3. Carrots, beets, and squash
4. Teddy and Osito
5. brothers and sisters
B. 1. cleaned and peeled
2. laughed and giggled
3. waited and watched
4. weeds and waters
5. writes and edits
C. 1. buys and reads, CP
2. authors and illustrators, CS

### Page 124
A. 1. teacher, students;  The teacher and her students visited the ocean.
2. Seagulls, Pelicans;  Seagulls and pelicans flew overhead.
3. Seashells, Seaweed;  Seashells and seaweed littered the sand.
4. Carlos, Tanya;  Carlos and Tanya ran on the beach
B. 1. paints, draws;  The artist paints and draws sea life.
2. collect, decorate;  I collect and decorate driftwood.
3. swim, dive;  Seals swim and dive near the pier.

### Page 125
A. 1. a   2. b   3. a   4. c   5. b
B. 1. c   2. a   3. c   4. b   5. b

### Page 126
A. 1. simple
2. compound
3. compound
4. simple
5. simple
6. compound
B. 1. Connor had seen many parks in his life, but he never had seen a park like this one.
2. Dad brought a pair of binoculars, and Nate used them to look for animals.
3. He saw his first live bear, and the hair stood up on his arms.
4. It was an exciting moment, but it only lasted a second.
5. The bear was no bear at all, and Felicia was embarrassed.
6. He hadn't seen a bear, but he kept looking.

### Page 127
A. 1. One day we were in the park, and we saw two ducks swimming by.
2. We watched the ducks for a while, but they disappeared into the tall grass.
3. The ducks might have gone to a nest, or they could have swum to the shore.
4. We walked along the grassy bank, but we could not find them anywhere.
5. We sat down on the dock, and out came the ducks again.
6. One adult duck led six ducklings around the pond, and the other adult followed behind the babies.
B. 1. but   3. and   5. or
2. but   4. and
C. Answers will vary.

### Page 128
A. 1. b   2. b   3. a   4. b   5. a
B. 1. a   2. b   3. a   4. b   5. c

### Page 129
A. 1. farmer, house, road
2. farmer, wheat, soybeans, corn
3. fields, crop
4. crops, rows
5. plants, farmer, weeds, bugs
B. 1. John Varley, Terra, Ontario
2. Varley Farm, Rising J Horse Ranch
3. Mr. Varley, Sally
4. Joker
5. October, Varley Farm, Harvest Celebration
C. 1. the street,  park
e.g. We walked down Oak Street to Blair Park.
2. aunt, the city
e.g. My Aunt Ellen lives in Winnipeg.

### Page 130
A. 1. story, celebrations ; *Toronto Life*
2. movie, poodles ; *Three Dogs on a Summer Night*
3. campfire ; "She'll Be Comin' 'Round the Mountain"
4. friend, grandparents ; August, John, Germany
5. family, beach ; Victoria Day
B. Common nouns: newspaper, city, day, magazine, park, book, month
Proper nouns: The Sun News, Calgary, Tuesday, Cobblestone, Yellowstone National Park, Young Arthur, July

**Page 131**
1. b   3. b   5. a   7. b   9. a
2. c   4. c   6. c   8. c   10. a

**Page 132**
A. 1. door, cap, bat, game   4. team
   2. bat, shoulder   5. day, foul, homer
   3. fence, dugout
B. 1. uncles, feet   4. brothers, sisters, cousins
   2. bases   5. teams, playoffs
   3. players
C. 1. (season); teams, players; awards
   2. (hitter), (catcher), (teammate); games
   3. (mother), (father), (assembly); parents
   4. (glove); achievements

**Page 133**
A. 1. (homework), (night), (story); friends
   2. (home); friends
   3. (cat); dogs, birds, pals
   4. adventures, pets, buddies
   5. (teacher), (story); classes
B. Singular nouns:
   1. chair   3. tooth   5. foot
   2. mouse   4. sheep   6. man
   Plural Nouns:
   1. chairs   3. teeth   5. feet
   2. mice   4. sheep   6. men
C. Answers will vary.

**Page 134**
1. b   3. b   5. c   7. b   9. a
2. c   4. a   6. c   8. a   10. b

**Page 135**
A. 1. The Grade 4s; (they)
   2. Ada; (she)
   3. Juan, Jill, and I; (We)
B. 1. the author; her
   2. the Grade 4s; them
   3. information; it
C. 1. (I), you   2. (You), me   3. (he), us

**Page 136**
A. 1. We; S   4. I; S   7. them; O
   2. us; O   5. it; O   8. She; S
   3. You; S   6. her; O
B. 1. They sent a postcard to us.
   2. It was addressed to him.
C. Answers will vary.

**Page 137**
A. 1. a   2. c   3. b   4. a   5. b
B. 1. a   2. b   3. a   4. b   5. b

**Page 138**
A. 1. my   3. their   5. her   7. Our
   2. his   4. my   6. your
B. 1. My   3. her   5. our
   2. their   4. his   6. my

**Page 139**
A. 1. mine   3. yours   5. her
   2. your   4. ours
B. 1. our   4. my   7. your
   2. her   5. his   8. our
   3. their   6. My or His
C. Answers will vary.

**Page 140**
1. d   3. b   5. d   7. b   9. c
2. c   4. c   6. b   8. d   10. a

**Page 141**
A. 1. wrote   4. weave   7. tie   10. wished
   2. painted   5. knits   8. learned
   3. twisted   6. stretched   9. made
B. 1. hopped   3. slurped
   2. pounded   4. sewed
C. Answers will vary.

**Page 142**
A. 1. use   3. imagine   5. amazes
   2. tie   4. invented
B. 1. lounge   3. gulp   5. staple
   2. gallop   4. drag

**Page 143**
A. 1. b   3. a   5. a
   2. c   4. b
B. 1. b   3. a   5. a
   2. b   4. b

**Page 144**
A. 1. past   5. present   9. future
   2. past   6. future   10. present
   3. future   7. present   11. past
   4. past   8. past
B. 1. Gum acted as an eraser.
   2. Unfortunately, pure rubber cracked in cold weather.
   3. Goodyear licensed the process to shoe companies.

**Page 145**
A. 1. wears   4. hurt   7. buys
   2. make   5. cause   8. want
   3. teaches   6. places
B. With Most Singular subjects: laces, designs, reaches, erases
   With Plural Subjects: lace, design, reach, erase

**Page 146**
A. 1. c   2. a   3. c   4. b   5. c
B. 1. a   2. c   3. b   4. a   5. c

**Page 147**
A. 1. will happen   6. will handle
   2. has equipped   7. was talking
   3. was polishing   8. had helped
   4. had tinkered   9. is wearing
   5. was gathering   10. will need
B. 1. had (asked); past
   2. will (drop); future
   3. is (learning); present
   4. will (enjoy); future
   5. has (eaten); past
   6. are (taking); present

**Page 148**
A. 1. was cooking   4. is tasting
   2. had added   5. will add
   3. have prepared   6. have arrived
B. 1. will bake   4. had planted
   2. has picked   5. have tossed
   3. is picking   6. are planning
C. Answers will vary.

**Page 149**
1. a   3. c   5. b   7. b   9. a
2. a   4. a   6. c   8. b   10. c

**Page 150**
A. 1. (I) am (reader)
   2. (books) are (nonfiction)
   3. (bookstore) is (one)
   4. (books) are (interesting)
   5. (owner) is (knowledgeable)
   6. (name) is (Terry Baldes)
   7. (Mr. Baldes) was (inventor, scientist)
   8. (windows) were (attractive)
   9. (event) was (appearance)
   10. (friends) are (admirers)
B. 1. is   3. were   5. were
   2. was   4. are
C. Answers will vary.

**Page 151**
A. 1. was, S   5. were, P   9. were, P
   2. were, P   6. are, P   10. was, S
   3. are, P   7. is, S   11. am, S
   4. is, S   8. are, P
B. 1. is   2. are   3. are   4. is
C. Answers will vary.

**Page 152**
1. c   3. c   5. a   7. a   9. b
2. b   4. b   6. b   8. b   10. a

**Page 153**
A. 1. bought   4. rode   7. took
   2. made   5. shook   8. thought
   3. came   6. heard   9. broke
B. 1. heard   4. broke   7. shook
   2. made   5. rode
   3. bought   6. came

**Page 154**
A. 1. have chosen    6. have gone
    2. has brought    7. had heard
    3. have eaten    8. have ridden
    4. has hidden    9. has bought
    5. had taken
B. 1. heard    4. ridden    7. brought
    2. taken    5. chosen
    3. gone    6. bought

**Page 155**
A. 1. b   2. a   3. c   4. a   5. b
B. 1. a   2. c   3. a   4. b   5. c

**Page 156**
A. 1. (colorful), (dark); many
    2. (small); few
    3. (strange), (unusual); one
    4. (mysterious)
    5. (big), (dark); four
    6. (rare), (new)
    7. (tiny), (large), (cold)
    8. (amazing); several
B. Sample answers are given.
    1. small, mysterious
    2. big, large
    3. sandy, small, long
    4. new
    5. underwater, several, many
C. Answers will vary.

**Page 157**
A. Sample answers are given.
    1. big, hungry
    2. fuzzy, orange, little
    3. missing, tasty
    4. plastic, red; red-headed, young
    5. more, tasty, good
B. 1. gray, shaggy, dark   4. soft, shady
    2. some, droopy      5. enormous, large
    3. little, quiet
C. Answers will vary.

**Page 158**
1. a    3. b    5. a    7. a    9. b
2. c    4. b    6. b    8. a    10. c

**Page 159**
A. 1. older    4. quieter    7. brightest
    2. loudest    5. higher    8. saddest
    3. biggest    6. softer
B. 1. hottest; more than two
    2. warmer; two
    3. colder; two
    4. tallest; more than two
    5. longer, two
    6. friendliest; more than two
    7. younger; two
    8. liveliest; more than two

**Page 160**
1. funniest      7. more challenging
2. funnier      8. most challenging
3. busier      9. more tiring
4. busiest      10. most tiring
5. more exciting    11. more delicious
6. most exciting    12. most delicious

**Page 161**
1. a    3. b    5. a    7. a    9. a
2. b    4. a    6. b    8. a    10. b

**Page 162**
A. 1. (of) mountains, rivers, and lakes.
    2. (on) the walls (of) his room
    3. (at) the scenes (in) the pictures
    4. (on) a camping trip
    5. (in) a backpack and knapsack
    6. (from) his father's mug
    7. (in) the mountains (for) hours
    8. (at) the Lost Lake
    9. (on) their journey
    10. (at) a quiet place (for) the night
    11. (in) a tent
    12. (from) the wind and rain
    13. (to) his father
    14. (on) their camping trip
B. 1. Answers will vary.

**Page 163**
A. 1. in    3. on    5. at
    2. with    4. for    6. into
B. Answers will vary.
C. Answers will vary.

**Page 164**
1. a    3. b    5. c    7. a    9. c
2. c    4. a    6. c    8. b    10. b

**Page 165**
A. 1. Tucker, lives; present
    2. It, opens; present
    3. Tucker, collected; past
    4. mouse, filled; past
    5. Tucker, sits; present
    6. He, watches; present
    7. boy, worked; past
    8. They, sell; present
B. 1. crowd, passes; singular
    2. Trains, run; plural
    3. Papa, waits; singular
    4. station, feels; singular
    5. People, rush; plural
    6. Mama, Papa, make; plural

**Page 166**
A. 1. Crickets, (make)
    2. males, (produce)
    3. I, (listen)
    4. You, (hear)
    5. Mario, (finds)
    6. mother, (calls)
B. 1. Mario wants the cricket for a pet.
    2. He wishes for a pet of his own.
    3. Crickets seem like unusual pets to his mother.
    4. Maybe insects scare her!

**Page 167**
A. 1. b        3. a        5. a
    2. b        4. b
B. 1. c        3. c        5. b
    2. a        4. b

**Page 168**
A. 1. "I really like tall tales!"
    2. "Davy Crockett is my favourite character,"
    3. "Who likes Sally Ann Thunder Ann Whirlwind?"
B. 1. "I am a big fan of hers."
    2. I added, "Sally can even sing a wolf to sleep."
    3. "How did Sally tame King Bear?"
    4. "Sally really ought to be in the movies,"
C. 1. "What kind of person is Sally?" asked Davy Crockett.
    2. The schoolman replied, "Sally is a special friend."
    3. "She can laugh the bark off a pine tree," added Lucy.
    4. The preacher said, "She can dance a rock to pieces."
    5. "I'm very impressed!" exclaimed Davy.
D. Answers will vary.

**Page 169**
A. 1. "Well,        3. "Yes,
    2. "Oh, Ed,      4. "Thank you,
B. 1. "Kim, your posters for the talent contest are terrific!"
    2. She replied, "Thank you, Doug, for your kind words."
    3. Our teacher asked, "Meg, will you play your guitar or sing?"
    4. "Oh, I plan to do both," said Meg.
    5. "Will you perform your juggling act this year, Roberto?"
    6. "No, I want to do a comedy routine,"
C. 1. "Kit, which act did you like best?" asked Mina.
    2. He replied, "Oh, I enjoyed the singing pumpkins and the tap dancing elephants."
    3. "Well, I liked the guitar player," said Mina.
D. Answers will vary.

## Page 170
1. b    3. b    5. a    7. a    9. a
2. a    4. c    6. b    8. c    10. b

## Page 171
A. 1. shouted, (Later)
   2. hit, (Yesterday)
   3. got, (soon)
   4. tried, (earlier)
   5. went, (Then)
B. 1. fell, (everywhere)
   2. piled, (up)
   3. were trapped, (inside)
   4. tunneled, (out)
   5. traveled, (there)
C. 1. never, when         3. inside, where
   2. underground, where  4. Soon, when

## Page 172
A. 1. talked, (happily)
   2. squawked, (sharply)
   3. greeted, (warmly)
   4. guided, (expertly)
   5. wrote, (regularly)
   6. recorded, (faithfully)
   7. responded, (personally)
   8. looked, (eagerly)
   9. jumped, (quickly)
   10. snorkeled, (easily)
   11. saw, (clearly)
   12. gazed, (intently)
   13. surrounded, (Swiftly)
   14. chased and nipped, (playfully)
B. Sample answers are given.
   1. bellowed loudly.
   2. swam gracefully.

## Page 173
A. 1. a    2. b    3. b    4. c    5. a
B. 1. c    2. b    3. a    4. a    5. b

# WRITING

## Page 176
Sentences will vary.

## Page 177
A. (left to right) S, P; S, P; P, P; S, P; S, S;
P, S; P, P; S, S; B. 1. Half a loaf is better than
none. 2. One good turn deserves another.
3. One rotten apple spoils the whole barrel.
4. The show must go on. 5. Every cloud has
a silver lining. 6. The early bird catches the
worm. 7. A rolling stone gathers no moss.
8. Haste makes waste.

## Pages 178–179
1. S; 2. E; 3. S; 4. Q; 5. C; 6. E; 7. C; 8. E;
9. Q; 10. C; 11. S; 12. Q; Sentences will vary.

## Page 180
1. Did you know that the whale shark can
grow to a length of 18 metres? 2. That's
about as long as two school buses parked
end to end! 3.These huge creatures are not a
threat to humans like some other sharks are.
4. Whale sharks float near the surface to
look for plankton and tiny fish. 5. Imagine
how amazing it must be to swim alongside
a whale shark. 6. There are an estimated
20,000 known species of fish in the world.
7. Is the dwarf pygmy goby the smallest of
all these species? 8. This species of goby is
one centimetre when it is fully grown! 9. This
tiny fish makes its home in the massive
Indian Ocean.

## Page 181
1. Are numbers that cannot be divided evenly
by 2 called odd numbers? 2. Can all even
numbers be divided evenly by 2? 3. Is 0
considered an even number? 4. Are numbers
that have 0, 2, 4, 6, or 8 in the ones place
even numbers? 5. Do odd numbers end in 1,
3, 5, 7, or 9? 6. Is the number 317,592 an
even number because it ends in 2? 7. Is the
sum always an even number when you add
two even numbers? 8. Is the sum of two odd
numbers also an even number? 9. Does the
same rule apply if you subtract an odd
number from an odd number? 10. Can you
figure out all the rules for working with odd
and even numbers?

## Page 182
Think about the fastest car you've ever seen
in the Indianapolis 500 race. That's about
how fast a peregrine falcon dives. It actually
reaches speeds up to 280 kilometres an
hour. How incredibly fast they are! Peregrine
falcons are also very powerful birds. Did you
know that they can catch and kill their prey in
the air using their sharp claws? What's really
amazing is that peregrine falcons live in both
the country and in the city.  Keep on the
lookout if you're ever in New York City.
Believe it or not, it is home to a very large
population of falcons.

## Page 183
Answers will vary.

## Page 184
Sentences will vary.; The simple sentence
will be: The team cheered.

## Page 185
Answers and sentences will vary.

## Page 186
1. My sister Annie has always participated in
sports, and many say she's a natural athlete.
2. Soccer, basketball, and softball are fun,
but she wanted a new challenge. 3. My sister
talked to my brother and me, and we were
honest with her. 4. I told Annie to go for it,
but my brother told her to stick with soccer or
basketball. 5. Will Dad convince her to try
skiing, or will he suggest ice skating?

## Page 187
1. The Caspian Sea, the world's largest lake,
covers an area about the same size as
Japan. 2. The Komodo dragon, a member of
the monitor family, can grow to a length of 10
metres. 3. Our closest star, the sun, is
estimated to be more than 15,000,000°C.
4. Ronald W. Reagan, 40th president of the
United States, worked as a Hollywood actor
for almost 30 years. 5. Prince Edward Island,
the province that grows the most potatoes,
harvests more than one billion kilograms
each year. 6. Hank Aaron, major league
baseball's all-time home-run hitter, broke
Babe Ruth's record in 1974.

## Page 188
1. My brothers built a tree house in the old
oak tree in our backyard. 2. Jim made a
sturdy rope ladder for the tree house. 3. Kyle
bought a gallon of brown paint. 4. Kyle and
Jim finished painting the walls in an hour.
5. Jim painted a "no trespassing" sign on the
tree house door. 6. A curious squirrel leaped
from a branch into their tree house. 7. The
unexpected visitor startled my unsuspecting
brothers. 8. The frightened squirrel leaped
out of the tree house in a big hurry.

**Page 189**
1. While I waited for my parents to get home, I watched a movie. 2. My brother was in his room because he had homework to do. 3. Before the movie was over, the power went out. 4. Since this happens all the time, I wasn't concerned. 5. I didn't mind the dark at first until I heard a scratching sound. 6. When I found my flashlight, I started to look around. 7. I was checking the living room when I caught Alex trying to hide.

**Page 190**
Sentences will vary.

**Page 191**
1. I'd like a bike, a pair of in-line skates, and a snowboard for my birthday. 2. Well, my friend, you can't always have what you want when you want it. 3. No, but I can always hope! 4. My friends and I skate all year long and snowboard during the winter. 5. I used to like skateboarding, but now I prefer snowboarding and in-line skating. 6. What sports, games, or hobbies do you enjoy most, Jody? 7. I learned to ski last year, and now I'm taking ice-skating lessons. 8. Skiing, ice skating, and skateboarding are all fun things to do. 9–12: Examples will vary.

**Page 192**
1. While Gina answered the phone, Marta watched for the bus. 2. Just as Gina said, "Hello," the caller hung up. 3. Unless they hurried, the girls were going to miss the one o'clock show. 4. By the time they got to the corner, the bus had already come and gone. 5. After the girls had waited a half hour, the next bus to town finally showed up. 6. Since they missed the earlier show, the girls decided to catch the four o'clock show. 7. Since Gina bought the tickets first, they wouldn't have to stand in line later. 8. Even though it was early, Gina and Marta were at the theatre by three o'clock. 9. Once they were inside, they bought a tub of popcorn and drinks.

**Page 193**
Possible sentences: 1. Did you know that the United States is the top meat-eating country in the world? Each person consumes about 118 kilograms of meat each year. Beef is the most commonly eaten meat. 2. Have you ever noticed that Abraham Lincoln faces right on a U.S. penny? He is the only president on a U.S. coin who does. Sacagawea faces right on the new dollar coin, but she was not a president. 3. It would be fantastic to have a robot to do all my chores, help do my homework, and play games. I really think the day will come. Unfortunately, it won't come soon enough for me.

**Page 194**
How would **you** like to go to school on Saturdays? If you lived in the **country** of Japan, that's just where you'd be each Saturday morning. I have a **friend** who lives in Japan. Yuichi explained that **students** attend classes five and one-half **days** a week. The **half** day is on Saturday. I was also surprised to **learn** that the Japanese school **year** is one of the longest in the world—over 240 days. It begins in the **month** of April. While we have over two months off each **summer**, students in Japan get their **vacation** in late July and August. School then **begins** again in fall and ends in March. The people of **Japan** believe that a good **education** is very important. Children are required to attend school from the age of six to the **age** of fifteen. They have elementary and middle **schools** just like we do. Then most **students** go on to **high** school for another three years. Yuichi says that students work very **hard** because the standards are so high. He and some of his friends even **take** extra classes after school. They all want to get into a good **college** someday.

**Page 195**
Starting Over
Today started off badly and only got worse. Everyone in my family woke up late this morning. I had only 15 minutes to get ready and catch the bus. I dressed as fast as I could, grabbed an apple and my backpack, and raced to get to the bus stop on time. Fortunately, I just made it. Unfortunately, the bus was pulling away when several kids pointed out that I had on two different shoes. At that moment, I wanted to start the day over.

**Pages 196**
Sentences and topics will vary.

**Page 197**
Topic sentences will vary.

**Page 198**
Topic sentences will vary.

**Page 199**
**Topic sentence:** Tony Hawk is an extraordinary skateboarder.

**Supporting sentences:** He turned professional when he was only 14 years old. Now in his thirties, Tony has won more skateboarding contests than anyone else has. He even made history in 1999 by landing a trick called the "900" at the Summer X Games.

**Closing sentence:** Tony Hawk may just be the greatest skateboarder in the world. Paragraphs will vary.

**Page 200**
**Topic sentence:** Yesterday our science class went on a field trip to a pond.

**Unrelated supporting sentences:** Next month we're going to the ocean.; That will be fun.; One of the boys accidentally fell in.; He was really embarrassed.

**Page 201**
Supporting sentences will vary.

**Page 202**
Paragraphs will vary.

**Page 203**
1. O; 2. F; 3. F; 4. O; 5. F; 6. O; Fact and opinion sentences will vary.

**Page 204**
Paragraphs will vary.

**Page 205**
Responses and paragraphs will vary.

**Page 206**
Responses will vary.

**Page 207**
1. Max had forgotten to check the pot of stew heating up on the stove. 2. Effects: the stew boiled over; the bottom of the pot was scorched; smoke filled the kitchen; dinner was ruined; and Max was in trouble; Paragraphs will vary.

**Page 208**
Paragraphs will vary.

**Page 209**
Overused words in paragraph: good, nice, little, big, bad, hard, afraid, sad; Synonyms will vary.

**Page 210**
Verbs: 1. went; 2. ran; 3. blew; 4. cleaned; 5. laughed; 6. ate; 7. liked; 8. slept; 9. looked; Synonyms will vary.; Exact verbs and sentences will vary.

**Page 211**
Responses will vary.

**Page 212**
Responses will vary.

**Page 213**
Responses will vary.

**Page 214**
Responses will vary.

**Page 217**
Responses will vary, but all should include commas and quotation marks around the direct words of speakers.

**Pages 218–219**
1. Chester Greenwood; 2. 3; 3. Who was Chester Greenwood?; 4. 5; Outlines will vary.

**Page 220**
Responses will vary.

# CHARTS, TABLES & GRAPHS

## Mathematics

### Page 220
1. c
2. b
3. d
4. a
5. b

### Page 221
1. 150 centimetres
2. 11 kilograms
3. Teresita and Pablo
4. Size 5
5. The sizes get larger, or the numbers increase.

### Page 222
1. b
2. a
3. c
4. d

### Page 223
1. a
2. d
3. b
4. d

### Page 224
1. a
2. a
3. b
4. c

### Page 225
1. Computer
2. 30
3. Automobile and telephone
4. 20

### Page 226
1. a
2. c
3. b
4. b

### Page 227
1. 2
2. Nova Scotia
3. 1
4. 16

### Page 228
1. b
2. d
3. b
4. c

### Page 229
1. 5
2. 3
3. Nature
4. 31
5. The Science badge is probably most difficult because it has been earned by the fewest scouts.

### Page 230

### Page 231
1. Science museum
2. 5
3. Water park and amusement park
4. Amusement park
5. Example: The water park would get the fewest votes; the science museum would get a lot more votes.

### Page 232
1. d
2. a
3. d
4. b
5. c

### Page 233
1. 21
2. Thursday
3. 8
4. 29
5. About 13 books

### Page 234
1. 16 cm
2. 5 cm
3. 20 sq. cm
4. 3.5 cm
5. Example: The area of a square increases rapidly as the sides of the square become longer.

## Reading/Language Arts

### Page 235
1. c
2. a
3. d
4. c
5. a

**Page 236**
1. Hiking, camping
2. 4
3. Lilac Lake and Mead Canyon
4. Mead Canyon
5. Underwood Park

**Page 237**
1. a
2. c
3. b
4. c

**Page 238**
1. Amy Grows Up
2. $2.95
3. 5
4. Dinosaur Dig, $4.50

**Page 239**
1. b
2. a
3. d
4. d

**Page 240**
1. c
2. a
3. b
4. d

**Social Studies**

**Page 241**
1. 2
2. July
3. 5
4. Spring
5. April

**Page 242**
1. Verrazano-Narrows
2. Mackinac Straits, Michigan
3. California, 1937
4. 1067 metres
5. Delaware Memorial and Tacoma Narrows

**Page 243**
1. Regina
2. 1871
3. New Brunswick and Nova Scotia
4. black-capped chickadee
5. Nova Scotia
6. wild rose
7. Alberta and Manitoba; great horned owl and great grey owl

**Page 244**
1. Logs are chipped into small pieces.
2. Wood pulp is cleaned and beaten into slush.
3. Step 4, Screen
4. Heat is used to cook the wood chips and to dry the web.

**Page 245**
1. 60 houses
2. Franklin County
3. Langham County
4. 25 houses
5. The answer should show $4\frac{1}{5}$ house symbols.

**Page 246**
1. c
2. d
3. b
4. c
5. b

**Page 247**
Examples of Correct Responses:
1.

2.

**Page 248**
1. b
2. d
3. d
4. b
5. a
6. c

**Page 249**
1. About 1200
2. About 400
3. About 2400
4. 1940–1960
5. Example: The population grew steadily from 1900 to 1980, and then it began to decline.
6. Probably between 2,000 and 2,200

**Page 250**
1. a
2. c
3. d
4. c
5. Example: Winding became unnecessary in 1930 when electric clocks were invented.

**Science**

**Page 251**
1. 5:26 am
2. August 4
3. June 23
4. 10 minutes
5. July 14
6. The sun rises later each day and sets earlier.

**Page 252**
1. 19°C, 5°C
2. Tuesday
3. Friday and Saturday
4. Partly cloudy
5. 3.75 cm
6. Example: It was warm until Wednesday, and then it got cooler each day. It got cloudy and rainy on Thursday and Friday.

**Page 253**
1. b
2. c
3. b
4. d
5. a

## Page 254
1. Ana
2. Earl
3. Hanna
4. Danielle
5. Example: In each year, names alternate between male and female. In even-numbered years, the first name is male. In odd-numbered years, the first name is female.

## Page 255
1. 80 kph
2. 40 kph
3. Cheetah
4. 64 kph
5. Elephant, deer, zebra, lion, cheetah

## Page 256
1. c
2. d
3. a
4. c
5. a

## Page 257
1. 37°F
2. 64°F
3. July
4. January
5. 47°F
6. Example: The average temperature rises steadily each month from January through July, and then it drops steadily from July through December.

# ADDITION, SUBTRACTION, MULTIPLICATION & DIVISION

## Page 260
1. 19; 2. 42; 3. 54; 4. 35; 5. 66
6. 165; 7. 245; 8. 368; 9. 768; 10. 1,323
What sickness can't you talk about until it's cured? Laryngitis

## Page 261
102 + 49 = 151; 311 + 219 = 530
315 + 669 = 984; 452 + 266 = 718
167 + 267 = 434; 202 + 179 = 381
177 + 114 = 291; 372 + 109 = 481
345 + 166 = 511; 201 + 99 = 300
99 + 246 = 345; 397 + 119 = 516
245 + 345 = 590; 548 + 328 = 876
756 + 145 = 901
219 + 79 = 298
Taking It Further: 750, 900, 1,050

## Page 262
A. 13, 14; B. 18, 14; C. 16, 12; D. 15,14;
E. 15, 15; F. 15, 13; G. 17, 17; H. 19, 15;
I. 17, 14; J. 15, 20; K. 20, 22; (6 + 3) + 7=16 pieces

## Page 263

| 18 | 18 | 17 | 19 | 15 |
|----|----|----|----|----|
| 16 | 18 | 15 | 15 | 17 |
| 17 | 18 | 18 | 16 | 16 |
| 17 | 22 | 18 | 15 | 19 |
| 17 | 15 | 18 | 18 | 18 |

## Page 264
A. 3,569, 9,876; B. 9,982, 7,949, 7,860, 91,798; C. 86,992, 90,749, 89,994, 77,787;
D. 581,998, 774,862, 567,990, 694,939, 959,596; 29,028 feet

## Page 265
A. 15,981, 19,341, 10,397, 8,990; B. 12,349, 12,188, 11,929,10,984; C. 18,990, 16,767, 20,320, 16,971; D. 17,759, 15,984, 14,487, 18,510; 39,661 feet

## Page 266
Z. 1,371; B. 632; R. 1,211; Q. 1,522; S. 1,201;
X. 761; I. 9,107; C. 4,053; Y. 10,155;
A. 14,024; Y. 9,122; L. 103,468; P. 76,076;
E. 82,373; F. 92,228; D. 539,396; Q. 651,951;
R. 1,059,472; THEY ARE BIRDS OF PREY.

## Page 267
H. 9,122; L. 12,548; I. 18,975; A. 17,531;
E. 10,322; O. 17,200; C. 18,506; T. 14,123;
M. 13,590; N. 130,752; U. 111,110;
Y. 182,920; R. 136,131; THE BALD EAGLE IS FOUND ONLY ON THE NORTH AMERICAN CONTINENT.

## Page 268
W. 7,901; T. 12,300; P. 7,148; N. 12,885;
O. 11,695; E. 15,019; H. 15,994; R. 10,404;
S. 9,207; ! 9,816; A. 8,915; U. 11,303; ONE WEARS TROUSERS. THE OTHER PANTS!

## Page 269
A. 6,741 + 3,382 = 10,123, 9,443 + 9,817 = 19,260, 4,578 + 5,361 = 9,939, 2,227 + 6,973 = 9,200; B. 3,841 + 4,064 = 7,905, 7,024 + 9,438 = 16,462, 9,810 + 9,385 = 19,195, 7,426 + 7,923 = 15,349; C. 1,773 + 158 = 1,931, 3,654 + 6,474 = 10,128, 4,284 + 3,821 = 8,105, 8,863 + 2,317 = 11,180;
D. 3,948 + 9,265 = 13,213, 9,759 + 8,724 = 18,483, 7,558 + 9,948 = 17,506, 4,595 + 6,628 = 11,223; 38,369 + 42,510 = 80,879 pieces

## Page 270
A. $92.83; G. $92.53; U $114.60; O. $63.87;
B. $72.25; N. $170.78;  E. $157.35;
R. $69.37; M. $168.72; C. $765.09;
S. $980.05; T. $670.09; D. $477.07;
Y. $616.34; F. $1,216.40; W. $1,000.68;
BECAUSE MONEY DOESN'T GROW ON TREES!

## Page 271
1. 1,804; 2. 689; 3. 1,063; 4. 2,133; 5. 3,489
6. 8,234; 7. 7,538; 8. 8,292; 9. 5,429
10. 10,439
What's the best thing to eat in a bathtub? Sponge cake

## Page 272
1. Deluxe Scraps
2. Kibble or Mouse Crumbs
3. Mouse Crumbs
4. Table Scraps and Mouse Crumbs
5. Crumbs & Cheese and Deluxe Scraps
Super Challenge: Woovis can't buy three items with $5. The cheapest three items cost a combined $5.67.

## Page 273
A. $69.95; B. $118.00; C. $23.88;  D. $18.58;
E. $178.75; F. $5.25

## Page 274
N. 3; T. 10; B. 9; L. 15; U. 14; E. 7; D. 0; O. 1;
L. 8; I. 6; W. 5; D. 12; R. 11; N. 13; I. 16; O. 2;
H. 4; TWO HUNDRED BILLION

## Page 275
2237 m.p.h.; A. 5, 5; B. 2, 9; C. 9, 9; D. 8, 2;
E. 1, 6; F. 5, 8; G. 3, 2; H. 9, 8; I. 6, 7; J. 3, 9

## Page 276
5,104, 9,221, 4,732, 6,528; 803, 1,161, 3,106, 3,114; 9,159, 112, 2,106, 236; 1,515, 337, 8,613, 241

## Page 277
464, 63, 416; 73, 179, 699; 240, 164, 119; 506, 376; 479 is left standing.

## Page 278
E. 3,338; E. 4,729; H. 2,579; T. 4,818; A. 8,858; R. 3,689; H. 7,046; N. 857; C. 2,491; B. 3,875; E. 5,252; L. 5,583; S. 874; I. 1,988; IN THE BLEACHERS!

## Page 279
First Column: 5,708, 4,834, 1,052, 491, 3; Second Column: 7,187, 5,708, 2,812, 1,034, 7; Third Column: 8,245, 6,879, 2,980, 1,383, 4; Fourth Column: 4,609, 2,656, 818, 126, 9; Panthers

## Page 280
E. 51,411; I. 3,228; R. 41,164; E. 2,497; P. 30,702; H. 9,166; T. 7,805; L. 13,041; A. 6,748; G. 16,378; S. 11, 907; ! 9,477; HE'S A LIGHT SLEEPER!

## Page 281
8,604; 26,416; 41,658; 73,278; 4,316; 9,156; 9,493; 5,289

## Page 282
Across: 2. 1807; 6. 90,213; 8. 35,975; 9. 1,321; 10. 17,496; 11. 2,072; 12. 686,552; 14. 1,829; 15. 6,317; Down: 1. 3,131; 3. 6,956; 4. 7,761; 5. 45,044; 7. 37,127; 10. 12,697; 13. 666,372

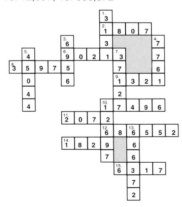

## Page 283
A. 36.1; B. 43.48; C. 19.40; D. 78.9; E. 51.59; 265.7; Mary visited Regions B and C.

## Page 284
Asteroids, 24–23; Comets, 98–96

## Page 285
A. 367 kilometres; B. 2,289 kilometres; C. 3,787 kilometres; D. 657.7 kilometres; E. 3,627 kilometres; F. 899 kilometres

## Page 286
4, 9, 54, 20, 42; 24, 4, 40, 27, 8; 48, 45, 0, 15, 63; 64, 28, 81, 0, 12; 25, 36, 49, 10, 32; 6 x 7 = 42 balloons

## Page 287
HE WAS HIRED AND FIRED ON THE SAME DAY!; HE HAD TO BRING IT BACK!

## Page 288
I. 328; O. 819; S. 168; H. 276; J. 146; E. 497; L. 159; R. 720; C. 366; N. 55; A. 128; F. 369; T. 490; E. 208; P. 320; THE CAPITAL OF COSTA RICA IS SAN JOSE.; 99 kilograms of coffee

## Page 289
A. 144, 168, 292; B. 399, 567, 168; C. 196, 512, 456, 315, 184, 492; D. 864, 462, 747, 768, 112, 495; 604 metres

## Page 290
A. 256, 448, 350, 260, 340; B. 243, 534, 300, 276, 192; C. 294, 312, 576, 612, 216; D. 215, 291, 182, 237, 147

## Page 291
A. 1,389, 3,692, 1,552, 3,150, 988, 2,416; B. 2,275, 4,902, 2,637, 504, 1,664, 1,176; C. 610, 4,075, 6,860, 1,395, 1,878, 756; 2,072 kilometres

## Page 292
A. 560, 3,000, 27,000, 440, 240, 12,000; B. 490, 36,000, 5,400, 42,000, 3,500, 360; C. 48,000, 480, 240, 4,500, 44,000, 400

## Page 293
1. 2,300; 2. 3,400; 3. 9,300; 4. 17,600 5. 9,500; 6. 16,200; 7. 24,500; 8. 14,400 9. 45,000
What are the cheapest ships to buy? "Sale"boats

## Page 294
1. 11,000; 2. 24,000; 3. 30,000; 4. 56,000; 5. 100,000; 6. 144,000; 7. 210,000 8. 256,000; 9. 360,000; 10. 375,000
Why did the spider join the baseball team? To catch "flies"

## Page 295
973 x 8 = 7784; 380 x 6 = 2280 909 x 7 = 6363; 178 x 4 = 712 272 x 8 = 2176; 319 x 4 = 1276 592 x 7 = 4144; 711 x 7 = 4977 699 x 6 = 4194; 716 x 8 = 5728 340 x 5 = 1700; 234 x 1 = 234 443 x 4 = 1772; 841 x 8 = 6728 361 x 6 = 2166; 246 x 4 = 984 588 x 9 = 5292; 741 x 8 = 5928 508 x 7 = 3556; 799 x 8 = 6392 247 x 7 = 1729; 300 x 9 = 2700 650 x 9 = 5850; 348 x 9 = 3132 948 x 9 = 8532
Taking It Further: 222

## Page 296
6,916, 20,130, 19,012, 5,836, 11,284; 7,692, 9,048, 82,890, 22,635, 8,144; 12,663, 7,161, 72,648, 28,744, 42,780; Stormy, Black Beauty, Midnight, Lola's Lad, Lightning, Dusty

## Page 297
G. 1,536; T. 938; S. 1,431; I. 4,992; A. 2,739; D. 3,528; M. 1,092; E. 840; N. 1,992; R. 3,450; K. 4,896; H. 5,208; NIGHTMARES!; 744 kilograms

## Page 298
3,066, 1,323, 3,960; 630 feet; 2,814, 2,425, 1,064; 454 feet; 6,723, 2,160, 5,135; 305 feet; 6,536, 3,640, 3,071; 601 feet; Gateway Arch should be circled.; 6,050 people

## Page 299

45 x 22 = 990; 89 x 23 = 2047
75 x 13 = 975; 68 x 26 = 1768
80 x 26 = 2080; 61 x 23 = 1403
75 x 23 = 1725; 48 x 48 = 2304
96 x 42 = 4032; 77 x 23 = 1771
49 x 71 = 3479; 24 x 20 = 480
96 x 26 = 2496; 65 x 13 = 845
45 x 31 = 1395; 54 x 28 = 1512
34 x 28 = 952; 47 x 23 = 1081
59 x 29 = 1711; 16 x 36 = 576
55 x 52 = 2860; 65 x 21 = 1365
27 x 57 = 1539; 45 x 22 = 990
Taking It Further: a. 2; b. 1; c. 5

## Page 300

57 x 73 = 4161; 98 x 34 = 3332
23 x 13 = 299; 30 x 42 = 1260
21 x 61 = 1281; 44 x 20 = 880
87 x 33 = 2871; 79 x 12 = 948
81 x 14 = 1134; 55 x 13 = 715
58 x 42 = 2436; 25 x 13 = 325
60 x 33 = 1980; 61 x 11 = 671
72 x 32 = 2304; 41 x 23 = 943
16 x 34 = 544; 53 x 73 = 3869
27 x 34 = 918; 71 x 17 = 1207
49 x 52 = 2548; 83 x 17 = 1411
25 x 46 = 1150; 95 x 36 = 3420
25 x 17 = 425; 62 x 12 = 744
23 x 45 = 1035; 26 x 35 = 910
37 x 11 = 407; 24 x 20 = 480

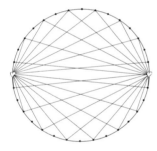

a. 9; b. 7; c. 2; d. 2

## Page 301

A. 15,566, 10,836, 9,944, 3,679, 24,786,
26,015; B. 20,520, 23,352, 18,788;
C. 23,528, 21,682, 78,948; D. 19,614,
17,342, 62,853; 37,716 steps

## Page 302

A. $44.62; M. $19.75; I. $131.84; O. $30.60;
A. $117.76; T. $181.26; F. $63.36; D. $87.42;
E. $546.05; S. $683.56; R. $65.25;
H. $574.36; AT THE FIFE AND DIME STORE!

## Page 303

A. $4.92; B. 18,816; C. 1,305;
D. $19.95; E. 10,582; F. $17.88

## Page 304

A. 6, 9, 8, 5, 9, 3; B. 9, 9, 7, 7, 6, 9;
C. 4, 3, 8, 8, 4, 9, D. 8, 7, 6, 3, 1, 5; 1928

## Page 305

A. 4, 7, 3, 5, 6, 7, 8, 5, 8; B. 5, 4, 3, 8, 4, 6,
3, 8, 9; C. 6, 5, 3, 7, 6, 9, 3, 9, 6; D. 9, 9, 7,
7, 3, 7, 4, 8, 6; 8 ÷ 1 = 8, 16 ÷ 2 = 8, 24 ÷ 3
= 8, 32 ÷ 4 = 8, 40 ÷ 5 = 8, 48 ÷ 6 = 8, 56 ÷
7 = 8, 64 ÷ 8 = 8, 72 ÷ 9 = 8

## Page 306

14 ÷ 7 = 2; 28 ÷ 7 = 4; 63 ÷ 7 = 9; 49 ÷ 7 = 7
84 ÷ 7 = 12; 70 ÷ 7 = 10; 21 ÷ 7 = 3; 42 ÷ 7 = 6
7 ÷ 7 = 1; 35 ÷ 7 = 5; 77 ÷ 7 = 11; 56 ÷ 7 = 8
70 ÷ 7 = 10; 63 ÷ 7 = 9; 14 ÷ 7 = 2; 28 ÷ 7 = 4
14 ÷ 7 = 2; 7 ÷ 7 = 1; 77 ÷ 7 = 11; 63 ÷ 7 = 9
77 ÷ 7 = 11; 56 ÷ 7 = 8; 7 ÷ 7 = 1; 35 ÷ 7 = 5
Taking It Further: 10 squares

## Page 307

24 ÷ 6 = 4; 27 ÷ 3 = 9; 36 ÷ 6 = 6; 28 ÷ 4 = 7
32 ÷ 4 = 8; 40 ÷ 8 = 5; 7 ÷ 7 = 1; 18 ÷ 9 = 2
9 ÷ 9 = 1; 16 ÷ 8 = 2; 32 ÷ 4 = 8; 20 ÷ 4 = 5
42 ÷ 7 = 6; 63 ÷ 9 = 7; 16 ÷ 4 = 4; 81 ÷ 9 = 9

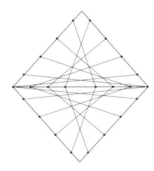

Taking It Further: 54, 45, 36, 27, 18; 42, 35,
28, 21, 14

## Page 308

A. 70, 900, 90, 900, 800; B. 600, 80, 900, 80,
80; C. 500, 90, 800, 60, 80

## Page 309

E. 9 R3; I. 9 R2; S. 9 R4; O. 4 R4; T. 3 R5;
N. 7 R5; P. 6 R3; I. 7 R3; O. 4 R3; A. 8 R6;
T. 8 R2; S. 6 R1; H. 5 R3; ! 6 R3; R. 5 R2;
N. 9 R7; NO, ON THE STAIRS!

## Page 310

14 ÷ 6 = 2R2; 15 ÷ 9 = 1R6; 86 ÷ 7 = 12R2
41 ÷ 6 = 6R5; 37 ÷ 6 = 6R1; 33 ÷ 9 = 3R6
15 ÷ 2 = 7R1; 23 ÷ 6 = 3R5; 13 ÷ 3 = 4R1 54
÷ 7 = 7R5; 45 ÷ 7 = 6R3; 15 ÷ 8 = 1R7
66 ÷ 9 = 7R3; 63 ÷ 8 = 7R7; 28 ÷ 3 = 9R1
33 ÷ 7 = 5R5; 19 ÷ 2 = 9R1; 53 ÷ 6 = 8R5
27 ÷ 5 = 5R2; 62 ÷ 7 = 8R6; 76 ÷ 9 = 8R4
80 ÷ 9 = 8R8; 17 ÷ 4 = 4R1; 11 ÷ 6 = 1R5

## Page 311

1. 4; 2. 2; 3. 6; 4. 5; 5. 8; 6. 3 remainder 2
7. 6 remainder 6; 8. 9 remainder 2
9. 8 remainder 1; 10. 15 remainder 2
What kind of tools do you use for math?
"Multi"pliers

## Page 312

T. 52; U. 51; M. 91; C. 82; A. 92; E. 81; O. 71;
S. 62; N. 84; D. 72; C. 82; I. 53; W. 61; M. 31;
! 22; IT WANTED TO CATCH THE MOUSE!

## Page 313

A. 75; B. 82; C. 108; D. 82; E. 27; F. 36;
G. 106; H. 94; I. 76; J. 78; K. 54

## Page 314

880 ÷ 2 = 440; 996 ÷ 3 = 332; 576 ÷ 4 = 144
502 ÷ 2 = 251; 992 ÷ 2 = 496; 603 ÷ 3 = 201
903 ÷ 3 = 301; 392 ÷ 2 = 196; 982 ÷ 2 = 491
897 ÷ 3 = 299; 738 ÷ 6 = 123; 742 ÷ 2 = 371
990 ÷ 3 = 330
Taking It Further:

```
         432
    2 ) 864
      −  8
         06
      −   6
          04
      −    4
           0
```

## Page 315

O. 64 R2; G. 63 R4; K. 95 R3; R. 42 R2;
L. 52 R3; A. 83 R1; M. 58 R3; P. 88 R2;
S. 87 R2; T. 59 R2; C. 44 R1; A CARPOOL!

## Page 316

Z. 742; N. 583 R3; T. 262 R3; S. 748;
B. 618 R6; P. 356; D. 394; C. 542 R6; U. 857;
O. 921; A. 921 R4; Y. 672; SUNDAY!;
91 R1 days

## Page 317

A. 43, 13, 12, 38; B. 18, 15, 33, 10;
C. 18, 18, 27, 46; 206 bones; 350 bones

## Page 318

S. 604; U. 908; W. 50 R10; X. 130; G. 20 R16;
B. 308; R. 20 R6; J. 902; A. 601; E. 20 R22;
Y. 320; T. 705; STAR WARTS!; 237 pieces
of popcorn

## MATH

### Page 321
1. 3,462; 2. 98,724; 3. 8,749
4. 128,467; 5. 617,823; 6. 618,397

### Page 322
1. forty two; 2. sixty eighth
3. six thousand two hundred thirty four
4. thirty four; 5. one hundred forty five
6. seventeen; 7. ninety three

### Page 323
1. 496, 23; 2. 49, 63; or 43, 69
3. 23, 496; or 26, 493; or 93, 426; or 96, 423
4. 732, 469; 5. 23, 64, 97; or 23, 67, 94; or 24, 63, 97; or 24, 67, 93; or 27, 63, 94; or 27, 64, 93; 6. 674, 392

### Page 324
1. 9,875; 2. 12,346; 3. 93,876
4. 13,579; 5. 951,876; 6. 123,648

### Page 325

### Page 326
1. 10; 2. 20; 3. 50; 4. 90; 5. 200
6. 400; 7. 600; 8. 300; 9. 500; 10. 700
What did the farmer get when he tried to reach the beehive?
A "buzzy" signal

### Page 327
1. Exact Answer; 2. Estimate
3. Exact Answer; 4. Estimate
5. Estimate; 6. Exact Answer
7. Estimate; 8. Exact Answer
How Would You Estimate...
Answers will vary. Ask students to explain their estimation method in their writing.

### Page 328
1. 1; 2. 4; 3. 22; 4. 26; 5. 34
6. 57; 7. 115; 8. 124; 9. 60; 10. 215
How can you make the number seven even?
Take away the "s."

### Page 329

### Page 330
1. T; 2. R; 3. R; 4. B; 5. O
6. O; 7. E; 8. O; 9. F; 10. E
What do cheerleaders like to drink?
Lots of root beer

### Page 331
$19 + 37 = 56$; $33 + 47 = 80$; $51 + 39 = 90$
$49 + 22 = 71$; $48 + 23 = 71$; $78 + 12 = 90$
$67 + 13 = 80$; $29 + 27 = 56$

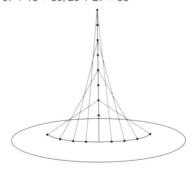

Taking It Further: a. 3; b. 9; c. 7; d. 85; e. 4; f. 26

### Pages 332–333

| T | H | E | Y | A | L | R | E | A | D | Y |
|---|---|---|---|---|---|---|---|---|---|---|
| 1/5 | 3/8 | 4/6 | 6/8 | 1/2 | 2/9 | 2/3 | 4/6 | 1/2 | 1/3 | 6/8 |

| H | A | V | E | B | I | L | L | S. |
|---|---|---|---|---|---|---|---|---|
| 3/8 | 1/2 | 5/6 | 4/6 | 6/12 | 3/4 | 2/9 | 2/9 | 3/5 |

### Page 334
$3/20 + 2/20 = 1/4$; $2/16 + 2/16 = 1/4$
$1/14 + 1/14 = 1/7$; $1/9 + 2/9 = 1/3$
$1/4 + 2/4 = 3/4$; $4/9 + 2/9 = 2/3$
$4/10 + 2/10 = 3/5$; $1/5 + 2/5 = 3/5$
$6/12 + 5/12 = 11/12$; $4/10 + 5/10 = 9/10$
$4/12 + 7/12 = 11/12$; $1/10 + 8/10 = 9/10$
$4/14 + 6/14 = 5/7$; $6/10 + 2/10 = 4/5$
$4/8 + 2/8 = 3/4$; $4/8 + 3/8 = 7/8$;
$2/10 + 3/10 = 1/2$; $1/6 + 2/6 = 1/2$
$1/16 + 1/16 = 1/8$; $3/40 + 7/40 = 1/4$

### Page 335
$7/8 - 1/8 = 3/4$; $9/10 - 1/10 = 4/5$
$2/4 - 1/4 = 1/4$; $3/5 - 1/5 = 2/5$
$8/9 - 2/9 = 2/3$; $7/11 - 5/11 = 2/11$
$7/12 - 1/12 = 1/2$; $7/8 - 2/8 = 5/8$
$7/12 - 3/12 = 1/3$; $14/15 - 9/15 = 1/3$
$12/15 - 2/15 = 2/3$; $9/10 - 8/10 = 1/10$
$7/6 - 4/6 = 1/2$; $18/20 - 3/20 = 3/4$
$9/18 - 2/18 = 7/18$; $7/8 - 6/8 = 1/8$
$11/13 - 1/13 = 12/13$; $4/5 - 3/5 = 1/5$
$15/18 - 1/18 = 7/9$; $13/16 - 1/16 = 3/4$
$4/9 - 1/9 = 1/3$; $7/8 - 4/8 = 3/8$; $3/4 - 1/4 = 1/2$

### Page 336
1. 1/2 white, 1/2 black
2. 4/7 black, 3/7 white
3. 1/4 black
4. 2 red socks, 4 green socks
5. 2/5 red
Super Challenge: 5 yellow socks, 7 red and white socks

## Page 337
Here is the correct ranking from highest to lowest:
1—Tony Gwynn (.368); 2—Mike Piazza (.346); 3—Barry Larkin (.319); 4—Kirby Puckett (.314); 5—Frank Thomas (.308); 6—Mo Vaughn (.300); 7—Barry Bonds (.294); 8—Cal Ripken, Jr. (.262); 9—Ken Griffey, Jr. (.258); 10—David Justice (.253)

## Page 338
ACROSS: A. 3.7; C. 4.38; E. .55; F. .6; G. .9; J. .57; K. 7.16; L. 4.3
DOWN: A. 3.14; B. 78.29; C. 4.5; D. 8.1; F. .2704; H. 24.3; I. 1.7; J. .36

## Page 339
1. $1.55; 2. 23¢; 3. $2.45; 4. 48¢; 5. $12.70
6. $3.51; 7. 32¢; 8. $10.65; 9. 83¢; 10. $2.57

## Page 340

## Page 341
1. 52; 2. 12; 3. 100; 4. 20; 5. 365; 6. 36
7. 16; 8. 24; 9. 10; 10. 2; 11. 4; 12. 5,280
13. 60; 14. 1,000
Answer: TWENTY AFTER ONE

## Page 342
1. scale; 2. ruler; 3. clock; 4. teaspoon
5. thermometer; 6. measuring cup
7. yardstick; 8. measuring tape

## Page 343
1. a and e (4); b and c (30); d and g (16)
2. a and d; 3. a, b, and d; 4. 124

## Page 344
1. perimeter: 20; area: 9
2. perimeter: 24; area: 13
3. perimeter: 22; area: 11
4. perimeter: 24; area: 15
5. perimeter: 32; area: 23
6. perimeter: 44; area: 48

## Page 345
1. eight; 2. acute; 3. perimeter; 4. area
5. square; 6. cube; 7. triangle; 8. circle
9. polygons
Answer: IT ATE MARS BARS.

## Page 346

1. 6.

2. 7.

3. 8.

4. 9.

5. 10.

What is the last thing that the trapeze flier wants to be?
The fall guy

## Page 347
Children can examine each angle in the letters MATH and determine whether it is right, acute, or obtuse.

## Pages 348–349
Tessellate patterns will vary.

## Page 350
Taking It Further:

0.2    1.7  2.5    4.9

## MAPS

**Pages 352–353**
1. state border
2. Cheyenne
3. Nevada
4. Montana, Idaho
5. Idaho
6. southeast
7. northwest
8. southeast
9. north
10. southwest

**Page 355**
1. four
2. Southern Hemisphere
3. Prime Meridian
4. north
5. equator
6. It's an imaginary center line on which Earth turns.
7. North America, Asia, Europe, or Africa
8. Asia, Australia, Africa, Europe, and Antarctica

**Page 357**
1. A world map is flat, a globe is round.
2. Mercator
3. Robinson
4. Mercator
5. Robinson; answers will vary.

**Pages 358–359**
1. Washington Monument
2. D1
3. Virginia Avenue
4. D1, E1, E2
5. Potomac River
6. E2
7. B2
8. State Department
9. B3
10. A2

**Pages 360–361**
1. Anchorage
2. 30° N
3. Brasilia
4. equator
5. Nairobi
6. Addis Ababa
7. northern latitudes
8. About 10 degrees
9. 35°N and 35°S
10. 70

**Page 362–363**
1. north to south
2. west
3. Manaus
4. 30°E
5. Kinshasa
6. Prime Meridian
7. It is on the other side of Earth.
8. 15°W and 45°E
9. false
10. true
11. true
12. true

**Pages 364–365**
1. a
2. b
3. b
4. a
5. 300 miles
6. 300 miles, about 500 kilometres
7. about 450 miles
8. 400 kilometres
9. about 800

**Pages 366-367**
1. 1.5 kilometres
2. 3 kilometres
3. 3.3 kilometres; 6.6 kilometres
4. Map A
5. Map B
6. Map B
7. Map A: 300 miles; Map B: 150 miles
8. Map B just shows part of Texas.
9. Beaumont, Fort Worth
10. 300 miles
11. Map A

**Page 369**
1. desert
2. northern part
3. Small; it would be hard to live in the desert.
4. light green
5. mostly woodland and shrub
6. Algeria, Egypt

### Crossword Answers

**Pages 370–371**
1. volcano
2. mountain
3. hill
4. plain
5. valley
6. plateau
7. canyon
8. isthmus
9. cape
10. peninsula
11. gulf
12. bay
13. strait

**Pages 372–373**
1. 300-600 metres
2. Cougar Ridge; 1500 metres
3. green
4. about 1200 metres
5. about 750 metres
6. the north side; 1500 metres
7. at 750 metres
8. the east side, 1200 metres
9. Answers will vary.

**Page 374**
1. 0 to 300 metres
2. Hawaii
3. mountains
4. 0-300 metres
5. Nihau, Molokai, Lanai, Kahoolawe

**Page 375**
1. Haiti, Dominican Republic
2. green
3. Dominican Republic; mountains
4. 0 to 300 metres
5. 300 to 1500 metres
6. northwest

**Pages 376–377**
1. Harness and Saddlemaker, C4
2. Apothecary, I3
3. Cooper, E2
4. Printer, F3
5. Windmill, E2
6. Wetherburn's Tavern, G4
7. Milliner, G3
8. Blacksmith, F4
9. Bake Shop, H3
10. Silversmith, H3

**Page 379**
1. southeast
2. 50s
3. Minneapolis
4. Los Angeles, Miami
5. Possible answer: warm coat
6. rain and a cold front
7. San Francisco
8. yes

**Page 381**
1. Warm or hot summers, cold winters; Wet
2. Southeast; Pacific Coast; Hawaii
3. three
4. Cool summers, cold winters; Wet. Cool summers, cold winters; Very dry. Cool summers, mild winters; Wet.
5. Hot summers/mild or warm winters; Wet
6. Cool summers, cold winters; Wet
7. drier

**Pages 382–383**
1. northwest
2. red dot
3. Supe Valley
4. Andes
5. inland
6. Thailand, Laos; Vietnam
7. Siem Reap
8. northwest
9. about 200 kilometres
10. Tonle Sap

**Pages 384–385**
1. Montana, Wyoming, Idaho
2. five
3. west
4. Yellowstone River
5. Yellowstone Lake
6. about 80-90 kilometres

**Page 386**
1. 0°
2. Ecuador, Colombia, Brazil
3. Southern Hemisphere
4. 80°W
5. woodland and shrub
6. along the western coast
7. forest and farmland
8. near the Amazon River

**Page 387**